THE BIGGEST CON

''Inflation, our public enemy No. 1, will, unless whipped, destroy our country, our homes, our liberty, our property . . . as surely as any well armed wartime enemy.''

President Gerald Ford
Before a Joint Session of the Congress,
October 8, 1974

Since it is our own government that causes that inflation —our own government is that enemy.

IRWIN A. SCHIFF

THE BIGGEST CON

How The Government Is Fleecing You

Foreword by John Chamberlain

Freedom Books
HAMDEN, CONNECTICUT

Illustrations and Graphs by Emanuel Zeid
Cover by Danial Brown

Manufactured in the United States of America

ISBN 0-930374-01-0

PRINTING HISTORY
Arlington House Edition — Published April, 1976
Freedom Book Edition — Published August, 1977
Freedom Book, Second Printing — December, 1977

This book contains the complete text of the original, hardcover edition published by Arlington House, plus a new addendum specially written for this edition.

Library of Congress Cataloging in Publication Data

Schiff, Irwin A.

The Biggest Con.

Includes index
1. United States—Economic policy—1971-
I. Title
HC106.7.S33 1977 338.973 77-81568

Contents

To my parents, Jacob and Anna Schiff, who, like millions of others, immigrated to these shores, not seeking or expecting a public subsidy but seeking only those rewards that freedom, hardwork, thrift and self-reliance could bestow. May this spirit and these virtues be restored to American life to serve as inspiration for my two children, Peter and Andy, their generation and future generations of Americans.

Foreword

The word ''blockbuster'' is used indiscriminately. But, it is surely the right word for Irwin Schiff's account of how our uneconomists (his word for the Keynesians who believe in the universal solvent of the free lunch) have flooded us with unmoney to the point where recovery has become almost impossible without a truly terrifying bankruptcy.

What is new about Mr. Schiff's work is that he shows how scores of mistakes, no one of which is necessarily lethal by itself, can react on each other to bring an end to the efficacy of any temporary palliatives. A law of critical mass becomes involved.

Long ago, John T. Flynn and Edna Lonigan proved the fraudulent nature of a Social Security system that builds up no backlog of investments capable of meeting its obligations. We might have survived this theft if the purchasing power of our money hadn't been systematically leached by additions to dead-horse debt that must now be reckoned in the trillions. The government-induced energy crisis complicates everything by a factor we have not yet fathomed.

Legal ratchet actions prevent any fall-back to positions that might enable producers to reduce their costs, revive their attraction for investors, and come out of it with an annual profit, Union wages and fringe benefits remain on the escalator. The minimum wage has put a whole generation of young blacks on the relief rolls. The Employment Act of 1946 forces Congress to spend endlessly in the vain hope that work can be made for everybody.

Meanwhile, the federal, state and municipal payrolls become padded with thousands of non-producers. Mr. Schiff figures that only sixteen out of every hundred people in the U.S. are actually busy producing things to eat, use and wear. The rest do engage themselves in some necessary services, but we have thousands of teachers who function mainly in trying to keep order in schools that are not wanted by students who might be better off in a system that would allow for teen-age apprenticeships in going trades. We have hundreds of statisticians who keep records that nobody reads, or who provide the justification for government activity that nobody wants.

In a grand peroration, Mr. Schiff accuses our Federal government of compelling citizens to participate in a chain letter (social security); of illegally shifting wealth through inflation; of hiding the true extent of the National Debt; of saddling a lower standard of living on people by the destructive burdens it imposes; and of using the Federal Reserve to force what amounts to counterfeit money on the banks. The citizen is required to swear to things on his tax return that no two people can interpret the same way. We are, so Mr. Schiff suggests, contributing to our own destruction by paying taxes to a government that engages in so many unlawful and criminal activites that it makes the Mafia look lily-white by comparison. This poses a nice question for the taxpayer: If you cooperate with a thief, doesn't that make yourself the perpetrator of an unlawful act?

How long before all the evil fowl will come home to roost? Mr. Schiff gives us five years, providing we do not turn on our government in the meantime and shrink it down to size. Can this be done? He is the eternal optimist when he says that if enough people will heed his diagnosis he thinks it can.

—John Chamberlain

Introduction

An article in the *Wall Street Journal* of March 29, 1974, carried ominous implications for America. Headlined "Fed's Sheehan Warns Against Big Effort to Squeeze Inflation," it concerned a speech by John E. Sheehan, then a governor of the Federal Reserve System, before a meeting of groups representing security analysts.

According to the article, Sheehan said the time had come to answer charges that the "Fed alone is responsible for inflation." He was reported to have disagreed sharply with economists such as Milton Friedman of the University of Chicago and William Wolman of Argus Research Corporation who had blamed the Fed for the inflation by the latter's expanding the money supply faster than productivity.

The *Wall Street Journal* story contained the following eyebrow-raisers:

> Mr. Sheehan didn't argue with this [the economists'] analysis. "There isn't any lack of understanding on our board, nor lack of courage either," he said heatedly. But he added that a sharp *cutback in money expansion would stall the economy and "would result in 15 to 20 percent unemployment by year-end, with 35 to 40 percent black unemployment and zero employment for black teen-agers.*
>
> "Milton could go to his farm (in Vermont) and sit this out but when he comes back *he will find the cities burned down and the University of Chicago along with them,"* said Mr. Sheehan. [Italics mine.]

Most disturbing was that neither the Fed nor the federal government, as indicated by Governor Sheehan's remarks and observable government action, was doing anything substantial to prevent the anticipated conflagration, while his statements evoked other shocking inferences. For example:

1. Since the Federal Reserve System cannot inflate *ad infinitum*, the inflationary bubble will eventually burst. Expansion of the money supply by the Fed and the resultant inflation are therefore not *eliminating* the threat to our cities, only *postponing* it.

2. The Fed's generating of inflation is, by Sheehan's admission a way of shifting wealth from those who save to those who live in the nation's cities, where this shifted wealth "bribes" city dwellers from "burning down the cities." This shifting is accomplished by increasing the supply of paper money and federal debt in order to make increased welfare payments possible while the resultant inflation shrinks the value (purchasing power) of all accumulated savings.

3. Why after 200 years should our government suddenly feel compelled to cause inflation in order to keep a segment of our population from burning down our cities?

Governor Sheehan has not been the only prominent public official to make dire predictions recently about what may be in store for America. In May 1974 Arthur F. Burns, chairman of the Board of Governors of the Federal Reserve System, declared that a continued high rate of inflation threatened to bring "a significant decline of economic and political freedom for the American people." Prominent voices from the private sector of the economy have also joined the ominous chorus. AFL-CIO president George Meany has said:

> There is every indication that the U.S. is heading into a depression, possibly worse than in the 1930s, with business failures and widespread unemployment. I thought we had eliminated the major causes of a depression in this country during the Roosevelt days . . . but despite that, I can see a depression coming unless there is a quick turnaround.

In September 1974 President Ford underscored the gravity of the coming crisis when he stated at the close of the White House conference on inflation that "the very future of our political and economic institutions, indeed, our whole way of life is literally at stake." Such expressions of doom and gloom concerning the economy from public leaders would have been unthinkable a generation ago, even two years ago.

As of 1975, over 50 million Americans (not counting veterans and those collecting unemployment) were on the public dole—in excess of 30 million receiving Social Security benefits and more than 20 million on welfare and various other government wage continuation and retirement programs—all requiring tax dollars for their solvency. This situation did not exist in 1929. Then the U.S. government was solvent, and, theoretically, could aid the private sector. But now the U.S. government is *broke*: it has been forced into bankruptcy *three times* in the *last four years,* while encouraging vast segments of our population to depend on it for their economic welfare. Many of these people are now in no position either financially or temperamentally to care for themselves. What will they do when the U.S. government can no longer honor its financial promises to them (or more accurately, redirect tax receipts from others to them)? This is not unlikely, as this book will show. Thus the situation facing the U.S. today is far more crucial than in 1929, with greater dangers, both internally and externally.

In the hope that there may still be time to rescue a rapidly deteriorating economy, this book attempts to explain how we arrived where we are, and suggests ways to reverse the course that is bringing us to national disaster.

To this end, complicated charts and statistics have been kept to a minimum. Seemingly complicated economic and monetary principles are clarified so that the reader will see among other things how the U.S. government (1) steals from the public annually an amount five times greater than the total cost of all crime —including the cost of its suppression, (2) runs the world's largest counterfeiting operation, (3) operates the world's largest pyramid club since Ponzi, (4) violates Public Law 89-809 by routinely reporting only 10 percent of the national debt, (5) legislates unemployment, and (6) caused the energy crisis.

I hope that this book will serve as a practical guide to help you protect yourself and your country.

Irwin A. Schiff
Ft. Lauderdale, Florida

1

The U.S. Money Swindle

All the perplexities, confusions and distresses in America arise not from defects in their constitution or confederation, not from want of honor or virtue, so much as from downright ignorance of the nature of coin, credit and circulation.

—John Adams in a letter to Thomas Jefferson, 1787

Money has ceased to exist in the American economy. ''Conventional wisdom'' to the contrary notwithstanding, Mr. Average American literally has *no money* in the bank, *none* in the stock market, *none* in his wallet or pocketbook. Preposterous, you say, *but it is true!* U.S. politicians, contrary to the Constitution and the U.S. criminal code, have conned all citizens out of their money savings. This monetary swindle was perpetrated despite a reasonably literate electorate, despite our well-developed financial and banking institutions, and despite our many institutions of higher learning and the nation's extensive network of information media. Now, just how did such a thing happen? Answering this question, first of all, requires a quick review of some basic monetary facts of life.

What Is Money?

To appreciate the scope of the Big Swindle, it is necessary to understand what ''money'' is and what it isn't. Money, like the wheel, was one of mankind's most important inventions. Before the development of money all exchanges were on a barter basis—the trading of one good directly for another. For example, if a hatmaker needed a pair of shoes, he had to find a shoemaker who needed a hat, an exceedingly inefficient method of exchanging goods.

Fortunately, society discovered that there was usually one commodity which would be accepted in exchange for all goods and services, and so this commodity became money. Because of the development of money, which facilitated and accelerated the exchange of goods and services and made division of labor possible, productivity increased and thus living standards rose. The sounder a nation's money, the more efficient would be its economy and the faster would its standard of living grow.

In ancient times sheep and cattle served as money. Roman legionnaires received their pay in salt. Pins, before they were mass produced, served as money for minor sums. American Indians used beads, called wampum, for their money. American GIs in Europe after World War II discovered that cigarettes could be used as money.

Ideally, money performs four major economic functions.

1. Money serves as the *unit of account;* it is the unit in which all other values are expressed. By all goods and services having a value in money, they can be related in value to each other, thus eliminating the near impossible task of evaluating goods and services directly to each other, as in barter. For example, how many heads of lettuce would equal a pair of shoes? Or, how many wooden bowls would equal a jacket, or how many hours of chopping wood would equal ten loaves of bread? By expressing the value of all these goods and services in money—their "price"—we can easily relate them to each other.

2. Money serves as a *medium of exchange,* thereby facilitating the exchange of goods and services. By expediting and simplifying trade, money makes possible a more extensive division of labor with increased specialization, thereby making society more efficient and elevating its living standard.

3. Money serves as a *store of value.* Money not spent immediately can be saved and stored for later use, and ideally it should buy as much later as it would if spent currently. When money has this quality—the maintenance of its purchasing power—saving is encouraged. When society saves, capital creation occurs, since capital can only be created out of stored savings.[1] As capital is created, society's ability to produce an expanding quantity of goods is also increased, so again sound money enhances a society's ability to raise its standard of living.

4. Money serves as a *unit of deferred payment.* Money, of course, can be loaned to others who may have a greater immediate need for it than its owner. However, the lender expects to be repaid in money that will buy the same amount of goods and services as the money he lent. To the degree that money loses value through inflation, interest rates will rise to compensate for this loss in purchasing

[1]See pages 265-266.

power. Money that does not lose value will encourage lower interest rates thereby making possible projects requiring long-term financing at economical interest rates. Thus, again, *sound* money contributes to society's economic progress.

What About the Role of Gold?

By trial and error, civilizations discovered those commodities which best served as money. In most societies, the commodities that evolved were gold and silver. Gold was desired because of its versatility and its unique properties. First of all, it had a rich and warm color and was capable of being highly polished. It was the only metal that neither tarnished nor rusted. It could be extruded to the fineness of a hair and beaten to the thinness of tissue paper. Since gold concentrated considerable value in a small area, it made transportation of one's wealth relatively simple. Imagine having to leave a country hurriedly when all of one's wealth was in cattle! Since gold was malleable, it was easily divisible and could accommodate exchanges of lesser value. Gold could be easily measured and its quality could be readily determined. These latter qualities, of course, made loaning money possible since it was easy to establish that the loan was repaid in the same type of money that had been loaned.

Some other commodities—oil, coal, diamonds, even soybeans—have been suggested as substitutes for gold. I have found among people a hostility toward gold, reminiscent of William Jennings Bryan and his fears that mankind was being "crucified on a cross of gold." The antigold hysteria of the 1890s is still very much with us—witness the U.S. government's campaign to replace gold with Special Drawing Rights (SDRs), claiming that there was not enough gold with which to conduct world trade; witness statements by high government officials that gold is a "barbaric metal." Far from being barbaric, the metal has preserved purchasing power far better than "barbaric" Federal Reserve notes, printed on government presses.

Those seeking a substitute for gold labored under a misunderstanding. They believed that governments designated gold money, and all government needed to do to change it was to decide on a different form of money. This is simply not the case. Government did *not* create money; it merely recognized officially the money that was functioning in the marketplace. It was the people, not government, that decided on what to use for money.

It cannot be overemphasized that people the world over were not compelled to use gold as money. They gravitated to gold because it served all the requirements demanded of money better than any other commodity. As gold is already used and valued throughout the world and has proven itself by over 2000 years of service, why should our government think it necessary to switch to another form of money?

Now that we have examined the nature of legitimate money, let's look into "banking" and the function of "monetary reserves." When a medieval merchant arrived in a city for, say, a trade fair, he obviously did not wish to carry his gold around or leave it at the inn where he was staying. Consequently, he sought the local goldsmith who, for a modest fee, would store it for him. When a merchant placed his gold with the goldsmith, he received a receipt as evidence of his claim to the stored gold. When merchants conducted their business, they could transfer these paper receipts instead of transferring the gold itself. Others would then circulate these receipts because it was more convenient than transferring gold. So these warehouse receipts for gold became "paper money"—more accurately, a "money substitute."

It is precisely at this point that 99 percent of the people lose all their understanding concerning money, which is why they can be so easily victimized by government dishonesty. It is, therefore, extremely important for the reader to grasp the difference between money, and paper (or coin) money substitutes. The paper warehouse receipt for money is obviously not money but merely a paper substitute for money that is stored. Money substitutes are correctly referred to as currency and society's total stock of money and official money substitutes (stored and circulating) may be called its total currency supply (loosely called the money supply). However, its actual money supply can only be its total stock of gold and silver, if those are its monetary metals. If money is based on another commodity, then its total money supply would be the total physical supply of *that* commodity.

If, for instance, $100 worth of gold were deposited with a goldsmith and a warehouse receipt for $100 were issued, what would the total money supply be? If the money substitute was counted as money, one might conclude that the "money supply" had been expanded to $200—$100 worth of paper and $100 worth of gold. But the money supply is still only $100, the value of the gold. As you will see, it is even possible to have $200 of paper money substitutes circulating backed by only $100 of gold in which case one might conclude that the money supply had been expanded to $300. In both cases, however, the money supply has stayed exactly the same but the amount of currency, money substitutes, has been expanded. In the first instance, the amount of circulating currency was $100 and the amount of money $100. In the second instance, the amount of circulating currency was $200 while the amount of money was still $100.

It is people's inability to differentiate between money and money substitutes that causes them to be continually swindled by the government. Historically, this is a game that governments never tire of playing and citizens never seem to catch on to.

Now, the value and quality of real money—gold, silver, wampum, salt, etc.—can be easily understood since its value is tangible and relatively certain, which is why it served as money in the first place. However, the value and quality of paper money substitutes can vary from being absolutely worthless (as "worthless as a continental") to being one honest step away from the real thing. It is a government's sneaky ability to progressively make its money substitutes worth less (usually in response to some short-term political need) that destroys nations, empires, and civilizations. It is America's tragic misfortune that its currency can now serve as a virtual testtube example of how politicians can, in stages, totally destroy a nation's currency supply.

Now, there are two general types of money substitutes: (1) receipts for money that have been deposited for storage (of the type we have just described), and (2) mere promises to pay money, sometimes called "bank notes." Obviously a note to pay money is only as good as the maker's ability to redeem his note in real money, if payment in real money is demanded. Thus, a note "money substitute" can only be as good as the maker's supply of real money relative to his notes outstanding. The fact is that even when "money substitutes" become intrinsically worthless either because they have become backed by empty warehouses or bankrupt creditors and governments, they will continue to circulate simply by force of habit. Government monetary treachery relies on a people's irrational willingness to accept and circulate worthless "money substitutes" while being under the illusion that they are accepting and saving real money.

For example, during October 1923, Germans were still trading in marks even though their value had fallen to less than 1/50 millionth of a penny. So, with this firmly in mind, let's return to our goldsmith.

The goldsmith, who had initially charged a fee for storing gold, soon noticed that his storeroom always contained an ample supply of gold since his receipts continued to circulate with relatively few being presented for redemption. The goldsmith discovered that a portion of this dormant gold could be loaned to others showing an economic need for it and having the capacity to repay it, plus interest, before it was needed for redemptive purposes. Soon the goldsmith was making more money loaning out other people's gold than he was at goldsmithing—so he became a "banker."

In time, bankers developed a skill for judging the community's need for gold, based upon local economic conditions and the travel habits of the local merchants. From this, they determined how much gold they should have on hand in order to redeem all receipts that might be presented. Based on his assessment of the situation, a banker might call in some loans and suspend making others and, so, his actual supply of gold to outstanding paper might be as high as 100 percent or as low as 25 percent or even lower. Note that the banker did not need to have a dollar in gold for every dollar in receipts issued. All that was required was that he have *enough* gold to honor all possible receipts when presented, and the confidence of the public that this would always be the case. The amount of gold, of course, served to limit the amount of paper that could be circulated and the ratio of gold to currency became known as the *gold reserve*.

Obviously the smaller the reserve, the greater was the ratio of loans and the greater the banker's profit. However, the smaller the reserve, the greater the risk of not being able to honor currency presented for redemption. If holders of currency suspected that this might happen, the banker could face a "run" which might end forever his ability to generate banking profits. So, the banker's desire to maximize profits by having the smallest possible reserve was tempered by the need for higher reserves in the interest of safety and stability. Thus, a banker's ability to weigh needs efficiently would promote not only his welfare, but the community's welfare. Since the banker was not only storing the community's gold (and now paying interest for the privilege) but prudently extending credit, he was allocating the community's limited supply of capital on a businesslike basis. Obviously, bankers made mistakes when allocating the limited supply of capital, but those who made the least mistakes remained in business longest and their judgments and experience benefited the community.

How the U.S. Government Destroyed the Nation's Money Supply

The authority for the U.S. government's involvement with money is vested in Article 1, Section 8, of the U.S. Constitution: "Congress shall have the power to coin money and regulate the value thereof." Note that the Constitution does not say that Congress shall have the power to "make" or "create" money; it specifies to *coin* it. Congress was empowered to take gold and silver, which the nation then recognized as money, and put them in *coin* form. When the Constitution refers to coining money, it means *full-bodied money*—that is, where the value of the metal in the coin corresponds to the value expressed on the coin's face. This full-bodied character of legitimate money is what distinguishes it from counterfeit money.

When a counterfeit coin is passed, the counterfeiter's gain and the recipient's loss is the difference between the value of the metal in the coin and the face of the coin. If, for example, a counterfeiter made a coin containing metal equal in value to the face of the coin, no crime would technically be committed because, when the coin was passed, a fair exchange of values would have occurred. Of course, no counterfeiter makes full-bodied money because there's no profit in it. Counterfeiting is a crime because counterfeit coin contains less intrinsic value than represented by its face and so robs those to whom it is passed.[1]

Let us now examine the types of coins that the United States Mint is producing and see whether they are the type authorized by the U.S. Constitution. If you examine the currently minted U.S. dollar, half-dollar, quarter, and dime, you will discover a reddish stripe around the coin's outer rim. This is the copper core of the coin showing through the outer edge. The silvery appearance of these coins is the result of a nickel layer which has been bonded to the coin's copper core. These coins have a serrated rim, while the penny and the nickel have smooth rims.[2] Why did the U.S. bond nickel to copper in manufacturing these higher denomination

[1]If a monetary system issues at least one full-bodied coin, it can issue minor coins which are not full-bodied as long as these are exchangeable at par for those that are full-bodied.

[2]These serrated rims are called mill marks and are placed on silver and gold coins to prevent their being "clipped"—that is, to prevent portions of the metal from being scraped from the coin's outer edges before it is passed. No such marks were put on the penny or the nickel since no one would bother to "clip" coins made of a base metal. Since all U.S. coins are now made of base metals, they need not have mill marks. The only purpose that mill marks serve on present U.S. coins is to perpetuate the deception that somehow U.S. coins are legitimate money.

coins? Since these coins are 91.67 percent copper, why weren't they minted to look like copper? Had the United States government honestly minted the dollar, half-dollar, quarter, and dime, the public would have rejected them. If the government had tried to pass copper-colored, smooth-rimmed coins as quarters, most people would have laughed them off as being big pennies, so a way had to be found to get the public to accept copper for silver. Nickel was, therefore, bonded to copper to give it the appearance of silver, the substance of which our then full-bodied money was made. Since this new "money" possesses nowhere near the value indicated on its face, it is not legitimate and full-bodied and should be considered as merely "token money." (See Figure 1 for a comparison of the intrinsic value of U.S. silver coins and the currently minted "tokens.")

Please refer to Figure 2, where you will find the *Webster's New Twentieth Century Dictionary's* definition of "counterfeit." Note how aptly this describes currently minted U.S. copper coins: "made in imitation of something else with a view to defraud by passing the false copy for genuine or original." Obviously, counterfeit coins are now being made by the U.S. government. Heretofore, only private individuals engaged in such activity.

Consider the following. Suppose a counterfeiter made quarters containing 10 cents worth of silver, thereby earning a profit of 15 cents on every coin he made and passed. Suppose he were caught and arrested. At his trial he could argue that since the quarters he made contained 10 cents worth of silver, while the federal government's quarters contained only a penny's worth of copper, he was indeed making and putting into circulation money that was ten times better than the

Figure 1

VALUES OF OLD SILVER COINS COMPARED TO NEW CLAD TOKENS

Based on their Metallic Content on December 31, 1974

DENOMINATION	Discontinued Silver Coins (90% silver—10% copper)	Currently Minted Cupro-nickel-clad Tokens (91.67% copper—8.33% nickel)
Dollar	$3.54	4 cents
Half-dollar	$1.65	2 cents
Quarter	$ .83	1 cents
Dime	$ .33	.04 cents

Source: U.S. Mint

Note: The intrinsic value of the old dime was eight times greater than the new "dollar," while even the value of the current penny on that date (.047 cents) was greater than the new "dime." The adulteration and deterioration of U.S. money merely reflects the deterioration in U.S. political leadership—at this point, U.S. "coins" could just as well be made of plastic, like poker chips.

Figure 2

Webster's New Twentieth Century Dictionary, Second Edition, describes the word *counterfeit* as follows:

coun'tẽr feit (-fit) a. (OFr. *contrefait;* LL. *contrafactus*, counterfeit, pp. of *contrafacere; contra*, against, opposite, and *facere*, to make.)
1. forged; false; fabricated without right; made in imitation of something else with a view to defraud by passing the false copy for genuine or original: as, a *counterfeit* coin, a *counterfeit* deed or bond.
2. pretended; sham; feigned; dissembled; as, *counterfeit* sorrow.
Syn.—bogus, deceptive, false, fictitious, forged, fraudulent, mock, sham, spurious.

coun'tẽr feit, n. 1. a cheat; an imposter. (Archaic)
2. one thing made like or resembling another; specifically, an imitation without lawful authority, made with intent to defraud by passing the false for the true; as, the note is a poor *counterfeit*.
3. a copy of likeness, as in painting, sculpture, etc. (Archaic)

coun'tẽr feit, v.i. and v.t. 1. to make an imitation of (money, pictures, etc.) usually with intention to deceive or defraud.
2. to pretend.
3. to resemble or make resemble.

government's. He could appeal to judge and jury: "Since I am circulating money that is better than the government's, what crime have I committed?" The government could only respond that "counterfeiting is an activity now reserved solely for the government and it is the government's *monopoly* of counterfeiting that you are guilty of violating."

This will explain why "real" U.S. money is selling at such a premium and why it is advertised on the financial pages of our nation's newspapers and journals. Since real money, gold and silver, is no longer provided by the government, it must be bought at a premium from private sources. With gold selling at $150 an ounce, a U.S. $20 gold piece has the intrinsic value of 150 paper dollars. The fact that it is selling for considerably more than this is because of its numismatic value and the premium that gold coins command. An old silver quarter contained .1808 ounces of silver and, therefore, had an intrinsic value of 24 cents when their counterfeits were introduced by the government.

The sharp appreciation in the paper value of gold and silver coins is an example of how honest money provides protection against runaway inflation. As inflation increases the cost of goods and services, it increases the value of the gold and silver contained in these coins. If gold goes to $500 an ounce, a $20 U.S. gold piece will be worth 500 paper dollars. If silver goes to $10 an ounce (as in my opinion it will—if the program outlined in Chapter 14 is not adopted), a silver quarter will be worth $1.80. Paper money obviously cannot appreciate in value with inflation. Neither can the bogus coins now minted by the U.S. government.

Since a U.S. quarter contains only about a penny's worth of copper, even if copper increased 500 percent in value, the intrinsic value of the U.S. quarter would still only increase to 5 cents. These coins would still be overvalued some 400 percent. Since currently produced U.S. money cannot offer protection against inflation, it can no longer fulfill two of the four requirements demanded of money. It can no longer serve as a reliable store of value or as a means of deferred payment.

Correctly understood, the U.S. government's coinage operation violates Article 1, Section 8, of the U.S. Constitution. The Constitution empowered Congress to "coin money," not to produce worthless tokens.

The government's coinage operation also violates Title 18, Section 1001, of the U.S. criminal code which reads as follows:

> Whoever, in any matter within the jurisdiction of any department or agency of the United States knowingly and willfully falsifies, conceals or covers up by any trick, scheme, or device a material fact or makes any false, fictitious, or fraudulent statement or representations, or makes or uses any false writing or document knowing the same to contain any false, fictitious or fraudulent statement or entry shall be fined not more than $10,000 or imprisoned not more than five years or both. June 25, 1948, c. 645, 62 Stat. 749.

Since the design, composition and structure of U.S. cupro-nickel coins is nothing more than "a trick, scheme, or device" to conceal their true value, character, and composition, *all persons who have been and are now involved in their authorization should be prosecuted under this statute*.

The Destruction of U.S. Paper Currency (Money Substitutes)

Using gold and silver exclusively as money has certain disadvantages. Weight might make it impractical, if not impossible, to transport and transact large sums. Government, therefore, provides a useful monetary service when it acts as a depository for the nation's money and issues paper receipts for the money stored in the treasury. Thus, a nation's legitimate paper money supply (currency) is nothing more than warehouse receipts for gold and silver stored in the national treasury, on exactly the same basis as those warehouse receipts first issued by goldsmiths in the Middle Ages. Figure 3 is an example of what was once honest U.S. paper currency—a *gold certificate.* This type of U.S. currency, first issued in 1863, changed very little from the type of receipt originally issued by those medieval goldsmiths. Note that it states "this certifies that there have been deposited in the Treasury of the United States of America ten dollars in gold payable to the bearer on demand." Gold certificates circulated in the United States until 1934 when the New Deal took away the citizen's right to own gold, a right Americans had enjoyed since the Pilgrims first stepped on Plymouth Rock.

Figure 4 is a similar warehouse receipt, only for silver. *Silver certificates* were discontinued in 1963.[1] Given this type of paper currency, those who ran the U.S. government were discouraged from printing unlimited quantities of paper currency since they could be compelled to redeem it with gold or silver. Thus, such currency prevented government from wantonly creating quantities of paper with which to pay its bills. Such a practice would inflate the currency supply, drive up prices, and rob citizens by reducing the purchasing power of the currency they already held. *Inflation,* correctly understood, is a device used by government to acquire revenues in lieu of direct taxation, and is achieved by debasing the nation's currency and stealing from the nation's savers (see Chapter 2).

In its campaign of currency debasement, the U.S. government gradually switched from honest paper currency (shown in Figures 3 and 4) to the dishonest and fraudulent kind it now circulates. Federal Reserve notes, the only type of paper currency in circulation today, came into being as a result of the Federal Reserve Act of 1913.[2] Changes that have occurred on the face of the Federal Reserve note dramatically reveal how the ability of Federal Reserve notes to serve as legitimate money substitutes was effectively terminated and how the total destruction of the U.S. money supply was engineered.

Federal Reserve notes, when first authorized, were not considered lawful money. This simple fact can be established from the very wording that appears on their face. Figure 5 is a specimen of the type of note originally issued by the Fed. It is simply a note, an IOU—nothing more. Since it is only a note, it must state how it is to be redeemed. These original Federal Reserve notes stated that they would be redeemed in "gold" at the U.S. Treasury or "in gold or lawful money at any Federal Reserve Bank."

When the note stated that it would be redeemed in "lawful money," it was emphasizing that it was not to be regarded as "lawful money." What was the "lawful money" in which Federal Reserve banks would redeem their notes? Gold and U.S. notes. Strange as it seems, even gold certificates were not accorded legal tender status until 1920, while silver and silver certificates did not attain it until 1933.

[1]And redemption suspended on June 24, 1968.

[2]See page 260 for an understanding of why Federal Reserve notes came into being and the purpose of the original act.

Figure 3

HONEST UNITED STATES CURRENCY

THIS CERTIFIES THAT THERE HAVE
BEEN DEPOSITED IN THE TREASURY OF

IN GOLD COIN PAYABLE TO THE BEARER ON DEMAND

U.S. GOLD CERTIFICATE 1863-1934

Figure 4

THIS CERTIFIES THAT THERE IS ON DEPOSIT
IN THE TREASURY OF

IN SILVER PAYABLE TO THE BEARER ON DEMAND

U.S. SILVER CERTIFICATE 1886-1963

When the Gold Reserve Act of 1934 made it illegal for Americans to own gold, the gold clause was removed from Federal Reserve notes and a new redemption clause appeared (see Figure 6). This new clause read: "This note is legal tender for all debts, public and private, and is redeemable in lawful money at the United States Treasury, or at any Federal Reserve Bank." Two things should be noted from the changes in the redemption clause. Suddenly Federal Reserve notes became "legal tender";[1] since this was not a characteristic of Federal Reserve notes when they were originally issued, how or why did they suddenly earn this "legal tender" status? And, Federal Reserve notes are still redeemable in "lawful money," further evidence that the notes themselves were still not regarded as being "lawful money." What was the "lawful money" with which the Fed banks would redeem their notes? Apparently, silver coins, silver certificates, and U.S. notes. These notes continued to circulate until discontinued by the government in 1963.

In 1963 the redemption clause on Federal Reserve notes was totally destroyed as shown by Figure 7, an example of the type of U.S. currency now in circulation. Note it contains no redemption clause. It only says: "This note is legal tender for all debts, public and private." In other words, the Fed is under no obligation to redeem its paper IOUs. Even "will pay to the bearer on demand" has disappeared. The situation is analogous to a creditor who's under no obligation to honor his debts. Since all Federal Reserve notes are now nonredeemable, they are in effect *IOU-nothings* of the Fed. It makes absolutely no difference to the Fed whether it issues a note for $10, $100, $1000 or $1,000,000 since the Fed does not create any obligation on its part to redeem in anything other than another piece of paper it is capable of printing.

Currently issued Federal Reserve notes do not even conform to the "Uniform Negotiable Instruments Act," which states that a note "to be negotiable" (1) must be in writing and signed by the maker or drawer, (2) must contain an unconditional promise or order to pay a certain sum in money, (3) must be payable to order or to bearer, and (4) where addressed to a drawee, he must be named or otherwise indicated therein with reasonable certainty.

The language used on the Federal Reserve notes in Fig.5&6 conforms to the first 3 requirements(the 4th being unnecessary for "bearer"paper) while that shown in Figure 7 does not. So what does this mean? It means that Federal Reserve notes are *not notes at all and are not negotiable as defined by law!* How could this fact have escaped the notice of the entire U.S. Bar, including our Supreme Court Justices? Surely, somebody must have completed a course on negotiable instruments and should, therefore, have protested the government's action in flooding the nation with non-negotiable "legal tender."

Since the U.S. Treasury does not issue any real money, no U.S. "legal tender" has any intrinsic value. The only value possessed by U.S. coins and paper currency

[1]The Thomas Amendment to the Agricultural Adjustment Act of 1933 made all forms of currency, and apparently even small change, unlimited legal tender.

Figure 5

REDEEMABLE IN GOLD ON DEMAND
AT THE UNITED STATES TREASURY
OR IN GOLD OR LAWFUL MONEY
AT ANY FEDERAL RESERVE BANK

WILL PAY TO THE BEARER ON DEMAND

A LEGITIMATE FEDERAL RESERVE NOTE 1913-1934

Figure 6

THIS NOTE IS LEGAL TENDER FOR ALL DEBTS
PUBLIC AND PRIVATE AND IS REDEEMABLE IN
LAWFUL MONEY AT THE UNITED STATES TREASURY
OR ANY FEDERAL RESERVE BANK

WILL PAY TO THE BEARER ON DEMAND

FEDERAL RESERVE NOTE 1934-1963

Figure 7

UNITED STATES UNMONEY

FEDERAL RESERVE "NOTES" CURRENTLY ISSUED

THIS IS A "NOTE" TO PAY NOTHING!

...IT IS A FRAUD!!

is that the U.S. Government will accept them in payment of taxes. Therefore, what circulates within the American economy is *not* money but script in which taxes are levied, and it is because of this assigned value that it is used and accepted in commercial transactions. If the U.S. government were to require citizens to pay their taxes in something else, like peach pits for example, U.S. paper money would immediately lose *all value* and the nation would begin calculating its wealth in peach pits. The fact that no U.S. coins contain gold or silver and all U.S. paper certificates are IOU-nothings raises some very perplexing questions for all U.S. citizens.

Before getting to those questions, there is one other form of paper money to consider. Figure 8 is an old, lucky $2 bill which is no longer in circulation. Why did they disappear? Notice from the bill's heading that it is not a Federal Reserve note, but a *United States note*. These were descendants of the notes originally issued by the North, in limited supply, to finance (the South, of course, issued its own irredeemable "Confederate Money" which, because it lost the war, ended up worthless) the Civil War. Yet, even the bill authorizing them barely made it out of Congress (since their unconstitutionality was readily apparent) even though their issue was made a matter of *national survival* and

Figure 8

U.S. NOTE CIRCULATION DISCONTINUED

FEDERAL RESERVE NOTE

passed solely out of "... apprehension for the safety of the Republic ..."[1] There now was no *monetary* difference between U.S. notes and Federal Reserve notes. Compare the wording on the notes shown in Figure 8—you will see that they had become one and the same. So, U.S. notes *had* to be removed from circulation to hide this fact from the public.

Now, there *was* one important distinction between these two notes. U.S. taxpayers were never charged interest when U.S. notes were created since they were run off and distributed directly by the government. Federal Reserve notes, on the other hand, came into being more subtly. The U.S. government would print up some U.S. bonds and take them to the Fed and *borrow* Federal Reserve notes, leaving the bonds as collateral,[2] with the government paying the Fed interest on the bonds deposited. However, since the "currency" the Fed gives to the government is irredeemable paper of the same quality that the U.S. government can print itself, why doesn't the government print all the money it needs directly and save the taxpayers all that interest? The answers to these questions can only be: (1) If the government were to print its money directly, the cat (that the U.S. government simply prints its money) would be out of the bag. Since few understand how Federal Reserve notes came into being, the country can continue to be hoodwinked into not realizing that the U.S. government, in reality, prints money when it prints government bonds. It is interesting to note that the original Federal Reserve Act prohibited this type of transaction since government bonds were not then deemed to be fit collateral for Federal Reserve notes. (2) Since the process of the government printing bonds and the Fed printing notes is far more complicated and costly than printing U.S. notes directly, this arrangement apparently fits the thinking and requirements of the Washington bureaucracy. Now, the fact that no U.S. coins contain gold or silver and no U.S. paper currency can be converted into gold and silver, raises the following interesting questions:

1. Is there any lawful "legal tender" circulating in the economy?[3] This would depend on whether the U.S. government has the authority to make anything it wishes a tender of valuable consideration? In my view *it does not have that right*. If the U.S. government can compel a citizen to accept trinkets in payment for his house, the government would, in my judgment, be depriving him of his property

[1] From the majority opinion written by Chief Justice Salmon P. Chase (8 Wall 625) declaring fiat, U.S. notes, unconstitutional—and ironically it was Chase who, as Lincoln's Secretary of the Treasury, had spearheaded the drive for their adoption! Note that it was only after U.S. notes became *redeemable in gold* (on January 1, 1879) that they were declared Constitutional (Julliard v. Greenman 110 U.S., 421, [1884]). And, even then, it is the *dissenting opinion* in this case, delivered by Justice Stephen J. Field, which history has clearly vindicated.

[2] Technically, the government does not borrow directly from the Fed, but indirectly, through the Fed's "open market" activities. However, the readers' understanding of government monetary shenanigans will be far more simplified but no less accurate, if he considers that the government borrows directly from the Fed. (See pages 260-263.)

[3] A tender, that is, of good and valuable consideration.

without due process of law. But, if the government does not have the right to make trinkets legal tender, then by what authority can it make bits of paper, having even less intrinsic value, legal tender?

2. Since Federal Reserve notes were never "lawful money," then they must have been "unlawful money." Does this mean that all U.S. currency is in effect unlawful? It is obvious when the face of an original Federal Reserve note is compared with the face of a current one, that the original notes were far superior paper. Despite the superiority of these earlier notes, they were not regarded as legal tender. Why, therefore, are current Federal Reserve notes of much poorer quality legal tender if the earlier notes were not? Is it because there was greater monetary integrity and understanding in the United States in 1913 than there is today?

3. No one in America earns any *real money*. Since no one earns any money, is anyone legally *required to pay income taxes?*

4. Section 10, Article 1, of the U.S. Constitution states that no state shall "make anything but gold and silver coin a tender in payment of debts." Since there is no official gold and silver coin or paper that is redeemable in gold and silver coin, can state and municipal courts legally compel persons to pay their debts?

5. Since the Constitution only empowers Congress to "coin money and regulate the value thereof," can Federal Reserve notes circulate as "legal tender" since they are the product of the Federal Reserve System which is technically independent of Congress?

6. Since Federal Reserve notes are no longer convertible into lawful money, how can they serve as lawful money themselves? Thus, it would seem that payment in money which itself is not lawful cannot be made legal tender, despite pretensions to legal tender printed on them. Historically, Federal Reserve notes were legal tender because they were convertible and redeemable in lawful money. But since they are no longer redeemable, they are worthless. Since they have no real value, how can one be compelled to accept them? This principle has already been upheld in *First National Bank of Montgomery* v. *Jerome Daly in the County of Scott, State of Minnesota.*[1]

Recapping, therefore, it is clear that only gold and silver can constitutionally be regarded as *money,* while all forms of paper money and less than full-bodied

[1]December 9, 1968. Being in arrears in his payments, the First National Bank of Montgomery foreclosed on his mortgage, purchased the property at a Sheriff's Sale, and brought suit to regain possession of the property on which it had granted Mr. Daly a $14,000 mortgage in 1964. Daly, however, contended that since the bank "created the money and credit upon its own books by a bookkeeping entry . . ." there was no legal consideration to support the mortgage deed, and, therefore, alleged ". . . that the Sheriff's Sale passed no title to the plaintiff." The jury found in favor of Daly and permitted him to keep his property, awarded him $75 in costs, and also voided his debt. In a supporting memorandum, the judge in the case, Martin V. Mahoney, a Justice of the Peace, stated: "Plaintiff's act of creating credit is not authorized by the Constitution and laws of the United States, is unconstitutional and void, and is not lawful consideration in the eyes of the law to support anything upon which any lawful rights can be built."

coins serve only as *substitutes* for money—and as such are correctly referred to as *currency* or *tokens—not money*. However, since the U.S. government no longer requires that real money be exchanged for money substitutes, Americans not only do not have any money, they also do not have any currency (a money substitute for which no money will be substituted can hardly be termed a money substitute). Correctly understood, therefore, a new term must be employed to accurately describe American "legal tender"—an appropriate term, I suggest, would be—*UNMONEY!*

2

Inflation: The Government's Silent Partner

Inflation is one of the least understood words in the English language. The U.S. government and most of the nation's economists and financial "experts" have convinced the public that inflation is an illusive economic force that manages to propel prices continually upward despite efforts to contain them.

We are, of course, told that this mysterious force is a problem plaguing not only America but many other countries, and from this we are to conclude that inflation is a universal problem that befuddles economists and statesmen the world over. High government officials almost daily express bureaucratic concern about the tragic effects of inflation, especially on the nation's senior citizens and those living on fixed incomes.

To prove their determination to stop inflation, government policymakers impose wage and price controls. The controls do no good, but at least the policymakers show that their hearts were in the right place.

One way that the government attempts to combat inflation is by admonishing American workers asking for "inflationary" wage hikes. Of course, many high officials and politicians never consider that granting higher government salaries is inflationary. But the government really gets angry and goes all out to "help" the consumer when American businesses raise prices. Government officials tell the offending businesses in no uncertain terms that price increases are inflationary and must be rolled back. If a business does not voluntarily roll back prices, our government simply uses a little muscle in the consumer's behalf. This is known as "jawboning" or "arm twisting" and is applied all in the "spirit" of free enterprise. When the 1974 automobile prices were released, some increases were as high as $175 per car—increases of nearly 5 percent. Much of these increases were for the safety devices mandated by the U.S. government. Despite this, official Washington said that such price increases were inflationary and urged the auto industry to roll them back. At about the same time, though, the U.S. Postal Service unobtrusively raised first-class postage from 8 to 10 cents—a 25 percent rate increase. Now, why wasn't the Postal Service "jawboned" to roll back its prices?

Another technique the government employs in fighting inflation is that of telling us inflation is *our* fault. We, the consuming public, simply want too much. We demand more and more, and as long as we do, inflation is the price we must pay. Remember President Lyndon Johnson urging American housewives back in '66 to fight inflation at the checkout counter of the supermarket? However, if spending *less* can really fight inflation, why hasn't the government applied this policy to its own spending habits? After all, the U.S. government is by far the nation's biggest spender. And now our present political leadership has seen fit to treat us to a new spectacle, an "Economic Summit Meeting" attended by 800 delegates representing all segments of the economy to help the President deal with inflation. This had been preceded by a "presummit meeting" of twenty-eight of the nation's "leading" economists, presumably to prep the President for the larger conference to follow. What President Gerald Ford overlooked, however, is that most of the "experts" at the first conference had advised former presidents to promote inflation and, in fact, had helped to make inflation academically respectable. The result of this conference was a clarion call *for even greater doses of inflation*. It was to the Ford administration's credit that this call was rejected. "Jawboning," price controls, Summit Conferences—why haven't these government efforts to stop inflation worked? Why do we have the highest rates of inflation in the nation's history?

How the Government "Fights" Inflation

There is nothing mysterious about inflation. The government could stamp it out tomorrow if it really wanted to. After all, inflation is conceived by government, nurtured by government, perpetuated by government. *Inflation is government's silent partner. Inflation permits government to bestow increased "benefits" on taxpayers without the apparent need for increased taxes. Inflation permits government to retire huge debts without being inconvenienced by honest repayment.* Since the present value of the government debt is approximately $5 trillion (see Chapter 3), inflation of only 10 percent will effectively wipe out $500 billion of that debt. *Inflation creates an illusion of prosperity.* People can be persuaded that they are becoming richer even as they are forced to work harder, and they and the nation become poorer.

Inflation effectively increases tax rates and tax levels without the need of increased taxing authority. With the graduated income tax, inflation automatically forces people into higher tax brackets. So, while inflation does not increase spendable income, it increases tax revenues. For example, assume a taxpayer earns $10,000 a year and spends all of it on goods and services. (To keep it simple, let's disregard the impact of taxes on just this portion of his income and expenses.) Let us assume an inflation of 10 percent which will increase wages and expenses proportionately. His income will now be $11,000 and his expenses $11,000. If this were all there is to it, the taxpayer would not appear to have suffered any loss, if you overlook the impact on his savings. But, wait, at this income level federal income and Social Security taxes (we shall now consider the impact of taxes on just this portion of income) will probably take about 30 percent of his salary increase, leaving only $700 to pay for the $1000 increase in expenses. Thus, inflation has enabled government to secure more of the taxpayer's spendable income without any official increase in taxes. The taxpayer is really poorer, but now paying *more* in taxes.

In determining one's estate tax liability, one is permitted to exclude the first $60,000 of property from the taxable estate. This $60,000 exemption was first adopted in the 1947 Revenue Act. Since then, of course, inflation has increased some 400 percent, thus effectively reducing the estate tax exemption to $12,000. Thus, federal estate taxes have been effectively increased without the authority of law. This same principle, of course, applies to personal exemptions, gift taxes, and so forth, and all manner of government tax exemptions and tax exclusions. Inflation has the effect of lowering all these exclusions and exemptions in the government's favor.

As you can see, inflation is government's wondrous genie, performing all sorts of economic and monetary magic for its master. The capital gains tax provides dramatic evidence of how the government profits from inflation, for inflation provides government with the means to (1) tax assets that should go untaxed, and (2) extract increased taxes where they are unwarranted. Let's assume that a house bought in 1940 for $5000 sells in 1975 for $18,000. Forgetting any other extraneous considerations, the government would claim that the seller had a gain of $13,000 on this sale and would assess a capital gains tax accordingly. The fact of the matter is that the seller had an economic loss, yet he is compelled to pay a "gains tax." Since prices have increased at least 500 percent since 1940 (see Figure 9), in order for the seller to receive the same *purchasing power* from the sale of the house as when he bought it, he would have to receive at least $30,000. In fact, he received only $18,000—60 percent of the initial purchasing power. This loss is, of course, understandable and to be expected since the owner used the house for 24 years. The house should have a *lower* value in 1975 than it had in 1940. But the government's ever-industrious genie has caused the house to appear to be worth more when it is actually worth less. In this way, government can extract unwarranted taxes at the time of its sale. Logically, capital appreciation

Figure 9

THE EFFECT OF INFLATION ON PRICES

Commodity	1945	1975	Percent Increase
Average Cost Nonfarm Dwelling	under $5,000*	$37,500**	650
Bus and Trolley Fare	.08	.35	335
Minimum Wage	.40	2.10	425
Men's Dress Shirt	3.50	9.50	170
Ice Cream Cone	.05	.35	600
Daily Newspaper	.02	.15	650
Soda Pop	.05	.25	400
Corned Beef Sandwich	.20	1.75	775
Hot Dog	.10	.60	500
Cup of Coffee	.05	.25	400
Movie	.35	2.00	470
Per Diem Hospital Cost***	9.00	144.00	1,500
Weekly News Magazine	.15	.75	400
2 Hostess Cupcakes	.05	.25	400
Post Card (to mail)	.01	.08	700
AVERAGE PRICE INCREASE			605
GOVERNMENT'S CONSUMER PRICE INDEX	54.2(6/45)	160.6(6/75)	196

These examples of price changes do not take into account changes in quality, size, or improvements in efficiency. If they did, price disparities would be greater than indicated. It should also be noted that since price changes are inaccurate indications of inflation, it is unnecessary to compile an extensive list in order to suggest accuracy. Even one product (two Hostess cupcakes, for example) is a reflection of hundreds of other prices for both goods and services which go into their manufacture, delivery, and sale, and thus they could alone serve as a fairly reliable indicator of inflationary pressure. To the extent that the nation looked to them rather than to the Consumer Price Index as its official index of inflation, taxpayers would not only save millions in unnecessary bureaucratic salaries but would also, as the figures suggest, acquire a more reliable index.

*The median values for nonfarm, owner-occupied dwellings according to the 1940 and 1970 U.S. census, were $3,000 and $17,100 respectively.

**The median sale price for all new, one family homes sold in December 1974. Source: U.S. Department of Commerce circular C25-74-12.

***Average hospital stay was shortened from 9.1 to 7.5 days.

should be adjusted for artificial inflationary increases, even using the government's own inaccurate statistics.

When government monetary policy shrinks the value of the dollar, prices respond by moving up.[1] Since a dollar is the yardstick by which all wealth is measured and taxed, measuring one's wealth with smaller dollars creates the illusion of greater wealth and compels the payment of higher, unwarranted taxes.

Now, there are two types of "dollar shrinkages"—official ones and unofficial ones. On December 18, 1971, and February 12, 1973, we had two official ones called "devaluations":[2] the former was 8.57 percent and the latter 10 percent. Almost daily, as the dollar shrinks in value, causing prices to appear to be going up, we have unofficial devaluations. When the government reported, for instance, that the Consumer Price Index for '74 had risen by 12.2 percent, it should have reported that government monetary policy has "shrunk" the dollar by another 12.2 percent. But by asserting that prices had gone up rather than accurately reporting that the dollar's value had gone down, the government is able to mislead the public as to what is really going on.

Let's look at the consequences of an official dollar devaluation. When the U.S. government officially devalued its currency by 10 percent on February 12, 1973, it declared that $1000 on February 11, 1973, was worth only $900 on February 12. Why was this loss not taken into consideration by all the nation's accountants and tax attorneys when calculating their clients' tax liabilities? A taxpayer who had $10,000 in the bank on February 11 was told by his government that on February 12 it was officially worth only $9000. Since this individual had an official loss of $1000, he should have deducted it as a loss on his 1973 income tax return. This deduction should have been applied as well to all of his fixed dollar assets such as bonds, the cash value of life insurance, bank accounts, etc. As a result of this official devaluation of U.S. currency, prices *had* to move up (that is, prices for *all* goods, domestic and imported) to compensate for the loss in the dollar's purchasing power created by the official devaluation.

A loss of purchasing power to the taxpayer is the same when caused by the government reducing the value of a taxpayer's money as when a taxpayer loses money directly. If the latter is tax deductible, why not the former?

While it would seem that a taxpayer should be able, in all equity, to adjust the value of his assets to reflect both official and unofficial devaluations in computing his tax liability, he should have the constitutional right to make the adjustment to reflect official devaluations of the dollar. For example, applying this adjustment to our example of the house that sold for $18,000 in 1975, in the light of the devaluations of 1971 and 1973, the U.S. government had officially proclaimed that 1975 dollars were 18.57 percent smaller than 1940 dollars. This being the position of the U.S. government, the $18,000 received in 1975 were by the

[1]Or they move down by less than they otherwise would.

[2]See Chapter 5.

government's admission equivalent to only $14,658. Capital gains taxes, therefore, should be calculated to show a gain of only $9,658 and not $14,000 (overlooking entirely, of course, the fact that a loss had actually been suffered if unofficial devaluations were taken into consideration).

That such an adjustment should be allowed, in all equity, by the U.S. government can be determined from the rules of the International Monetary Fund. When the IMF was established at Bretton Woods in 1944, capital subscription quotas for each member included the proviso that if any nation devalued its currency in terms of gold, it must pay the Fund an *additional* quantity of its money sufficient to indemnify the Fund against its devaluation losses in terms of gold. What the IMF was, in effect, saying to the world's monetary authorities was, "If you want to swindle your nationals through devaluation manipulations, OK. But, don't think you can pull that on us." So while the U.S. must indemnify the IMF, which holds $825 million of U.S. bonds, for their losses due to U.S. currency devaluation, no such compensation is made to U.S. taxpayers to cover their losses. Therefore, these losses should at least be tax deductible. Is there no end to how the U.S. public allows itself to be fleeced by its own government?

Who's Really to Blame?

Inflation comes from one source—and only that source, government, can stop it. Whenever there's inflation, government is spending more than it collects in taxes and/or is increasing the supply of money and credit relevant to the production of goods and services.

All governments find that paying their bills by creating inflation is safer politically than increasing taxes. When government's inflationary policy succeeds in forcing prices up by an uncomfortable degree, the government simply blames other segments of the economy and even the consumer for the higher prices. For its scapegoats government singles out "middlemen" or "big business" who are causing "inflation" in pursuit of "unwarranted high profits." Since there are fewer middlemen and big businessmen than, for example, farmers or laborers, they are a safer target for the government. Of course, no economic segment is to blame for inflation, except society in general for being so naive as to entrust the nation's currency to politicians and their appointees. Apart from the government, however, much of the nation's inflation can be blamed on the banks and insurance companies.[1] These powerful institutions should have exerted pressure on government to guard the purchasing power of the billions of dollars entrusted to them by the nation's savers. In 1974, with an inflation of at least 18 percent,[2] insurance companies permitted the government to wipe out nearly $38 billion in the purchasing power of insurance cash values and over $320 billion from the face value of

[1] They could have refused to purchase government bonds while publicizing for the benefit of their depositors and insureds the true nature of inflation.

[2] Officially only 12.2 percent, but that, of course, is a lie.

existing policies. Since insurance companies only wrote $207 billion in new face value insurance in 1974, approximately 50 percent more insurance was wiped out that year because of inflation than was written by all insurance companies combined. Insurance companies should have been duty-bound to protect insurance values since they sell insurance on the strength of a ''guarantee,'' but they have done little to pressure government to exercise monetary restraint so that their ''guarantees'' would be meaningful.

The Economics Of Inflation

Let us now return to the subject of inflation. What exactly is inflation? Look at the word *inflation* and you will see that its root is *inflate*—like to inflate a balloon. In inflation it is the currency supply that is being inflated, like a balloon. Who controls the currency supply. Who's inflating it? Why, the *government*. So it is the government that creates inflation, inflating the quantity of currency and credit. As the quantity of money and credit is inflated relevant to the supply of goods and services, prices *must* rise. So, price increases are not inflationary, they are merely the *effects of inflation* created by government. To find out who causes inflation, find out who controls a nation's currency supply. Since, in the United States, as in other countries, the government controls the currency supply, it is the government that does the inflating by permitting the currency supply to grow. This principle could easily be seen at work in Germany following its defeat in World War II. Until national currencies were reestablished American cigarettes served as money. However, as more GIs occupied an area and brought more cigarettes, ''inflation'' in terms of cigarettes set in, so prices (in cigarettes) went up.

The federal government would have you believe that it promotes prosperity by expanding the currency supply and easing credit. But this is not true. However, let's for now omit considering what will or will not cause prosperity or depression and concentrate on why prices rise or fall—in other words what causes inflation or deflation?

Note that Figure 10 does not include the *total* U.S. money[1] supply—I omitted bank deposits. For the sake of simplicity, we need only examine the U.S. *physical* supply of money to find the source of our inflation. Notice how money in circulation was inflated while our supply of real money, gold and silver, was vanishing. In 1930 there was about a dollar's worth of gold for every dollar in circulation (forgetting silver backing). Yet by 1974 it had dwindled to 15 cents in gold for every dollar in circulation.[2] Severe price increases were, therefore the

[1]Since we all now know the difference, the reader will be understanding when he notes that the author, in the interest of simplicity, has used the word ''money'' in its popularly understood context.

[2]*Pick's 1973 Currency Yearbook,* taking into consideration external liquid liabilities and demand deposits as well as money in circulation, arrived at a gold reserve of 3.5 percent as of the end of March 1973, and characterized this as a ''rather flimsy reserve for a currency of alleged worldwide importance.'' The reserve has grown flimsier since.

Figure 10

**A SUMMARY
OF
THE CHANGES IN THE U.S. SUPPLY
OF
UNMONEY-MONEY-CURRENCY-BULLION**

	In Circulation*		Stored Bullion In U.S. Treasury** (Backing for Currency)	
Year	Total (In Billions)	Per Capita (In Dollars)	Gold (In Millions of Ounces)	Silver
1915	$ 3.3	$ 33	100	9
1920	5.5	51	140	20
1925	4.8	41	215	24
1930	4.5	36	225	17
1935	5.5	44	260	483
1940	7.8	59	571	2,365
1945	27.0	191	571	1,877
1950	27.0	179	686	1,734
1955	30.0	183	617	1,717
1960	32.0	177	543	1,899
1965	40.0	204	490	1,000
1970	54.0	265	314	66
6/73	68.0	322	276	46
6/75	82.0***	384	275	44****

Note how the introduction of unmoney enabled the government to inflate the currency supply by over 750 percent per capita between 1935 and June 1975, during which time America's supply of *real money* dropped approximately 40 percent per capita. This, essentially, is the heart of the nation's inflation and the principal cause of its rising prices.

* Including currency held by the U.S. Treasury and in bank vaults.

** Bullion figures were derived from U.S. Mint sources—however, certain assumptions were still required. For example—the government usually carried bullion in dollars which had to be converted into ounces. Silver inventories for some years prior to 1930 were carried at cost, so estimates of the Treasury's cost had to be made.

*** No consideration is given to the monetary value of earlier U.S. coins which, prior to 1934, were largely gold and silver, and prior to 1966, silver. This would add additional value to earlier figures in comparison to the approximately 7 billion of inferior cupro-nickel coins included here.

**** Does not include 212.7 million ounces transferred to the strategic stockpile pursuant to act of June 24, 1967. (81 Stat. 77)

natural result of such an *irresponsible* monetary policy.

The government greatly benefits from an inflationary policy. Politicians gain because inflation increases substantially government revenues and creates an illusion of prosperity. Much of American prosperity over the last 15 years was bought by squandering the nation's gold and silver supply and going into debt to the rest of the world to the tune of $100 billion. Inflation cloaks indicators of our real economic problems. When the government inflates the currency supply by printing more "money" and by expanding the availability of credit, such as FHA financing, it is "inflating the supply of 'money' and credit." When the government does this, price increases are inevitable. Price increases themselves are *not* inflationary, they are the *effects* of government-engendered inflation. When U.S. officials insist that price increases are inflationary, they are misrepresenting to the public the real cause and effect.

Getting to the Nitty-Gritty on Why Prices Rise

Better understanding of why prices rise requires grasping the concept that rising prices, mistakenly termed inflation, are caused by more money chasing fewer goods. When an economy has more money and fewer goods the money will be used to bid up the prices of the available goods. So, anything that increases the supply of money and reduces the quantity of goods is inflationary, anything that reduces the supply of money and increases the quantity of goods is deflationary. To fight rising prices effectively, therefore, one must either *reduce* the supply of money in relationship to the supply of goods or *increase* the supply of goods in relation to the supply of money. In its fight to curb inflation, has the U.S. government done either of these? Absolutely not. Examination of U.S. monetary and fiscal policies will show that all U.S. government activity has been not only to increase the currency supply but actually to reduce the quantity of goods and services coming to market. In other words, all U.S. economic and monetary influence has been exerted in the interest of increasing inflationary pressures.

Many federal laws were designed to discourage and prevent goods and services from reaching market. For example, for years the U.S. government has paid farmers about $4 billion a year *not* to grow food. Removing this amount of agricultural products from the economy pushed food prices upward and living standards downward. Consider too, that the government sends out checks to over 30 million Social Security recipients each month (see Chapter 4). Many of these recipients are encouraged not to work under penalty of losing Social Security benefits. Consequently, because of this penalty for working, the economy loses whatever economic contributions these recipients might make. The government eliminates their productivity while giving them paper dollars with which to bid up the productivity of others. The government, of course, exerts the same type of influence on people on welfare.

The federal government's minimum wage law is another example of how government economic interference increases inflationary pressures. This law is inflationary not because it forces wages and prices up as some might think (see Chapter 9), but because it artificially creates a legal standard of productivity, a "minimum standard for productivity" higher than many are capable of achieving. Consequently, many workers are simply cut from the nation's work force, thereby denying to society their productivity.

The U.S. government knows it creates inflation but simply refuses publicly to accept responsibility for it. For example, both Henry Fowler, then Secretary of the Treasury, and William McChesney Martin, then Chairman of the Federal Reserve System, when testifying before the U.S. Senate Committee on Banking and Currency urged removal of the 25 percent gold reserve requirement from Federal Reserve notes. At that time, the U.S. Treasury reached the point where the reserve requirement interfered with the government's ability to continue inflating the currency supply—which is why the statutory requirement was there in the first place. When the Federal Reserve System started in 1913, district banks were required to maintain a 40 percent gold reserve behind those paper Federal Reserve notes and a 35 percent gold reserve against deposits. In 1945 gold reserve requirements both for notes and deposits were dropped to 25 percent. In 1965 the gold reserve requirement for deposits was eliminated and, as a consequence of the type of testimony illustrated in the following paragraph, gold backing of Federal Reserve notes was eliminated in 1968. With gold backing of Fed notes and bank deposits eliminated, the total debasement of U.S. currency was completed. Now, the U.S. government and the Fed could print unmoney without end. (See Chapter 13 for further discussion.)

Secretary Fowler told the Senate Banking and Currency Committee that the government must generate more inflation because "an expanding U.S. economy needs an expanding supply of currency." (See Note I, Appendix C, for fuller presentations of government testimonies.) Notice how Fowler uses "expanding [the] supply of currency" as a euphemism for *inflating* the money supply. Monetary events since then show just how deceptive Fowler's comments were. *The 1975 Economic Report of the President* noted (page 68) that ". . . currency grew at a 9.9 percent rate from December 1973 to December 1974 . . ." while noting (page 37) that the nation's "GNP in 1974," given the government's GNP inflation deflator of 10 percent had sustained ". . . a 2 percent *decline* in output." Who, therefore, needed this expansion of currency—Secretary Fowler, the *economy*, or the U.S. government?

William McChesney Martin, then Chairman of the Federal Reserve System, testified:[1]

[1]*Hearings before the Committee on Banking & Currency*, U.S. Senate, 90th Congress, 2nd Session on S.1307, S.2815, S.2857. Washington: p. 37.

. . . the Board of Governors of the Federal Reserve System recommends prompt enactment of legislation to repeal the statutory provisions that now require each Federal Reserve bank to maintain reserves in gold certificates of not less than 25 percent of its Federal Reserve notes in circulation. Some change in this requirement this year or next will be *unavoidable as the volume of our currency grows* in response to the demands of a growing economy, as Secretary Fowler has already pointed out. Its repeal now would help to make absolutely clear that the U.S. gold stock is fully available to serve its primary purpose as an international monetary reserve. [Italics mine.]

Where Fowler uses "expanding the currency supply" to describe the need for inflating the money supply by creating additional quantities of worthless Federal Reserve notes, Martin sees the need to *increase* the "volume of our currency."

However, Martin was wrong on two counts. Like Fowler, he erred when he suggested that "the volume of our currency grows in response to the demands of a growing economy." Our currency grew and continues to grow because of the demands of government, not in response to the demands of the economy. Martin was wrong when he suggested that the primary purpose of the U.S. gold stock is to be "fully available to serve its primary purpose as an international monetary reserve." The primary purpose of the U.S. gold stock was to satisfy the public's need for sound money. It was because U.S. currency had a tradition of integrity that it was accepted as an international standard of value. This is now no longer true. Destruction of the integrity of U.S. currency at home has damaged its acceptability abroad. However, since the U.S. government halted convertibility of the dollar for gold in 1971, our gold stock is no longer "fully available to serve" as an "international monetary reserve." So, what is its "primary purpose" now, Mr. Martin?

Why All Theories That Blame Inflation on Factors Other Than Government Monetary Policy Are Wrong

At this point, some may be wondering about other types of inflation mentioned in recent years—such as *cost-push, demand-pull,* and *the wage-price spiral*. These terms and their theoretical assumptions were largely developed by Keynesian "economists."[1] They have enabled Keynesians (read: inflationists) to escape the consequences of their theories and blame the resultant high prices on the consumer. Most politicians find Keynesian explanations for inflation irresistible because they get them off the hook for causing inflation in the first place. Attempts to explain price increases by way of cost-push inflation are foolish, because a fundamental law of economics is that *supply and demand determine prices*. This law, the bedrock of economics, has never been refuted successfully. Note that "cost" does not appear anywhere in this law governing prices. This, of course, means that

[1] See Chapter 12 on the uneconomists.

cost, and that includes wages—the cost of labor—has no effect on prices. Thus, there can be no such things as cost-push inflation or a wage-price spiral. I shall offer you an example to demonstrate this law. Remember the hula hoop craze? At their height hula hoops became scarce and people paid up to two to three dollars apiece for them. Now, let's assume it costs 30 to 40 cents to manufacture one. Manufacturers would charge 75 cents, a dollar or whatever the traffic would bear. Cost was immaterial to them as they tried for the maximum possible based upon the heavy demand. In response to this demand, manufacturers rushed to produce hula hoops, even paying a premium to secure the necessary materials. Then the craze fizzled. Did this mean that if a retailer paid $1.25 for a hoop, he could automatically sell it for $1.75 or even $1.25? Did the cost of the hoop determine its price at the time? Of course not. When the craze ended, you couldn't give hula hoops away, and if all you could get for a hoop was 25 or 50 cents, that's what you sold it for, even though it might have cost 75 cents or a dollar to make.

Suppose demand for hula hoops is such that given their supply the public is only willing to pay 50 cents for them. If this price is too low for them to be manufactured profitably, hula hoops will no longer be made. Supplies, therefore, will dwindle. Hula hoops will become scarce. They might even become collector's items. Serious buyers will soon vie for the dwindling supply and soon would be bidding up their price. That is how cost affects prices.

Increased demand, of course, has immediate impact on prices, but for this demand to be effective and cause price increases, it must be accompanied by *money* to translate this demand into effective bidding for goods and services. Demand-pull inflation is an inanity, since it is the "money" printed by government and placed in the hands of the consumer that does the pulling not the consumer's naked demand.

The cost-push theory attempts to explain rising prices on the basis of rising costs. The rationale is: rising costs force up prices, which in turn force up costs, which again in turn force up prices, and so on—that is why prices keep escalating. This reasoning is also implicit in the wage-price-spiral concept. Exponents of these theories assume that increasing costs force up prices and overlook the fact that *cost and price are one!* The cost to the consumer of a gallon of gasoline is the price charged at the local pump. The cost of a pound of nails to a builder is the price charged by the hardware store. The cost of a house to a homeowner is the price charged by the builder. Cost and price are synonymous, only viewed from two different angles. For costs to push up prices would be a feat comparable to one pulling himself up by his own bootstraps. Attempting to explain rising prices on the basis of rising costs is tantamount to saying "prices go up because prices go up" or "costs go up because costs go up." Such specious reasoning is apparent in the wage-price-spiral concept. Since wages are themselves a price, the price for labor, the wage-price spiral translates into "price-price spiral"—a distinction without a difference. Thus, in my view, theories that explain inflation on the basis of demand-pull, cost-push, and wage-spiral only underscore the lack of understanding of economics by their respective proponents.

Price controls cannot stop inflation, and their advocates simply reveal their lack of comprehension of the subject of inflation. Price controls merely attack the symptoms of inflation—high prices—not the causes. And while they will even be ineffective in mitigating the symptoms of inflation, they will create economic distortions which will, together with all the bureaucratic red tape that any such system of controls must necessarily produce, hinder and reduce total productivity—and thus actually contribute to the inflation!

A recent TV special on inflation is a good example of the misinformation that is rampant. On October 7, 1974, the PBS network produced a special entitled "Inflation—The Money Merry-Go-Round." The panelists[1] were Walter Heller, John Kenneth Galbraith, and Milton Friedman. Here's a sampling of the discussion.

Announcer: Let me get a very quick answer from all of you on one question that we don't seem to have dealt with. Is this wage-price spiral that we get into an inevitable by-product of our society today? Is it always going to be that way? Are wages always going to go up?

Friedman: There is no wage-price spiral . . .

Galbraith: (interrupting, good naturedly) Absolutely, your instincts are absolutely sound and pay no intention to Friedman's answers. (Audience laughter)

Friedman: . . . because there is no wage-price spiral, the wage-price spiral is an invention of the people in Washington who want to shift the blame to somebody else and to blame the greedy trade unions and the grasping businessmen for what is really the consequence of misgovernment in Washington.

Galbraith: Milton, I . . .

Friedman: What is called the wage-price spiral is a consequence of the prior inflationary policies of the federal government. Now the federal government is not doing it at random, they are doing it because the public at large makes it politically profitable to spend more and to tax less.

Galbraith: Milton, I've done more to publicize the wage-price spiral than anybody in Washington. Don't blame this on the politicians.

Friedman: (laughing) Okay, I withdraw that.

Heller: I want to say two things on this. Number one, it is not a wage-price spiral today; it is a price-wage spiral. Prices were pushed up, real incomes were pushed down and labor is recouping, and we're in the midst of it right now. Now what we have to hope—we're moving from soft-core inflation to hard-core inflation. We're moving from inflation that came from a food price explosion—supply side—from oil, from commodities prices, and so forth.

Galbraith: And demand?

Heller: Demand was high, but demand certainly isn't a factor today. We don't have excess demand in the economy. There is a lot of excess capacity. And so, that is not our problem. But just let me finish this thought . . .

[1]A former chairman of President's Council of Economic Advisers and two prominent university economists.

Friedman: We certainly do have excess money demand.

Heller: Ahh . . . disagree. But let me just finish by saying that those of us who are concerned about the price-wage spiral are worried that this inflation that is beginning to ebb, in terms of the world wide commodity pressures and in terms of the pop-up effect of what we were talking about before, of taking off phase IV controls, that that unfortunately is being picked up in the wage settlements and perpetuated.

Now, if we had a believable anti-inflationary policy, labor would not have had to convert all of that inflation into its wage settlements. But, we don't have a believable anti-inflation policy, so we do have a price-wage spiral.

So, here you have it: Galbraith and Heller believe not only in a wage-price spiral but Heller, practicing one-upmanship, asserts that it has become a price-wage spiral. In other words, according to Heller, the *price-price spiral* has now become a *price-price spiral.*

Is the Consumer Price Index a Reliable Measure of Inflation?

Now, let's consider the spurious notions associated with the U.S. Government's Consumer Price Index. This index purports to measure the degree of inflation by changes in prices. Since it is the government that is causing the inflation, to expect it to provide accurate statistics concerning the degree of inflation it is causing is like expecting the Mafia to furnish accurate statistics on crime. Government statistics are designed to mislead, not inform, the public concerning the full extent of the inflation that government is inflicting upon them. Inflation, as shown in Figure 9, is far greater than the CPI figures indicate.

Price increases do not measure inflation, they only reveal its effects. They remain an inaccurate measure, because a substantial portion of inflation is hidden by technological advances and changes in quality. For example, an average nonfarm dwelling prior to 1945 sold for under $5,000. Today, the price would be in excess of $37,500. Does that mean that inflation has only increased the cost of housing by 650 percent? No, the rate of inflation is much higher because if today's house were built with the same level of technology as that prior to 1945, with the same skills, materials, building methods, and craftsmanship, it would in all probability sell for well over $60,000—showing a rate of inflation of over 1,100 percent, not 650 percent.

Government figures purporting to show the rate of inflation through price changes fail to take into consideration the downward pull on prices exerted by increased efficiency. Prices have increased—*despite increases in productive efficiency, despite* advances in technology, and *despite* development of new and more economic materials.

My father was a carpenter, and during the late 1930s and early 40s I would accompany him to the "job." On all these jobs, which were usually one-family houses, I never once saw a piece of power equipment. If a door had to be trimmed, muscle power was used to propel a ripsaw through seven feet of solid lumber. Wood then was planed and sanded, and joints were mitered. Lumber yards then carried a variety of wood—oak, cherry, mahogany, cedar—where now you find mostly spruce and pine. You do not need me to point out the difference between workmanship of yesterday and today. But what must be pointed out is that if the workers of 30 years ago had access to the materials, techniques, and equipment available today and wished to build with the quality of workmanship found acceptable today, houses would have sold then for $2000, not $5000.

Not too long ago, I bought a candy bar for 15 cents that had for many years sold for only a nickel. "Well," I noted, picking the candy bar from the case, "its price has only increased 200 percent." However, when I removed the oversized wrapper, I discovered the candy was actually a third its nickel-priced size. Its price, therefore, had soared not 200 percent, but 600 percent. CPI statistics do not, of course, reveal price increases of this type.

CPI figures are not adjusted upward to compensate for improved technology, changes to inferior materials, and poorer workmanship, but they are adjusted downward to adjust for quality improvement. For example, suppose that the price of an iron was increased from $12 to $13 but it now contained a thermostat for settings for different fabrics. The U.S. government might conclude that the thermostat was worth a dollar, and so their statistics might show that the price of the iron did not increase at all. I suppose if things were really tough, I wouldn't put it past the government to conclude that the thermostat was worth $1.50, so the price of the iron would actually be reduced by 50 cents. The point is that government statisticians have a good deal of arbitrary leeway that enables them to produce all kinds of figures—after all, who's to check on them?

In line with this, several years ago I was discussing with some friends why government's cost of living figures were always so much lower than those developed by private sources and what could be observed with the naked eye. The father of a friend, who owned a lumber yard, interrupted. "Every year," he said, "I get a call from some government agency wanting to know what our price is for ¾ inch tongue and groove flooring. We had that stuff lying around for years and we never get any calls for it, so its price hasn't changed in years." Flabbergasted, I pursued the subject. He told me that he was never asked the price of plywood or two-by-fours which, at that time, had risen sharply in price. Here apparently was the government incorporating into its lumber statistics the price of a type of lumber no longer used. Thus, the government was able to hide increases in lumber prices by including in its sampling the cost of a type of lumber whose price it knew to be stable.

The way one can approximate annual price increase (again, not the rate of inflation) is simply to ask any businessman, home builder, store owner, druggist: "Approximately how much higher are your costs now than they were a year ago?" You will routinely be quoted increases of 20, 30, even 50 percent and higher.

This quick, uncomplicated method of measuring inflation by way of price changes is as reliable as any because price increases do not really measure inflation. The CPI leaves so much out that it is unreliable, serving no purpose other than perhaps that of creating work for numerous government statisticians and others who report and interpret misleading statistics.

Why Deflation Is the Normal Course for Price Movements in a Free Enterprise Economy

All things being equal, the natural course for prices is to decrease, not increase; in other words, deflation, not inflation, is the natural trend for prices. As business recovers its fixed charges, it can lower prices as it now needs primarily to cover only its variable costs. Increases in efficiency and the introduction of newer, more economic materials will also contribute to lower prices. Figure 11 illustrates this fact in no uncertain terms. Please note that prices decreased rather substantially between 1800 and 1915, over a period of 115 years. This was a period of tremendous economic growth for America and should explode completely the myth that the American economy needs or has ever needed inflation or an expanding money supply for its prosperity. This fairy tale has been repeated so often by Keynesian "economists" and American politicians that a majority of Americans have incredibly come to believe it, despite all the concrete evidence to the contrary.

However, note the sharp increases in prices that have accompanied each war. All governments prefer to pay for wars by resorting to inflationary methods of financing rather than by direct taxation, since it is initially less painful. This does result in sharp price increases during wartime and accounts for the "war prosperity." But wars, as should be evident, cannot be prosperous, since much of what the economy produces is simply destroyed with comparatively little produced for civilian consumption. Since there is a sharp increase in the amount of currency, however, this creates the illusion of prosperity which many people, even economists confuse with increasing real wealth.

Deflations following wars and depressions are the economy's way of correcting the price abuses and inflation generated by government during wartime. The free economy must battle with the government to bring prices down and back into line, while the government, through its inflationary policies, keeps forcing them up. The "Great Depression," as it was called, was not the result of any deficiency in our free enterprise, competitive system (as was charged and used as false justification for those New Deal "reforms"), but was the direct result of the socialization of the nation's currency, achieved as the result of the Federal Reserve Act of 1913, which encouraged an expansion of the nation's supply of currency

Figure 11

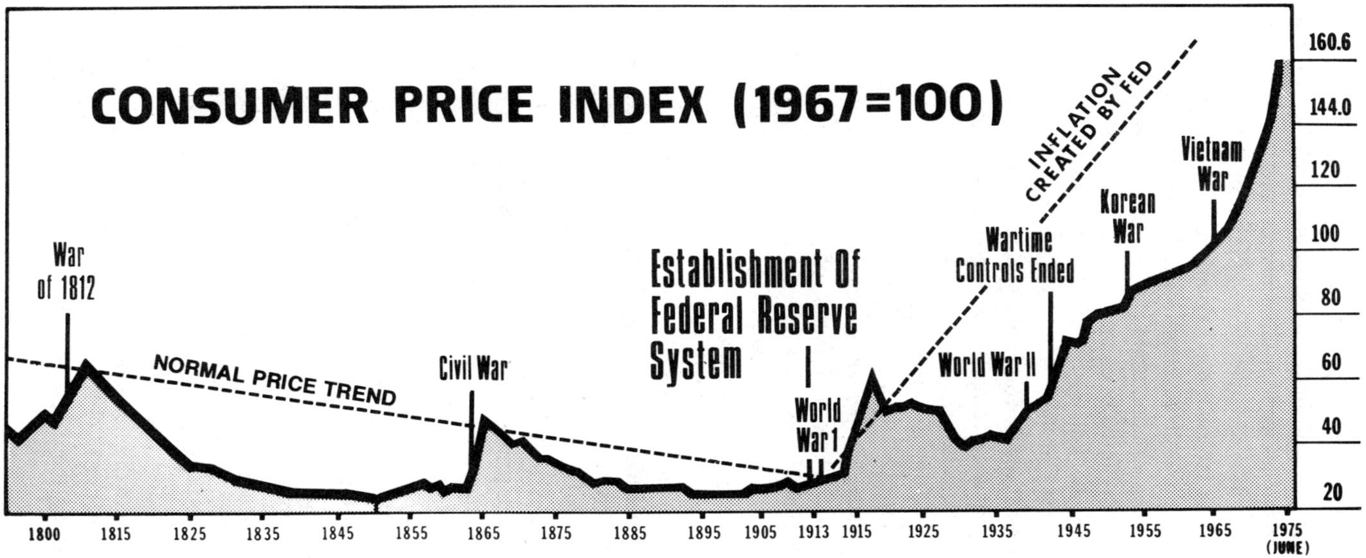
CONSUMER PRICE INDEX (1967=100)
INFLATION CREATED BY FED
NORMAL PRICE TREND
War of 1812
Civil War
Establishment Of Federal Reserve System
World War 1
World War II
Wartime Controls Ended
Korean War
Vietnam War
160.6
144.0
120
100
80
60
40
20
1800
1815
1825
1835
1845
1855
1865
1875
1885
1895
1905
1913
1915
1925
1935
1945
1955
1965
1975 (JUNE)

and credit, and by the government's decision to finance World War I not out of current taxation but with inflation. So, the real payment for World War I was delayed and postponed and hit the economy and the people in 1929, when the phony credit and price structure erected to finance World War I collapsed. Please note that so far we have not had a comparable price correction following World War II. However, look at the amount of inflation America has had since the end of World War II. This inflation again can be attributed to the creation of the Federal Reserve which was initially created to add elasticity to our money supply and ended up adding not elasticity, but constant expansion. The chart shows that prices between June 1945 and June 1975 increased by 196 percent. This would indicate that a 1975 dollar is really worth only 34 cents in 1945 money. However, since the prices in the CPI were compiled by a government agency and for the reasons mentioned earlier, these prices are understatements. Figure 9 indicates that prices between June 1945 and June 1975 rose by at least 500 percent. This means that, in terms of 1945 currency, we now have not a 34-cent dollar, as the CPI indicates, but a 17-cent one. This 500 percent increase in prices over 30 years calculates to a compounded annual rate of inflation of 6.2 percent. However, this does not consider the downward pull on prices exerted by advances in technology and increases in productive efficiency. The increased availability of power equipment—more computers and calculators, new fibers and fabrics and the impact of the petrochemical industry, to name several at random—have enabled industry to operate more efficiently than 30 years ago. Such advances in efficiency should have benefited the consumer in the form of lower prices, but they were instead absorbed by inflation, which was thus made to look less virulent than it actually was. This figure is just an arbitrary assumption on my part, but I suggest that such increases in efficiency could have accounted for at least a 1 percent annual decrease in prices. This 1 percent, when added to the 6.2 percent determined earlier, indicates that the U.S. has experienced a minimum annual rate of inflation over the last 30 years of 7.2 percent.

I am amazed that no one has asked why the tremendous increases in labor-saving devices over the last 30 years, the development of low-cost synthetic fibers, the refinement of production techniques, and the substantial increases in capital have not yielded lower prices for goods and services for the consumer? Since the consumer has not benefited price-wise from all of this technology, who has? The workingman? According to the Bureau of Labor Statistics, as of January 1, 1975, the average weekly earnings of nonagricultural production workers was $154.45. Adjusting this to the 17-cent dollar, we get $25.74[1] in 1945 wages. Average 1945 wages for comparable employees was approximately $42.00. This indicates that production workers did not benefit wage-wise from all of this increased technology. As of December 31, 1974, the Dow Jones Industrial Stock Average stood at 616.24. Adjusting these dollars to the 17-cent dollar means that the D.J. was

[1]If we adjusted this for income and Social Security taxes, this, of course, would be smaller still.

around 103 in terms of 1945 dollars. Since the D.J. closed in 1945 at 192.07, the market was approximately 46 percent lower on December 31, 1974, than it was on December 31, 1945. So, the investor has not benefited from all of this increased technology. Well, if the consumer, the worker, and the investor have not benefited from all of the increased technology since 1945, who has?

The vast benefits that should have come to the consumer, the worker, the investor, and the saver because of the vast increases in technology over the last 30 years were confiscated by the U.S. government through its taxing powers and used to encourage and support economic idleness in an ever-expanding army of Americans.

The government, through the use of tax dollars, vastly expanded the number of nonproductive bureaucrats, promoted a false concept of retirement which removed millions of Americans from the nation's workforce and in so doing, pinned their future welfare on false hopes, created a vast, nonproductive "student" population, and encouraged many millions of Americans to trade self-reliance and productivity for a public dole.

Want to know why in many families both the husband and wife have to work to keep their family's economic nose above water, or why you may have to moonlight and work 54 hours a week? It's because many are not only producing to provide for themselves and their families, they are compelled to produce a good deal more for the benefit and support of those people our government has encouraged not to produce anything at all.

As I have already indicated, if government did not create inflation, the economy would sustain a steady rate of deflation. Now, deflation would create hardships for debtors, and so I personally would have no objection if government created a certain amount of inflation to compensate for the deflationary tendencies of an efficient economy. In other words, the Treasury could ensure price stability so that no segment of society benefits from (or is penalized by) changes in the price level. Inflation now benefits the debtor since inflation allows him to pay off his debts with cheaper money. Conversely, deflation would penalize the debtor by compelling him to pay his debts in money of increased value. Since the federal government is the biggest debtor in the nation, owing some $5 trillion, it pursues a monetary policy which will benefit the debtor class, since even a 1 percent increase in inflation permits the government to "wipe out" $50 billion of its debt. Strange as it seems, the debtors are not the middle- or lower-income levels; they are the upper-income classes. It is the lower and middle classes that put their savings in the bank. It is the upper economic classes that borrow these savings from the bank. Middle and lower classes have their savings largely in government bonds, savings accounts, cash value life insurance, pensions, and other dollar assets. Many of these financial institutions will then make these funds available to those in the higher economic brackets, enabling them (because of their borrowing power) to acquire businesses, larger homes, and increase their control over industry and natural resources.

As inflation shrinks the value of currency, it increases the relative value of equity investments. Thus, inflation is a process by which purchasing power is shifted from the middle and lower classes, who have their savings in fixed dollar investments, to the upper classes who have the bulk of their wealth in equities and natural resources.

So, unlike Robin Hood who stole from the rich to give to the poor, the government steals from the middle and lower classes to give to the rich. It is interesting to consider, therefore, that it is those politicians who most passionately plead the cause of the working man and who are most loyally supported by organized labor who advocate political and economic policies that *maximize* inflation.

Ironically, it is those politicians who are supported by the working class who actually serve the economic interests of the wealthy[1] the most and those of the working man the least.

[1]But in the end, all are made to pay the bitter price for inflation.

3

The U.S. Public Debt and How the Government Conceals It

At the end of World War II, America stood alone like an economic and financial colossus astride the globe. The U.S. Treasury held $25 billion worth of gold and 2 billion ounces of silver, a substantial amount of foreign currency, and practically no external debts. Thirty years later and with a larger population, the U.S. Treasury's gold supply is down to $9.6 billion,[1] the nation's silver stock is depleted, and the nation has little foreign currency and owes the world over $117 billion in liquid liabilities ($39 billion owed to the U.S.).[2] Figure 10, of course, shows the decline of U.S. gold and silver stock—the nations's only supply of legitimate money. This decline in the nation's money supply is comparable to an individual's shrinking bank account.

The U.S. public debt, which is larger than the combined debt of all other nations in the world, has now reached astronomical proportions and is far greater than Americans realize. The President's 1976 budget only reports the national debt as $538.5 billion as of June 30, 1975, when, in reality, the national debt is *over $5 trillion* or *ten times greater* than reported.

[1]Government figures will show this to be $11.5 billion. This higher figure is arrived at by inflating our gold reserve by the arbitrary increase in the gold price from $35 per ounce to $42.20 per ounce. If we wish to consider our present gold holdings at $11.5 billion, then we must consider that we started with $30 billion.

[2]*Federal Reserve Bulletin,* April 1975, p. A61, A66.

The public does not realize the full extent of the U.S. national debt because the government neither reports nor publicizes it honestly. The government conceals the extent of its indebtedness by citing only its "funded" or "bonded" debts, while failing to report its "unfunded" and "contingent" liabilities. Unfunded government liabilities can be understood by considering the situation of a soldier discharged from the service with a government pension of $300 per month. The government, of course, does not issue him a series of bonds which he must redeem each month. However, the government's financial obligation to pay, in this situation $300 a month, is as great an obligation as if the government redeemed a $300 government bond each month. However, in the case of a veteran's payment, no government bonds are issued; the government's liability, therefore, is "unfunded" in contrast to bond redemptions where a bond is issued and reported as part of the national debt.

It is possible to determine actuarially the present value of all veterans' benefits that will run into the future by using mortality tables as explained on page 109. Government actuaries had developed an unfunded liability to veterans, as of June 30, 1973, of over $200 billion. (This sum can be seen in Note A, page 22 of Figure 14.) Thus this one item omitted from the Treasury Department's official report of the national debt as of June 30, 1973, hid the fact that the debt was in reality approximately 50 percent greater than the government admitted. The national debt as officially reported is only the tip of the iceberg of what the U.S. government really owes, or more accurately, what the U.S. government has committed the U.S. taxpayer to pay.

One of the last pieces of legislation for which Senator Leverett Saltonstall of Massachusetts was responsible was Section 402 of Public Law 89-809, (see Figure 12). The purpose of this law, Saltonstall's letter to me indicates (see Figure 13), was to compel the government to reveal not only its direct (bonded) debts but its indirect liabilities so those like the Senator and the public might know to what extent the government was getting the taxpayers in hock. What the government was getting away with by not reporting its unfunded and contingent liabilities was tantamount to a private corporation reporting as its total indebtedness only those formal bonds it had issued as outstanding, while omitting from its balance sheet such liabilities as unpaid taxes, accrued and unpaid salaries, monies owed trade creditors, liabilities that might develop due to a pending lawsuit, and other such contingent liabilities. This type of accounting from a private corporation would never be tolerated by the government or the public, but official Washington employs this type of deceptive accounting when reporting its indebtedness to the public. So, the vaunted U.S. debt ceiling which only sets limits on the *bonded* indebtedness of the government helps control total government indebtedness as revolving doors might contain a prison break.

By now, many readers will still find it hard to accept the extent to which their government has been deceiving, fleecing, and using them. I must, therefore, apologize for subjecting the reader to the tedious analysis of the following government report. But, please remember that this is probably the first time that a

Figure 12

PUBLIC LAW 89-809
SEC. 402. REPORTS TO CLARIFY THE NATIONAL DEBT AND TAX STRUCTURE.

The Secretary of the Treasury shall, on the first day of each regular session of the Congress, submit to the Senate and the House of Representatives a report setting forth, as of the close of the preceding June 30 (beginning with the report as of June 30, 1967), the aggregate and individual amounts of the contingent liabilities and the unfunded liabilities of the Government, and of each department, agency, and instrumentality thereof, including, so far as practicable, trust fund liabilities, Government corporations' liabilities, indirect liabilities not included as part of the public debt, and liabilities of insurance and annuity programs, including their actuarial status. The report shall also set forth the collateral pledged, or the assets available (or to be realized), as security for such liabilities (Government securities to be separately noted), and shall also set forth all other assets specifically available to liquidate such liabilities of the Government. The report shall set forth the required data in a concise form, with such explanatory material (including such analysis of the significance of the liabilities in terms of past experience and probable risk) as the Secretary may determine to be necessary or desirable, and *shall include total amounts of each category according to the department, agency, or instrumentality involved.* [Italics mine.]

Approved November 13, 1966.

report on the *true* status of the U.S. *public debt* has ever been made *public*. I maintain that all of the statistics that you have ever seen in government budgets, Federal Reserve reports, almanacs, encyclopedias, textbooks, financial and credit analyses in connection with the U.S. national debt *have all been woefully inaccurate–and have generally understated that indebtedness by about 90 percent*. All the more reason why the following pages are to be studied carefully.

The "Statement of Liabilities and Other Financial Commitments of the United States Government as of June 30, 1973" has been reproduced here (see Figure 14). Only 100 or so mimeographed copies are usually prepared, the bulk of them remaining with the Treasury Department. Some copies are sent to Congress; none are officially released to the public or to the media. This, of course, will explain the public ignorance regarding the true nature of the national debt and should establish a *prima facie* case of conspiracy against the government for its efforts to conceal the facts from the public.

In the following pages, I shall attempt to prove that the report, supposedly compiled in compliance with Public Law 89-809, (1) violates that law, and (2) was prepared in a manner to veil the extent of the government's indebtedness through actuarial tricks, schemes, and devices in direct violation of Title 18 of Section 1001 of the U.S. Criminal Code.

Let us now move to the report itself. Please refer to Note A, page 2. This, you will note, is the first entry of government liability listed in the report and is shown to be $458,142,000,000. It is listed as the "public debt on June 30, 1973, as

Figure 13

82 DEVONSHIRE STREET, ROOM 608
BOSTON, MASSACHUSETTS 02109

October 8, 1974

Irwin A. Schiff, Esquire
2405 Whitney Avenue
Hamden, Connecticut 06518

Dear Mr. Schiff:

I am in receipt of your letter of September 18 regarding the bill that I filed about the Government's "Statement of Liabilities and Other Financial Commitments" which later became law.

The purpose of this law is a simple one. It is to give the members of the Congress and the public once or twice a year the total liabilities of the Government - direct net debt and indirect liabilities from endorsements and subsidies of the various commissions, such as, "Fanny Mae".

I have not seen a copy of the Government's statement for several years. I agree with you that the one I did see made it very difficult to get a comprehensive and simple understanding of the Government's financial position. I do not know whether the Government has deliberately avoided putting totals on its liabilities.

As a former member of the Senate Appropriations Committee for a number of years, I felt that the law would be helpful to that committee for its work concerning the budget.

Very sincerely yours,

Leverett Saltonstall

LS:j

Figure 14

<u>Statement of Liabilities and Other Financial Commitments of the United States Government as of June 30, 1973</u>

This report is compiled in accordance with Section 402 of Public Law 89-809 approved November 13, 1966 (31 U.S.C. 757f). It shows the liabilities of the Federal Government as of June 30, 1973 (Section I), and amounts representing financial commitments which may or may not subsequently become liabilities, depending upon a variety of future conditions and events (Sections II, III, and IV).

A word of caution about the use of the data is essential. The four sections of the report deal with basically dissimilar types of commitments which cannot be aggregated in any meaningful sense. Within Sections III and IV, even the individual line items are largely dissimilar and not susceptible to meaningful addition. A

The "Liabilities" in Section I represent existing liabilities to pay for such things as (1) money borrowed, (2) goods and services actually received, and (3) adjudicated claims. The existence of the liability in each of these categories is certain and unconditional in all material respects and the amount owing is fixed or reasonably determinable, but simply has not yet been paid.

The "Undelivered Orders" in Section II represent obligations for goods and services ordered but not yet received and other legal commitments against appropriations, all pursuant to Section 1311 of the Supplemental Appropriation Act of 1955 (31 U.S.C. 200). These commitments will mature into liabilities in Section I when the goods and services ordered are delivered or when other performance stipulations have been fulfilled. The maturation of undelivered orders in Section II into Section I liabilities is a normal expectancy in the regular course of events in a relatively short time and the amounts of the undelivered orders are a reasonable measure of such future liabilities.

The "Long-Term Contracts" in Section III represent commitments of a general nature which have some similarity to those in Section II but differ from the latter insofar as (1) they are not legal commitments against appropriations, (2) maturation to a liability stage is of longer range nature, and (3) they are more susceptible to cancellation or modification and hence are much less susceptible to use as a measure of future liabilities.

The "Contingencies" in Section IV represent commitments which have the basic characteristic of uncertainty (1) as to whether the conditions or events implicit as a matter of conjecture will ever occur to cause any liability to be incurred or (2) if they do occur, as to when, with what frequency and to what degree.

Clearly, there is a vast difference between items in Section I -- where the liability is certain and the amounts relatively precise -- and Section IV -- where the possible future liability is highly speculative, and may never arise and where the amounts, if they can be projected at all, are stated for the most part in terms of maximum theoretical risk exposure (the upper limit of the Government's financial commitment) without regard to probability of occurrence and without deduction for existing and contingent assets which would be available to offset potential losses. C

The explanatory notes accompanying the data, particularly for Sections III and IV, are intended to assist interested parties in assessing broadly any risk of probable loss; for most of the items in Section IV, quantitative assessment becomes highly illusory.

Department of the Treasury
Fiscal Service
Bureau of Accounts
January 1974

Summary Statement of Liabilities and Other Financial Commitments
of the United States Government as of June 30, 1973
(In millions)
(Details may not add to totals due to rounding.)

Section	Description	Total	Applicable to other Government funds	Applicable to the public
I.	Liabilities:			
	The public debt on June 30, 1973, as published in the daily Treasury statement (Schedule 1)........	$458,142 A	B $124,210 1/	$333,932 C
	Agency securities issued and outstanding (Schedule 2)........	11,109	1,996	9,113
	Total public debt and agency securities........	469,251	126,206	343,045
	Net public debt transactions in transit as of June 30, 1973........	-6	-	-6
	Deposit fund liability accounts (Schedule 3)........	3,653	-	3,653
	Checks and other instruments outstanding (Schedule 4)........	7,075	-	7,075
	Accrued interest on the public debt, not due (Schedule 4)........	2,874	-	2,874
	Unamortized premium from sale of public debt securities (Schedule 4)........	107	-	107
	Other liabilities on the books of the Treasury (Schedule 4)........	317	-	317
	Accounts payable and accruals on the books of Government agencies (Schedule 5)...	37,426	6,377	31,049
	Total liabilities........	520,697	132,583	388,114 D
II.	Undelivered orders (obligations incurred under law against appropriations and funds for goods and services not yet received) (Schedule 6)........	102,095	5,908	96,187 E
III.	Long-term contracts (subject to future modification or cancellation in advance of delivery of goods or services) (Schedule 7)........	8,916	-	8,916 F

Summary Statement of Liabilities and Other Financial Commitments
of the United States Government as of June 30, 1973--Continued
(In millions)

Section	Description	Maximum theoretical measure of contingency
IV.	Contingencies:	
	Government guarantees, insuring private lenders against losses (Schedule 8)	$157,753
	Insurance commitments (Schedule 9)	1,021,915
	Actuarial status of annuity programs (Schedule 10)	2/
	Unadjudicated claims (Schedule 11)	5,762
	International commitments (Schedule 12)	7,605
	Other contingencies not included above (Schedule 13)	17,502

Note: The data presented in this report were compiled from reports submitted by the agencies in accordance with Department Circular No. 966, Revised, dated December 20, 1972, and Treasury Fiscal Requirements Manual Transmittal Letter No. 95. In several instances, incomplete data have been submitted by certain agencies since their accounting systems have not yet been developed to the point where they are able to provide the required information. In other instances the data furnished were on the basis of estimates by the reporting agencies.

1/ Includes $825 million of public debt securities held by the International Monetary Fund.

A 2/ Because the various annuity programs have been computed on different actuarial bases, it is not possible to compute a total. Details of individual programs are given in Schedule 10.

Schedule 1 - The Public Debt
as of June 30, 1973

Public debt securities held by	Amount of public debt securities outstanding	
Government Accounts:		
Legislative Branch:		
United States Tax Court:		
Tax court judges survivors annuity fund	$348,500.00	
The Judiciary - Judicial survivors annuity fund	8,148,000.00	
Funds appropriated to the President:		
Overseas Private Investment Corporation	127,590,000.00	
Department of Agriculture:		
Milk market orders assessment fund	1,033,000.00	
Rural Telephone Bank	6,969,000.00	
Department of Commerce:		
Federal ship financing fund	42,580,000.00	
War risk insurance fund	5,531,000.00	
Gifts and bequests	125,000.00	
Department of Defense	1,017,075.00	
Department of Health, Education, and Welfare:		
Federal old-age and survivors insurance trust fund	34,945,623,000.00	
Federal disability insurance trust fund	7,803,229,000.00	
Federal hospital insurance trust fund	4,172,365,000.00	A
Federal supplementary medical insurance trust fund	699,631,000.00	
Other	81,500.00	
Department of Housing and Urban Development:		
New communities guarantee fund	8,338,000.00	
Federal Housing Administration fund	1,138,377,500.00	
Rental housing assistance fund	8,571,000.00	
Participation sales fund	877,116,000.00	
Guarantees of mortgage-backed securities fund	8,082,000.00	
National insurance development fund	80,986,000.00	
Department of the Interior	914,500.00	
Department of Labor:		
Unemployment trust fund	10,956,747,000.00	
Other	31,000.00	
Department of State:		
Foreign service retirement and disability fund	64,562,000.00	
Conditional gift fund, general	190,000.00	
Department of Transportation:		
Coast Guard	22,650.00	
Highway trust fund	5,550,051,000.00	
Department of the Treasury	2,968,157,273.61	
General Services Administration	2,481,500.00	
Veterans Administration:		
Servicemen's group life insurance fund		
Veterans reopened insurance fund	252,993,000.00	
Veterans special life insurance fund	352,638,000.00	
National service life insurance fund	6,427,365,000.00	B
United States Government Life Insurance fund	689,705,000.00	
General Post Fund, National Homes	1,429,000.00	
Other independent agencies:		
Civil Service Commission:		
Civil service retirement and disability fund	30,490,779,000.00	
Employees health benefits fund	188,607,000.00	
Employees life insurance fund	1,242,781,500.00	
Retired employees health benefits fund	36,381,000.00	
Emergency Loan Guarantee Board:		
Emergency loan guarantee fund	4,315,000.00	
Federal Deposit Insurance Corporation	5,635,828,500.00	
Federal Home Loan Bank Board:		
Federal Savings and Loan Insurance Corporation	2,906,576,000.00	
National Credit Union Administration:		
National credit union share insurance fund	27,089,000.00	
United States Postal Service	1,084,912,500.00	

Schedule 1 - The Public Debt
as of June 30, 1973-Continued

Public debt securities held by	Amount of public debt securities outstanding
Other independent agencies--Continued	
Railroad Retirement Board:	
Railroad retirement holding account	$3,785,000.00
Railroad retirement account	4,516,586,000.00
Railroad retirement supplemental account	38,531,000.00
Small Business Administration:	
Lease and surety bond guarantees revolving fund	5,630,000.00
Total held by Government accounts	123,384,829,998.61
Non-interest-bearing public debt securites held by:	
International Monetary Fund	825,000,000.00
The public:	
Interest-bearing	332,968,564,345.17
Non-interest-bearing	963,210,968.31
Total held by the public	333,931,775,313.48
Total public debt securities	458,141,605,312.09

Schedule 2 - Agency Securities Outstanding
as of June 30, 1973

Issuing agency	Total agency securities outstanding	Agency securities held by Government accounts	Agency securities held by the public
Department of Defense:			
Family housing mortgages	$1,480,837,746.68	$192,026,359.67	$1,288,811,387.01
Homeowners assistance mortgages	2,710,852.15	--------------	2,710,852.15
Department of Housing and Urban Development:			
Federal Housing Administration fund	411,650,450.00	58,106,850.00	353,543,600.00
Government National Mortgage Association:			
Participation sales fund	4,480,000,000.00	1,695,350,000.00	2,784,650,000.00
Department of Transportation:			
Coast Guard - Family housing mortgages	2,628,311.13	--------------	2,628,311.13
Department of the Treasury:			
Federal Farm Mortgage Corporation (in liquidation)	65,200.00	--------------	65,200.00
Other independent agencies:			
Export-Import Bank of the United States: 1/			
Agency securities	2,221,056,159.37	--------------	2,221,056,159.37
Federal Home Loan Bank Board:			
Federal Home Loan Bank Board - Revolving fund	4,910,680.00	--------------	4,910,680.00
Home Owners' Loan Corporation fund	203,425.00	--------------	203,425.00
United States Postal Service	250,000,000.00	--------------	250,000,000.00
Tennessee Valley Authority	2,255,000,000.00	50,760,000.00	2,204,240,000.00
Total agency securities	11,109,062,824.33	1,996,243,209.67	9,112,819,614.66

1/ Pursuant to an act approved August 17, 1971 (12 U.S.C. 635(a)), the net outlays of this Bank were reclassified outside the unified budget, effective as of the close of business August 16, 1971.

Schedule 3--Government's Liabilities for
Deposit Fund Accounts
as of June 30, 1973

Agency	Amount
Legislative Branch	$5,176,697.28
The Judiciary	15,475,019.19
Executive Office of the President	247,718.51
Funds appropriated to the President	60,793,512.73
Department of Agriculture	117,143,627.88
Department of Commerce	8,876,701.91
Department of Defense	414,091,195.30
Department of Health, Education, and Welfare	70,113,636.49
Department of Housing and Urban Development	25,212,316.01
Department of the Interior	971,546,131.32
Department of Justice	37,545,510.69
Department of Labor	9,475,699.90
Department of State	2,985,380.71
Department of Transportation	7,720,582.54
Department of the Treasury	1,283,178,357.88
Atomic Energy Commission	270,171,508.07
Environmental Protection Agency	815,101.84
General Services Administration	9,155,637.63
National Aeronautics and Space Administration	49,201,765.63
Veterans Administration	61,379,385.76
Other independent agencies	153,567,488.23
District of Columbia	79,579,488.97
Total Deposit Fund Liabilities	3,653,452,464.47

Note: Excludes holdings of public debt and agency securities and participation certificates which are shown as liabilities of the Government in other schedules of this report.

Schedule 4--Other Liabilities on the Books of the Treasury
as of June 30, 1973

Description	Amount	Explanatory notes
Checks and other instruments outstanding:		
Accrued interest due and payable on the public debt	$123,206,099.53	
Disbursing officers' checks 1/	6,939,198,116.47	1/ Includes postal money orders outstanding.
Military Payment Certificates 2/	12,927,531.06	2/ Military payment certificates are issued in certain overseas areas by military finance officers in lieu of dollar instruments to discharge obligations incurred under appropriations of the Department of Defense.
Total checks and other instruments outstanding	7,075,331,747.06	
Accrued interest on the public debt: 3/		
Accrued interest payable - not due	2,873,983,129.82	3/ This liability does not include interest on savings bonds of any series. The liability for interest on savings bonds which are sold at a discount is included in the public debt principal on the basis of the increment in redemption value. The liability for interest on other savings bonds is recorded when the interest checks are issued with a corresponding liability for interest due and payable (equivalent, in this case, to checks outstanding).
Accrued interest on deferred public debt subscriptions - not due	16,499.39	
Total accrued interest on the public debt	2,873,999,629.21	
Unamortized premium from sale of public debt securities: Public debt interest premium	107,331,978.57	
Undistributed and other deferred credits 4/	317,336,063.87	4/ Represents deposits in the Treasurer's Account and cash held outside Treasury in accounts of certain collecting officers not classified on June 30.
Total other liabilities on the books of the Treasury	10,373,999,418.71	

Schedule 5 - Accounts payable and accruals
on the books of Government agencies
as of June 30, 1973
(In millions)

Agency	Funded			Unfunded— Due the public	Total due the public
	Total	Due Government agencies	Due the public		
Legislative Branch	$103	$12	$91	$8	$99
The Judiciary	18	-	18	-	18
Executive Office of the President	8	4	4	1	5
Funds Appropriated to the President	1,290	867	423	86	509
Department of Agriculture	1,713	341	1,372	231	1,603
Department of Commerce	396	64	332	120	452
Department of Defense	8,937	2,320	6,617	1,878	8,495
Department of Health, Education, and Welfare	7,815	126	7,689	300	7,989
Department of Housing and Urban Development	1,415	618	797	31	828
Department of the Interior	282	71	211	58	269
Department of Justice	90	13	77	83	160
Department of Labor	95	5	90	777	867
Department of State	110	9	101	32	133
Department of Transportation	787	52	735	111	846
Department of the Treasury	1,842	30	1,812	168	1,980
Atomic Energy Commission	334	245	89	129	218
Environmental Protection Agency	437	20	417	-	417
General Services Administration	407	326	81	39	120
National Aeronautics and Space Administration	613	142	471	53	524
Veterans Administration	1,268	36	1,232	216	1,448
Other independent agencies	4,751	1,076	3,675	396	4,071
Total	32,709	6,377	26,332	4,717	31,049

Schedule 6 - Undelivered Orders
as of June 30, 1973
(In millions)

Agency	Total	Obligations to other Government accounts	Obligations to the public
Legislative Branch	$78	$32	$46
The Judiciary	3	-	3
Executive Office of the President	39	*	39
Funds appropriated to the President	13,705	2,770	10,935
Department of Agriculture	4,704	21	4,683
Department of Commerce	1,387	40	1,347
Department of Defense	32,078	1,909	30,169
Department of Health, Education, and Welfare	9,990	306	9,684
Department of Housing and Urban Development	9,720	1	9,719
Department of the Interior	1,032	23	1,009
Department of Justice	1,117	24	1,093
Department of Labor	1,904	4	1,900
Department of State	68	3	65
Department of Transportation	9,380	150	9,230
Department of the Treasury	59	28	31
Atomic Energy Commission	1,508	-	1,508
Environmental Protection Agency	3,925	471	3,454
General Services Administration	552	15	537
National Aeronautics and Space Administration	648	51	597
Veterans Administration	328	26	302
Other independent agencies	9,871	34	9,837
Total	102,095	5,908	96,187

* Less than $500,000.

Schedule 7 - Long-term Contracts
as of June 30, 1973
(In millions)

Agency	Annual rental or cost	Remaining life of contracts (years)	Costs of remaining portion of contracts	Explanatory notes
Department of Agriculture:				
Forest Service	$3	1/4-3 1/4	$6	
Commerce Department:				
Maritime Administration..................	170	20	3,400	Operating differential subsidy contracts are made generally for 20 years. Annual payments under these contracts over the past 10 years have ranged from $112 million to $227 million. Subsidies under the contracts are paid subject to final adjustments at the end of operators' recapture periods which are established by contracts generally as 10-year terms. Operating differential subsidy contracts provide for the payment of the difference in the voyage costs of American-flag ships as compared with the voyage costs if the same ships were operated under foreign flags over designated strategic trade routes. Each contract specifies the maximum number of voyages which may be made on each designated route, but this number may be changed from time to time by contract amendment. No limitations are specified as to the maximum amount of payments.
Department of Defense:				
Panama Canal Company	-	22	32	Electric power contract with an autonomous agency of the Republic of Panama.
Department of Housing and Urban Development:				
Federal Housing Administration	-	-	98	Incompleted portion of contracts for property repairs.
Department of Transportation:				
Coast Guard	3	1	3	Letter agreements with foreign countries to operate and maintain Loran Stations in the host nation for the benefit of the United States. These agreements have been in effect for 6 years or more, and can be cancelled by giving appropriate notice (at least 1 year).

Schedule 7 - Long-term Contracts
as of June 30, 1973--Continued
(In millions)

Agency	Annual rental or cost	Remaining life of contracts (years)	Costs of remaining portion of contracts	Explanatory notes
General Services Administration:				
Building leases	$ 287	1/12-20	$ 1,615	7,141 building leases, including 2,100 leases expiring in fiscal year 1974 which have an annual rental of $44.7 million and a potential liability of $25.2 million.
Building lease-purchase contracts	2	12-30	31	Includes principal and interest, assessments and taxes and estimated payments in lieu of taxes in determining cost of remaining portion of contracts.
Other long-term contracts	1	1/12-4 1/3	1	
United States Postal Service	214	0-29	1,631	Contracts for leasing postal facilities.
Veterans Administration....................	2	-	2	Equipment rentals.
Tennessee Valley Authority	141	11 1/2-15	2,097	Includes long-term power fuels contracts, power plant lease, and other contracted commitments.
Total................................			8,916	

Note: Data for Department of Defense (other than Panama Canal Company) and certain other agencies not available.

Schedule 8 - Government Loan and Credit Guarantees
as of June 30, 1973
(In millions)

Agency and program	Amount of contingency			Less: Amount shown as undelivered orders in Section II	Net amount of contingency	Explanatory notes
	Total	For guarantees and insurance in force	For commitments to guarantee or insure			
Funds appropriated to the President: Agency for International Development:						
Housing guaranty fund..........	$277	$277	-	-	$277	Includes extended risk guarantee contracts for housing signed as of June 30, 1973.
Foreign military sales funds......	244	244	-	-	244	Represents guarantees of credit for sales of defense articles and services.
Overseas Private Investment Corporation....................	218	191	$27	$91	127	This corporation offers U.S. lenders protection against commercial and political risks by guaranteeing payment of principal and interest on loans made to eligible private enterprises in foreign countries.
Department of Agriculture: Farmers Home Administration:						
Agricultural credit insurance fund........................	2,874	2,735	139	139	2,735	This fund is used to insure farm ownership loans and soil and water conservation loans. Loans may be insured or made to be sold and insured.
Rural development insurance fund	1,509	838	671	671	838	This fund is used to make, sell, or insure water facility loans, rural electrification and telephone loans, industrial development loans, and community facility loans.
Rural housing insurance fund....	6,180	5,869	311	311	5,869	This fund is used to insure rural housing loans, farm labor housing loans, and loans for rural rental and cooperative housing. Loans are made to persons of low income and others in rural areas.

Schedule 8 - Government Loan and Credit Guarantees
as of June 30, 1973--Continued
(In millions)

Agency and Program	Amount of contingency: Total	Amount of contingency: For guarantees and insurance in force	Amount of contingency: For commitments to guarantee or insure	Less: Amount shown as undelivered orders in Section II	Net amount of contingency	Explanatory notes
Department of Commerce:						
Economic Development Administration:						
Economic development revolving fund..........................	$48	$48	-	-	$48	Outstanding guaranteed loans disbursed by financial institutions to private borrowers for working capital in connection with projects in redevelopment areas.
Maritime Administration:						
Federal ship financing fund, revolving fund................	2,579	1,260	$1,319	-	2,579	U.S. Government securities and cash of $97,104,901 were held in escrow by the Government in connection with insurance of loans and mortgages which were financed by the sale of bonds to the public prior to the completion of construction of ships under mortgage commitments.
National Oceanic and Atmospheric Administration:						
Federal ship financing fund, fishing vessels...............	12	12	-	-	12	Represents insurance of loans for construction or purchase of fishing vessels.
Department of Health, Education, and Welfare:						
Medical facilities guarantee and loan fund.......................	455	47	408	-	455	Guarantees in force represent medical facilities guaranteed loans.
Student loan insurance fund.......	2,099	2,099	-	-	2,099	Guaranteed loans - reinsured. Estimate of expected losses is $130 million. Funds are requested and appropriated by Congress to cover losses recognized during year in which claims are received.

Schedule 8 - Government Loan and Credit Guarantees
as of June 30, 1973--Continued
(In millions)

Agency and Program	Amount of contingency: Total	For guarantees and insurance in force	For commitments to guarantee or insure	Less: Amount shown as undelivered orders in Section II	Net amount of contingency	Explanatory notes
Department of Housing and Urban Development:						
Low-rent public housing program.	$11,783	$11,783	-	-	$11,783	Represents guarantees of bonds and notes issued by local housing authorities to private investors.
New communities guarantee fund..	294	198	$96	-	294	Guarantees of loans issued by private developers to finance land acquisitions and development costs of new communities.
Federal Housing Administration..	93,432	86,877	6,555	-	93,432	Insurance of loans for financing the production, purchase, repair, and improvement of residential properties. The FHA is indemnified against loss by trust agreements, performance bonds, and personal demand notes to the extent of $1 million.
Urban renewal fund.............	3,651	3,651	-	-	3,651	Guarantee of non-Federal loans.
Department of Transportation:						
Federal Aviation Administration:						
Aircraft loan guarantees......	11	11	-	-	11	Represents guarantee of one aircraft loan.
Federal Railroad Administration:						
Railroad loan guarantees......	275	171	104	-	275	Represents a guarantee of $68 million on a loan made to the National Rail Passenger Corporation and guarantees of $103 million on trustee certificates of railroad companies undergoing reorganization.
Urban Mass Transportation Administration:						
Washington Metropolitan Area Transit Authority bonds......	445	445	-	-	445	Principal and interest on bonds and other evidences of indebtedness of the WMATA may be guaranteed by the Secretary of Transportation. Periodic payment of one-fourth of the net interest cost to the Authority is provided.

Schedule 8 - Government Loan and Credit Guarantees
as of June 30, 1973--Continued
(In millions)

Agency and Program	Amount of contingency			Less: Amount shown as undelivered orders in Section II	Net amount of contingency	Explanatory notes
	Total	For guarantees and insurance in force	For commitments to guarantee or insure			
General Services Administration:						
Defense production guarantees ..	$ 49	$ 5	$44	-	$49	Guarantees are given on loans made by public and private financing institutions to facilitate performance of defense production contracts.
Expenses, disposal of surplus and related personal property..	2	2	-	-	2	Mortgage sold with full recourse to the U.S. Government secured by real property.
Real property activities	633	633	-	-	633	The GSA building construction program includes projects financed by purchase contracts under the Public Buildings Amendments of 1972.
Veterans Administration:						
Loan guaranty revolving fund ...	25,372	24,420	952	-	25,372	Represents the guaranteed portion only of total loans of $47,165 million made to veterans for purchase of homes, farms, and business property; the remainder of $22,745 million is nonguaranteed; cumulative gross claims of $1,698 million were paid through fiscal year 1973 out of $50,841 million guarantees issued. Salvage operations (acquisition and resale of security properties) have resulted in recovery of all but $94.8 million of the total claim payments.
Other independent agencies:						
Emergency Loan Guarantee Board:						
Emergency loan guarantee fund.	250	150	100	-	250	The Board may guarantee loans made by private lenders if necessary in order to prevent adverse and severe effects on the economy, if credit is not otherwise available on reasonable terms.
Export-Import Bank of the United States.................	4,576	1,784	2,792	$1,525	3,051	Represents loans sold with recourse and medium-term guarantees.

Schedule 8 - Government Loan and Credit Guarantees
as of June 30, 1973--Continued
(In millions)

Agency and Program	Amount of contingency			Less: Amount shown as undelivered orders in Section II	Net amount of contingency	Explanatory notes
	Total	For guarantees and insurance in force	For commitments to guarantee or insure			
Other independent agencies--Continued Interstate Commerce Commission....	$42	$42	-	-	$42	Loan guarantees to railroads under Part V of the Interstate Commerce Act, as amended. This guaranty program ended as to receipt of new applications, on June 30, 1963. All applications pending on that date have been processed, and the proceeds of all the guaranteed loans have been fully disbursed. The appraised value of collateral pledged is $66.1 million.
National Credit Union Administration: National credit union share insurance fund................	4	4	-	-	4	The fund has guaranteed the loans purchased by successful credit unions from liquidating credit unions at a price to permit payoff to members at par.
Small Business Administration: Business loan and investment fund...........	3,393	2,673	$720	$222	3,171	Represents guaranteed portion of loans held by private lenders as follows: business loans $2,755.5 million, displaced business loans $1.4 million, economic opportunity loans $89 million, local development company loans $52.4 million, and investment company loans and debentures of $200.8 million. The nonguaranteed portion of loans, or participants' share is $426.1 million.
Disaster loan fund.............	6	5	1	1	5	The nonguaranteed portion or participants' share is $671,000.
Total	160,713	146,474	14,239	2,960	157,753	

Schedule 9 - Insurance Commitments
as of June 30, 1973
(In millions)

Agency and Program	Amount of insurance in force	Amount of commitments to insure	Less: Amount shown as undelivered orders in Section II	Net amount of contingency	Explanatory notes
Funds appropriated to the President: Overseas Private Investment Corporation	$3,509	$2,990	-	$6,499	This corporation insures U.S. investors against political risks of expropriation, inconvertibility of local currency holdings and damage from war, revolution, or insurrection.
a) Department of Agriculture: Federal Crop Insurance Corporation .	854	-	-	B 854	Represents the gross or maximum amount of 1973 crop insurance coverage provided. For fiscal year 1974 it is estimated that premiums of $46 million will exceed indemnities of $41.5 million by $4.5 million.
Department of Commerce: War risk insurance revolving fund: Builders' risk insurance	33	-	-	33	Conditional liabilities for prelaunching war risk builders' risk insurance on two vessels.
Insurance under binder contracts ..	18,000	-	-	18,000	Represents the estimated insurance exposure under binder contracts. 1,100 contracts for hulls, 1,039 for protection and indemnity, and 779 for insurance on crew life and personal effects; and post-launching war risk builders' risk insurance policies; all of which become effective in the event of the outbreak of war.
Department of Health, Education, and Welfare: Student loan insurance fund	1,915	296	-	A 2,211	Represents Federal insurance program. Loss on insurance in force is estimated to be $172 million. The loss will be requested, appropriated by Congress, and recognized in the year in which claims are received.

Note: Data on indemnity agreements issued by Department of Defense not available.

Schedule 9 - Insurance Commitments
as of June 30, 1973- Continued
(In millions)

Agency and Program	Amount of insurance in force	Amount of commitments to insure	Less: Amount shown as undelivered orders in Section II	Net amount of contingency	Explanatory notes
Department of Housing and Urban Development:					
Federal Insurance Administration:					
Crime insurance	$77	-	-	$77	This insurance program enables businessmen and residents of homes and apartments to get crime insurance in States where crime insurance is difficult to get or excessively costly. Citizens of States designated to need the Federal program may purchase the Federal policies through any licensed insurance agent or broker.
Flood insurance	4,000	-	-	4,000	This insurance program enables persons to purchase insurance against losses resulting from physical damage to or loss of real or personal property arising from floods or mudslides. After communities are designated eligible, Federal insurance policies may be purchased from any licensed insurance agent or broker.
Riot reinsurance	125,000	-	-	125,000	This reinsurance program helps property owners in urban areas get insurance protection on property in areas subject to riots or civil disorders. Federal reinsurance is available for companies participating in Fair Access Insurance Requirements (FAIR) plans under supervision of the State insurance authority. These companies agree to provide coverage on insurable property. Owners who cannot get insurance in the private market are referred to the FAIR plan headquarters, the property is inspected, the rate determined, and the policy is issued if requirements are met.
Department of Transportation:					
Aviation war risk insurance revolving fund	42,085	$4,721	-	46,806	Insurance in force of $42,068 million is covered by an indemnity agreement with the Department of Defense. Hull insurance in force of $17 million is covered by FAA. Commitments to insure are binder agreements to provide insurance in a state of emergency.

Schedule 9 - Insurance Commitments
as of June 30, 1973--Continued
(In millions)

Agency and Program	Amount of insurance in force	Amount of commitments to insure	Less: Amount shown as undelivered orders in Section II	Net amount of contingency	Explanatory notes
Atomic Energy Commission	$125,000	-	-	$125,000	Atomic Energy Commission has about 250 indemnity agreements in effect. Maximum liability coverage provided by an agreement is $500 million for a nuclear incident.
Veterans Administration:					
From appropriations	27	-	-	27	
U.S. Government life insurance fund	704	-	-	704	This fund holds $690 million of public debt securities.
National service life insurance fund	27,513	-	-	A 27,513	This fund holds $6,427 million of public debt securities and agency securities of $310 million.
Service-disabled life insurance fund	1,304	-	-	1,304	
Veterans special life insurance fund	5,295	-	-	5,295	This fund holds $353 million of public debt securities.
Veterans reopened insurance fund	1,310	-	-	1,310	This fund holds $253 million of public debt securities.
Export-Import Bank of the United States	924	$1,912	$747	2,089	Represents short- and medium-term insurance and war risk consignment insurance.
Federal Deposit Insurance Corporation	435,300	-	-	B 435,300	Represents estimated insurance coverage of total deposits in insured banks as of June 30, 1973. This corporation holds $5,636 million of public debt securities.
Federal Home Loan Bank Board:					
Federal Savings and Loan Insurance Corporation	204,574	-	-	C 204,574	Represents estimated potential insurance liability of the corporation. This corporation holds $2,906 million of public debt securities and agency securities of $141 million.
National Credit Union Administration:					
National credit union share insurance fund	14,980	-	-	14,980	Represents estimated insurance liability of insured credit unions. The fund holds $27 million of public debt securities. The estimated loss for the fund is $700,000.
Small Business Administration:					
Lease and surety bond guarantee revolving fund	241	98	-	339	The nonguaranteed portion is $27 million.
Total	1,012,645	10,017	747	1,021,915	

Schedule 10 - Actuarial Status of Annuity Programs
as of June 30, 1973
(In millions)

Agency and Program	Valuation date and valuation period	Valuation interest rate	Actuarial liabilities	Actuarial assets	Actuarial deficiency (-) or surplus (+)
Department of Commerce:					
National Oceanic and Atmospheric Administration:					
Retired pay, commissioned officers.....	6/30/73	5%	$26	-	-$26
Department of Defense:					
Retired pay............................	6/30/73	3½%	137,136	-	-137,136
Panama Canal Company:					
Retired benefits to certain former employees..........................	6/30/73	-	12	$12	-
Note: Non-United States citizen employees who retired prior to October 5, 1958, are not covered by the Civil Service Retirement System but do receive retirement benefits under a separate annuity plan.					
Department of Health, Education, and Welfare:					
Social Security Administration:					
Federal old-age and survivors insurance trust fund...........................	D 7/1/73(1973-2047)	E 6%	4,745,381	C 4,683,399	A -61,982
Federal disability insurance trust fund...............................	7/1/73(1973-2047)	6%	780,554	666,683	-113,871
Federal hospital insurance trust fund...	7/1/73(1973-1998)	6%	414,358	432,605	+18,247

Note: The actuarial liabilities and assets have been computed over the valuation periods indicated, taking into account the assets at the beginning of the periods indicated and the present values of all income and outgo items during the period.

These estimates are prepared on the bases used by the Congress in making provision for financing the program -- bases regarded by the Congress and the trustees of the trust funds as the correct ones to use in a social insurance program -- namely, that future young workers will be covered by the program as they enter the work force. If the estimates were to be prepared on the assumption that no workers were to be covered B in the future other than those who were age 23 and over in the middle of 1973 (that is, contrary to the basis on which the Congress has provided for financing the program), there would be a deficiency of $2,118 billion for the OASDI program, computed on the dynamic assumptions basis, rather than the level-earnings assumptions basis customarily used in prior years.

No long-range data are furnished for the Federal supplementary medical insurance trust fund, since this program is operated on a 1-year term insurance basis, with the premium rate being adjusted by the Secretary of Health, Education, and Welfare so as to finance the cost of the program. Therefore, this system is not susceptible to long-range actuarial analysis, and it has no actuarial deficiency on this basis, but rather only for the existing situation as to incurred liabilities and funds on hand.

Schedule 10 - Actuarial Status of Annuity Programs
as of June 30, 1973--Continued
(In millions)

Agency and Program	Valuation date and valuation period	Valuation interest rate	Actuarial liabilities	Actuarial assets	Actuarial deficiency (-) or surplus (+)
Department of Labor:					
Federal Employees' Compensation Act....	6/30/73	-	$1,062	-	-$1,062
Note: Actuarial liabilities for Federal Employees' Compensation Act represent estimated future costs for death benefits, disability compensation, medical, and miscellaneous costs for compensated cases on rolls as of June 30, 1973.					
Department of State:					
Foreign service retirement and disability fund....................	6/30/73	5%	1,101	$ 374	-727
Veterans Administration:					
Compensation and pensions fund........	6/30/73 (FY 1974-FY 2000) B	-	205,279	-	-205,279 A
Note: This is an estimate of compensation, pensions, and other benefits costs as shown in the long-range plans of the agency.					
Veterans insurance and indemnities....	6/30/73 (FY 1974-FY 2000)	-	584	-	-584
Note: This is an estimate of the claims costs as shown in the long-range plan of the agency.					
Civil Service Commission:					
Civil service retirement and disability fund....................	6/30/73	5%	154,609	85,933	-68,677
Railroad Retirement Board:					
Railroad Retirement System............	6/30/73	5-3/4%	43,690	36,852	-6,838

Note: The above data pertain only to the regular benefit program for which financing is handled through the Railroad retirement account. The Supplemental annuity program financed through the Railroad retirement supplemental annuity account has been excluded because it is financed on a pay-as-you-go method with the contribution rates subject to change quarterly.

Actuarial data are as of June 30, 1973 but reflect effects of Public Law 92-336 (1972 social security amendments providing 20-percent increases in benefits effective in September 1972, expanded wage base for payroll taxes, and automatic future adjustments in benefit levels and taxable wage base for cost-of-living changes) which was signed into law on July 1, 1972. Figures exclude effects of future cost-of-living increases.

The actuarial valuation was made under an open-end approach, that is, account is taken of the expected income and outgo with respect to individuals who will enter railroad service in the future. For the closed group of former and present employees, the actuarial figures would show a substantial deficit.

The liabilities include allowances for administrative expenses and for the net costs due to the Board's participation in the administration of Part A (hospital insurance) of the medicare program.

The assets include railroad retirement taxes (exclusive of medicare taxes), expected gains from the financial interchange with social security (OASDHI) and interest on the funds on hand on the valuation date.

Schedule 10 - Actuarial Status of Annuity Programs
as of June 30, 1973-Continued

(In millions)

Agency and Program	Valuation date and valuation period	Valuation interest rate	Actuarial liabilities	Actuarial assets	Actuarial deficiency (-) or surplus (+)
Tennessee Valley Authority:					
Retirement System:					
Fixed benefit fund................	6/30/72	4-1/2%	$517	$417	-$100
Note: The amount shown for actuarial assets represents the book value of assets held by the fund plus the present value of prospective TVA contributions for currently accruing benefits. The amount shown for the actuarial deficiency represents the present value of prospective TVA contributions for past service benefits.					
Variable annuity fund.............	12/31/72	4%	81	81	-
Note: The amount shown for actuarial assets represents the market value of assets held by the fund.					
Tax Court of the United States:					
Tax Court Judges Survivors Annuity Fund--This fund was established under 26 U.S.C. 7448, and is used to pay survivorship benefits to eligible widows and dependent children of deceased judges. Participating judges pay into the fund 3% of their salaries or retired pay to cover creditable service for which payment is required and such additional funds as are needed are provided through appropriations. No actuarial status of the fund is available as of June 30, 1973. Eighteen judges are participating in the fund, and two eligible widows are receiving survivorship annuity payments. This fund holds $348,500 of public debt securities.					

Note: Because the various annuity programs have been computed on different actuarial bases, it is not possible to compute a total.

a)

Schedule 11 - Unadjudicated Claims
as of June 30, 1973
(In millions)

Agency	Total amount of unadjudicated claims	Less: Amount included in Section II	Net amount of unadjudicated claims	Explanatory notes
Legislative Branch:				
General Accounting Office	$18	-	$18	Freight and passenger transportation claims of carriers against the United States and other claims.
Funds appropriated to the President:				
Office of Economic Opportunity	2	$2	-	
Department of Agriculture:				
Commodity Credit Corporation	2	2	-	
Forest Service	23	-	23	
Department of Commerce:				
Maritime Administration:				
Vessel operations revolving fund	4	-	4	Composed of 202 claims. Based on previous experience, it is anticipated that settlement of these claims will be made for amounts substantially less than the gross amount of the claims.
Other	25	-	25	Composed of 27 claims. Based on previous experience, it is anticipated that settlement of these claims will be made for amounts substantially less than the gross amount of the claims.
Department of Defense:				
Corps of Engineers	115	-	115	
The Panama Canal Company	7	-	7	The maximum liability which could result from outstanding claims and lawsuits is estimated at $7 million.
Canal Zone Government	2	-	2	The maximum liability which could result from outstanding claims and lawsuits is estimated at $2 million.
Department of Health, Education, and Welfare:				
Social Security Administration:				
Federal old-age and survivors insurance trust fund	161	-	161	Benefits payable on all claims filed, but not yet adjudicated.
Federal disability insurance trust fund	130	-	130	Do
Federal hospital insurance trust fund	815	-	815	Claims that have not yet been paid, whether or not yet filed.
Federal supplementary medical insurance trust fund	752	-	752	Includes incurred but unpaid benefits only.

Schedule 11 - Unadjudicated Claims
as of June 30, 1973--Continued
(In millions)

Agency	Total amount of unadjudicated claims	Less: Amount included in Section II	Net amount of unadjudicated claims	Explanatory notes
Department of Health, Education, and Welfare--Continued				
Health Services and Mental Health Administration:				
Buildings and facilities	$1	-	$1	Construction contractor claims.
Howard University	5	-	5	Estimated contractor claims for delays and design errors in contract documents for Howard University, Washington, D.C.
Department of Housing and Urban Development:				
Low-rent public housing programs	-	-	-	Suits and claims against the Housing Assistance Administration were negligible as of June 30, 1973. However, contractors' suits were pending against local housing authorities, but estimated amounts are not available. Any payments by the local housing authorities arising from these suits will result in additional project development costs and an increase in this agency's annual contributions to local housing authorities.
Department of the Interior:				
Bonneville Power Administration	9	-	9	Appeals from contractors ($6.35 million) and tort claims ($2.35 million).
Bureau of Mines:				
Helium operations	475	-	475	Secretary of Interior has determined these crude helium purchase contracts to be cancelled. Northern Helex, annual payment of $9.5 million, filed suit on breach of contract. National Helium, Cities Service, and Phillips Petroleum, annual payment of $38 million, are operating under an injunction.
Department of Justice:				
Office of Alien Property	16	-	16	Represents the maximum amount this Office would be required to pay to individuals whose property was vested under the Trading with the Enemy Act during World War II and have filed claims or brought suits against this Office for the recovery of their property. The maximum estimated payment in 1974 is $12 million (which includes $0.4 million for income and estate taxes and administrative expenses). In 1975, the maximum estimated payment is $5 million (which includes $0.2 million for income and estate taxes and administrative expenses).

Schedule 11 - Unadjudicated Claims
as of June 30, 1973--Continued
(In millions)

Agency	Total amount of unadjudicated claims	Less: Amount included in Section II	Net amount of unadjudicated claims	Explanatory notes
Department of Labor:				
Federal Employees' Compensation Act	$13	-	$13	Represents estimated future medical and compensation costs for cases reported as of June 30, 1973. The Office of Workmen's Compensation Programs also administers five other compensation acts covering employees in private employment. Compensation for these acts is covered by private insurance. While OWCP administers several small trust funds in connection with these private acts, contingent liability is less than one-half million dollars, and so is not reported here.
Department of Transportation:				
Coast Guard	1	-	1	Claims by contractors stated at the maximum limit of risk, not the expected cost.
Federal Aviation Administration	779	-	779	Excludes claims transferred to the General Accounting Office and the Department of Justice.
Department of the Treasury:				
Internal Revenue Service	1,752	-	1,752	Claims for refunds, overassessments, refund suits, and interest.
Bureau of Customs	120	-	120	Estimate based on fiscal year 1973 drawback payments and refunds of duties and miscellaneous receipts.
Bureau of the Mint	1	-	1	Construction claims by contractors.
Federal Law Enforcement Training Center	1	-	1	Post construction claims by contractors.
Atomic Energy Commission	11	-	11	
General Services Administration	42	-	42	Claims filed by contractors or vendors for additional amounts due, tort claims for personal injury or property damage, etc.
National Aeronautics and Space Administration	4	-	4	In addition to these claims there are 13 pending claims for patent infringements, the amounts of which are not specified by the claimants; therefore, the maximum limit of risk and the expected probable risk are not now known.

Schedule 11 - Unadjudicated Claims
as of June 30, 1973--Continued
(In millions)

Agency	Total amount of unadjudicated claims	Less: Amount included in Section II	Net amount of unadjudicated claims	Explanatory notes
Veterans Administration:				
Loan guaranty revolving fund	$25	-	$25	Represents 1,244 claims, average amount $20,000.
Other independent agencies:				
Indian Claims Commission	260	-	260	
United States Postal Service.............	193	-	193	Pending suits and damage claims.
Smithsonian Institution	2	-	2	Contractor claims for suspension of work costs at Hirshhorn Museum and Sculpture Garden, Washington, D.C.
Total	5,766	$4	5,762	

Schedule 12 - International Commitments
as of June 30, 1973
(In millions)

International organization	Amount	Explanatory notes
Inter-American Development Bank..................	$1,570	Represents the unpaid authorizations to invest in callable capital stock of $1,224 million, and paid-in capital stock of $347 million.
Asian Development Bank..........................	100	Represents the U.S. subscriptions to callable capital stock authorized by Public Law 89-369, approved March 16, 1966.
International Bank for Reconstruction and Development..................................	5,826	Represents the unpaid authorizations to invest in callable capital stock, as authorized by 22 U.S.C. 286.
World Food Program.............................	2	The United States has pledged up to $3 million for the fifth period (1973-74). An amount of $1.5 million has been requested in the fiscal year 1974 to meet the second half of the 2-year pledge.
Indus Basin Development Fund....................	47	Under the IBDF agreement as amended in April 1964, the United States pledged to contribute $651.8 million, (consisting of $295.6 million in grants, $121.2 million in loans, and $235 million in Pakistan rupees), as its share of total commitments of $1.580 billion for construction of works in Pakistan. Thus far, the United States has paid in $250.6 million in grants, $119 million in loans, and $235 million in rupees. The U.S. unappropriated commitment is $47.2 million.
Agreement of Friendship and Cooperation Between the United States and Spain..................	9	An agreement was signed August 6, 1970 for a period of 5 years, with an option for extension for another 5 years. The agreement of friendship and cooperation also called for assistance in cultural-educational and scientific programs. Funds will be expended as mutually agreed upon by the United States and Spain.

Schedule 12 - International Commitments
as of June 30, 1973--Continued
(In millions)

International organization	Amount	Explanatory notes
Southeast Asia Ministers of Education Organization	$7	The United States pledged contributions at the Southeast Asia Ministers of Education meeting in Manila in November 1966. The six centers established and funded are in varying stages of development.
North Atlantic Treaty Organization (Malta)	28	As a result of an agreement signed March 26, 1972, between the United Kingdom and Malta, the Government of Malta receives payment of 14 million pounds sterling (about $37 million) for a 7-year period. The U.S. annual share in NATO supporting assistance funds will be $9.5 million.
Organization of American States: Capital Markets Development Program	1	This is a fund for fostering development of capital markets in Latin America. Studies made under this program are to result in recommendations concerning (1) desirable changes in national economic and institutional policies and practices, and (2) use of financial and technical assistance needed to support such efforts. The United States paid $2 million in FY 1970, $1 million in FY 1972, $1 million in FY 1973, and $1 million in FY 1974 for this program.
Inter-American Export Promotion Center	1	The Center began operations in 1969 as part of a drive to expand and diversify Latin American exports. The goal is to expand and diversify nontraditional exports, thereby helping to accelerate the economic integration and growth of Latin America. The Center furnishes short courses on export practices and provides technical assistance through national export promotion centers.

Schedule 12 - International Commitments
as of June 30, 1973--Continued
(In millions)

International organization	Amount	Explanatory notes
Organization of American States--Continued Special Development Assistance Fund	$ 5	This is a continuing program, funded by voluntary contributions of OAS members. It supports multilateral technical assistance, research, and training activities. SDAF funds are used for activities such as natural resources work, tax policy formulation and reform, public administration, social development, and support for eight Inter-American training centers. SDAF support is 66% from the U.S. and 34% from other members. The U.S. pledged up to $5 million during FY 1974 subject to availability of funds and at a 66/34 ratio.
Special Multilateral Fund	9	This fund was initiated in 1968 in response to the Declaration of the Presidents in 1967 concerning the need for expanded multilateral programs in education, science, and technology. Funded by voluntary contributions of OAS members, it supports two programs directed by two specialized committees comprised of distinguished educators and scientists of Latin America. The science program encourages research and new techniques in soil research, metallurgy, food technology, and nuclear energy. The education program focuses on curriculum and education technology including adult education. For FY 1973 the U.S. pledged $9 million which will be due if matched at the 66/34 ratio by other members' contributions during FY 1974.
Total	7.605	

Schedule 13 - Other Contingencies
as of June 30, 1973
(In millions)

Agency	Amount	Explanatory notes
Legislative Branch:		
General Accounting Office..................	$4	Transportation and previously reported suits. There are 850 court cases brought by household goods forwarders against the U.S. but due to the nature of filings no reasonable estimate of the potential liability of the Government can be given.
Funds appropriated to the President:		
Agency for International Development:		
Alliance for Progress fund................	104	Represents funds committed for loans that have not been signed into loan agreements.
Cooley loan program.......................	3	Dollar equivalents of local currencies committed for loans that have not been signed into loan agreements.
Housing guaranty fund.....................	38	Represents contracts of guaranty authorized, but not yet executed by AID and the prospective investors.
New development loan fund.................	102	Represents funds committed for loans that have not been signed into loan agreements.
Other Public Law 480 loans................	27	Represents line of credit not implemented by project agreements.
Department of Agriculture:		
Farmers Home Administration:		
Agricultural credit insurance fund.........	316	The fund is liable for an estimated amount of interest due investors on net amount of contingent liability for periods subsequent to June 30, 1973.
Rural development insurance fund...........	187	Do.
Rural housing insurance fund..............	307	Do.
Forest Service.............................	14	
Department of Defense:		
Corps of Engineers.........................	688	Unfinanced continuing contracts.
Panama Canal Company.......................	5	
Department of Housing and Urban Development:		
Federal Housing Administration..............	173	Contingent insurance claims partially offset by contingent assets of $153 million.

Schedule 13 - Other Contingencies
as of June 30, 1973--Continued
(In millions)

Agency	Amount	Explanatory notes
Department of Justice:		
Office of Alien Property	$4	Estimated amount of transfer to the War Claims Fund in the U.S. Treasury for payment of awards issued by the Foreign Claims Settlement Commission in settlement of claims of American citizens for loss of property in Germany during World War II.
Atomic Energy Commission	721	Cancellation provisions of contracts for supply of electric power and natural gas for production facilities.
General Services Administration:		
Federal telecommunications fund	2	Terminating charges if communications installations are discontinued before a certain period has expired.
National Aeronautics and Space Administration	65	Cancellation provisions of contracts relate to the supply of electric power and communications services. Cancellation provisions relating to some 3,300 mortgages.
Veterans Administration:		
Readjustment benefits	13,185	Estimate of costs for the period fiscal year 1974 through fiscal year 1979 based on data used in the fiscal year 1975 preview estimates.
Other independent agencies:		
Export-Import Bank of the United States	1,157	Unsigned loan agreements.
Small Business Administration:		
Business loan and investment fund	132	Reflects undisbursed commitments which have not matured into valid obligations, and pending legal actions.
Disaster loan fund	261	Do.
U.S. Information Agency	7	
Total	17,502	

published in the daily Treasury statement (Schedule 1)'' and was the only figure that was officially released and thus picked up by all the reporting media as being the national debt as of that date. However, the report then continued with another 31 pages of unfunded and contingent government debts and obligations of which *not a penny* ever found its way into any Treasury statement and thus is missing in all statistics which purport to show the U.S. public debt as of June 30, 1973. *It is in these additional, unreported and unpublicized 31 pages that 90 percent of the U.S. public debt is to be found.*

Thus, the first element in the government's concealment of the true size of the U.S. debt is in instilling the idea that only the first entry on the first page of a 32-page list of U.S. government liabilities accurately reflects the government's financial condition. Additional evidence of this cover-up (which violates Public Law 89-809 and Section 1001 of Title 18 of the U.S. Criminal Code) can be found from the misleading statements and inaccurate figures in the report.

First of all, as Note B, page 2, reveals, $124 billion of the outstanding government bonds are owned by the government itself. Please refer to pages 4 and 5 for a breakdown of the $124 billion bonds as owned by the various government departments and trust funds. As explained on page 111 of this book, government bonds owned by government agencies are not assets of these agencies at all, but represent notations of money collected in the past from these agencies and already spent by the government. These bonds are no more valuable than mere journal entries showing money that the U.S. government could have invested and saved but didn't. Moreover, they represent monies *owed* by Uncle Sam to these ''trust funds.'' We can also properly eliminate government bonds owned by the government itself from the national debt because money the government owes itself is like money that one may owe oneself. As one cannot properly owe himself money, neither can the U.S. government properly owe itself money. So, the real U.S. bonded indebtedness as of June 30, 1973, is Note C, page 2—$333.9 billion, not $458.1 billion.

However, there were a number of other obligations owed to the public as of June 30, 1973. These when added to $333.9 billion of bonded debt total (see Notes D & E on page 2) $484 billion—a sum already greater than Note A, even though we discarded the $124 billion government bonds owned by the government agencies. I did not include the $8.9 billion of indicated government liabilities shown in Note F because these liabilities contained so many uncertainties that I eliminated them from consideration rather than try to determine a reasonable degree of dollar liability. Note E has been included since it appears to be monies *bona fide* owed the public comparable to monies owed one's trade creditors.

So far, we have only considered the smallest part of the government's debt. Now let us explore an area of government indebtedness that the public does not even know exists. Please refer to page 3 of the report where the government's contingent liabilities are supposedly grouped by class. Please note that there is *no total given for these liabilities* or, for that matter, none in the entire report, even though the law stated specifically (Figure 12, Note A) that the report ''shall include *total* amounts of each category according to the department, agency, or instrumentality involved.''

Why are no totals shown for the figures in this report? Because it states that the figures are too ''dissimilar'' and cannot be ''aggregated in any meaningful sense'' (see Note A, page 1). I contend that these figures were made to *look* dissimilar so that the government could avoid aggregating them in *any* sense.

Please note page 3, Note A: ''Because the various annuity programs have been computed on different actuarial bases, it is not possible to compute a total.'' This is nonsense. For one thing, there is no reason why the various government annuity programs need to be computed on ''different actuarial bases,'' because this means only differences in the assumption of one of two variables—expected mortality and the expected interest earned on the fund's assets. Since none of the government's trust funds *owns* any real assets (only government bonds), none earns interest (how can the government pay interest to itself?). So, ''computed on different actuarial bases'' really amounts to assuming differences only in mortality for those covered in each fund, which is a dubious practice because why should the government assume mortality differences in the various annuity programs? The government could use the same mortality table for all its annuity programs. But, even if these trust funds are calculated on different actuarial bases, totaling them would still be simple. Each annuity fund would develop its own dollar liability, based upon whatever actuarial assumptions it makes. For example, Trust Fund A, using mortality Table Z and interest assumption of 3½ percent develops a liability of $1 million. Annuity Trust Fund B, using a different mortality Table X and a different interest assumption of 6 percent, develops a liability of $2 million. Therefore, the total liability of these two annuity programs is $3 million, and this is an accurate total even though both of these programs were ''computed on different actuarial bases.'' *The government's contention that total liabilities for the annuity programs cannot be shown because they were computed on ''different actuarial bases'' is sheer rubbish and a flagrant attempt on its part to avoid the law's intent.*

All insurance companies, of course, have outstanding policies and annuities calculated on different actuarial assumptions. Imagine the reaction of a state insurance commissioner if a company claimed that it could not supply a total of its insurance liabilities as a check against its current assets because its policies were ''computed on different actuarial bases''! The insurance commissioner would claim, and rightly so, that such a contention was proof that the company was too incompetent to operate and would shut it down immediately.

In the case of the government, however, it wasn't that the persons concerned were too incompetent to come up with a total, it was that they were too clever —clever enough to realize that if they did supply an accurate total for these annuity programs, and if the figure got out, ''all hell would break loose.''

Uncovering the Government's Unfunded Social Security Liabilities

Note A, page 22, is part of Schedule 10, which lists the actuarial status of annuity programs. Note that the present value of future veterans' benefits totals more than $205 billion. That is the present liability of future veterans' benefits as of June 30, 1973, and is equivalent to 45 percent of what the government reported its national debt to be as of that date. Note that the funds show no "actuarial assets," and, therefore, the "actuarial deficiency" is equivalent to the total "liability." This is a relatively simple entry which will be helpful for comparative purposes with the entries for Social Security liabilities, which could have been shown in this straightforward manner but were made complicated, if not incomprehensible, to cloak their inaccuracy.

Note A, page 21, indicates three figures which purport to show the actuarial deficiency for the three Social Security programs. This deficiency totals $157.6 billion, which in itself is greater than 30 percent of the reported national debt. But wait—note the line (see Note B) buried in the footnote:

> If the estimates were to be prepared on the assumption that no workers were to be covered in the future other than those who were age 23 and over in the middle of 1973 (that is, contrary to the basis on which the Congress has provided for financing the program), there would be a *deficiency of $2,118 billion* for the OASDI program, computed on the dynamic assumptions basis, rather than the level-earnings assumptions basis customarily used in prior years. [Italics mine.]

What is the right deficiency—$2.118 trillion or $.157 trillion? The difference is not minor! The larger figure is about 1,300 percent larger than the other that had been used as the deficiency and would amount to a government liability nearly 400 percent greater than the entire admitted national debt as *officially* reported. How can the U.S. government justify using the smaller liability figure when the report (Note B, page 1) states "amounts, if they can be projected at all, are stated for the most part in terms of *maximum theoretical risk exposure* (the upper limits of the government's financial commitment)" [Italics added]. Since Social Security liabilities account for over half the liabilities in the budget, why haven't they been stated in "terms of maximum theoretical exposure"? This would be the $2.118 trillion figure which, contrary to that statement, has been buried in a footnote and in language too technical and misleading for the average layman.

An analysis of this report will show that the government on the one hand, *overestimates* certain obvious liabilities at such illogical maximum levels (such as insurance liabilities at their total face amount), so as to cover up and hide the *understatement* of its most important, largest, most awesome, and most complicated liability—Social Security.

Note the $5.6 trillion of actuarial assets shown for the three Social Security

Funds (Note C, page 21). When I first saw this figure, I couldn't understand what these assets could be since I knew that the only assets that Social Security could legitimately claim were those $47 billion worth of government bonds owned by the Social Security Administration (Note A, page 4). I was, therefore, nonplused by how Social Security could have suddenly acquired some $5 trillion in assets or an increase of some *12,000 percent*. I called the actuarial department of the Social Security Administration and was put in touch with the senior actuary who was instrumental in preparing these figures. When asked the nature of the "$5 trillion assets apparently owned by the Social Security System," the actuary replied that these were "actuarial assets" and did not really represent assets in the usual sense. "But the report states 'assets.' " I persisted! "What kind of assets are they?" The individual was evasive, saying that these were actuarial calculations developed solely to *comply with the law* and were not necessarily meaningful figures in a strict insurance sense—since this was, after all, "social insurance," not regular insurance. When I finally extracted it, *the $5.6 trillion represented potential future Social Security receipts!* Since when are *potential future receipts* ever shown on a balance sheet as assets which can be applied against current liabilities? Remember this statement of government direct and indirect liabilities is entitled "Statement of Liabilities and Other Financial Commitments of the United States Government as *of June 30, 1973*"—so what right have *potential future receipts,* projected to the year 2047, to be in a report of the government's liabilities as of June 30, 1973? This can only distort the government's liability picture as of that date.

But wait. Why are the liabilities of the fund shown as "7/1/73 (1973–2047)," Note D, page 21? Social Security actuarial assets represent all of the receipts that the System expects to receive to 2047 for the OASDI and the disability trusts, and to 1998 for the hospital trust fund, while the actuarial liabilities represent estimated payments running to 1998 and 2047. Remember that in order to develop such figures, the actuaries had to calculate all Social Security income and outgo for some 70 years. Social Security actuaries had to determine liabilities for people not even born while at the same time calculating benefits in amounts not fully known or determined since future benefit levels are subject to increases or decreases. So, the figures for future liabilities and income are speculative. Why, ask yourself, did the government go through all of this extra calculation when the law required only a statement of the government's assets and liabilities as of June 30, 1973? Obviously, any assets or liabilities that Social Security may receive after that date (such as new workers entering the System) are of no concern as of the date of the report. So why would the government assume liability for payments for which it has no liability? Why assume liabilities for people yet unborn, while treating as an asset money not received or even legally owed? Why did the government even bother to get into such a calculation, since such calculation is more complicated and less accurate, containing as it does such a host of variables, than showing the assets and liabilities of the Social Security System as of June 30, 1973? Why didn't the government simply calculate the Social Security liability as it calculated the veterans' liability (as shown in Note A, page 22)? All future Social Security liabilities could have been calculated to reflect only those covered as of June 30, 1973, and then have included as assets of the Social Security System only those "make-believe" assets that the System had as of that date—namely the $47 billion of government bonds mentioned previously. Such a direct and accurate entry would reflect the true financial condition of the Social Security System *as of the date of the report*.

The government did not do this because it would have to show a Social Security liability of $2.118 trillion, the figure that was buried in the footnotes instead of the comparatively puny liability of $.157 trillion.

How would the inclusion of future Social Security receipts along with future Social Security disbursements serve to reduce the appearance of the government's current Social Security liabilities? Assuming that one was born in 2000, by 2023 he would be, by the plan's assumption, working full time and contributing to the System. He would be presumed to be contributing to the Social Security trust fund until 2047, the cutoff date used for calculating receipts and disbursements. Thus, as incredible as it sounds, this report, which was to reflect the government's liabilities as of June 30, 1973, treated as an asset receipts presumed to be received from some yet unborn and unnamed individuals for 24 years. Why should our government have included such a calculation? By 2047 the above individual would be only 47, far from the retirement age needed to collect his Social Security retirement benefits. So, the government, while picking up as an asset the theoretical contributions, would not have to pick up any offsetting liabilities. Thus, through inflated future receipts and deflated future liabilities the government was able to develop a considerable amount of actuarial "assets" with few offsetting actuarial liabilities and this actuarial "surplus" was used to offset the very real current Social Security liability that existed as of the date of the report. If any insurance company ever calculated its liabilities and assets on this basis, its officers would be carted off to jail.

Furthermore, the Social Security calculations and assumptions contradict the representations made in the first page of the report. Look at Note C, page 1, which states that government liabilities would be stated "without deduction for existing and contingent assets which would be available to offset potential losses." The government has done exactly what it said it would not do—offset current Social Security liabilities with contingent future assets.

In brushing aside the more accurate Social Security liability of $2.118 trillion on the basis that such an evaluation is "contrary to the basis on which Congress has provided for financing the program," the report is an unabashed attempt to reinforce creditability for the lower figure on the basis of Congressional actuarial ignorance, since the man in the street reading the report will not have the foggiest notion of what "dynamic assumptions" mean relative to "level-earnings assumptions.'' The statement is even more misleading since there is no basis for financing this program, Congressional ignorance notwithstanding.

How Overstatement of Other Government Liabilities Conceals Understatement of the Government's Trust Fund Liabilities

Many persons have pointed out why Social Security benefits are not worth the taxes charged the public, especially for younger workers entering the system. While this is certainly true, I am more concerned with showing what in my judgment amounts to an intent by the government to deceive the public on the very nature and solvency of the Social Security System and to conceal the status of the System's current liabilities. Not only has the government attempted to hide the extent of its Social Security liabilities by the methods discussed above, it has also tried to do so under its own actuarial assumptions. Refer to Note B, page 22. In indicating its veterans'liabilities, the government projected liabilities to the year 2000 while projecting Social Security income and liabilities to 2047. (I think the fact that the hospital trust fund was made to project its liabilities only to 1998 was done only to introduce another inconsistency and thus reinforce the image that the report consisted of funds calculated on ''different annuity bases'' that could not be totaled.) If the VA figures were calculated consistent with Social Security figures, VA liabilities would have far exceeded the amount shown, since these liabilities are only calculated for 24 years. VA liabilities are obviously larger (how much larger I cannot say) than shown for there are 25-year-old veterans who will, in all probability, receive benefits beyond the year 2000, the cutoff date to which the government arbitrarily calculated its liabilities. To this extent, the government's figure of $205 billion actually understated its potential veterans' liabilities. But the point is that the government calculated its Social Security obligations to the year 2047—so why, in the interest of consistency, didn't it calculate VA liabilities for the same length of time? The reason is that because of the way in which the government calculated its Social Security liabilities, the *longer* the period of time selected, the *less* the government's liabilities would appear, while the *longer* the period for the VA calculation, the *larger* they would appear. So, the government arbitrarily chose to run its Social Security calculations 47 years longer than its VA calculations. Such an arbitrary selectivity for the purpose of reducing the appearance of government liabilities violates Section 1001 of the U.S. criminal code which enjoins government officials from resorting to ''tricks'' and ''devices'' and from making ''false statements'' and ''misrepresentations.''

But this is not all. Notice the figure in the column entitled Valuation Interest Rate. The rate for Social Security, Note E, page 21, is 6 percent, while the rate shown for the ''Retirement Pay, Department of Defense'' is 3½ percent, while the ''Retired Pay, Commissioned Officers'' of the ''National Oceanic and Atmospheric Administration'' is 5 percent. Here we find the government using three different interest assumptions in calculating the public liability contracted by the government in the public's behalf—when not one of the three interest assumptions is even justified.

"Interest assumption" reduces the amount of money theoretically required (and thus reduces a fund's calculated future liability) in the trust fund, since this represents interest earnings on the trust fund's assets and would be available in addition to the trust fund's principal to pay future benefits. So, the higher the rate of interest one assumes a fund will earn, the lower its future liability will appear. Interestingly, neither of the 3½ and the 5 percent interest assumptions is valid since these trust funds have no assets at all. Since both of these funds should not calculate further liabilities based upon an interest assumption, their future liabilities should be greater than the amounts shown. Actuaries have a rule of thumb which states that every 1 percent increase in an interest assumption reduces a fund's liability by 10 percent. Therefore, a simple calculation indicates that proper adjustments in these two funds would increase the government's liability by about $50 billion.

As I pointed out, the higher the interest assumption, the lower a trust fund's future liability will appear. This brings us to the Social Security assumption that the System will "earn" 6 percent interest on its assets. First of all, a 6 percent interest assumption is not a conservative estimate for a pension, and I doubt if there are many private pension programs that would assume a higher rate than this. What would the government's liability be if it had assumed a lesser interest assumption? Below is what the government might have stated its Social Security liabilities to be had it used a more conservative interest assumption.

Government's liability assuming a 6 percent assumption:	$2.1 trillion
Government's liability assuming a 5 percent assumption: This interest assumed in the following government programs: Foreign Service, Civil Service retirement.	$2.3 trillion
Government's liability assuming a 4 percent assumption: This interest assumed in TVA variable annuity program.	$2.5 trillion

So, the government is not presenting its Social Security liability in terms of its "maximum theoretical exposure" as the report proclaims. What theoretical interest assumption the Social Security System employs is immaterial, since the *Social Security System should not use any interest assumption in calculating its future liabilities*. The reason for this is really quite simple. The purpose of Public Law 89-809, Section 402, which furnished the legal basis for this report in the first place, is for the government to account accurately for the extent to which the government (it must be continually recognized that the U.S. public debt is actually the debt of the U.S. taxpayer) has incurred present and future debts on the taxpayer's behalf. Now, the interest assumption used in connection with the Social Security calculations is the theoretical interest that U.S. taxpayers have to pay on U.S. government bonds held by the Social Security trust fund. To the extent that a higher interest assumption on the part of the Social Security trust fund appears to lower future Social Security liabilities, to the very same extent it increases the taxpayer's future interest liability—which is neither shown nor accounted for in this report. So, while the government is apparently handing the nation's taxpayers a lower Social Security bill, because of a higher interest assumption used in its Social Security calculations, it is at the same time handing them a higher bill for interest charges since the taxpayers must pay both parts of the Social Security bill—principal and interest.

So, what does the current Social Security liability look like minus the bogus interest assumptions? $3.3 trillion! Numbers this high have no real meaning. So, let's give some concreteness to the government's Social Security liability as of the date of this report. The government collected tax revenues of about $247 billion for the year 1973. Thus, government had already mortgaged, just for current Social Security liabilities without regard to any future Social Security liability, better than 13 years of its total revenue at current levels. Let's put it another way. The maximum annual government expenditure during World War II was the $98.3 billion reached in 1945. So, what the government had already promised to those currently covered under the Social Security program, as of June 30, 1973, equaled about 33 years of expenditure at the maximum level reached during World War II.

What is so astounding about Uncle Sam's arithmetic is that while the government was willing to offset potential Social Security liabilities with potential Social Security income from sources yet unborn, it apparently was unwilling to reduce other liabilities where it had good expectations of collecting and where substantially greater liability to the government existed. (See, for example, Note A, page 18, "Student Loan Insurance Fund.") Note that the government shows as its "net amount of contingency" the amount that it has guaranteed and *intends* to guarantee! The government has guaranteed student loans of $1.9 billion while $296 million waits to be insured—this is the *same* amount that the government has shown as its liability contingency. Obviously, a good portion of these loans will be repaid. In its explanatory notes, the government even indicates that it only expects $172 million of the amount guaranteed to develop into losses. Isn't it then lunacy for the government to assume as a potential liability $2 billion and not $172 million? Since the government assumes no repayment of any of its loan guarantees and assumes as a "contingency" $296 million of loans not as yet insured, clearly the government is overstating its liabilities in this area.

Note that throughout this schedule of "Insurance Commitments," the government "net amount of contingency" (column 5) appears at the full face amount of all the "insurance in force" (column 2). As far as insurance is concerned, this is as fatuous as showing the contingencies for loans equal to the full amount of all guaranteed loans. If a fire insurance company has a million dollars of insurance in force, its liability is only the assets required to cover a reasonable portion of its liability exposure based on the statistical probability of loss.

Please note Note A, page 20. See how the government lists as its potential liabilities as of June 30, 1973, the face amount of all the National Service Life Insurance Policies, totaling $27.5 billion. Is it really logical to assume that this insurance can mature as a death claim on June 30, 1973? The only liabilities the government has to account for as of June 30, 1973, are (1) the total cash value of all outstanding policies, (2) the present value of any annuity or monthly payments selected by insureds or beneficiaries as a result of a death claim or the cash surrender of the policies, and (3) the present value of any waiver of premium benefits or disability benefits which have matured as a claim.

The report of June 30, 1973, does not realistically reflect the government's liabilities. Against its realistic liabilities, as I have outlined, the government indicates that it owns some $7 billion of "Public Debt Securities" (Note B, page 4). So the government doesn't have a cent in real assets with which to pay the billions of dollars of real liabilities needed as a result of its veterans' insurance programs.

The government carries as its full liability the $435 billion of savings deposits it "insures" (Note B, page 20). But can all these deposits mature as a claim as of June 30, 1973? If all banks collapsed on that date—though highly unlikely—how could the government's assets shown as $5.6 billion of government bonds, the equivalent of 1½ percent of its stated liabilities, cover deposits? What the government statement of liabilities should reflect is the total amount of premium collected and held by the government against possible bank failures, then show for informational purposes the total of these deposits. If the government's liability as of the date of the statement is indeed $435 billion, this liability *alone* would be greater than the reported national debt! It is obvious that such a liability is absurd, for how could the government expect to discharge such a liability with a reserve of only $5.6 billion? Suppose bank losses were 10 percent of deposits (they were 40 percent during 1929-32), or $43 billion, would losses in excess of the $5.6 billion in bond assets have to be met out of current taxation? But how? The budget has a deficit now! Would this then mean a larger deficit? If so, how large? Since the government is showing its contingency as $435 billion, could it pay a $43 billion loss, forgetting how it would manage to pay its full contingency loss of $435 billion? For that matter, how could the government even pay a loss of $5.6 billion for which it says it holds "public debt securities"—that is, government bonds? Why, it would theoretically have to tax the public to redeem the bonds that the Federal Deposit Insurance Corporation holds in order to provide funds for the bankrupt banks. In other words, the government must raise funds to pay losses below $5.6 billion in the exact same way it must raise funds to pay losses in excess of $5.6 billion—by levying additional taxes to reimburse the banks for such losses. So, FDIC insurance is a sham. *There are no real assets insuring bank deposits*. If there were, the government could not double the amount of deposits that it insures from $20,000 to $40,000. Since the U.S. government has no assets to insure these $435 billion of deposits, and since it really has no tax-gathering potential to raise this amount (which would amount to taxing the public so as to reimburse the public for its bank losses), it intends to print whatever unmoney is needed to reimburse the depositors for any losses they sustain.

Another example of how our government distorts and exaggerates its insurance liabilities can be found in Note B, page 18. Here the net contingency is shown as $854 million. However, the note says that only $46 million was collected in premiums, with crop losses of only $41.5 million expected. The only real liability that the government is accountable for is the premium it has collected, so the government's reflection of its true liability should be as follows:

Estimated losses due to crop guarantees	$41.5 million*
Premiums held against losses	$46.0 million
Estimated surplus or deficiency	$ 4.5 million

*This represents estimated losses on $854 million of insured crops.

Instead of showing a loss contingency of $854 million, this entry should show a $4.5 million surplus. The total amount insured should appear as the note, and not, vice versa as the government has shown.

It is important for the nation's taxpayers to understand the degree to which their government violated Section 402 of Public Law 89-809. This law requires that the Treasury Department submit a report showing the "aggregate and individual amounts of the contingent and unfunded liabilities" and further shall include "total amounts." The government's excuse for not complying with the law's requirements for "totals" is on the first page of the report, where it states that figures were not susceptible to "meaningful calculation" and that they could not be "aggregated in any meaningful sense." This excuse reappears in paragraphs 5 and 7 and in the statements of Note A on page 3 and Note A on page 23. I have already cited the fatuousness of the government's contentions. Each and every government liability, regardless of how remote, tenuous, or complicated, can be reduced to a simple numerical expression, and these expressions can constitute a meaningful total. Insurance companies do it all the time. The Social Security Administration alone has 20 actuaries, who could have done the necessary calculations for a meaningful total in one afternoon—and I am sure that the total would come within 5 percent of the government's actual liabilities. If the U.S. government can put men on the moon with such mathematical precision, why can't it provide a "meaningful total" of dissimilar dollar liabilities?

The calculation shown in Figure 15 took me about an hour and while it may not be 100 percent accurate, it more accurately reflects government liabilities as of June 30, 1973, than the $458 billion figure shown in government statistics.

As I stated at the beginning of this chapter, the national debt for 1975 will be *over $5 trillion*. Although the government's report of its 1975 funded, unfunded, and contingent liabilities is not available at the current time (December 3, 1975), I

SECTION IV

THE ONLY HONEST SUMMARY OF LIABILITIES AND OTHER FINANCIAL COMMITMENTS OF THE U.S. GOVERNMENT AS OF 6-30-73

As prepared by Irwin A. Schiff

From Information Assumed to be Accurate

DESCRIPTION	REASONABLE MEASURE OF TAXPAYERS' LIABILITY (IN BILLIONS)
Contingencies	
Government guarantees, insuring private lenders against losses (Schedule 8)	
An assumption of a 10 percent loss on $157.7 billion of debt guarantees	$ 15.7
Insurance commitments (Schedule 9)	
An assumption of a 5 percent loss on $1,021.9 billion of face commitments	$ 50.0
Actuarial status of annuity programs (Schedule 10)	
This figure disregards (with the exception of TVA retirement calculations) all government bonds held (approximately $85 billion) and eliminates any interest assumptions, since "reserves" are nonexistent. In essence, therefore, this figure reflects the total amount of future taxes required to pay future benefits for those covered as of June 30, 1973	$3,787.0
Unadjusted claims (Schedule 11)	
Assume 50 percent liability on $5.76 billion	$ 2.8
International commitments (Schedule 12)	
Assume 100 percent liability	$ 7.6
Other contingencies not included above (Schedule 13)	
Assume 90 percent liability since one item alone is $13 billion and appears to be a definite obligation	$ 15.0
Total of contingent and unfunded liabilities (i.e. Statutory debt)	$3,878.1
Other debts owing to the public and International Monetary Fund	
As shown in Section 1 as $388.1 and Section 11 as $96.1 (omit Section 111)	$ 484.9
Total debt of the U.S.: Funded, unfunded and contingent (bonded & statutory)	$4,363.0
That is	$4,363,000,000,000.00
As of 6/30/73, the government implied that the total U.S. debt was	$ 458,142,000,000.00

THUS, AS OF THE DATE OF THE REPORT, THE U.S. GOVERNMENT ONLY ADMITTED TO DEBTS OF APPROXIMATELY 10 PERCENT OF WHAT IT ACTUALLY OWED AND SO FAR NOT ONE GOVERNMENT OFFICIAL HAS BEEN CRIMINALLY INDICTED!

Figure 15

have been reliably informed that the report will show unfunded social security liabilities of $2.71 trillion, an increase of $592 billion over the $2.118 trillion shown in the 1973 report, while the government's funded indebtedness to the public will climb from $343 billion to $397 billion, for an increase of $54 billion. Thus, increases in just these *two items* of government indebtedness, totaling $646 billion, without even adjusting the 1975 social security liability for the specious "interest" assumption, will, when added to my estimated June 30, 1973 liability of $4.362 trillion, bring the government's funded, unfunded, and contingent liability as of June 30, 1975 to $5.008 trillion.

How the U.S. Government "Pays" Its Debts

The concept of the U.S. "national debt," like so many other terms used by the U.S. government, is a form of Newspeak, the language of George Orwell's *1984*. This is the process by which government distorts the meaning of words so as to confuse and tighten its grip on society. For example, if government outlawed and eliminated *freedom* from the vocabulary, the state of freedom itself would disappear, so that people would not even know that they were being subjugated. This distortion of language to achieve the purposes of a totalitarian state has to some extent been employed in America. Americans have been conditioned to call socialism *free enterprise,* Social Security *insurance,* and worthless paper and metal tokens *money*.

The U.S. government employs Newspeak when it refers to its practice of "borrowing money" to finance government deficits. There was a time when our government really did borrow. It not only borrowed legitimately, it even balanced its budget and provided for surpluses in order to pay off past debts. At one time, our government managed itself with some degree of fiscal integrity, much as any honest person who tries to live within his means and meet his obligations.

Of course, during emergencies, governments, like individuals, can go into debt. But when our government went into debt, as when a family went into debt, it paid back what it borrowed and managed to reduce its overall indebtedness. If a family spends more than it earns in some years, then its indebtedness must be balanced by other years when it earns more than it spends, using the difference (the surplus) to repay previous debts. With this in mind, please note Figure 16, which shows the government's funded debt for every five years from 1900 to 1974.[1] Please note how the government reduced its total indebtedness between 1900 and 1915 and reduced its per capita indebtedness by over 30 percent. To help finance World War I, the U.S. government went deeply into debt as shown; its funded debt increased by $23 billion, reaching $24.3 billion, while per capita indebtedness soared 1,800 percent.

Now notice how the government systematically reduced its indebtedness. The

[1]The chart doesn't take into consideration the federal unfunded and contingent liabilities, which for the years shown, grew at an even greater rate than the federal funded debt.

total national funded debt was actually reduced to $16.2 billion by 1930, for a reduction of 33 percent, while the per capita debt was reduced 42 percent. Here we see an example of the government honestly repaying what it owes. After 1930, however, the picture changed—*radically*.

As the New Dealers who came to power in 1933 explained it, government could *pump prime* the economy by spending more in depressions than it took in. This "deficit spending" would put additional federal money into the economy, so the theory went, and would stimulate consumer spending, which in turn would stimulate business activity, which in turn would stimulate business and business payrolls, which in turn would stimulate additional consumer spending—and on it would go until the economy would "spend" itself right out of the depression. If anyone asked these eager New Deal economists how government deficits were to be repaid, their stock reply was: "Why, during periods of prosperity, the government will create budget surpluses with which to pay off these depression deficits." So, during periods of good times this technique supposedly would take the steam out of an "overheated economy" while propelling the economy upward during bad times. "Such use of 'compensatory fiscal monetary management' will eliminate the booms and busts so characteristic of an unmanaged free-enterprise economy," confidently proclaimed the New Dealers.

Figure 16

THE U.S. FUNDED DEBT More Commonly Known As THE NATIONAL DEBT

YEAR	GROSS (billions)	PER CAPITA
1900	$ 1.3	$ 17
1905	1.1	14
1910	1.1	12
1915	1.2	12
1920	24.3	228
1925	20.5	177
1930	16.2	132
1935	28.7	226
1940	43.0	325
1945	258.7	1,849
1950	257.4	1,697
1955	274.4	1,660
1960	286.3	1,585
1965	317.3	1,631
1970	382.6	1,866
1972	437.3	2,112
1973	468.4	2,230
1974	486.2	2,290[1]

[1]Please note that this only covers the funded debt. While the U.S. unfunded debt was negligible prior to 1940, it would increase 1974's per capita federal indebtedness to over $20,000 (which when added to per capita state, municipal, and personal indebtedness, places [with rare exceptions] every man, woman, and child in America, somewhat in hock).

Well, this sounded like good economic theory—but it wasn't. Falling prices in themselves stimulate the economy since they encourage spending by consumers who had been discouraged by higher prices. Putting more money in consumers' hands merely forces prices higher and accomplishes little from their standpoint. More inflation and higher prices, however, do the government some good since they generate higher tax revenues, which is exactly what the government wanted to accomplish—that is, bolster government tax revenues, not the economy.

From a practical political point of view, politicians will simply *not* create budget surpluses during the years of supposed prosperity to balance the deficits they say they will temporarily create during depressions. Giving politicians the right to create deficits but expecting them to use that power prudently is wishful thinking of a most dangerous sort.

Americans have certainly been led to believe that the 1950s, 1960s, and 1970s were prosperous years in contrast to the Depression-pocked 1930s. If this is so, where were all the budget surpluses? In the last 19 years, the U.S. has only managed to have two surpluses.[1] Figure 17 shows the history of surpluses and deficits since 1934 when conscious deficit spending was made respectable. In three of those years—1968, 1971, and 1972—the deficits were, in themselves, greater than the entire 1933 U.S. funded debt of $22.5 billion when the New Deal started, while the "official" 1975 and '76 deficits are 2 or 3 times greater.

This, of course, does not even take into account the unfunded liabilities created during this period. If unfunded liabilities are taken into consideration, they, of course, would wipe out all supposed budgetary surpluses. So, it can be accurately stated that the U.S. government has had no *surplus* budget since the theory of deliberate government deficits was propounded as a tool & technique for stimulating the economy. Moreover, what was supposed to be only a temporary measure has become standard government operating policy. The only real question is the *size* of the budget deficit.

Since the U.S. government now makes no effort whatsoever to reduce its indebtedness, but goes merrily along piling debt on top of debt, it cannot be said to "borrow" in the accepted sense of the word.

As stated previously, if one spends more than one earns, making up the difference in borrowed money, the following year or so one must earn more than one spends, using the difference to repay what has been borrowed. No one can go on *ad infinitum* increasing one's total indebtedness without any need to reduce it. Total government debts soared from approximately $20 billion in 1930 to nearly $5 trillion in 1975, for an increase of *25,000 percent* in just 42 years. Since the government obviously does not pay back what it borrows, it does not *borrow*. How can one go on year after year spending more than one earns? There are only three ways that this can be done—borrow, receive charity, or steal. Since the U.S.

[1]And even these surpluses were frauds since if surplus Social Security revenues had been put in a trust fund as the Government claimed, the government would have had to report a $5.5 billion operating *deficit* for fiscal 1969. (Government deficits were, in reality, much greater than the government reports since they apply surplus Social Security revenues towards reducing operating deficits.)

Figure 17

FEDERAL SURPLUSES AND DEFICITS

YEAR	RECEIPTS	EXPENDITURES	SURPLUSES	DEFICITS
1934	3.015	6,645		−3,630
1935	3,706	6,497		−2,791
1936	3,997	8,422		−4,425
1937	4,956	7,733		−2,777
1938	5,588	6,765		−1,177
1939	4,979	8,841		−3,862
1940	6,879	9,589		−2,710
1941	9,202	13,980		−4,778
1942	15,104	34,500		−19,396
1943	25,097	78,909		−53,812
1944	47,818	93,956		−46,138
1945	50,162	95,184		−45,022
1946	43,537	61,738		−18,201
1947	43,531	36,931	6,600	
1948	45,357	36,493	8,864	
1949	41,576	40,570	1,006	
1950	40,940	43,147		−2,207
1951	53,390	45,797	7,593	
1952	68,011	67,962	49	
1953	71,495	76,769		−5,274
1954	69,719	70,890		−1,170
1955	65,469	68,509		−3,041
1956	74,547	70,460	4,087	
1957	79,990	76,741	3,249	
1958	76,636	82,575		−2,939
1959	79,249	92,104		−12,855
1960	92,492	92,223	269	
1961	94,389	97,795		−3,406
1962	99,676	106,813		−7,137
1963	106,560	111,311		−4,751
1964	112,662	118,584		−5,922
1965	116,833	118,430		−1,596
1966	130,856	134,652		−3,796
1967	149,552	158,254		−8,702
1968	153,671	178,833		−25,161
1969	187,784	184,548	3,236	
1970	193,743	196,588		−2,845
1971	188,392	211,425		−23,033
1972	208,649	231,876		−23,227
1973	232,225	246,526		−14,301
1974	264,847	268,343		−3,495
1975	280,921	325,133		−44,212
1976 est.	300,800	374,900		−74,100

government does not borrow (for it does not reduce its indebtedness), or exist on chairity, it must be stealing. The only question to be answered then is: How does it steal and from whom?

How and from Whom the Government Steals
(How the Government "Pays" its debts)

As already pointed out in Chapter 2, the government, by issuing counterfeit money and guaranteeing debt, inflates the unmoney supply. This process of inflation reduces the purchasing power and hence the value of all existing stocks of unmoney and claims to unmoney, while correspondingly increasing the unmoney value of tangible wealth. Thus government inflationary practices continually and unconstitutionally shift dollar wealth from creditors to debtors, from savers to spenders, from the holders of dollar assets to the holders of real assets.

Let's assume, for example, that you had $1,000 in the bank from January 1 to December 31, 1974.[1] Since the government's inflationary policies caused the C.P.I. index to increase by 12.2 percent, during 1974 the $1,000 on December 31 will only buy (even when measured by the government's conservative index) what $878 would have purchased a year previously. This loss of $122 in purchasing power is just as real as if a burglar had entered your home with a gun and stolen it from you directly.

Let us examine how the government steals in this manner from the most defenseless and vulnerable members of society—the nation's elderly, who must rely on their accumulated savings and pensions to see them through their retirement years.

Let us assume that the government discovered that it did not have enough revenue to meet its Social Security commitments, and so did the only honest thing it could do under the circumstances and announced a cut in benefits. Let us further assume that it was determined that a 10 percent cutback was required, so that a recipient who would normally receive a $300 monthly check would now receive one for $270.00. Such a direct and forthright reduction in Social Security benefits would undoubtedly set off a large public outcry. What politician would dare vote to reduce Social Security benefits even if fiscal circumstances demanded it? But our government is broke and is unable to legitimately pay the Social Security benefits our politicians have so generously, but irresponsibly, promised. So what do our courageous legislators do—they deficit spend, printing up more paper checks in order to meet the government's unrealistic Social Security commitments. Assuming that the government's inflationary activities cause prices to rise by 10 percent, a $300 Social Security check will now buy only what $270 bought before, and thus the government has effectively engineered a 10 percent reduction in Social Security benefits by indirect rather than direct means. Recipients, who will now receive effectively smaller Social Security checks, will be encouraged by the

[1]Or in other fixed dollar assets, such as bonds, cash value life insurance, and annuity pensions.

culprits in Washington to blame the merchants, the middlemen, or global problems for this shrinkage in the value of their Social Security checks.

As the government, by the use of inflation, swindles from those on Social Security, so it also swindles government bondholders.

Assuming a holder of a U.S. "savings bond" earned 5½ percent in bond interest, inflation of 11 percent would mean that the bondholder is actually losing 5½ percent in purchasing power annually and is therefore not earning a thing on his bond. However, to add insult to injury, the government will tax the bondholder on his nonexistent "gain," when in all equity he should be entitled to a tax deduction for *his losses!* To get some idea of the magnitude of the government's swindling operation, we need only refer to the crime study of the President's Commission on Law Enforcement and Administration of Justice. For the year 1965, this study revealed that the total cost of all crime in the U.S., including the cost of the police, the courts, and private costs related to crime, amounted to $20.98 billion. Crimes against property, including commercial, unreported theft of $1.4 billion, robbery, embezzlement, fraud, forgery, arson and vandalism, amounted to $3.932 billion.

Since, as of June 1974, the total U.S. debt was at least $4.7 trillion, the 12.2 percent rate of inflation wiped out $569 billion of present and future government debts. Thus, in 1974, the government, by generating inflation, embezzled from its current and future creditors far more than it collected in taxes—indeed, the government stole through inflation an amount approximately 20 percent greater than its entire admitted debt.

Relating the government's criminal activities to private crime is truly startling, since what the government stole via inflation in 1974 was 29 times greater than the entire *cost* and *suppression* of all crime in the U.S. in 1965[1] and 152 times greater than all crime directed against property. Stealing by inflation most resembles embezzlement, and the law enforcement commission found that embezzlement losses in 1965 were $200 million; so what the U.S. government embezzled in 1974 from its creditors was 300,000 percent more than what was embezzled privately in the U.S. in 1965.

These figures certainly suggest that there would be a sharp reduction in crime in this country if we simply released all of the nation's crooks, thieves, embezzlers, swindlers and con artists, and simply locked up the politicians.

There will be those, who, despite the evidence, will undoubtedly be critical of my blanket labeling of our federal politicians as crooks and swindlers. Well, after personally witnessing the economic hardships that befall our elderly when inflation rots away their savings, it's pretty hard to be tolerant and good natured toward those responsible. While I realize that there have been some responsible lawmakers who have tried to prevent the government's inflationary activities, their numbers are so small as to make exceptions unimportant.

[1]"The Challenge of Crime in a Free Society," The President's Commission on Law Enforcement and Administration of Justice, Washington, 1967.

Since my purpose is to reveal the extensive criminal nature of federal activities, I feel no need to be sidetracked or diverted by having to qualify minor exceptions to this activity. Those congressmen and government officials to whom my charge does not apply will, I am sure, be understanding, since they are fully aware of the urgency of the situation—and the importance of explaining its cause as simply and directly as possible.

Is the surreptitious taking of an individual's purchasing power through the use of a government printing press any less effective than when it is done with a gun and a mask? Is counterfeiting less of a crime when practiced by the government than when it is carried out by private individuals? I think not.

It is precisely because our senators and congressmen are generally undeserving of the respect and the restraint accorded them that enables them to perpetuate the charade that somehow they are fit to lead and govern in accordance with our historic traditions. Only when this myth is effectively exposed will the country be able to return to limited, constitutional government and a free enterprise competitive system. Only then will we be able to turn away from the disastrous economic course in which they are leading us. Unfortunately, "contempt of Congress" is now a charge to which all thinking Americans are compelled to plead guilty.

If additional proof is needed to justify the criminal labels I have affixed to our federal politicians, I offer no less an authority than Secretary of the Treasury William Simon. In a speech at Southern Methodist University in early September 1974, Simon stated: "Either we get higher taxes directly, or the resulting budgetary deficits produce inflation, which is the most insidious and indiscriminate tax of all." Now, Secretary Simon is, of course, 100 percent accurate when he characterizes inflation as a "tax," since that is precisely what it is. Secretary Simon is also the most forthright Secretary of the Treasury to serve in that capacity in several generations. No former Secretary has ever had either the intelligence or the courage to admit that (1) deficit spending produces inflation, and that (2) the resultant inflation is, in effect, a federal tax.

What Simon was correctly referring to is, that if one had $1,000 in the bank and inflation of 10 percent eroded $100 of its value, then that individual, along with paying regular taxes, simply paid an additional "inflation tax" of $100. However, while Simon's statement is technically correct, he overlooks one significant detail that I refuse to overlook. I would ask the Secretary the following: "Granted, Mr. Secretary, that inflation is merely another federal tax. However, for every tax that the government imposes, there is a constitutional authorization. Where, Mr. Secretary, is the government's constitutional authority for levying an 'inflation tax'?" Neither Secretary Simon, nor anyone else, can produce any authorization, since none exists. The U.S. government was never empowered to extract revenue (and shift wealth) by means of an "inflation tax"; thus all government inflationary activities are obviously unconstitutional and therefore illegal. Since the U.S. government persists in levying this tax illegally, taxes extracted by the use of inflation amount to nothing less than embezzlement on the part of the federal government.

4

Social Security: The World's Biggest Chain Letter

Leaving the government's currency flim-flam and fleecing by inflation, let's consider another multibillion-dollar fraud, Social Security.

Let me stress at the outset that there are *no monetary reserves* available to the Social Security System out of which future benefits can be paid. All past Social Security taxes collected by the government have been spent like regular taxes and never treated any differently. They were never deposited in any trust fund despite the many statements and assurances by the government that this was being done.

Government officials over the years have told the American public that Social Security is an "insurance program" employing sound principles of funding and financing. Nothing could be farther from the truth.

Let me offer some examples of how the government goes about "informing" the public about the structure and financial condition of the Social Security System. Figures 18, 19, and 20 are from Social Security publication No. SS1-50, and entitled "Your Medicare Handbook." Please note that *insurance* is used *six* times on the cover of the booklet (Figure 18), and on page 3 (Figure 19), it appears *eighteen* times. The usage of the word insurance is amazing when one considers that Social Security is not insurance. These numerous uses of the word, in my view, only emphasize the Social Security Administration's flagrant attempt to mislead the American public. Note the following statement in Figure 19: "Your Medicare Health Insurance Card shows the protection you have." "Insurance"

Figure 18

Your Medicare Handbook

Health Insurance

SOCIAL SECURITY ACT

NAME OF BENEFICIARY
JOHN Q PUBLIC

CLAIM NUMBER 000-00-0000-A — SEX MALE

IS ENTITLED TO — EFFECTIVE DATE
HOSPITAL INSURANCE 1-1-73
MEDICAL INSURANCE 1-1-73

SIGN HERE John Q. Public

HEALTH INSURANCE
UNDER
SOCIAL SECURITY

SSI-50
February 1974

HOSPITAL INSURANCE (PART A)
MEDICAL INSURANCE (PART B)

Figure 19

Like Medicare, your handbook has two parts. . .

PART A

• The *first* section describes *hospital insurance*, often called *Part A* of Medicare. This is the part that helps pay for your care when you are in the hospital and for related health services, when you need them, after you leave the hospital.

PART B

• The *second* section describes *medical insurance*, often called *Part B* of Medicare. This is the part that helps pay your doctor bills and bills for other medical services you need.

Your Medicare health insurance card shows the protection you have

The people at the hospital, doctor's office, or wherever you get services, can tell from your health insurance card that you have both hospital and medical insurance and when each started. This is why you should always have your card with you when you receive services.

When a husband and wife both have Medicare, they receive separate cards and claim numbers.

If you ever lose your health insurance card, the people in your social security office will get you a new one.

This is your personal health insurance claim number. It must be shown on all Medicare claims exactly as it is shown on your card—INCLUDING THE LETTER AT THE END.

This shows you have hospital insurance.

This shows you have medical insurance.

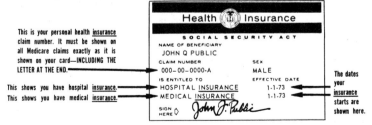

The dates your insurance starts are shown here.

3

Figure 20

Hospital Insurance—Part A of Medicare

You Get a Personal Record of Benefits Used

You don't have to bother about trying to keep track of how many "days" or "visits" you use in each benefit period. The notice you receive from the Social Security Administration after you have used any hospital insurance benefits will tell you how many benefit "days" and "visits" you have left in that benefit period. But, very few people who enter a hospital or extended care facility, or use home health services, need these services long enough to use all the benefits they have for a benefit period. So most people will never run out of "days" or "visits," because a new benefit period will almost always start with full benefits available again the next time they are needed.

EXAMPLE:

Mr. L was in the hospital for 2 weeks and then went home.

After Mr. L has been at home for 75 days, he returns to the hospital. When Mr. L is admitted this time, he is in a new benefit period. That means he is again eligible for up to 90 hospital days because more than 60 days have gone by since he was last in a hospital or other facility that mainly provides skilled nursing care. The benefit days Mr. L used the time before do not matter because he is in a new benefit period.

How Hospital Insurance Benefits Are Financed

The hospital insurance program is financed by special contributions from employees and self-employed persons, with employers paying an equal amount. These contributions are collected along with regular social security contributions from the wages and self-employment income earned during a person's working years.

67 Until 1972, the contribution rate for the hospital insurance program is six-tenths of one percent of the first $7,800 of earnings. It will increase gradually until 1987 when it will reach the final rate of nine-tenths of one percent.

These contributions are put into the Hospital Insurance Trust Fund from which the program's benefits and administrative expenses are paid. Funds from general tax revenues are used to finance hospital insurance benefits for people who are covered under the program but are not entitled to monthly social security or railroad retirement benefits.

In addition, the law provides that the various dollar amounts for which the patient is responsible be reviewed annually. These dollar amounts include the first $40 of hospital charges in each benefit period and different per-day amounts after certain periods of benefit use in hospitals and extended care facilities. These are described on the following pages. The law also provides that if this annual review shows that hospital costs have changed significantly these amounts must be adjusted for the following year. However, no change in these amounts may be made before 1969.

serves no useful purpose in this sentence. The sentence should have read "Your Medicare card shows the protection you have."

Note the heading on the Medicare card—"Health Insurance." It would have been more accurate to simply title it "Medicare." Note the use of the phrase "name of beneficiary" on it. In insurance terminology, the beneficiary is a third party designated to receive a policy's benefits; it is never used to signify the *owner* or the *covered person*. *Covered person* or *name* would be a more accurate term. But the Social Security Administration chose to use insurance terminology even if incorrectly.

Note the first paragraph on that page "Part A": "The first section describes hospital insurance, often called Part A of Medicare." This could have read: "The first section describes the *hospital benefits* of Medicare, often called Part A." Part B should read: "The second section describes the *medical benefits* of Medicare, often called Part B." But, again "insurance" appears unnecessarily in both paragraphs.

In the section where the arrows are used in the lower left-hand portion, "insurance" is used *four* times. The card states "Is entitled to Hospital Insurance/Medical Insurance." It should read that the covered person is "entitled to Hospital Benefits and Medical Benefits." Although a person is normally entitled to *benefits*, he *pays* for *insurance*. Since insurance was already used on the Medicare card, good writing would dictate that the word "benefit" should be used, instead of "insurance." But "insurance" *is* used—and not just a few times, but 211 times in the 26 pages of this pamphlet.

What Is Insurance?

Insurance has three general characteristics. (1) Insurance is a contract between an insuror and the insured whereby the insuror agrees to indemnify either the insured or a third-party beneficiary designated by the insured. The benefits itemized in the contract are enforceable in a court of law and are not subject to unilateral change. (2) Insurance attempts to relate the premiums and the costs of the insurance to the benefits and the risk involved—that is, the greater the risk, the higher the premium, or cost. Actuarial science is employed to achieve equity and financial stability. (3) Insurance companies are required to deposit premium income into a "reserve." This reserve is kept in cash accounts and the securities of *other* institutions. This reserve enables insurance companies to guarantee to pay the promised benefits. To determine the adequacy of its reserves, a company (a) assumes that it receives no new premiums and incurs no new liabilities after the evaluation date, and then (b) calculates whether the assets on hand, plus the interest they can earn in the future, are sufficient to meet future claims. If they are, then the company's insurance and pension liabilities are adequately funded. Let's apply this principle to a pension situation. Suppose a company had promised ten men aged 65 a $100 per-month pension for life. Mortality tables might show that the life expectancy of a man age 65 is 13 years. Obviously, some men in that group will not live that long, while others might outlive this period considerably. But for the purposes of establishing adequate reserves, we can rely on the known life expectancy for each man. So, starting at age 65, we can expect to pay each man $100 per month ($1,200 per year) or $15,600 over his life expectancy. Thus, we have committed ourselves to paying out nearly $156,000 to these ten men. Does this mean that, in order to discharge these future obligations, we must have $156,000 in our "reserve"? No, since while we are making these monthly payments, those assets in the reserve will be earning interest. If we assume that the assets in our reserve will earn 6 percent, we must have $108,140 in the reserve to pay the promised benefits. If we assume that our assets will only earn 4 percent, then we must begin with a larger reserve of $121,488.

Insurance company reserves are periodically examined by the insurance departments of the various states. If they're found to be deficient the company is suspended from doing business. It is actuarial reserves that differentiate insurance guarantees from other mere promises to pay. Applying the term insurance to a financial program which does not fund its future liabilities in the manner just described is to use the term erroneously, if not fraudulently.

Is Social Security Insurance?

Let's examine Social Security in terms of the general characteristics of insurance.

1. Is there a legal, enforceable contract between the U.S. government and the citizen concerning Social Security benefits? No. Social Security benefits can be changed or terminated at any time by Congress, and the government's right to confiscate individual Social Security benefits has been upheld in the courts (see *Fleming v. Nestor,* 80 S. Ct. 1367 [1960]).

2. There is, of course, little attempt to relate costs, risks, and benefits within the Social Security System. Wage earners pay the same OASDI taxes regardless of age, health, and degree of medical and disability risk involved. Recipients of Social Security benefits routinely have these benefits increased without ever having paid additional premiums.

3. How about reserves? The public, of course, is constantly reminded of the Social Security "trust fund." What constitutes this trust fund? Cash in a multitude of banks? Corporation stocks and bonds? Not at all. The U.S. Treasury reported that, as of June 30, 1973, the Federal Old Age Survivors Insurance Trust Fund, the Federal Disability Insurance Trust Fund, and the Federal Hospital Insurance Trust Fund collectively owned about $48 billion worth of government bonds, held in the "insurance trust funds" in order to help "defray" Social Security liabilities. This is the assumption that most people would make. However, this assumption is erroneous for government bonds are worthless in the hands of the government

and are of no help to the government in meeting future Social Security liabilities. The only value that these bonds have is to help the government conceal the nature of these "insurance trust funds."

Why All Government Bonds Held in So-Called Government "Trust Funds" Are Worthless

Most people regard a bond as an asset. If a government bond is an asset in the hands of a private citizen, then it is thought also to be an asset in the hands of the government. Quite the contrary. A bond is not an asset when held by the maker of the bond. For example, suppose you gave someone an IOU (you, of course, recognize that a bond is nothing more than a formal IOU). That individual could treat your IOU as his asset. You, of course, could not write yourself an IOU and treat it as your asset. But this is what the government does when it passes off its bonds as "assets" of government "trust funds." The fact that the government routinely reports that their trust funds own approximately $48 billion of government bonds is indicative of not what the trust funds *own* but what the government *owes* them. Money that the government must pay to the trust funds to redeem these bonds can *only* be secured by taxing the citizens again for Social Security revenue for which they *had already been taxed and which had already been paid.*

Interestingly, even if the Social Security trust funds contained *legitimate* securities, they would only be a pittance compared to the actual amount that the trust funds should hold in order to pay the promised benefits. As shown in Chapter 3, in the "Statement of Liabilities and Other Financial Commitments of the United States Government as of June 30, 1973," the government's liability was nearly $2.118 billion (actually it was $3.3 trillion). Since these trust funds collectively owned only about $48 billion in government bonds, assets in the "insurance trust funds" would have had to be increased by at least 4,300 percent for them to have been actuarially sound. Since the Social Security System does not have actuarially sound trust funds, Social Security cannot be insurance.

Suffice it to say that not only would the insurance commissioners of the various states shut down a company with an unfunded liability comparable to that of Social Security, but because of its reserve containing only notes of the company involved, they would also press charges against the company's officers for *fraud and grand larceny*. Insurance companies do not indiscriminately spend their premium income on projects and then leave their own IOUs (bonds) in the company till. If they did, they would be shut down and their officers carted off to jail.

All monies collected in the past through Social Security taxes have already been spent. This money was spent not only to meet past Social Security obligations, but to fight World War II, and the Korean and Vietnamese wars. It was used to bribe farmers not to grow food, finance Congressional junkets, support the U.N., and pay for landing on the moon. The bonds held by the Social Security trust funds are reminders of Social Security collections that have been spent on other projects.

Had the government taken past Social Security taxes and invested them in American corporate bonds, the cash flow of these bonds plus their redemption value would help meet current Social Security obligations. This might have given the country a legitimate Social Security trust fund, but this was not done.

As further evidence of the U.S. government's deceiving of the American public about Social Security, we need only consider statements such as the following by Maurice Stans, a former Director of the Budget and a former Secretary of Commerce. In the following interview, reprinted from *U.S. News & World Report,* January 16, 1967, Stans was asked if he would do away with the Social Security trust fund, and just handle Social Security as a direct obligation of the Treasury. To this he replied:

> I don't think it really makes any significant difference. There's now less money in the trust fund than is necessary to pay one year's benefits. We have long since abandoned the idea that President Roosevelt originally had when the Social Security fund was set up—the idea of keeping it on an actuarial basis so that the accumulated reserves would be equal at any date to the accrued retirement liabilities.
>
> We are now on a basis in which one year's collections from existing taxpayers are paid out in benefits to beneficiaries in the following year. So the trust fund has no particular significance as of now, except as an earmarking of taxes.

He was then asked:

> In what you said about the Social Security fund being adequate for less than one year's benefits, did you mean to imply that benefits are in danger in any way?

To which Stans answered:

> Oh, no—of course not. I merely imply that Social Security payments rest upon the general credit of the Government of the United States, upon its current taxing power, and not upon any accumulations in a trust fund to take care of you and me when we become eligible for benefits.

Considering Mr. Stans' accounting background, he is qualified to render a judgment on the "significance" of the government's trust fund, which he does well; however, he is hardly qualified to deliver an expert opinion concerning the *safety* of the payments that the System has promised to make. Stans should have responded to the second question by saying: "Yes, of course," since such an answer is implicit in his prior statement, which is why the question was asked. But, Social Security is sacrosanct, with few politicians daring to criticize it and expose it for what it really is.

Since the Social Security System does not operate on a legitimate reserve principle, as does insurance, then by what funding principle does it operate? The principle of the "chain letter"! Wage earners entering the bottom of the "chain" send their contributions, along with others moving up the "chain," to those workers who have made it to the top (those becoming eligible for benefits). Each new wave of entrants hopes, of course, that when it reaches the top, new waves of workers starting out at the bottom and those moving up will be forwarding benefits to them, thereby keeping the chain going. Is it conceivable that such an endless chain can really continue generation after generation? Look at what is happening. When Social Security was adopted, the maximum proposed tax was to be 3 percent withheld and 3 percent paid on a maximum salary of $3,000, *given a total proposed maximum tax of $180.* In 1975, with Social Security taxes at 5.85 percent, withheld and levied against payroll on a maximum salary of $14,100, the maximum tax reached $1,650. In only 35 years, therefore, the maximum tax has soared over 800 percent. At this rate of increase (and Social Security taxes have been *increasing* at an *accelerating* rate), those who are now 25 could find the maximum tax at age 60 to be $13,000.

In the light of Stans' statements and in light of what we have learned so far, let's examine Figure 20, page 7 of *Your Medicare Handbook.* Please note its many errors and misleading statements. Notice the paragraphs beneath the caption "How Hospital Insurance Benefits are Financed" and in the first paragraph of that section the phrase, "with employers paying an equal amount." The Social Security Administration has always conveyed the impression to the American wage earner that he only pays half of the cost of Social Security and his employer pays the other. This is not true. The worker pays the *entire cost* of his Social Security. This becomes obvious when one understands the principle that a worker must produce enough to pay the entire cost of his employment, which includes direct and indirect wages. Also, money paid by employers in Social Security taxes reduces the amount that can be paid in wages. In any case, employers will treat Social Security taxes as simply another cost and pass it on in terms of higher prices. Therefore, the American worker must bear the entire cost of Social Security either in terms of lower wages or by paying higher prices.

Notice this line in the third paragraph: "These contributions are put into the Hospital Insurance Trust Fund from which the program's benefits and administrative expenses are paid." This statement is false because all Social Security receipts are immediately mixed with regular tax revenues where they all become available to meet various government expenditures.

Note in the second paragraph that Social Security *taxes* are *contributions. Contributions,* however, are voluntary payments. Social Security payments, as the IRS will speedily remind you, are *taxes* not *contributions.* This again is another Newspeak technique.

Please refer to Figures 21 and 22, the cover and page 8 of the IRS 1975 "Employer's Tax Guide," respectively. Note how the government, when writing to employers concerning Social Security, consistently uses *taxes* when describing Social Security *payments. Taxes* appears 30 times in only two columns on page 8. Not once is *contribution* used. However, when the government produces pam-

Figure 21

Department
of the
Treasury
Internal
Revenue
Service

Third Class Bulk Rate
Postage and Fees Paid
Official Business
POSTMASTER: This matter must be forwarded and delivered without payment of postage due. If undeliverable after forwarding handle as specified in section 159.41B.

Circular E

Employer's Tax Guide

New Income Tax Withholding Rates and Tables

This revision of Circular E contains the revised rates and tables prescribed by the Department of the Treasury in accordance with the Tax Reduction Act of 1975 for withholding income tax from wages paid after April 30, 1975 and before January 1, 1976. The rates and tables take intc account the new personal exemption credit, the increase in the standard deduction, and the new earned income credit.

A new Form W–4 (Revised April 1975), Employee's Withholding Allowance Certificate, is on pages 49 and 50. This new form with the revised table should be used by employees to determine the correct number of withholding allowances for itemized deductions that they are entitled to claim under the new law. Copies of Form W–4 are available at Internal Revenue District offices.

Please display the poster on page 51 of this circular on your bulletin board so that your employees will be aware of how the new law affects their tax withholding.

Social Security Tax Base Increases

The maximum amount of wages subject to social security (FICA) taxes has been increased to $14,100 for wages paid in 1975.

Magnetic Tape Reporting

Employers required to file wage and information documents are encouraged to do so on magnetic tape rather than on paper forms. See section 23, on page 10 for details.

Publication 15
(Rev. April 1975)

Figure 22

18. Depositing Withheld Income Tax and Social Security (FICA) Taxes

Note. If any date shown falls on a Saturday, Sunday, or legal holiday, substitute the next regular workday.

Generally, you must deposit withheld income tax and social security taxes in an authorized commercial bank or a Federal Reserve bank. Include a Federal Tax Deposit Form 501 with each deposit. If you employ agricultural labor, you must include Federal Tax Deposit Form 511 with each deposit of the taxes on their wages.

The amount of taxes determines the frequency of deposits. Your liability for these taxes accrues when wages are **paid,** not when your payroll period ends. The following rules and examples show how often you must make deposits:

(1) If at the end of a quarter, the total undeposited taxes are less than $200, you are not required to make a deposit. You may either pay the taxes directly to the Internal Revenue Service along with your quarterly Form 941 or 941E, or make a deposit.

Example: At the end of the second quarter, the total undeposited taxes for the quarter are $170. Since this is less than $200, you may either pay the entire amount directly to the Internal Revenue Service with your quarterly Form 941 or 941E, or make a deposit.

(2) If at the end of a quarter, the total undeposited taxes are $200 or more, you must deposit the entire amount on or before the last day of the next month. If the undeposited amount is $2,000 or more, see rule 4 below.

Example: Your taxes for each month of the second quarter are $75. You must deposit $225 on or before July 31

(3) If at the end of any month (except the last month of a quarter), your cumulative undeposited taxes for the quarter are $200 or more and less than $2,000, you must deposit the taxes within 15 days after the end of the month. (This does not apply if you made a deposit for a quarter-monthly period that occurred during the month under the $2,000 rule in 4 below.)

Example A: Your taxes for each of the first two months of the second quarter are $300. You must deposit $300 within 15 days after both April 30 and May 31.

Example B: Your taxes for each of the first two months of the second quarter are $150. You must deposit $300 within 15 days after May 31.

Example C: Your taxes are $500 for each month of the second quarter. You must deposit $500 within 15 days after both April 30 and May 31, and $500 on or before July 31.

8

(4) If at the end of any quarter-monthly period, your cumulative undeposited taxes for the quarter are $2,000 or more, you must deposit the taxes within 3 banking days after the end of the quarter-monthly period. (Quarter-monthly periods end on the 7th, 15th, 22d, and last day of any month.) To determine banking days, exclude any local banking holidays observed by authorized commercial banks as well as Saturdays, Sundays, and legal holidays. You will meet the deposit requirements if: (a) you deposit at least 90 percent of the actual tax liability for the deposit period, and (b) if the quarter-monthly period occurs in a month other than the third month of a quarter, you deposit any underpayment with your first deposit that is required to be made after the 15th day of the following month. Any underpayment of $200 or more for a quarter-monthly period that occurs during the third month of the quarter must be deposited on or before the last day of the month.

Example A: During April your taxes for each quarter-monthly period are $3,000. You must deposit $3,000 within 3 banking days after April 7, 15, 22, and 30.

Example B: During the second quarter your taxes for each quarter-monthly period are $700. You must deposit $2,100 within 3 banking days after April 22, May 15, June 7, and June 30.

Summary of Deposit Rules for Withheld Income Tax and Social Security Taxes

Deposit rule	Deposit due
1. If at the end of a quarter the total undeposited taxes are less than $200:	No deposit required. Pay balance directly to the Internal Revenue Service with your quarterly return, or make a deposit if you prefer.
2. If at the end of a quarter the total undeposited taxes are $200 or more:	On or before last day of next month. If $2,000 or more, see rule 4.
3. If at the end of any month (except the last month of a quarter), cumulative undeposited taxes for the quarter are $200 or more, but less than $2,000:	Within 15 days after end of month. (For the first 2 months of the quarter no deposit is required if you previously made a deposit for a quarter-monthly period that occurred during the month under the $2,000 rule in item 4, below.)
4. If at the end of any quarter-monthly period, cumulative undeposited taxes for the quarter are $2,000 or more:	Within 3 banking days after the quarter-monthly period ends.

19. Using Government Depositories

How to Deposit Taxes.—Fill in a pre-inscribed Federal Tax Deposit Form 501 or Form 508, depending on the type of tax you are depositing, according to instructions.

Send each Federal tax deposit form and a single payment covering the taxes to be deposited to any commercial bank qualified as a depository for Federal taxes, or to a Federal Reserve bank. Make checks or money orders payable to the bank where you make your tax deposit. Contact your local bank or Federal Reserve bank for the names of authorized commercial bank depositories.

The timeliness of deposits is determined by the date the bank receives them. A deposit received by the bank after the due date will be considered timely if you establish that you mailed it 2 or more days before the due date.

How to Obtain Federal Tax Deposit Forms.—The Service will automatically send you pre-inscribed Federal tax deposit forms after you apply for an identification number. If you need additional forms, order them from the Internal Revenue Service Center where you file. Be sure to show your name, employer identification number, address, periods for which the forms are needed, and type of tax. **Request forms early.**

If your branch offices make tax deposits, obtain a supply of Federal tax deposit forms and distribute them to the branches so they can make deposits when due.

Do not use another employer's pre-inscribed forms. If you have not received Federal tax deposit forms by a deposit due date, mail your payment to the Internal Revenue Service Center where you file your return. Make it payable to the Internal Revenue Service and show on it your name, identification number, address, kind of tax, and period covered.

Deposit Record.—Before making a deposit, enter the payment amount on the form and stub, and record the check or money order number and date. Keep the stub for your records. The Service will not return the deposit portion of this form to you, but will use it to credit your tax account by means of your employer identification number.

How to Claim Credit for Overpayments.—If you deposited more than the correct amount of taxes for a quarter, you may elect to have the overpayment refunded, or applied as a credit to your next return. Show the appropriate

phlets for public consumption (see Figures 18, 23, and 24 containing 26, 17, and 27 pages respectively), *taxes* is never mentioned, but *contributions* is used repeatedly. How should we account for this reverse terminology?

Please note Figure 23, a copy of page 7 from a pamphlet of the Department of Health, Education and Welfare, coded No. (SSA) 73-10033, and entitled "Social Security Information for Young Families." The final paragraph states:

> Financing of Social Security is examined each year by the Boards of Trustees of the trust funds. The latest report shows that the program is soundly financed both for the short-range and long-range future.

As was noted earlier, the Social Security System had unfunded liabilities of $2.118 trillion, which had increased from the previous year's liabilities by over $300 billion. This one year's increase in its unfunded liabilities was greater than the entire federal budget for that year, while the total unfunded liabilities of the Social Security System was nearly five times greater (even using the government's own understated figures) than the entire reported national debt! This, therefore, hardly qualifies as a program that is "soundly financed both for the short-range and the long-range future." *Social Security obligations are not "financed" at all, as the pamphlet unabashedly claims.*

Figure 24 is a reproduction of pages 22 and 23 of HEW pamphlet 75-10035 issued November 1974 and entitled "Your Social Security." These two pages contain no less than *thirty-one* misstatements of fact and/or misleading inferences regarding Social Security.

The many misstatements in the three Social Security pamphlets cited are good examples of how the government and the Social Security Administration have deliberately misled the American public regarding Social Security's solvency and character.

To that extent, these pamphlets are blatant violations of Section 1001, Title 18, of the U.S. criminal code, a section I cited earlier. The statement in pamphlet 73-10033 that "the latest report shows the program [Social Security] is soundly financed both for the short-range and long-range future" is so blatantly false, given the Treasury Department's report of June 30, 1973, that those who approved this pamphlet should receive disciplinary action immediately. And, of course, both "Your Medicare Handbook" and "Your Social Security" are fraught with statements that are false, fictitious, and fraudulent.

What Are "Social Forms of Insurance"?

When government actuaries and bureaucrats find themselves trapped by intelligent questions about Social Security's deficiencies, they try to evade the fact that Social Security is a Ponzi-like scheme by replying, "but Social Security is a social form of insurance and, as such, it is not susceptible to the same type of measure-

Figure 23

Kinds of work covered
Almost every kind of employment and self-employment is covered by social security. Some occupations and some kinds of earnings, however, are affected by special provisions of the law.

If the kind of work you do is listed below and you aren't sure if you are earning protection under social security, you may want to ask someone at your social security office for information on these special provisions:

▼
Family employment—work done by a child under 21 for a parent, work done by a spouse, or work done by a parent in the home of a child;

▼
Work in or about the private home of your employer;

▼
Student employment at a school or college;

▼
Farm work; or

▼
Employment in a job where you get cash tips.

Financing social security
Social security retirement, survivors, and disability benefits and hospital insurance benefits are paid for by contributions based on covered earnings.

If you are employed, the contributions are deducted from your salary, and your employer pays an equal amount; if you are self-employed, you contribute at a little over ⅔ the combined employee-employer rate for retirement, survivors, and disability insurance. The hospital insurance contribution rate is the same for employers, employees, and self-employed persons.

The maximum amount of yearly earnings that can count for social security and on which you pay social security contributions is $13,200 for 1974. The maximum will increase automatically in later years to keep pace with increases in average earnings.

The maximum in past years was: $3,000 a year for 1937-50; $3,600 for 1951-54; $4,200 for 1955-58; $4,800 for 1959-65; $6,600 for 1966-67; $7,800 for 1968-71; $9,000 for 1972; and $10,800 for 1973.

People now making social security contributions can be sure that funds will be available to pay their benefits when they become eligible. The schedule of contribution rates now in the law will provide income sufficient to pay all benefits under present law as well as administrative costs of the program now and into the future. Financing of social security is examined each year by the Boards of Trustees of the trust funds. The latest report shows that the program is soundly financed both for the short-range and long-range future.

ment and actuarial standards as private forms of insurance.'' Such assertions are absurd. Either something is insurance or it isn't.

What are ''social forms of insurance,'' if they are not insurance? They are simply forms of ''socialism'' (see Chapter 6, for discussion on socialism). ''Social forms of insurance'' is socialism sold to the public as an adjunct of the free-enterprise system, since its proponents use capitalistic terms, such as *insurance,*

Figure 24

Financing

The basic idea

The basic idea of social security is a simple one: During working years employees, their employers, and self-employed people pay social security contributions into special trust funds. When earnings stop or are reduced because the worker retires, becomes disabled, or dies, monthly cash benefits are paid to replace part of the earnings the family has lost.

Part of the contributions made go into a separate hospital insurance trust fund so workers and their dependents will have help in paying their hospital bills when they become eligible for Medicare. The medical insurance part of Medicare is financed by premiums paid by the people who have enrolled for this protection and amounts contributed by the Federal Government.

Contribution rates

If you're employed, you and your employer each pay an equal share of social security contributions. If you're self-employed, you pay contributions for retirement, survivors, and disability insurance at a somewhat lower rate than the combined rate for an employee and his employer. The hospital insurance contribution rate is the same for the employer, the employee, and the self-employed person.

As long as you have earnings that are covered by the law, you continue to pay contributions regardless of your age and even if you are receiving social security benefits.

Through 1977 employees and employers each pay 5.85 percent on the employee's wages. The total rate for self-employed people is 7.90 percent. The rates include .90 percent for hospital insurance under Medicare. The maximum amount of earnings that can count for social security purposes and on which you pay social security contributions is $14,100 in 1975.

Future rate increases are scheduled. In 1978 the employee and employer will each pay 6.05 percent. The rate for each will go to 6.30 percent in 1981 and 6.45 percent in 1986. The self-employed rate goes to 8.10 percent in 1978; to 8.35 percent in 1981; and to 8.50 percent in 1986. The hospital insurance part of the rate will be 1.10 percent in 1978; 1.35 percent in 1981; and 1.50 percent in 1986.

Funds not required for current benefit payments and expenses are invested in interest-bearing U.S. Government securities.

The Government's share of the cost for supplementary medical insurance and certain other social security costs come from general revenues of the U.S. Treasury, not from social security contributions.

How contributions are paid

If you're employed, your contribution is deducted from your wages each payday. Your employer matches your payment and sends the combined amount to the Internal Revenue Service.

If you're self-employed and your net earnings are $400 or more in a year, you must report your earnings and pay your self-employment contribution each year when you file your individual income tax return. This is true even if you owe no income tax.

Your wages and self-employment income are entered on your social security record throughout your working years. This record of your earnings will be used to determine

22 23

reserves, funding, and *premiums,* which are non-existent in a socialistic lexicon. "Social forms of insurance" is actually a cryptosocialistic term; it promotes socialism under the guise and within the framework of the free-enterprise system.

How Social Security Lowers America's Standard of Living

One of the tragedies of Social Security is that it has helped (and helps) to lower the American standard of living. One reason for this is that Social Security has spawned a large, nonproductive class of bureaucrats whose sole function is to service this vast system, while at the same time imposing uneconomic and unnecessary collection and record-keeping burdens on American industry.

I often wonder how many American businesses that are now forced to close their doors (thus creating unemployment and social *insecurity*) would remain open if only they had as working capital the money they had paid into Social Security during the last five years.

Another tragedy in connection with Social Security is that the government has convinced vast segments of the public that the System will be able to provide them with significant income during their later years. This, of course, will not be possible. An objective analysis of the assets and liabilities of the System, together with the growth rate of these liabilities, plus the declining growth rate and the declining productive base of the economy (in large measure due to the economy being saddled with such inane government programs and burdensome taxes) will point toward the System's collapse. The only question is: when? Therefore, many will be without the income they had expected. Had Social Security "contributions" not been compulsory, the money could have been invested elsewhere in the private sector. Substantial capital, in this way, would have been channeled into the private sector, increasing the country's industrial base, and creating more jobs and goods—in sum, generating real growth. Instead, this capital was channeled to Washington where it was largely dissipated by politicians and bureaucrats.

Perhaps the greatest tragedy of the Social Security System is that each month over 30 million recipients[1] of Social Security are told that if they earn more than a stated sum, they will lose part if not all of their benefits. How many millions of these recipients might, in fact, be capable and willing to work if only they were not discouraged and penalized from doing so by government? A nation's standard of living is determined by the total economic output of its citizens. If fewer people work, then the lower the nation's productivity and its standard of living become. Thus, since Social Security actually encourages, even compels, nonproductivity by a vast segment of the population, it is forcing a substantially lower standard of living on the entire nation.

[1]To recipients under 16, such prohibitions are, I grant, immaterial.

5

How and Why the Government Declared Bankruptcy and Concealed It

Within the past five years, the U.S. government has declared bankruptcy three times-on August 15,1971,December 18,1971 and February 12,1973. Incredible, you say?

To understand these events, requires some understanding of the word *bankruptcy*. Bankruptcy means settling with one's creditors for less than what one owes. It is a repudiation of one's debts and financial obligations. Settling with one's creditors for 90 or 95 cents on the dollar is no less a bankruptcy than settling with them for 2 or 5 cents on the dollar—the difference is only in degree.

In accordance with monetary arrangements made at Bretton Woods, New Hampshire, in 1944, the U.S. government pledged to the world's central banks that it would pay an ounce of gold for every 35 U.S. dollars (IOUs) presented for redemption. Since this promise was considered an iron-clad guarantee from a country presumed to be both rich and honorable, the nations of the world were willing to hold dollars on the same basis as they held gold in their national treasuries. Not only were dollars *as good as gold,* they were better. After all, gold earned no interest, developed storage and insurance costs, and was not so easily transferable. Central banks, therefore, amassed dollars, holding them as they would gold, as an asset against the issuance of their own national currencies. Since they could increase their own currency by an amount even greater than their reserves (gold and dollars), exportation of U.S. dollars had a multiplier effect, thus artifically inflating the world's currency supply.

Americans had a great thing going. While foreigners shipped us transistors, automobiles, calculators, motorcycles, and shoes, we shipped out paper notes. In this manner, we shipped out over $65 billion of paper IOUs while the world sent us over $65 billion in real wealth which, when added to the wealth we produced, provided Americans with a vast supply of goods and helped create an illusion of prosperity.[1]

After a while some of our foreign creditors became edgy. They saw America buying more of the world's goods on credit without trying to shore up its own gold reserves or its export potential to pay for all that America was "charging." So, America's creditors began cashing in their IOUs. That was the situation which caused our "gold drain," culminating on August 15, 1971, with the U.S. government repudiating its financial obligations and announcing to the world that it could no longer pay out gold to redeem American dollars. In effect this was a *declaration of bankruptcy*.

Again, the U.S. government engaged in Newspeak to conceal the dishonoring of its financial commitments by stating that it was ending the dollar's "convertibility" by closing the "goldwindow," cutting the dollar's "ties" to gold, and permitting the dollar to "float."

The average American (along with most financial commentators) did not understand the August 15 move. The government provided convincing, but misleading, reasons for its actions. But the cold hard fact was that it repudiated its financial obligation to redeem its paper IOUs for gold.

Suppose you bought merchandise either by charging or giving IOUs and owed an amount equal to 6½ times your liquid assests.[2] Within a short time, your creditors would begin demanding payment. You, of course, would now be in the position that President Nixon found himself on August 15, 1971. Assuming you could get away with some of the antics that governments do, you could (1) end your IOU "convertibility" into money, (2) close your "IOU window," (3) sever all money ties to your IOUs and debts, and (4) announce that you will allow your IOUs to "float."[3] So, you could have handled your obligations in the same way that the U.S. government handled its debts.[4]

[1]I say *illusion* because America was living "on-the-cuff." This was the Marshall Plan in reverse.

[2]The approximate ratio of U.S. gold to net foreign-held liquid dollar claims, but since our foreign creditors knew that we could never allow our gold stock to drop below $8 billion, the ratio was actually 26 to 1.

[3]Since you will not redeem your IOUs at par, they are now free to find their own value based upon what anyone will pay for them.

[4]While the U.S. government can compel its internal creditors to accept the "money" it creates, external creditors could insist on real money which the U.S. did not have in sufficient amount in relation to its debts.

What reason did President Nixon give for repudiating the United States' pledge of 1944 that the dollar was as good as gold? He claimed it was to "defend the dollar against the [international money]speculators."[1] However, his action neither defended nor saved the dollar. Actually, it buried it as an international standard of honesty and reliability. American politicians had showered the globe with dollars for years, until finally we didn't have enough gold at home to honor them.

Nixon's action was the culmination of four months of heavy selling of American dollars in Europe. This was aggravated by (1) the persistent U.S. gold loss, (2) the U.S.'s widening trade deficit, (3) the continued U.S. inflation, and (4) the lower interest prevailing in the U.S. than in West Germany.

In early May 1971, panic selling of American dollars climaxed when the Bundesbank (West Germany's central bank) was reported to have absorbed a billion of them on May 4th. On May 5th, it refused to accept any more. Several days later the central banks of Switzerland, Belgium, the Netherlands, and Austria followed suit.

During this period American tourists found to their dismay that the dollar was no longer so almighty. In some situations, Americans could not even spend their dollars or were forced to accept steep exchange discounts. When the currency exchanges reopened, the Swiss franc and German mark and other major European currencies no longer maintained their fixed parity with the dollar, but floated against the dollar, with their relative values now increased relative to the dollar. The American dollar had been devalued not by the United States, but by her creditors.

This "dumping of dollars" was the world's way of telling the United States that American goods were overpriced. It was U.S. goods, not dollars, that the world was rejecting. I could have forgiven President Nixon for suspending the convertibility of the dollar to save our remaining supply of gold, but only if in so doing he had leveled with the American public on *why* his action was necessary. He should have addressed the nation and the world as follows:

> My fellow Americans, the time for American self-deception is now at an end. The world is rushing to cash in U.S. dollars for gold, because our gold offers the world better value than our goods. Our nation created the assembly line, mass production flooded the world with low-cost, quality merchandise, but now by the world's standards, we have become a high-cost inefficient producer. Yes, we are able to export some computers, agricultural products, and heavy equipment such as airplanes, but look at the foreign cars that are entering this country. This is the type of merchandise that for so long American industry was able to export. But now foreign markets for American steel, American sewing machines, American tractors, and American radios have all but dried up. As of now, we cannot afford to pay for those things which we wish to import.

[1] This is tantamount to a company's management blaming bankruptcy on its insistent creditors, rather than on wasteful managerial policies that created more indebtedness than the business could afford.

> Therefore, my fellow Americans, the party is over. We have exhausted our credit and the world wants payment in kind. We have to go back to work. We cannot afford all the featherbedding, the extensive welfare programs, the fancy frills of government.
>
> I am imposing an austerity program to force down our internal price structure in order to make American goods more competitive so that we can pay for the things we must import. America is returning to work *full time*. Government payrolls will be slashed some 20 percent, all price supports will be eliminated, and all wage restrictions abolished. We can restore the convertibility of the dollar only when the goods we produce are priced so competitively that the nations of the world would rather use their dollars to buy our goods than use them to take our gold.

Nixon could have even reaped political advantage from the crisis by placing the blame for it squarely where it belonged—on the monetary blunders of the Kennedy and Johnson Administrations. Instead, he blamed "international speculators." He told the American public that while foreign goods and foreign travel would cost Americans more, that

> If you are among the overwhelming majority of Americans who buy American-made products in America, your dollar will be worth just as much tomorrow as it is today. The effect of this action [devaluation], in other words, will be to stabilize the dollar.

This was not true at all! The effect of ending dollar convertibility would be to drive up substantially the prices of *all* items—those produced domestically as well as those imported from abroad.

What Was the Practical Effect of Nixon's Action?

When President Nixon announced that the United States would no longer pay real money (gold) for its IOUs, this did not make dollars owned by foreigners worthless since the *private sector* would now be compelled to supply the convertibility that the U.S. government had rejected. If foreigners could no longer use their American dollars to acquire gold from our government, they could at least be used to acquire timber, oil pipe, agricultural products, real estate, and stocks from the U.S. private sector.

When President Nixon announced that dollars would no longer be redeemed for gold, the dollar immediately lost its position as a legitimate reserve currency and nations holding dollars were encouraged to spend them for American goods, rather than keep them as backing for their own currencies. Since the dollars owned by foreigners could only be spent in America, they would increasingly compete with American held dollars in the American marketplace and would begin exerting an upward pressure on the U.S.'s internal price structure. President Nixon had stated, of course, that this action would not affect such prices. But this was not true.

Shortly after these monetary events and governmental assurances, the United States began experiencing extensive shortages—a phenomenon in a peacetime economy. For example, Japanese businessmen used some of their U.S. dollars to buy U.S. beef, thereby forcing up prices and creating shortages.[1]

Many foreigners who couldn't buy our gold and didn't want our goods used their dollars to buy U.S. real estate and/or acquire interests in American businesses. With the dollar dropping substantially in value, foreigners were able to acquire American assets at discount prices.

Many shortages have resulted since people the world over began cashing in their paper IOUs and carting off more of our real wealth. So the American economy now has to produce goods and services for 210 million Americans and to pay for our past "on-the-cuff" purchases.

The following example illustrates what has been happening to America. Suppose one had purchased fuel all winter on credit. Finally, the fuel company requests payment. The debtor responds that although he has no money to pay his fuel bill, he would like to settle his indebtedness in some manner. Therefore, he suggests that the company use his IOUs in exchange for items in his house. In exchange for the IOUs, the company carts out a couch, and a few chairs, takes food from the cupboard, removes clothes from the closet—even draws gas from his automobile. The debtor's family now begins to experience all types of "shortages." With the cupboards bare, there is now a *food shortage.* With the gasoline siphoned from the automobile, there is now a *gasoline shortage*. However, the above debtor is really experiencing a *reduced standard of living, not shortages.*

How the U.S. Went Bankrupt *Again*—Alice-in-Wonderland Style

On December 18, 1971, the United States announced in connection with the Smithsonian monetary agreements that the dollar was to be "devalued" 8.57 percent, with the official price of gold raised from $35 to $38 per ounce. President Nixon announced this at the Smithsonian Institution, where over 400 members of the world press attended along with the ministers of the major nations. In his typical penchant for understatement, he said that the conference had concluded "the most significant monetary agreement in the history of the world."[2]

[1]I recall being a guest in someone's living room during a TV newscast during the beef boycott. American beef was shown being exported to Japan. The commentator stated that Japanese interests were buying beef and a good deal of Texas range land to ensure an adequate beef supply for Japan. My host's reaction was that this was a terrible state of affairs and that the government should do something about it immediately. I noticed then that we were watching the telecast on a Sony TV and that my host also owned a Japanese-brand hi-fi stereo. I pointed out that these were Japanese-made products and that the Japanese had received payment for them in U.S. paper dollars. I then asked my host why the Japanese shouldn't be allowed to spend their dollars any way they wished. "After all," I said, "if our government now says 'we will not give you the gold we promised in exchange for dollars,' then what are they to do with dollars they earned legitimately? If we do not now allow foreigners to exchange their dollars for goods, then we in effect stole the goods that they shipped to us to earn these dollars."

[2]Nixon significantly and unilaterally *broke* this agreement one year, one month and 24 days later when the U.S. *again* devalued its currency by another 10 percent.

Now, what is a devaluation? It is a complicated way in which a nation declares bankruptcy without revealing its true fiscal plight. For example, when the U.S. government increased the price of gold from $35 to $38 an ounce, it repudiated 8.57 percent of its external debts (or it was settling its debts for 91.5 cents on the dollar). Why? Prior to the devaluation, if one of Uncle Sam's creditors presented 35 paper dollar IOUs, he would theoretically receive an ounce of gold.[1] After the devaluation, the creditor would have to present 38 paper dollars to get the same ounce of gold. For 35 paper dollars he would, therefore, get 8.57 percent *less* gold than he would have received before the devaluation. This is what happens when a debtor settles with his creditors for an amount less than he owes—he, in effect, declares bankruptcy.

Now, when a government goes bankrupt and devalues its currency, it gives high-sounding reasons for doing so. The reasons usually advanced are (1) to stimulate exports, (2) to increase domestic employment, (3) to make one's goods more competitive in foreign markets, and (4) to prevent currency speculation. All of these merely hide the fact that the devaluing country simply piled up more debt than it could handle, had mismanaged its economy, and was compelled to settle with its creditors for something less than it really owed—in other words, it had to repudiate part of its debts.

Devaluation *lowers* a nation's standard of living because it compels the nation to export more of its wealth to pay for the same amount of imports. Since its goods are now cheaper to the rest of the world, more of its goods will flow out. Since the goods of the rest of the world have become relatively more expensive, less of the world's goods will flow in. So, a country with devalued currency will have less real wealth to distribute among its citizens, thus precipitating a drop in its standard of living. This is what has happened here as a result of the continual devaluations by the government of United States currency.

In keeping with our government's attempt to paint devaluation in positive terms and make a declaration of bankruptcy sound like smart business, President Nixon said that "the whole free world has won" and that the agreements would result in "a more stable world with more fair competition and more true prosperity." A tissue of half-truths and falsehoods indeed! For the reasons already enumerated, the U.S. consumer lost—but that wasn't Nixon's fault. He is to be faulted for not explaining the real reasons for and the consequences of his action. Two questions that should have been put to him in light of his statements: (1) If devaluing the currency accomplishes so much, why did you wait two years before taking action? (2) If 8.57 percent devaluation is so good, then why not one of 10 or 15 percent?

Since August 15, 1971, the United States government hadn't been exchanging gold for dollars at *any* price, so essentially what the government was now saying was, "before we were not selling gold for $35 an ounce, now we are not going to

[1]We say theoretically because as of August 15, 1971, as explained earlier, the government had repudiated its obligation to pay out *any* gold for dollars!

sell it for $38 an ounce.'' It is, of course, nonsense for the government to announce the *official price* for which it will not sell something, when what is at issue is the price at which the government *will* exchange gold for dollars—since this would establish the true value of the country's currency. When the U.S. government refuses to exchange gold for dollars at their official value, it means that the official value is pure fiction. The U.S. government refused to sell gold because it knew that gold would have to be priced substantially higher than the official price—thereby revealing that the dollar's value was *lower* than the government wished to admit.[1] The government's unwillingness to reveal the true value of its currency by exchanging it for gold can be traced to the same fraudulent mentality as revealed in its unwillingness to accurately report its unfunded & contingent liabilities

With all due apologies to Lewis Carroll it's an ''Alice-in-Wonderland'' world when a government announces the *official price* at which it *absolutely refuses to sell something*. It somehow reminds me of a man who told a soda jerk that he wanted some seltzer without chocolate syrup, and the soda jerk replied, ''Sir, we are all out of chocolate syrup, you will have to have it without strawberry syrup.'' Or a lady who asked a butcher how much he charged for liver, and he replied 89 cents a pound. ''Why so much?'' the lady inquired. ''The butcher across the street gets only 69 cents a pound.'' ''Then,'' the butcher asked, ''why don't you buy it across the street?'' ''Because he is out of liver,'' she replied. ''Well,'' the butcher retorted, ''when I am out of liver, I only get 59 cents a pound.''

The federal government makes the same kind of jokes, but on a grander, more majestic scale. On February 12, 1973, President Nixon scrapped the Smithsonian agreements and devalued the dollar again. On this occasion, the devaluation was 10 percent and the gold price was ''officially'' raised to $42.22 per ounce. George P. Shultz, then Secretary of the Treasury, stated that this devaluation was to ''lay the legislative groundwork for broad and outward-looking trade negotiations paralleling our efforts to strengthen the monetary system.'' He failed to mention that the action came after ten days of massive speculative assault against the dollar. I would have asked Shultz, ''How is the monetary system strengthened by weakening the dollar?'' In all fairness to Shultz, however, he did also urge Congress to exercise budgetary discipline to ''avoid a revival of inflationary pressure in the U.S.'' President Nixon again repeated the big lie, that while devaluation would raise the cost of some imports and increase the cost of tourism, ''as far as the great majority of Americans are concerned, it does not affect their dollars.''

Now here comes the ''funny'' part. Up until February 12, 1973, the U.S. was not prepared to sell gold at the official price of $38 per ounce. Yet, on that day, the government announced that it was *not* prepared to sell gold even at $42.22 per

[1] This was written before the U.S. started to auction off limited quantities of its gold. Since the minimum price the government would accept for gold was vastly in excess of its ''official price''—the government's action constituted an admission that its ''official price'' for gold was sheer fiction.

ounce. It could have, with equal logic, stated that it wouldn't sell gold at $60 or $75 per ounce. But, the government's official price is pure fiction, and it would be funny if the implications of the true value of gold being 300 percent higher than the "official" price were not so tragic. A gold price of $150 an ounce means that we are heading for an official devaluation of *at least 75 percent*, if things get no worse. The world has already devalued the dollar to that extent. All that remains is for Washington to admit it, officially.

Massive government spending—that is, spending beyond the economy's realistic capabilities—has caused government to debase the nation's currency in order to avoid paying for the massive debts it has incurred. And a tragic lesson that history teaches is that currency debasement and national decline go hand in hand.

6

Toward a United Socialist America?

It is amazing how few Americans know the difference between socialism, fascism, communism, and the system that has been responsible for America's growth, strength, and supremacy—free enterprise and competition. Many incorrectly characterize our economic system as *capitalism* or *laissez faire*. Laissez faire means leaving the economy alone, but that approach could lead to the growth of monopoly power. While the government should generally leave the economy alone, it should also, whenever necessary, break up monopoly growth as well as agreements designed to restrain and limit trade. Calling our system capitalism overlooks the fact that even socialist economies *require* capital—under our *old* system private individuals owned the capital; under socialism it is the state that owns the capital.

Under our former economic system *competition* was just as important as *free enterprise*. The force of competition ensures (1) that the best possible goods and services will be produced, (2) that the highest possible wages compatible with productive ability will be paid, and (3) that varying interest rates will direct capital to where it is needed most.

Artificial barriers that interfere with the free flow of capital and labor will hamper a free economy's ability to generate the maximum quantity of consumer goods and services and to elevate living standards. Government's legitimate function in a free economy is (1) to create an economic climate that will enable market forces to function, (2) to break up monopolies and agreements that hinder competition and limit productivity in order to increase prices, (3) to provide an efficient court system where business agreements can be adjudicated efficiently and equitably, and (4) to rid society of those members who insist on living off the labors of others through extortion, theft, and so on.

In some areas, of course, it is impossible, if not impractical, to have economic competition, such as in the area of public utilities. How many sets of water pipes or telephone poles from competing companies could a community afford or tolerate? In this instance, it's necessary to grant what amounts to *monopoly power*. But this can be supervised intelligently so that the consumer is not gouged. It should be recognized that even public utility monopolies compete and thus would not have unlimited economic power to force price increases on the public as consumers would, in many areas, to be able to choose between gas and electricity or between oil and coal. This would be true even if all four of these industries were monopolies. Competition between monopolies would generally dictate that profits would be maximized only by providing consumers with the best product and service possible.[1]

If there were only one steel company and one aluminum company, there would still be competition because, in certain areas, consumers would, depending upon price, choose one over the other. The companies would still be competing against other materials—for example, plastics, lumber, copper—and, of course, foreign producers of steel and aluminum. There should be no tariff barriers that deny the American consumer the right to buy products at the lowest possible prices. If, for some reason, an industry requires tariff protection it should be granted instead a direct subsidy from the U.S. government. In this way, *all* taxpayers would bear the responsibility of supporting the subsidized industry. For one thing, it is not equitable that only the users of a product be compelled to support an industry on behalf of the entire nation; for another, it would become evident which industries are being subsidized and to what extent.

So, even if General Motors is huge, size per se is not monopolistic. As long as consumers are free to buy Fords, Plymouths, Toyotas, Fiats, Rolls Royces, Volkswagens, and Ramblers, General Motors is not a monopoly: it must meet its competition to remain in business.

As stated earlier, an important economic function of government in a free enterprise economy is that of eliminating barriers to free trade, free negotiation,

[1]Obviously, I am now advocating this degree of monopoly power. I wish to point out that, even given this degree of monopoly (assuming the monopolies in question do not conspire among themselves concerning prices and markets), *competition* and the consumer's *freedom of choice* would still be powerful economic deterrents to the abuse of such economic power.

The areas where the consumer is really at the mercy of an abuse of monopoly power is in connection with U.S. government operation, such as the U. S postal monopoly and the U.S. money monopoly. With the former the consumer by law must accept deteriorating service at increasing prices. With the latter, by nationalizing then outlawing the ownership of gold, the U.S. government sought to eliminate its only real competition in the money field. With the competition eliminated, the government imposed its inferior "money" on the public.

and free entry into the labor market so that goods and services can reach the marketplace at their lowest prices. However, U.S. economic policy over the last 40 years has been the opposite. Practically every governmental intrusion into the economy has been to *promote monopoly* and to foist higher prices on the public. Let's consider some of the most recent examples.

1. *U.S. agriculture policy*. The government was empowered to impose fines and penalties in connection with its parity program covering more than 20 agricultural products. Government acreage restrictions were designed to force food prices higher than their previous prices on the open market. Since no private agricultural combine was powerful enough to become such an agricultural monopoly, the U.S. government obligingly assumed the role. However, this policy succeeds in increasing the price of many other items. Cotton subsidies raise the cost of clothing. Corn subsidies up the cost of feed for livestock, thereby increasing meat prices.

2. *Tariff duties*. Tariff duties inflate the prices of many imported items. For years import duties on sugar have created a domestic price more than twice that on the world market. Consequently government artificially has increased not only the price of sugar, but the price of all products requiring sugar.

3. *Wage laws*. Federal wage laws try to increase the cost of labor above the free market price. At the same time the federal government, for political reasons, refuses to use the Sherman Antitrust Act to curb the monopolistic power of labor unions and enforces union contracts that contain featherbedding provisions, limit productivity, and exploit the consumer.

4. *The Interstate Commerce Commission*. For years this regulatory agency has been an obstacle to lower transportation rates and fares.

Of Freedom and Free Enterprise

In a free enterprise system it is the entrepreneur (the one who combines all the factors of production—land, labor, and capital) who takes the economic risk, and it is he who should therefore benefit from any profit. If his venture fails, it is he who bears the financial loss. *Profit* is what is left after everybody else is paid—the banker his interest, the landlord his rent, the worker his wages. Generating profit is no easy task.[1] And, since the risks of entering business and remaining in business are great, the rewards must be commensurate with that risk. For if individuals are discouraged from assuming the economic risk, the creation of jobs and the ability of government to tax cease.

The more efficient the entrepreneur is in combining the factors of production, the greater his reward—and the greater society's gain. Since the factors of production are limited in quantity while society's economic wants are unlimited, the entrepreneur who can satisfy an economic want by employing as little of these factors as possible (creating maximum quality at minimum cost) will free re-

[1]For example, there were 9,345 business failures in the U.S. in 1973.

sources that can be used to meet society's other economic needs. This, then, is the entrepreneur's and management's function—to direct their attention and energies to produce goods and services as economically as possible in order to use the least amount and most economic of resources. When they perform this function well, their service to society is twofold: efficient creation of goods and creation of economic employment.[1]

To the extent that business is profitable, more capital will be available to increase efficiency and expand employment. The chief function of business in a free enterprise system, then, is to pursue profits as vigorously as possible, not to operate in a manner where profits are sacrificed to the "public interest."[2]

First of all, a company that manufactures a good product at a competitive price and provides employment for people would automatically operate in the public interest, if it did nothing else.[3] If a business operated primarily in the public interest, with profit-making the secondary concern, it would soon be out of business—much to the disadvantage of its employees and the consumer.[4]

Questions an Economic System Must Answer

All economic systems must solve three basic problems—what should be produced, who should produce it, and who should get it. In a free competitive systems these problems are not entrusted to fallible men who would make decisions based on their own interests and prejudices. Solution of these questions is left to the impersonal forces of the marketplace—supply and demand. Since the free enterprise and competitive system (from here on referred to as FEAC) employs no centralized planning mechanism to resolve these questions, it is often criticized as unsystematic, even chaotic. Quite the contrary: The law of supply and demand operates far more efficiently and equitably than human planning. In a FEAC system economic wants, needs, tastes, desires, and abilities all find their way to the marketplace where they are evaluated with computerlike speed and accuracy by a pricing mechanism that determines in *democratic* fashion what people want—and then (1) proceeds to allocate resources on a priority basis, based on prices people are willing to pay to have them produced, (2) determines a wage

[1]The U.S. government has never made a distinction between economic and uneconomic employment.

[2]We know, of course, about "profit-sharing" plans whereby the employer contributes to a retirement plan on behalf of his employees—this being in excess of normal wages and paid out of year-end profits. I wonder if employees would be so enthusiastic about this arrangement if it were also tied to a "loss-sharing" provision, so that if there were a year-end loss, the employees would *return* a portion of their wages. In all fairness and equity, if there is profit sharing, why not loss sharing?

[3]I am overlooking entirely any question of pollution and the possible destruction of the environment regarding these two factors, and I assume that there is no violation of criminal law.

[4]This is probably why those who usually urge that businesses be "socially responsible" or "operate in the public interest" are *not* businessmen.

scale, based upon society's needs and demands for specific skills, and (3) determines by open auction who gets the goods produced. The FEAC system materially rewards hard work, intelligence, drive, and creativity, thereby establishing economic incentive and motivation.

Some critics hold that this is "unfair," as some will be rewarded to a far greater degree than will others. What they overlook, however, is that life itself is "unfair." Is it "fair" that some are born strong and others weak? Or that some are born to parents who are responsible, while others are born to parents who are irresponsible? Is it "fair" that some are born of sound limb while others are born crippled? Since people are born *unequal*—physically, intellectually, morally—they will naturally acquire *unequal* amounts of worldly goods. A FEAC system, however, by its system of incentives and rewards, stimulates production and creativity so that even those born with physical handicaps and limited abilities can acquire far more goods and services (though the distribution may be unequal) than can be acquired by others having far greater skills and abilities but who live in an economy where incentive, initiative, and creativity are stifled. To suggest that the FEAC system is imperfect is to overlook the fact that no system, created by humans who are themselves fallible, can be perfect. However, the American experience provides ample proof that the FEAC system has provided far greater economic benefits—though in unequal portions—than other systems which in their zeal for economic equality have produced democratic poverty. Even the level of material comforts enjoyed by most of America's welfare recipients is beyond the reach of most who work full time in many parts of the world.

Along with supply and demand, self-interest and freedom of choice are part of the mechanism of a FEAC system; they constitute what Adam Smith (1723-1790) called the "invisible hand." An individual seeking only to promote his own welfare is, in most cases,

> led by an invisible hand to promote an end which was not part of his intention . . . . By pursuing his own interest he frequently promotes that of society more effectively than when he really intends to promote it. I have never known much good done by those who affected to trade for the public good. It is an affectation, indeed, not very common among merchants, and very few words need be employed in dissuading them from it.

U.S. economic history is replete with such examples.

Henry Ford did not intend to become a public benefactor. He simply wanted to make as much money as possible. The best way he knew was by building the best automobile and selling it at the lowest possible price. Since the American consumer, exercising his freedom of choice, would evaluate the practicality of Ford's Model T over other means of transportation—the more inexpensive his automobile, the more practical it would be over the competition, so the more cars he could sell.

When an American consumer exercises his free choice and buys a product from all those competing in the marketplace, he is "voting" for that product. Manufacturers must court the American consumer to "vote" for their product, since when the consumer stops voting in this manner, the product is compelled to "leave office." Thus, the free enterprise system is economic democracy with consumers exercising their voting rights 'round the clock.

So, in his pursuit of profit Henry Ford brought low-cost, private transportation to the world's working classes and in the process paid the highest daily wages up to that time for factory employment.

Thomas Alva Edison did not set out to be a public benefactor either. He just wanted to maximize profit. And in the pursuit of profit, by inventing the electric light, the Wizard of Menlo Park lighted the homes and streets of the world. Ford and Edison in their pursuit of profit did more to elevate the living standards and comfort levels of the world's working classes than all the social reformers, social planners, and economic theoreticians combined.

One need not be a Henry Ford or Thomas Edison to make this type of social and economic contribution. Joe Maboudi, a friend of mine who lives in New Haven, Connecticut, operates six discount stores. He often rises early in the morning and leaves for New York where he scours the market for bargains. Joe once told me that upon acquiring some merchandise, after driving a particularly hard bargain, he told the merchant the price at which he intended to sell, whereon the merchant responded, "Joe, you 'steal' the goods from me, then you let your customers 'steal' them from you."

Joe Maboudi, of course, does not work long hours because he conceives himself as some sort of public benefactor. Selling merchandise at rock-bottom prices is simply the best way he knows to become rich. However, in pursuit of riches he drives hard bargains from wholesalers for the ultimate benefit of his customers, for whom he provides low-cost, quality merchandise, while providing employment for over 75 people. So with hard work and by pursuing his own self-interest, Joe Maboudi does more to reduce poverty than all those politicians with their slogans, promises, and plans.

In order for a free enterprise system to function properly, however, remember, there should be as few artificial barriers as possible to impede the flow of capital, labor, and land resources. The law of supply and demand should be free to allocate resources to where market forces indicate they can be most economically employed. After all, it's the FEAC system that has produced our Fords, our Edisons and our Maboudis.

Now, How About Socialism?

Socialism differs from the FEAC system in two basic ways. (1) Under socialism the state runs the economy and owns the "means of production."

Factories, utilities, restaurants, gas stations—all businesses operate for one employer—the state (read: government). Business enterprises are run for the profit of the state, which theoretically uses these profits for the people. When socialists gain control of an economy they "nationalize" all businesses, sometimes confiscating them, sometimes compensating their owners at low, arbitrary prices or in long-term state bonds which begin depreciating as inflation sets in. (2) Furthermore, economic decisions and planning are not made by the impersonal forces of the market, but by centralized government agencies. These agencies function under the direction of commissars or commissioners and employ armies of bureaucrats who are equipped with rolls of red tape. These commissioners allocate and commit resources that do not belong to themselves but theoretically "to the people." Therefore, they do not risk their own capital but that of "the people." Thus, under socialism it is the "people" who bear the cost of economic risk and poor planning whereas in a FEAC system it is private capital that bears these risks.

Under socialism the responsibility of economic planning and society's economic direction is assumed by the state; under FEAC the government's primary economic function is to help safeguard a society where people are free to determine and meet their own economic needs. In a FEAC system, as opposed to a socialist one, the government is supposed to keep its hands off the economy. If some government participation in the economy is required, it should be at the lowest possible level—and at a minimum. However, it is self-deluding to encourage a "little" government participation in the economy. A little government intervention continues long after its initial purpose has been achieved. Can you conceive of a government agency saying, "We have accomplished our goal, let's close up shop and go home?" Limiting the growth of government is like limiting the growth of weeds: It's a full-time job.[1]

How does socialism deal with the basic economic problems we posed earlier when analyzing the FEAC system?

1. *What should be produced?* The state determines what should be produced, which boils down to what some commissioner or committee feels should be produced.

2. *Who should produce it?* The state assigns jobs based upon aptitude and preference, though an individual's political reliability and cooperation with the state often determine the type of work he is permitted to do.

3. *Who gets it?* In theory the one who needs it most. In practice it is the one with the most political influence (and who can also afford it).

What About Communism?

Communism is the revolutionary means of achieving socialism. All communists are socialists, but not all socialists are communists. Not really an objective economic and social theory, communism is only a means to an end. There are

[1]C. Northcote Parkinson, noted British humorist-historian, in his satire, *Parkinson's Law*, states that "government grows at the rate of 6 percent per year irrespective of the amount of work required of it."

many who somehow regard socialism as a mild form of communism. This view is incorrect.[1]

Socialists, or democratic socialists as they are sometimes called, seek to impose socialism through democratic means, by persuasion and the ballot box. Communists, however, maintain that since capitalists control the press, the government, etc., socialism can be achieved only through violent revolution. In accordance with Lenin's dictum, *the end justifies the means*.

Socialists, therefore, often are violently opposed to communists, though they agree on economic principles. They oppose violence and terror in furthering the cause of socialism. Nevertheless, the *ends* of the socialists and communists are the same—they differ only in the *means*.

There are some persons who profess a mild affinity for a degree of socialism, wanting only to nationalize the utilities or "heavy industry," or railroads or medicine. At what point, then, is an industry "heavy"? Nationalization of any business establishes the principle that private property can be confiscated and run by the state in the "interests" of the people. Once this principle is established, no property is safe from the same line of reasoning being applied to it. If one believes that the state can actually deliver medical care more efficiently than can a free economy, why shouldn't the state be able to deliver food better? Why not, therefore, "socialized food"?[2]

In the final analysis either you believe in the FEAC system, or you don't. You either believe in socialism, or you don't. The U.S. government is controlled by bureaucrats, the overwhelming majority of whom don't understand or trust the FEAC system. Socialists usually consider themselves superior to communists since they conceive of themselves as being democratic. This is a spurious distinction because nationalization—the confiscation of private property—is theft regardless of whether it is accomplished by the ballot box or by bullets.

By way of passing, it has been commonplace to characterize the ideological struggle between East and West as one of capitalism versus communism. This is a false dichotomy. It misleads the American public regarding its real enemies, domestic and foreign. First of all, as explained earlier, socialism and communism are capitalistic societies too. The Soviet Union has factories, public utilities, and machinery—all of which are *capital*. The U.S.S.R. tries to generate, increase, and attract capital (without having to give up much in exchange). In the United States capital (theoretically speaking, of course) is owned and controlled by private

[1]At the United Nations, for example, it will be noted that representatives of Eastern European "communist" countries always refer to themselves and their countries as being representative of socialism, not communism. Russia, is, of course, formally known as the Union of Soviet *Socialist* Republics. The term *communist* is conspicuously absent.

[2]An attorney friend of mine was complaining about the high cost of medical care and suggested socialized medicine as a solution. I asked him if socialized medicine could deliver better medical treatment, could "socialized law" deliver better legal services? Why pick on medicine? Obviously, he was not in favor of socialized law and so tried to draw a rather weak distinction between the two professions. Interestingly, indeed, how many who speak favorably about socialized medicine strongly object when the same reasoning is applied to their own occupations.

individuals. In the Soviet Union capital is owned and controlled by the state. So, really, the conflict is not between capitalism and communism but between a system of ownership of capital by individuals and of monopoly ownership of capital by the state. Actually, the struggle is between socialism and the FEAC system. If, indeed, we had an ideological enemy it was socialism, *not* communism. It was socialism and its insidiousness that the United States should have opposed. But the U.S. government has been ill-equipped to oppose socialism because the bureaucrats who run the key agencies favor and extoll centralized bureaucratic planning over the free market. Our political leaders have selected for economic advisers economists who invariably have been cryptosocialists.

Facing Up to Some Facts on Fascism

Fascism is one of the most misunderstood ideologies. Many leaders, businessmen, educators, or what have you place fascism on the extreme right of the political spectrum and socialism on the far left, as if a gulf existed between them. The semantic shorthand of "right" and "left" is misleading. The fact is that socialism and fascism belong on the same end of the political spectrum, whether left or right.

Some clarification of the left-right terminology is in order. In the French Assembly in the nineteenth century, republicans, who favored constitutional government and ending the monarchy, sat on the left; the monarchist, clerical, and militaristic parties were on the right. Anarchists were, therefore, called leftist. So, calling socialists *leftist,* when the left applied to republicans and even to anarchists, is perverting the original meaning of the term. Socialists believe in omnipotent government and in sacrificing minority rights for the "good of the people." Correctly understood, *left* should mean weak, decentralized government as characterized by the free enterprise system which provides a maximum of political and economic freedom. The extreme right should stand for strong central government, which results in less political and economic freedom. Given these definitions, then both fascism and socialism correctly belong on the *right*.

Socialists apply the fascist label to only their vilest enemies, unaware that they are referring to an ideology that is very similar to their own. While it is true that fascist states such as Nazi Germany persecuted ethnic and religious minorities, this is not a requisite nor is it an attribute of fascism. Certainly in Italy, the cradle of modern fascism, there was no persecution of minorities until 1938—19 years after the fascist party was founded—when Mussolini tried to gain Hitler's favor. So, persecution of minorities aside, fascism and socialism have the same ideological roots. After all, remember that Mussolini, father of fascism, edited *Avanti*, an Italian *socialist* newspaper. Remember, too, that Hitler rode into power on the shoulders of the National *Socialist* party.

An influential American economist, Stuart Chase, recognized several generations ago that socialism and fascism are indeed quite similar. In his book, *A New Deal,* published in 1932, on the subject of revolution, he stated:

> From many points of view, I sympathize with the first [revolution], the direct and singleminded attack. I believe it has been necessary and inevitable in Russia and it may some day be inevitable in this country. I am not seriously alarmed by the sufferings of the creditor class, the troubles which the church is bound to encounter, the restrictions on certain kinds of freedom which might result, nor even by the bloodshed of the transition period. *A better economic order is worth a little bloodshed.* [Italics mine.]

Now, let's see what Chase, the man who apparently supplied Franklin Roosevelt with the slogan for his administration, said about fascism. In the chapter entitled, "Dictators, Red and Black," he argued:

> Of one thing . . . I think we can be sure. Whatever the change, [the United States] is going in the direction of more collectivism, more social control of economic activity, more government interference, less freedom for private business . . . . The left . . . is the only possible direction . . . . To the left three roads branch. One of them we shall travel, but I do not know which. The first [communism] is the wild and stormy road of violent revolution. The second [fascism] is the stern, steel-walled road of a commercial dictatorship with political democracy swept down a gully and constitutional guarantees rolled flat. The third [the welfare state] is the road of change within the broad outlines of the law in the American tradition, with many a zooming curve but safely banked. The last is the road I prefer and I think the odds are in its favor—but this may be wish-fulfillment.

While Chase did not explain why he finds fascism objectionable, he clearly saw, unlike many political and economic thinkers of his day, that socialism and fascism belong on the same side of the political and economic spectrum.

Stripped of their semantic trappings, fascism and socialism both call for government direction and control of a nation's economy, as opposed to a minimum of direction and control in a FEAC system. Fascism and socialism differ only in degree and style. Unlike socialism, which takes legal title to the nation's means of production, a fascist government does not bother to take actual legal title but allows ownership to remain *technically* in private hands. Fascism prefers to control and direct industry by levying taxes and through government edict, thereby gaining control without needless nationalization. Socialists, by way of contrast, try to run the economy along Marxist lines and in so doing usually retard the standard of living otherwise obtainable.

Both fascism and socialism glorify a "higher good," rather than personal freedom. Fascism speaks of "the glory of the state"; socialism extols the "good of the people." Individual rights and liberties are sacrificed to these national gods.

What Do We Have in America Now?

Political and social forces keep a nation's economic system moving in one direction or another—toward greater centralized authority or toward less centralized authority and greater personal freedom. Lord Acton wrote somewhere that the struggle for liberty is the struggle to contain government power. For over the last 40 years Americans have been losing that struggle. The United States has been moving steadily toward greater centralized governmental power and authority, as its tax structure and the imposition of price controls on a peacetime economy have made painfully clear.

Suppose the government asked the American people to vote on whether the government should nationalize American business and industry. I assume the American voter would respond with an overwhelming *no*. However, I have yet to find an American who realizes that the bulk of American business has, in fact, been nationalized. Let me explain. Nearly all major U.S. corporations fall in the 48 percent tax bracket—that is, they pay 48 percent of their profits in excess of $25,000 (on the first $25,000 profits, the tax is 25 percent) to the federal government, before any dividends reach the stockholders. So, for example, for every $100 profit General Motors earns (whether distributed or not), the government takes $48. Even assuming that GM distributes the remaining $52 to its stockholders, the government will tax these profits again as a dividend.

Figure 25 graphically reveals the true status of American industry. For example, in 1972, American corporations generated approximately $126 billion in profits. However, $43 billion of this was needed by the corporations themselves in order to continue operations, leaving only $83 billion available for distribution to the "owners." Of this amount, government took $56 billion or 67 percent, while stockholders (the theoretical owners) received $28 billion, or approximately 34 percent. Moreover, government insisted on taxing these profits *again* when they were merely *received* by the stockholders (the "minority" stockholders, it now develops) as a dividend. Assuming that the average stockholder was in a 30 percent tax bracket (state and federal), government took another $8 billion of corporate profits, thereby receiving a total of $64 billion, or *77 percent of distributable profits!*

Figure 25

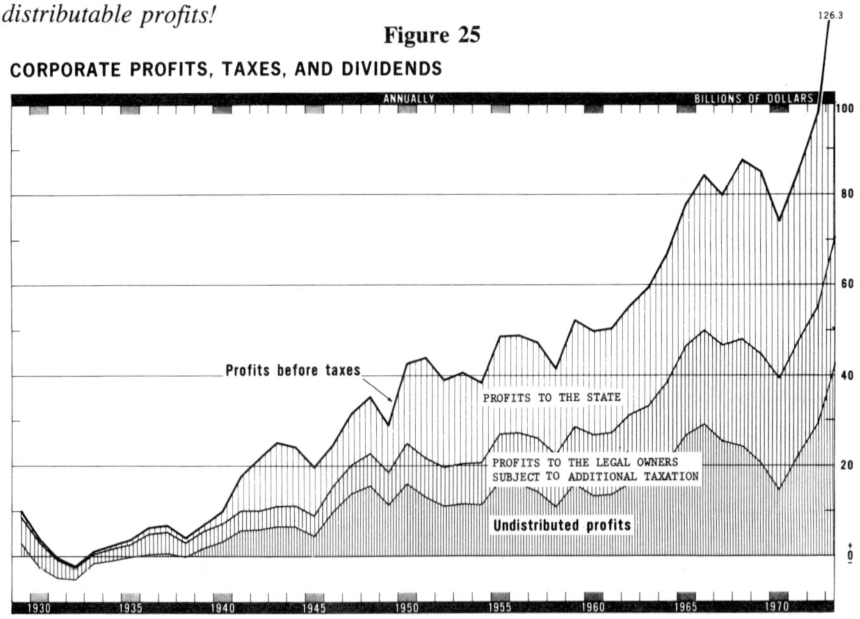

Source: Historical Chart Book--1974,
Board of Governors, Federal Reserve System, p50.

Suppose the state simply confiscated 77 percent of all the outstanding stock of American industry, and received its income not by the imposition of "taxes" but by the dividends received on this confiscated stock. Would the government's revenue be diminished? It makes little difference if we call what the state receives a "tax" or the "confiscated earnings" of the rightful owners. The point is that since the state receives and enjoys the bulk of American industry's profits, it is the state that really owns U.S. industry—not the stockholders!

True, the legal owners can make management decisions. But the purpose of all such decisions is to generate profits, so these decisions are made primarily for the state's benefit, since it is the state that will benefit from any increase in profits. It has not yet dawned on the public that the U.S. government has effectively nationalized American industry, simply because the nationalization has not been absolute. However, a 100 percent nationalization would be self-defeating. If the government took all of the profit, no one in the private sector would be foolish enough to invest any more capital, which then the government would be compelled to do. Also, if the government completely nationalized U.S. industry, it would be forced to operate it, and with the government's usual bureaucratic efficiency (e.g., the post office), it would obviously risk not only the 77 percent of the profit it now enjoys, but also the revenue it derives through withholding taxes, payroll taxes, processing taxes, excise taxes, and sales tax levies.

In any case, the right to enjoy income is tantamount to the right of ownership. Since it is the state that now enjoys the bulk of American industry's income, it is, in fact, the state that is the real equity owner, if not the legal owner, of American business.

This fact—the conversion of the equity ownership of American business from private to public hands through the government's abuse of its taxing power —cannot be emphasized too strongly. So, in the interest of additional emphasis, let's draw another analogy. Suppose you own a building. It is in your name. You operate and maintain it and enjoy all the income it furnishes. Suddenly you are compelled to turn over 80 percent of the building's profits to Mr. X. Mr. X informs you that nothing else is changed, the building continues in your name, you still operate it and are free to invest capital in it. Now who owns the building? Mr. X does. You are merely the caretaker, and your 20 percent can be considered as Mr. X's allowance to you for servicing and maintaining his profit, and for the bookkeeping and accounting services that you dutifully perform. This, of course, is the picture of most American business. So the next time you invest money in an American business, remember that you are investing in a business that is already nationalized.

The American public must wake up and realize that we are now living under a system that is a combination of socialism and fascism. It is doubtful that those lawmakers responsible for passing the Sixteenth Amendment to the Constitution, authorizing Congress to "levy and collect taxes on income," ever dreamed that they were providing future politicians with a tool for unconstitutionally altering the entire character of our economy and our nation.

7

U.S. Taxes– How They Have Converted the American Worker into a Serf

As taxes have transferred the ownership of American business from private hands to the state, so have taxes transformed the American worker from free man to serf. Since there is a lower social conscience among slaves and serfs than among free men, we should naturally expect a lower social and economic concern in America today than existed, say, fifty years ago when Americans were free.[1]

I realize that many people will automatically reject as absurd my contention that the American worker today is no more than a "slave." Many incorrectly associate slavery with confinement, flogging, and leg irons. The chief distinction, however, between a slave and a free man is that a free man owns what he produces, while a slave does not.

The slaves on the southern plantations had little incentive to produce since all they produced was taken from them. However, the slave owner was compelled to supply the slave with food, shelter, clothing, and medical care, if only to protect the value of his original investment. Slaves soon learned how little they needed to produce in order to secure the minimum level of subsistence that would be provided. Slave owners, therefore, realized very little excess productivity from their slaves, which is why slavery is such an inefficient economic institution.

[1]*Schiff's First Law of Social Behavior* states: "Strong government breeds weak citizens—weak government breeds strong citizens."

''Over the course of his lifetime, the typical slave field hand received about 90 percent of the income he produced.''[1]

During the Middle Ages serfs were required to turn over to their local lord 25 percent of their productivity, and for this the serf received protection. So, if the slave turned 10 percent of his productivity over to the slavemaster and the serf turned 25 percent of his productivity over to his local lord, what is the status of the American worker who routinely turns over 30 to 45 percent of his productivity to the state? Figure 26 will reveal how much is extracted by the state from the average American worker and how little is left over for his own discretionary use.

There are those who claim that a good deal of this tax money was taken by the government in order to provide benefits for the worker. One wonders if the worker would voluntarily purchase these ''benefits'' at the heavy price the government insists on charging.[2] In any case, history may decide that since the benefits were purchased at the expense of a massive depression and social chaos, the price extracted was a price the American public could hardly afford to pay. At issue here, however, is the question of freedom of choice. Does the American worker have the right to spend the money he earns as he sees fit or doesn't he? If I confiscate a substantial portion of another's income and use it to provide him with the benefits I think he should have, he is, essentially, not free.

If, at this point, one suggests that the majority of Americans are incapable of making such decisions for themselves and so need government to do it for them, he immediately becomes impaled upon the horns of dilemma. If the majority of Americans are indeed incapable of making decisions concerned with running their own lives and tending to their own welfare, how then can they be presumed to be sufficiently capable of making the more complex decisions required in selecting representatives who will? In other words, if American citizens are incapable of managing their own affairs, they are incapable of managing the more complex affairs of government --so why allow them to vote?

Why We Allow Ourselves to Be Fleeced

The process by which increasing levels of taxation have made virtual slaves out of America's working classes, I believe, was made possible because of the impersonal nature of money, and by taxpayers not directly associating money with the fruits of their own labor. For example, if an individual were to make seven chairs in his basement workshop and then set them out on his lawn, he would not tolerate for a moment the logic of a neighbor who said, ''I can't make chairs myself and since you obviously have more than you need, I think that I shall take two for my family.''

It is self-evident that no one save the maker of those chairs has any legal right or

[1]Robert William Fogel and Stanley L. Engerman, *Time on the Cross* (Boston: Little, Brown, and Company, 1974), pp. 5-6.

[2]I would be prepared to argue whether the taxes are needed to provide benefits for the taxpayer or jobs for bureaucrats.

Figure 26

Gross Income (Single taxpayer, one exemption)		$ 150.00*
Withholding taxes	$24.50	
Social Security taxes	8.78	
Social Security taxes levied against payroll	8.78**	8.78**
Total Gross Wages		$ 158.78
Total Taxes (direct)	$42.06	42.06
Net Wages(before deducting non tax deductible expenses)		$ 116.72
Deduct at least $3.00 a day for such items as transportation, lunches, clothing, cleaning, etc		15.00
Net Spendable Wages		$ 101.72
If a worker was to spend all of the $101.72, at least 20% would go to pay the cost of indirect Federal taxes, such as excise taxes, processing taxes, tariffs; and state and municipal taxes such as property and sales taxes. Since state and local taxes alone equal approximately 40% of Federal Taxes, 20% would be a conservative figure		20.34
Net Spendable Income		$ 81.38
1. Total value of worker's productivity		$ 158.78
2. Amount available for worker's personal, discretionary use for such incidentals as food, clothing, shelter, medical care, transportation, recreation, saving, investments, etc.		81.38
3. Amount of worker's productivity available for his discretionary use expressed as a percentage of his gross productivity		51%
4. Value of worker's productivity garnished by government taxation		$ 62.40
5. Government taxes expressed as a percent of worker's net spendable income		76% !

So many American workers are compelled to produce $76.00 for the government before they can have $100 to spend on themselves.

*According to the U.S. Bureau of Labor Statistics, the average gross weekly wages for nonagricultural workers was $145.43 in 1973 and $154.45 (estimated) for 1974.

**As explained on page 113, the worker pays the entire cost of Social Security.

claim to them, regardless of whether they are actually needed by him or not, or whether they might be needed by another more. Suppose, therefore, that instead of a neighbor, a representative of the U.S. government arrived and demanded the two chairs on the grounds that, "since you can make chairs while others cannot, it is your obligation to supply chairs to those who are unable to make them for themselves." Is there any doubt that no American would turn over anything he made to the government based on such reasoning? The government, I submit, would have a full blown revolution on its hands if it attempted to tax citizens directly, taking a portion of what they directly produced. But look what happens when taxes are levied and paid not in production, but in that common denominator of all production, that impersonal substance—*unmoney*. Suppose our chairmaker decided he no longer needed the chairs and so converted them to another asset, unmoney, in order to exchange it for another item he needed more. Suppose our chairmaker is in the 30 percent tax bracket and sells the chairs for $30 each, or $210 total. He suddenly owes the government $63 in taxes,[1] or the proceeds of two chairs. Our obedient, law-abiding citizen now does not even question the government's claim to the dollar value of the two chairs, and so he dutifully turns over to the government the dollar equivalent of the property he would have taken up arms to protect had the government dared lay claim to it *directly*.

Who's Being Gouged the Most?

It is those in the vast middle and lower income brackets who pay the bulk of the taxes. For example, using IRS figures for the year 1971, out of total tax receipts of $188.4 billion, only $13.9 billion, or about 7 percent, was collected in income taxes from those earning over $50,000 a year ($10,000 in 1945 dollars) while another $3.8 billion was collected in estate and gift taxes from those who might presumably be in the wealthy class. So, a grand total of $17.7 billion in federal taxes (or less than 10 percent of the total tax bill) can be said to have been paid by America's wealthy.[2]

Politicians have tried to persuade the American voter that there somehow is another fellow, of a vast "upper class," who is going to pick up the tab for all the federal spending programs. The somber truth is that the bill is handed to America's working men and women, and it's high time they understood that and that no "closing of loopholes" or "tax reforms" will change it.

The government disguises the extent of its tax-gathering activities by the

[1]I have not taken into account the cost to produce the chairs, since I do not want to detract from the principle involved.

[2]I do not cite these figures to suggest that higher taxes be imposed on those in upper income brackets. On the contrary, the government would actually increase tax receipts if lower tax rates were applied on the higher brackets. This would, therefore, reduce the taxes required of the middle and lower income levels.

variety of taxes it levies and the methods it uses to collect them. For example, consider the withholding procedure that was installed to make payment of income taxes as painless and inconspicuous as possible. I recall reading some years ago of a Southern manufacturer who tried to withhold federal taxes monthly rather than weekly. This resulted in most workers not receiving any paycheck at all at least one week each month, and emphasized painfully and clearly the extent to which they were compelled to *work* for government. If all American businesses followed this manufacturer's example for just six months, America's working men and women would drive from office any politicians who dared suggest another federal program for the "nation's workers." But, alas, I also recall reading somewhere that the government barred the manufacturer's action, making it mandatory that employers withhold taxes as they pay wages.

Americans now pay taxes on taxes. A few years ago, I bought some tires. On paying the bill, I noted that the clerk had added in the federal excise tax and, then to this total, computed the Connecticut sales tax. This meant that I paid state sales taxes for the *privilege* of paying federal excise taxes. I assumed, therefore, that the clerk had erred, instinctively feeling that paying taxes upon taxes was so inequitable as to be unreal. The clerk pointed out, however, that for some reason in connection with automobile tires, the excise tax was added on at the time of sale, unlike other products such as automobiles and alcoholic beverages, where they are already included in the retail price and not shown separately. So, he correctly pointed out, "you pay sales on top of federal excise taxes on those items." So, Americans indeed pay taxes on top of taxes.

Politicians also try to convey to the public the impression that the burden of a good portion of the nation's taxes can be shifted to the large corporations. It should be obvious, however, that any taxes corporations pay simply reduce the amount of capital they have for purposes of expansion and so again, these taxes come out of the pockets of U.S. workers and consumers. In any case, taxes become simply another production cost that is passed on to the worker and consumer in the form of higher prices. So he or she is deceived about the full extent of his or her tax bill because of the various hidden taxes, whether buying goods or services or when job hunting.

Consolidated Edison recently launched a campaign, which hopefully other American businesses will imitate. It sent out the following statement with its monthly bills:

> Beginning this month, your Con Edison bill will show approximately how much of each dollar we billed to customers in the preceeding 12 months went to taxes and fuel. For the year ending June 30, 1974, the amounts are 23 cents for taxes and 33 cents for fuel.
>
> The tax figure will reflect all taxes we pay, a total of nearly 500 million in the year ending June 30. These are mainly state and local taxes and include the sales tax which also appears as a separate item elsewhere on your bill.
>
> We don't enjoy serving as a tax collector. We would prefer that local and state

governments collect these taxes in some other way so that your Con Edison bill could be lower. But as long as we are required to collect these taxes they must be reflected in your bill.

It is indeed a tribute to the resourcefulness of politicians who, in devising a variety of taxes and methods for disguising and collecting them, have been able to con the average American into parting with so much of his productive effort. Had this level of taxation been attempted in the 19th century when Americans still understood the word freedom, a revolution would have ensued immediately. Can you even conceive of America's western pioneers being told they had to turn over 40 percent of what they produced to the government? Could our country have been built if it had been subjected to this level of taxation?

The Growth of Government Spending

In 1950, total expenditures for federal, state, and local governments was $70 billion; in 1972 they were $397 billion. In 1950 the GNP was $284.8 billion, while in 1972, it was $1,155.2 billion. Government expenditures, therefore, increased from nearly 25 percent of the GNP to 34 percent, for an increase of almost 40 percent. The increase, however, is even greater than these figures indicate because the GNP[1] is a misleading economic index and is not really an indication of *effective* economic output[2] since it even includes the salaries of our nonproductive politicians and bureaucrats whose swelling incomes distort meaningful GNP figures.

Figure 27 compares increasing government expenditures with *effective* GNP productivity and illustrates why America is experiencing all kinds of shortages and economic problems. It reveals the extent to which government is increasingly devouring the economy.

In 1950 total government expenditures were equivalent to 83.5 percent of the gross product of all U.S. manufacturing; however, by 1972, they equalled 98.53 percent of the *total* gross product of:

1) All U.S. manufacturing
2) All U.S. agriculture
3) All U.S. mining (including petroleum and natural gas production)
4) All U.S. communications
5) All electric, gas, and sanitation services

So, government is now spending more than the total GNP value of all the food we produce, all the minerals and fuel we extract, all the products of our factories,

[1]It would be more accurate to compare government expenditures to the Net National Product (the GNP minus capital consumption), which reveals that these expenditures climbed to 38 percent of the NNP.

[2]See page 243, Chapter 12.

Figure 27

THE GROWTH OF GOVERNMENT EXPENDITURES RELATED TO ECONOMIC PRODUCTIVITY

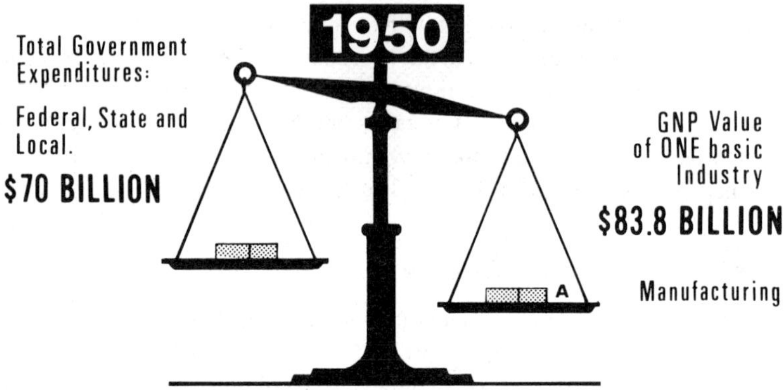

But LOOK at what has happened in only 22 short years!

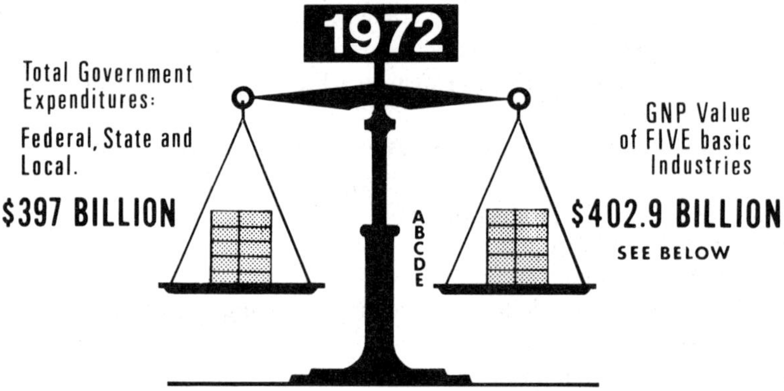

A–Manufacturing $290.7
B–Agriculture, Forestry and Fisheries 37.5
C–Mining (including Petroleum & Natural Gas) .. 18.2
D–Communications 28.5
E–Electric, Gas and Sanitation Services 28.0

$402.9

plus other basic services. Is it any wonder that the country is in serious economic trouble?

Since more and more of our economic activity is diverted to finance government activity, less and less is left to support the rest of the economy. All kinds of shortages must be expected because of this. In essence, shortages and a substantially lower standard of living are the price America now pays for government.

The American economy developed into the world's most powerful and efficient when government consumed only a meager portion of its national product; however, future historians may record that its demise quickly followed when government consumed too much.

The economic problems now facing America can be compared to a parasitic plant that has fastened itself onto a mighty oak. When the parasite covered only 10 percent of the tree, it was still possible for the tree to prosper; indeed, the parasite may hardly have been discernible as it grew among the tree's own branches. As the parasite grew, now covering 20 percent of the tree, it inflicted more damage. Dead leaves and branches began to appear; the oak's growth stopped. (The American economy exhibited a number of early symptoms of the parasitic growth of government: the persistent gold drain starting as early as 1958, our adverse balance of payments as early as 1960; later symptoms included the government's inability to maintain silver coinage and gold-backed currency.) However, the tree might still appear reasonably healthy (if one didn't examine it too closely). If the spreading fungus were even then destroyed, the tree would, in time, regain its former health.

But assume the parasite is permitted to continue to grow, soon wrapping its deadly tentacles around 30 percent, then 40 percent of the tree. At some point, that mighty oak must die, and then nothing will restore it to health.

Similarly all levels of American government, like the parasitic growth described above, have now grown to the point where they now threaten the very life of our economy. If Americans refuse to recognize this danger and permit this destructive growth to continue, our economy, and therefore our society, is doomed; and who can say what will replace it.

8

Taxes: The Arsenic in Our System

America is being poisoned by a tax system that (1) penalizes economic efficiency and destroys incentive while subsidizing inefficiency and encouraging unemployment, (2) diverts the nation's supply of capital to less efficient areas, (3) destroys jobs, (4) increases substantially the difficulty of the older workers to find employment, (5) promotes greater concentrations of economic power, (6) compels those entering business to make Uncle Sam a "silent partner" who puts up no capital yet demands more than half the profits, and (7) contributes directly to a lowering of public morality while increasing the influence of organized crime.

The Big Rip-Off

Every income tax system is potentially damaging to society. Despite this danger, however, an income tax might be necessary to provide government with the funds with which to conduct its legitimate business. Therefore, it becomes incumbent on legislators to be aware of its inherent dangers. Have our political leaders in Washington shown an awareness of this danger? Reference to U.S. tax schedules, past and present, shows the extent of their legislative irresponsibility.

Let's examine an extreme example, while recognizing that the same forces are at work, only to a lesser degree, at lower tax levels. From 1944 to 1964, a 90 percent tax applied to earnings over $100,000. In other words, a taxpayer with ordinary earnings of $100,000 was expected to give Uncle Sam 90 cents of every additional dollar he earned. From 1965 to 1970 this rate was lowered to nearly 70 percent, and again in 1970 to a maximum of 50 percent on earned income and a 70 percent rate on income from other sources.

Let's assume that a taxpayer was an actor during the 1950s, and that by March 1 he had already earned $100,000. Would he seriously pursue another $100,000, knowing he could keep only $10,000 of it? Would he seriously consider making a movie for $200,000, when in reality, he would be doing it for only $20,000? One having the talent and ability to command $200,000 will seek other ways of earning money where the tax impact will be lighter; or failing this, he might choose not to work at all.[1]

One method that actors used to keep the money that their talents earned for them was to seek earnings by way of "capital gains" rather than on the basis of straight salary, since the maximum tax on a capital gain was 25 percent, much lower than a 90 percent income tax. However, in order to pay the lower tax, an actor had to own an interest in the motion picture, and not be a salaried employee.

So, as a result of the confiscation of wages, it no longer became economical for movie stars to work for the large studios on a salaried basis. This is why major actors left their studios, or set up their own production companies, or demanded an interest in the movies they made, or even moved to countries where they could negotiate a lower tax rate.

Where once the man in the street could name 50 actors and actresses, today he would be hard pressed to name even 10. No, Hollywood's decline cannot be blamed just on changing tastes. Our government's unrealistic tax structure is also to blame.

Suppose that instead of attempting to tax individuals on a 90 percent basis Uncle Sam had only limited his greed to 25 percent. One might be willing to earn an additional $300,000, if in so doing he could at least keep $225,000. But is it realistic to expect that those who have the talent and ability to earn $300,000 would do so, if they had to give the government $270,000 while keeping only $30,000 for themselves? To expect that society can benefit to this extent is lunacy. Such levels of taxation merely destroy the creative efforts of those capable of attaining these income levels and force them to seek other ways to earn money.

While the degree to which a 90 percent tax bracket is counterproductive is obvious, the same negative forces will be at work all the way down the progressive tax ladder, only operating at lesser intensities. Recognizing this, our legislators in Washington, had they any economic intelligence at all, would have realized that they cannot burden an economy with tax rates that are so destructive to economic incentives. In essence, unrealistically high tax rates will actually impair and reduce

[1]In analyzing the economic impact of a 90 percent tax bracket, I am overlooking the larger moral issue of how an ethical society can even presume to have a legitimate claim on 90 percent of an individual's productivity! Is taxation merely a disguise to enable politicians to deprive citizens of their property without "due process of law" as provided by the Fifth Amendment?

the long-term ability of the economy to generate taxes, and thus actually increase tax burdens for all.

I personally feel that even a 50 percent tax rate is much too high, both from a moral point of view and from the standpoint of furnishing economic incentives. I feel that a maximum tax of 20 percent—one-fifth of what an individual produces—is sufficient tax for the federal government to learn to live with. It should be up to government to fashion a budget for itself based upon what the citizens of the country can realistically afford, rather than for citizens to be taxed for an amount that the government chooses to spend. It is government that must accommodate itself to the tax limitations of the economy, and not the economy that must accommodate to the financial appetite of government.

Let us examine how even a 50 percent tax bracket causes economic distortion. When businessmen consider expenditures for fixtures, advertising, new equipment, and so forth, each dollar spent may only represent 25 cents of their own after-tax money. If this amount were not spent, 75 cents might go to government in taxes anyway.[1] Conversely, if one works harder, one may only keep 25 cents out of every additional dollar generated by this extra effort.

The economic impact created by this is to encourage unnecessary and uneconomic expenditures while at the same time discouraging increased economic effort on the part of those capable of making it.

Would, for instance, the plush carpeting and draperies and furniture so characteristic of many of our offices be purchased if such expenditures were not tax deductible? If this type of expenditure were not tax deductible, many offices would be far more Spartan in their appearance. Expenditures would be treated far more seriously, and made more cautiously.

In this connection, somebody might raise the point that if you reversed this tax-induced propensity for businesses to spend, would you not be destroying the jobs that this increased spending creates? The answer is no! You would actually be creating more jobs and ultimately increasing consumer spending. If, for example, a $10,000 expenditure a firm contemplates for new furniture were not "subsidized" by the government (I use "subsidized" only in a distorted sense, since the government is not "giving" anything—it is merely thwarted from "taking") by being tax deductible, it might think twice before making such an expenditure. Indeed, it might decide that it could live with its old furniture. As a result, the $10,000[2] might remain in the firm's bank account, where it would be available to be loaned to other firms who could use the money for expenditures of a more

[1]For the sake of simplicity, I am not drawing any distinction between expenses which are immediately written off and those that might be capitalized and written off on a straight line or accelerated depreciation basis, since the end result is largely the same.

[2]I realize that my example overlooks the taxes that would, of course, be due if these expenditures were not made, but taking this into consideration would unnecessarily complicate and interfere with the principle I am attempting to illustrate.

pressing economic nature. In any case, the original firm—if guided by a more prudent fiscal policy—might accumulate in this manner $30,000 or $40,000 in additional capital. These additional reserves would be available to finance significant economic expansion, or to see the firm through a period of adverse business conditions.

In any case, total business spending has not diminished, nor have any jobs been lost. Spending has merely been shifted from less economic to more economic areas, while more permanent economic employment has been assured. And since taxes obviously encourage businessmen to make unnecessary and uneconomic expenditures, they lower substantially American industry's ability to produce goods and services at the lowest possible prices.

How Income Taxes Encourage Greater Concentration of Economic Power and Divert Capital from Productive Use to Stock Speculation

As explained earlier, a corporation pays 22 percent of its first $25,000 of corporate profits to the federal government and 48 percent on amounts in excess of $25,000. In addition, for example, the state of Connecticut levies an 8 percent corporation tax on profits; and so, in the Nutmeg State, the effective corporate tax is 28.2 percent on the first $25,000 of profits and 51.87 percent[1] on amounts over that. In addition, of course, when the after-tax corporate profits are distributed to the stockholders, they are again subject to taxes as dividends. For the sake of illustration, let's assume an average corporate tax of 50 percent on earnings in excess of $25,000 and a personal tax bracket of 50 percent for the owners of the following closed corporation.

Figure 28 illustrates how a pension or a profit-sharing proposal might be presented to the owners of a closed corporation by representatives of the insurance or securities industry interested in installing such a plan. By adopting a corporate pension plan or profit-sharing plan, you would have $8,000 working for the benefit of the *owner employees* and $2,000 working for the benefit of the other employees. Without a pension plan, only $2,500 would be available, after taxes, for the benefit of the working *stockholders* and *nothing* for the other employees. Which plan, Mr. Employee Stockholder, would you rather have: one that will provide you with $2,500, or one that will provide you with $8,000? They both cost the same.

While the percentage of the pension and profit-sharing money going for the benefit of stockholder-employee may appear discriminatory, according to the law it is not. Pension and profit-sharing contributions are based on an employee's age, salary, length of service, and social security benefits—a formula is generally

[1]Since state taxes are themselves deductible, the effective combined total is lower than the arithmetically combined rate.

Figure 28

PROPOSAL FOR PROFIT-SHARING OR PENSION PLAN FOR XYZ CORPORATION

Excess corporate profits	$ 10,000
LESS:	
State and federal corporate taxes	5,000
Profits available after taxes for stockholders dividends	5,000
LESS: Personal taxes—50 percent bracket	2,500
Net amount of corporate profits remaining for the benefit of stockholders after corporate and personal taxes	2,500
However, if $10,000 were tax sheltered in a corporate pension or profit-sharing plan, the following would result:	
Amount placed in corporate profit or pension plan	10,000
This amount would be tax deductible	
Amount allocated for the benefit of stockholder-employees	8,000
Amount allocated for the benefit of other employees	2000

determined which, based on these factors and applied uniformly to all employees, will simply create the maximum contribution for the benefit of owner-employees. After all, the success of a firm dealing in pension and profit-sharing plans is based on how skillful the firm is in developing formulas that provide the maximum percentage contribution for the stockholders and the minimum percentage for the other employees.

It was based upon proposals of this nature that the bulk of the pension and profit-sharing plans of small closed corporations were installed, but consider the economic impact.

Let's assume that the above business could have actually employed the $10,000 in its own operation. Obviously, however, it could not have done so, since after paying corporate taxes the firm would have had only $5,000 to invest, while additional earnings generated by this increase in investment would again be subject to high corporate tax rates. Money invested in the pension plan, however, is not only tax deductible, but the earnings in the fund accumulate tax free. So, instead of employing its capital within its business—for expansion purposes, for modernization, for product research and development (where the capital would be under the immediate control of management and where it would probably do the most economic good)—the firm manages to invest it in a pension or profit-sharing plan where it's used in all probability to buy the existing shares of larger corporations. Or, it might be used to buy debt securities of much larger corporations, or, what is even worse, to buy government bonds, where the capital would then serve no useful economic purpose at all.

For a FEAC system to function properly, the economy's limited amount of capital should flow to where it is needed most, free of artificial influences such as tax considerations. The best indication of where capital should be employed is where it will yield the highest rate of return. All things being equal, capital should flow in the direction of the highest yield. Let's return to the above example and see how tax considerations have distorted capital flow. Let's assume that the above corporation could develop a return of 15 percent on capital invested in its own business. So $10,000, if employed in the business, would generate $1,500 of additional profit and should economically be employed to expand this business. But $10,000, of course, would not be available for such investment, only $5,000 after taxes,[1] so the additional profit would be only $750 not $1,500. But this again would be taxed on a 50 percent basis, leaving only a $375 net return after taxes from the employment of $10,000 of original profit. If, however, the $10,000 of profit is invested in a pension or profit-sharing plan, where it is invested in government bonds or in stocks yielding 6 percent, the net yield to the corporate pension plan would be $600, which is much greater than the after-tax yield of $375. If taxes were not a factor, the $10,000 would be invested to generate 15 percent, but because of the impact of taxes, the capital is employed to earn only 6 percent. Thus, our tax structure *forces* capital to be employed less economically. This prevents the economy from producing the maximum amount of goods and services possible and contributes toward lowering our standard of living. Another consequence of this is that it creates artificial demand for the securities of our larger, public corporations and encourages capital to be used for stock speculation and stock trading rather than for creative purposes. (This has contributed to the large losses which pension and profit-sharing plans have suffered as a result of the severe drop in both the stock and bond prices.)

If an employer wishes to establish a pension or profit-sharing plan, that's one thing. But his decision should be made only after a careful weighing of the alternatives, and, as can be seen easily, impartial judgment is impossible because of the distorting impact of taxes. Thus, not only do taxes interfere with business judgement but they promote large corporations at the expense of small business by offering inducements to the latter to invest in the former thereby encouraging capital to be used less creatively, productively and competitively.

How Federal Estate Taxes Destroy Small Closed Corporations

Figure 29 contains the rates for one of the most destructive economic forces in American life today—the federal estate tax. These taxes have generally supplied the government with approximately the same amount of revenue that it has spent

[1]That is, overlooking any tax deductions and investment tax credits the additional employment of $10,000 might develop.

Figure 29

THE FEDERAL ESTATE TAX

Taxable estate equal to or more than— (1)	Taxable estate less than— (2)	Tax on amount in column (1) (3)	Rate of tax on excess over amount in column (1) (4)
			(Percent)
0	$5,000	0	3
$5,000	10,000	$150	7
10,000	20,000	500	11
20,000	30,000	1,600	14
30,000	40,000	3,000	18
40,000	50,000	4,800	22
50,000	60,000	7,000	25
60,000	100,000	9,500	28
100,000	250,000	20,700	30
250,000	500,000	65,700	32
500,000	750,000	145,700	35
750,000	1,000,000	233,200	37
1,000,000	1,250,000	325,700	39
1,250,000	1,500,000	423,200	42
1,500,000	2,000,000	528,200	45
2,000,000	2,500,000	753,200	49
2,500,000	3,000,000	998,200	53
3,000,000	3,500,000	1,263,200	56
3,500,000	4,000,000	1,543,200	59
4,000,000	5,000,000	1,838,200	63
5,000,000	6,000,000	2,468,200	67
6,000,000	7,000,000	3,138,200	70
7,000,000	8,000,000	3,838,200	73
8,000,000	10,000,000	4,568,200	76
10,000,000	----------------	6,088,200	77

on agricultural subsidies[1]—payments to farmers for not growing food. Therefore, it can be said that while taxes generated by estate tax levies have not benefited the American public, they have wreaked havoc on the economy and harmed the American worker and consumer.

Let's use a dramatic example of how this tax destroys local and family ownership of modest-size businesses, compels owners to sell out to larger public corporations, and accelerates the movement to greater industrial concentration while weakening the private competitive system. By effectively weakening the smaller, and usually more aggressive, business firms, our system of estate taxation assures the larger, more powerful corporations that they will have less competition, and thus they can be more complacent, more inefficient, and less competitive than they would ordinarily have to be.

Suppose an individual built up a soap and chemical manufacturing business worth $10 million; not a Procter & Gamble or a Colgate-Palmolive Company, but nevertheless a sizable firm that could be competitive with them in many areas. Let's assume that Mr. Smith started this business in 1945, at age 30, and now at 60 feels that he can retire and leave his business to his two sons to operate.

While Mr. Smith is now worth $10 million, this wealth is largely in illiquid assets such as plant and equipment, trucks, patents, and good-will, while in liquid assets Mr. Smith has about $300,000 of life insurance and about $300,000 in cash and other stocks and bonds.

As Mr. Smith contemplates retirement and makes plans for transferring the business, his accountant shows him the estate tax table (see figure) which indicates that at his death his estate would have to pay the federal government about $6,088,200 in estate taxes in order to bequeath his $10 million business to his two children.[2] In addition, state succession taxes would take another 5 percent (or $500,000), while legal and probate fees would be at least 2 percent (or $200,000), meaning his estate might have to raise $7 million in cash in the event of his death.

It is, therefore, impossible for Mr. Smith to consider leaving his business to his sons, since there is no way that these taxes can be paid without selling the business. Mr. Smith also realizes that he cannot risk death before disposing of his business since his estate would then be in a position of *having to sell* to raise money for taxes, and thus would be in a much weaker bargaining position. Mr. Smith realizes that his estate will have to be far more liquid before his death, so the logical remedy is to try and sell the business now, to a larger public corporation for stock and perhaps a long-term employment contract for himself and his two sons.

[1]For example, collection for estate taxes and gift taxes for the years 1971-73 (estimate) were $3.735 billion, $5.436 billion, and $4.6 billion, respectively, while "farm-income stabilization" payments for the same period were $3.651 billion, $5.146 billion, and $4.251 billion, respectively. These figures do not include the total agricultural subsidies, since they do not include that subsidy entitled "Food for Peace" that amounted to $918 million, $993 million, and $847 million for the years shown.

[2]I am overlooking the additional taxes that would be due on his other assets, which conceivably would take 77 cents out of every dollar.

Stock in a publicly held corporation would be far more liquid than the stock he currently holds in his family firm and could be sold to pay the estate taxes. So Mr. Smith sells out to a large public corporation. With the sale, the managerial and ownership ties between his family and the business are severed. Control of the family business within the local community has ended and so, in all probability, have the many services furnished by local businesses and professions. The accounting will probably be transferred to the acquiring firm's accountant, as will the insurance and numerous other services. Such is the destructive power of the federal estate tax and its capacity to force greater concentrations of economic power and absentee ownership on the American economy.

As the tax table indicates, one need not have a $10 million estate to be faced with forced liquidation in the event of death. Federal and state death taxes, plus probate and court fees, on a million-dollar estate can run to $400,000, 40 percent of what an individual has managed to create during his lifetime. If the bulk of this estate was a large nonliquid business asset, this might have to be sold in the same manner as described in the previous example in order to raise the cash needed to meet these heavy tax liabilities.

It would be one thing if the government, by confiscating this amount of wealth and forcing greater concentrations of economic power, did so in order to achieve some useful social purpose—but as the government figures themselves show, the taxes thus raised are wasted anyway.

How Higher Taxes Make It More Difficult for Older Americans to Find Employment

Government officials have found it necessary to enact legislation outlawing discrimination in employment because of age. What the American public has overlooked is the U.S. government's key role in creating this type of discrimination in the first place. Since taxes, even for the blue-collar worker, take such a large bite out of any salary increase, unions have for a long time pushed for a variety of nontaxable fringe benefits, rather than for straight salary increases. Examples of nontaxable benefits are group life insurance, group hospitalization insurance, group disability income protection, group major medical coverage, and pension plans. These benefits can, in many cases, equal a third of the direct salary paid as wages. Here's why having one's employer buy group life insurance is advantageous. In order to afford $100 of life insurance a worker might have to allocate $130 of his before-tax earnings (after paying income taxes of $30, he would have a net of $100 to pay his insurance premiums). His employer, however, could apply the entire $130 directly toward the purchase of insurance, so the employee receives more life insurance by the use of before-tax dollars spent by his employer than with after-tax dollars spent by himself. There are, of course, other benefits, but these are incidental to the immediate tax benefits involved and with the whole range of nontaxable employee benefits.

What the public should be aware of, however, is that providing these benefits carries social and economic price tags. A package of fringe benefits costs an employer considerably more for an older employee than for a younger one. Suppose an employer has a job opening paying $175 a week which could be handled just as well by a 25- or 50-year-old. The package of fringe benefits, however, that went with the job might cost $500 for an employee at age 25, while the cost of the same benefits for an employee age 50 might be $2,000. Obviously the cost to the employer of hiring the older worker is substantially higher than that of hiring the younger worker. Therefore, the employer is now compelled to pay the older applicant higher wages than the younger applicant for the same amount of work. Since the younger worker cost less than the older one, management, in trying to produce at the lowest costs, will tend to discriminate in favor of the former. If taxes were not so high, fringe benefits would not have developed as such an important component of wages and so a person's age would not have become such an important factor in labor costs. Therefore, it is government that has created this discrimination in employment, not the unfounded prejudices of employers.

How Income Taxes Distort the True Cost of Goods and Services

Because of their earning power, physicians reach a 50 percent tax bracket quickly. A physician filing a joint return moves into the 50 percent bracket when his taxable earnings are over $44,000. Surely $44,000 is not a considerable amount of earnings for a physician when you consider he might have spent 13 years plus a considerable amount of money learning his profession.[1]

Since, as pointed out earlier, a dollar is only worth 17 cents in terms of its 1945 purchasing power, taxable income today of $44,000 is equivalent to taxable income of only $7500 in 1945 dollars. Do you suppose our government could have successfully imposed a 50 percent tax bracket on that level of income in 1945? Now, what effect does this level of taxation plus inflation have on the cost of medicine or a physician's house call? Before 1945, a house call might have been $5, and since a physician's income was smaller then, he probably would have had to pay only 30 percent of this in taxes and would have netted $3.50 for a visit. How much would a physician have to charge now to match the same amount of purchasing power? Since the dollar today is worth only a sixth of what it was worth then, he would have to charge at least six times as much—or $21.00 after taxes. But since most doctors today are in a 50 percent tax bracket, he would have to charge at least $42 before taxes. So, given the impact of taxes and inflation, a physician would have to charge nearly $42 today to get about the same purchasing power he received from a $5 charge 30 years ago.

[1]Sanitation workers in many cities earn between $13,000 and $15,000 a year, with fringe benefits bringing it to over $20,000.

Physicians, I suppose, feel uncomfortable about charging $42 or more for a house call, which is why we are probably experiencing greater difficulty getting physicians who will make house calls. But it should be pointed out that this problem was caused by government—through its policies of inflation and taxation.

Instead of saddling the nation with Medicare, which can only increase the nation's total medical bill by forcing it to absorb the cost of an army of nonmedical personnel employed in nonessential tasks, the government could have lowered the cost of medical care for persons over 65 years of age by simply allowing physicians and all medical practitioners to exclude from their taxable earnings all fees received from persons over 65. Such favorable tax treatment of medical fees from people over 65 would have induced physicians to compete for this type of business by lowering their normal fees in order to attract and encourage this source of nontaxable income. This arrangement would have helped greatly toward lowering medical costs for people over 65 and would not have created an additional dollar of taxes or another roll of red tape.

The Direct Corrupting Influence of Excessive Taxation

One of the reasons why organized crime has become so powerful and able to enlarge its influence and control on American business (taking over many legitimate businesses through its loan-sharking activities) is that it remains the only segment of the "economy," apart from government, that can amass any cash (since it is relieved of paying taxes). In addition, the growth of the cash kickback and the "under-the-table-cash-payoff" is due to their being a source of nontaxable income and hence proportionally more valuable than income earned honestly which is then dishonestly taxed.

A further moral breakdown occurs when citizens, who would normally embrace the virtue of honesty with passion and consistency, are faced with the need of filling out their tax returns. After all, who would condemn a serf who attempts to hold out on his master? So, after one "lies and cheats" on the government, it becomes that much easier to carry this behavior into other areas of one's business and personal life.

How About Tax "Loopholes"?

Before leaving the subject of taxes, let's cover the issue of "loopholes," a favorite expression of our political con artists. The implication is that if a number of these "loopholes" were closed, the government would collect far more taxes from the rich and thus taxes from the average Joe might be reduced. "Closing tax loopholes" is often combined with the need for "tax reform," both expressions being a basic part of political campaign oratory.

First of all, even if the government collected more taxes from the rich, this would not reduce its appetite to collect taxes from those in lower brackets. It would simply provide our politicians with even more money to waste. In addition, the conventional definition of *reform* is:

> v. 1. To improve, as by alteration. 2. To abolish malpractice in. 3. To give up or cause to abandon immoral practices. *n.* 1. A change for the better. 2. A movement that attempts to improve social and political conditions without revolutionary change. 3. Moral improvement.[1]

So, to suggest that our tax system needs to be ''reformed'' is to imply really that all prior tax legislation was inequitable, misguided, and essentially ''immoral.'' While I would, of course, agree with this, this is not what politicians have in mind when they employ the phrase ''tax reform.'' They always imply that they mean only to ''change'' the tax system ''for the better.'' Generally, this means closing ''loopholes,'' which means collecting more taxes. So whenever politicians devise new methods of extracting taxes, they do so in the name of tax reform legislation. This is why every piece of tax legislation is always called ''tax reform.'' After all, applying the principles of Newspeak, *à la 1984,* how can anyone object to ''reform''?

What are ''loopholes''? A loophole implies an unintentional oversight or error by the authors of tax legislation through which wealthier taxpayers, with the aid of expensive tax attorneys, are able to avoid paying their share of taxes. Such a conception of a loophole is totally misleading. In essence, there are no loopholes—and if Congress should succeed in changing those ''tax incentives'' that our most irresponsible legislators insist on calling ''tax loopholes,'' prices for many of the items we buy will increase substantially, as will unemployment.

In order to encourage investments in certain areas, Congress provided tax incentives (itself an admission that taxes alone act as an economic deterrent) while other ''tax loopholes'' are derived from the economic nature of the investment itself. Tax-sheltered investments developed as a result of the basically punitive and destructive tax rates that our politicians insist on imposing.

Tax-free Municipal Bonds

Let's take the simplest ''tax loophole'' first—the tax-free status of municipal bonds. A wealthy individual could presumably buy $10 million worth of municipal bonds at 6 percent and therefore have $600,000 of nontaxable income.[2] Some find such a situation grossly unfair. However, our municipal bond buyer would obviously be in the 50 percent or better bracket, and if municipal bond interest were

[1]Copyright 1969, 1970 Houghton Mifflin Company. Reprinted by permission from *The American Heritage Dictionary of the English Language*, paperback edition.

[2]However, according to the Tax Reform Act of 1969, a taxpayer would now have to pay *some* tax. Since this book is not a tax guide, and since I only wish to convey principles, I shall not even attempt to explain how this so called ''loophole'' might have been modified by this very complicated section of the 1969 Act.

taxable, the bonds would only yield him 3 percent or less, instead of 6 percent. The reason that the municipal bond buyer bought bonds paying 6 percent, when he might have purchased others paying 10 or 12 percent, was that the interest earned on those other bonds would be taxed as ordinary income and therefore he is willing to accept a lower interest rate on the municipal bond. If this advantage were removed, bond buyers would demand higher interest rates from municipalities, and citizens would now find their property taxes increasing to pay these higher rates to municipal bond holders, who would then simply forward these increases to the federal government by way of income taxes. Politicians who suggest that terminating the nontaxability of municipal bond interest would close a "tax loophole" would simply be eliminating a source of cheap money for municipalities which is used to build schools, roads, sewers, etc. Not only that but such action would pass higher costs on to the taxpayer. But, even with their nontaxable return, municipal bond holders still get fleeced since the real rate of dollar depreciation (inflation) generally exceeds the interest (theoretically, that is) paid.

The Oil Depletion Allowance

The oil depletion allowance is related to the economics of removing oil from the ground since (1) oil is a wasting asset (at some point its flow will cease), and (2) it is impossible, because of various geological and mechanical factors, to predict how long and how much oil will flow from a given well. This obviously creates tax problems. For example, suppose $100,000 were invested to drill and complete an oil well (overlooking for a moment the after-tax cost resulting from the deductibility of the intangible drilling costs), which in its first two years of operation produced $20,000 in cash flow, after expenses.

Suppose the owners paid ordinary income taxes on this amount but in the third year the well ran "dry." If the owners were in a 50 percent tax bracket, they would have paid the government $10,000 in income taxes on a well from which they had not even recovered their drilling expenses. The government should in all equity allow the well owners to recompute their taxes for the previous years and allow them a refund for previously paid taxes. This the government does not permit. The well owner, therefore, is allowed to recover a percentage of the oil flow tax-free, which is regarded as a "return of capital" and is the notorious "depletion allowance." This percentage is recovered tax-free for the life of the well, while regular income taxes are paid on the balance. Currently, the depletion allowance is 22 percent of gross receipts.[1] This, together with normal depreciation allowances, might eliminate income taxes from approximately 30 percent of the cash flow. So, returning to our above example, the well owner who received $20,000 in cash flow, would now recover approximately $6,000 tax-free, while paying ordinary income taxes on the remaining $14,000 of revenue. So, while the well owner lost

[1]As amended by the Tax Reduction Act of 1975.

$47,000 after taxes,[1] Uncle Sam would have collected $7,000 in income taxes from a well that furnished no income, only losses. Here we see how the depletion allowance could generate income for the government from a well that generated only losses for the well owner. There will be times when the well owner benefits and recovers, tax free, far more than the cost of a well, but obviously cash flow from an oil and gas well does not lend itself to ordinary taxing methods.[2]

Since much of the cash flow from an oil and gas well is actually a return of capital, it should not be taxed. Characterizing such "tax-free" receipts as being the product of a "loophole" which should be "closed" is raising the level of political irresponsibility and ignorance beyond the point of tolerance.

"Close-the-tax-loophole" advocates wrongly assume that with the "loopholes" closed, the government would collect all the tax revenues that it theoretically loses because of them. They naively assume that with the tax incentives removed the same amount of capital would still be directed into these investment areas, which would hardly be the case. If the "tax loopholes" were closed, a considerable amount of the capital invested in municipal bonds, oil and gas wells, real estate, cattle, and the other tax-sheltered investments might simply be invested in stronger foreign currencies or in gold and silver.

No, with the "loopholes" closed, most Americans would still find that they would be paying the same high taxes as before. However, they would discover that because of the removal of investment and tax incentives, their municipal taxes would be higher, the costs of oil and natural gas would be higher, and rents would be higher. In other words, there would be higher prices, shortages, and less employment in those areas which had previously attracted investment capital because of "loopholes."

Taxpayers should realize that they are being conned when politicians suggest that closing "loopholes" will reduce their tax bill. The only way tax burdens can or will ever be reduced is by cutting or trimming Federal programs and agencies. All other claims and expectations are fallacious.

Here's a typical example of how politicians attempt to confuse the public concerning "tax loopholes." The *Miami Herald* of November 19, 1974, carried the following UPI dispatch, headlined "Proxmire Criticizes Tax Law":

> Washington—Sen. William Proxmire said Friday "a little-known loophole" in the tax laws will give corporations $6 billion to $9 billion in tax breaks this year.

[1]Though the well cost $100,000 to drill and complete, the after-tax cost because of the tax write-offs of the intangible drilling costs would be nearly $60,000. Deducting the after-tax recovery of $13,000 in revenue would still leave $47,000 tied up in a hole in the ground, having little value.

[2]Even if it were true that the statutory depletion allowance permitted oil and gas operators to escape taxation on a portion of their earnings, this would merely have amounted to a federal subsidy—a subsidy to secure for the nation vital supplies of oil and gas. What is so terrible about that? Hasn't the government, with less justification, granted lavish subsidies to the agricultural industry? How about the subsidies to the shipping industry, the educational industry—and let's not forget about the U.S. Postal Service?

> "The effect will be to swell the coffers of corporate treasuries at a time of unprecedented profits while it plunges the federal government deeper into debt and adds to inflationary pressures," Proxmire said.
>
> The loophole, according to Proxmire, allows a corporation, without the permission of the IRS, to shift its accounting treatment of inventories.
>
> "By using a system called last-in-first-out, a corporation can declare an inventory item at its present cost, rather than its original cost and escape paying taxes on the difference."

What is "last-in-first-out," sometimes known as the LIFO method of inventory valuation, as opposed to "first-in-first-out," or the FIFO method of inventory? Well, let's assume one sells sugar in hundred-pound bags. Of late, sugar has risen in price from about 10 cents a pound to 50 cents a pound. Let's assume, therefore, that a sugar merchant has in his inventory sugar bought at 10 cents a pound or $10 for a hundred-pound bag, as well as bags purchased for $20, $30, and $50. All of this sugar is of the same quality with the increased prices the result of inflation. Let's assume, too, that the merchant now sells a bag for $60. If he assumes that he sold the last bag he purchased, his profit would be $10; however, if he assumes that he sold the oldest bag, he would have a profit of $50. This, of course, makes quite a difference, since if the merchant is in a 50 percent tax bracket and assumes the latter valuation, he would be required to pay the government $25 in taxes. This would only leave him with $35 ($60–$25 in taxes), which would be insufficient to replace, at current prices, the bag that was sold. So, naturally, during a period of substantial inflation, it may be essential to adopt the "last-in-first-out" method of inventory, at least if one desires to remain in business.

While this example illustrates how inventory assumptions can affect taxable profits, over a period of time the same inventory assumptions will equalize profits. While the IRS does not allow arbitrary switching from one method to another, a firm may change its valuation methods, recognizing that it may have to justify that change to the IRS.

In any case, using the "first-in-first-out" method of accounting during a period of runaway inflation will develop artificial profits resulting from the increasing paper value of a firm's inventory, while actual operating profits might be decreasing. At the same time, of course, inflation will be increasing the replacement cost of fixed assets while high interest rates caused by the inflation will create a poor capital market that will impede a firm from acquiring outside financing to replace those assets. So, it becomes essential for a firm to retain as much earnings as possible, and a change of inventory valuation to eliminate artificial inventory profits therefore becomes important. With this in mind, any firm that does not switch, if it can, to the "last-in-first-out" method of inventory valuation during our current period of runaway inflation is probably getting poor accounting advice. The inflation, caused by government, will create an artificial picture of profits if inventory valuations are not changed. With these facts in mind, let's turn again to Proxmire's remarks.

First of all, he calls changing the method of inventory valuation a "little-known loophole.'' Nonsense! As any second semester accounting student knows, during a period of inflation a LIFO method of inventory evaluation will develop less initial taxable profits than will FIFO. Perhaps Senator Proxmire wanted to give the impression that he was so clever that he ''uncovered'' a little-known ''loophole.'' However, to call a change in inventory valuation a ''tax loophole'' is ridiculous. Proxmire realizes that the public conceives of a ''loophole'' as a small oversight in the law that wealthy taxpayers exploit to avoid their share of taxes. However, these changes to the LIFO method of inventory accounting are broad and open actions necessitated by the government's own inflationary activities.

Senator Proxmire states that this change of inventory valuation methods will ''swell the coffers of corporate treasuries at a time of *unprecedented profits* while it plunges the federal government deeper into debt and adds to inflationary pressure.'' Now, as a U.S. Senator, Proxmire certainly has the right to combine arrogance with ignorance. But here Proxmire even abuses that privilege. To blame private corporations for ''plunging the federal government deeper into debt'' when it is Proxmire and his merry band of legislative spendthrifts that are responsible for federal spending is to twist reason into a pretzel.

By referring to corporate ''coffers,'' the senator makes an obvious Marxian slip—that is, giving the impression that ''profits'' extracted from the ''exploited masses'' simply pile up unproductively in the counting houses of ''heartless capitalists.'' As I have already indicated, a substantial portion of current corporate ''profits'' are artificial and the result of inflationary increases in inventory. A tough question for the Wisconsin lawmaker would be: If this is truly a time of ''unprecedented profits,'' why was the stock market recently at its lowest level in twelve years? Changes in inventory accounting have become essential to eliminate artificial profits, and consequently unjustified taxes, in order to retain the capital necessary to replace inflated fixed assets and higher cost inventories.

All ''inflationary pressures'' are caused, of course, by this same destructive band of political con artists, not private industry. But it was Senator Proxmire who played a leading role in the removal of gold backing of U.S. currency (see Appendix C for samples of Proxmire's testimony). Since it was this act above all that was most responsible for our rampant inflation, Proxmire should be the last person to accuse anyone of causing inflation.

It should now be apparent how many totally misleading inferences are contained in this one short statement of Senator Proxmire's. What we might find in a longer statement simply boggles the imagination. It should also be apparent that there really are no ''loopholes'' in the tax law—save one. That one is the noose fashioned by the law itself, and from which the entire private economy hangs and twists. A way must soon be found, of course, to cut that loophole—while the victim is at least still breathing!

9

How Labor Laws Destroy Employment Opportunities

Did you know that it can be a federal offense to provide employment, or teach skills and trades? The legislation responsible for this economic and social situation is called the minimum wage law.[1] This allegedly benign law has hindered society's ability to pass trade skills from one generation to the next and has helped to reduce both America's ability to produce and to improve the quality of its production. Another consequence of this act is that it has helped to increase crime and public welfare. If the minimum wage were raised high enough, most Americans would have to resort to crime in order to survive.

U.S. labor laws do the following:

1. They make it illegal for many persons to work.
2. They compel millions of Americans to seek employment from two or more sources—that is, to "moonlight."
3. They contribute to a lowering of American standards of workmanship.
4. They create shortages for many types of skilled labor.
5. They interfere with the normal development of the division of labor.
6. They make a mockery of the 40-hour work week.

[1]More accurate, it is embodied in the provision of the Fair Labor Standards Act of 1938, as amended.

Assuming a minimum wage at $2 and hour[1] the minimum direct wage cost of a 40-hour employee is $80. However, payroll taxes alone will add at least 10 percent to this cost (Social Security, workmen's compensation, unemployment compensation), upping the direct labor cost to about $88 a week. Now, there are other indirect business costs that a worker's productivity must absorb—rent, tools, recordkeeping, and the collection of taxes, to name but a few.

No one can be employed over an extended period of time unless he produces enough to cover both his direct labor cost and his share of the overhead expenses. These overhead expenses could easily be 15 percent of the direct labor costs, further increasing the minimum level of productivity from $88 to $101.20 a week or $2.53 an hour.

However, we still have not accounted for the employer's profit for supplying employment in the first place. Let's suppose he wishes to earn 10 percent simply for assuming the risks involved in furnishing employment.[2] If we add a profit margin of 10 percent (which may be only 5 percent after taxes), we find that a federal minimum wage of $2 per hour is in reality a federal minimum rate of productivity of about $2.78 per hour and thus 40 percent higher than the actual minimum wage.[3]

Now, what specifically does a minimum rate of productivity of $2.78 an hour or $111.32 for a 40-hour week really mean? For all practical purposes, it means that it is illegal to be hired unless one is capable of producing, during 40 hours, goods and services worth at least $111.32. Suppose for various reasons one is only capable of producing goods or services worth $10 or $50 or $75—what then? What of those persons who cannot achieve the arbitrary, minimum standards of productivity established by law? Well, they can go on welfare or resort to crime, since these represent the only convenient and practical alternatives.

For example, suppose the owner of a large garage discovered a 17-year-old high school dropout wasting time practicing hook shots in some park playground. Suppose that after talking with the youth, the garage owner learned that he was unemployed and then struck up the following conversation.

[1]In January 1975, the minimum wage for employees covered prior to 1967 became $2.10 an hour, increasing to $2.30 by January 1976. For employees covered in 1967 or later, the minimum wage as of January 1975 is $2 an hour, increasing to $2.30 by January 1977. Minimum wage for "covered" agricultural workers is $1.80 an hour as of January 1975, increasing to $2.30 an hour by January 1978.

As one can see, different minimum wage rates currently apply for different employee categories while "covered employee" still excludes some workers from coverage. However, workers not covered under the federal law can be subject to state wage laws, which are often patterned after the federal model. In any case, approximately 70 percent of all workers are subject to the federal law, with a good portion of the balance subject to applicable state laws. In addition, the federal law set a minimum wage pattern for the nation, affecting even those employers not directly subject to the regulation.

[2]One of the risks being that employees are paid *before* the employer receives payment for their productivity.

[3]Note that this amount does not provide for "fringe benefit" costs such as paid vacations, sick leave, insurance and pensions, which in some cases amount to a third of the direct labor cost.

"Have you tried finding a job?"

"Yeah, but I just can't find anything."

"What can you do?"

"Well, nothin' special, but I'm willin' to learn."

"Why don't you go to a trade school?"

"Well, I always got into trouble in school, foolin' around with the other kids—besides, I need to make some money and that's hard to do while you're in school."

"But you've found that making money is a little harder than you figured, right?"

"Right!"

"Well, what are you doing to learn a skill or trade—you know that without any special skills it will be difficult for you to land a job and support yourself."

"I know that, but there doesn't seem to be anything I can do about it."

"Why not attend a private training school where you can learn a particular trade, like TV repair or bulldozer driving?"

"Well, that takes money and I don't have any to pay for any training."

"Would you like to be an automobile mechanic?"

"Sure, but how can I go about becoming one—I already told you I can't afford to pay anybody to teach me anything."

"Well, now, wait a minute—I own a large service station just six blocks from here. If you would be willing to come in every day we might make a fairly decent mechanic out of you in a year or two, if you applied yourself. Would you be willing to do that?"

"Yes, but why would you do that just to help me?"

"Well, while I would be training you, I'd expect that you would clean up around the station, wash cars, pump gas and, in general, make yourself useful. In addition, in connection with your training, you would be doing useful work for which I would receive compensation and this would compensate me for your training. As a matter of fact, I'll even provide you with $25 a week spending money, and as you improve your skills, you will be able to earn even more. Would you be interested in this arrangement?"

"Would I! When can I start?"

"NEVER," thunders Uncle Sam, never one to allow an untrained, unskilled youth to be "exploited." If that good samaritan garage owner wanted to take the unskilled youth off the streets, train him, and give him a skill and the opportunity to become economically self-reliant, at no expense to himself and society—the garage owner would be breaking the law!

If the garage owner wanted the youth to put in 40 hours, federal law would have required that he pay him the minimum of $80 (overlooking the additional direct and indirect labor costs). So, obviously he could not afford to train and pay him significant wages at the same time. Therefore, the youth is compelled to shoot basketballs in the playground until maybe a friend shows him how to steal TV sets, or how to snatch ladies' handbags for spending money. That's better than being "exploited" while learning a trade and contributing to society.

This is how our society attained "zero employment for black teenagers." I doubt there is another society where an official could say in all accuracy that a segment of its society—a young and healthy segment at that—had become *unemployable*. In short, we have permitted a whole segment of our society to be raised while denying it a *realistic* method of acquiring saleable skills. Who created such a condition? Why, the politicians who imposed a minimum level of productivity as a prerequisite for employment, thus effectively wiping out employment opportunities for those with little or no skills! We call this condition *hard-core unemployment*. The minimum wage law has also eliminated many services which some members of society might require, and other members of society might have furnished, but which had an economic utility lower than the minimum rates established by law.

For those who mistakenly believe that there are meaningful exceptions to the federal law granting relief from its folly, let's explore those exceptions. Most exceptions to the minimum wage law relate to a formal program of instruction under "work-study" arrangements and would not apply to the example of the high school dropout, where *hard-core* unemployment really exists and where the waste of human resources is so tragic.

The more comprehensive exception to the minimum wage law is a legislative attempt to mitigate the impact of the law on the physically and mentally handicapped and is embodied in title 29, part 524, of the Code of Federal Regulation, "Special Minimum Wages for the Handicapped Workers in Competitive Employment." This regulation attempts to solve in bureaucratic fashion the economic hardships *created* by bureaucratic interference.

> (d)(1) Except as otherwise provided in paragraphs (2) and (3) of this subsection the Secretary of Labor, to the extent necessary in order *to prevent curtailment of opportunities for employment,* shall by regulation or order provide for the employment under special certificates of individuals (including individuals employed in agriculture) whose earnings or productive capacity is impaired by age or physical or mental deficiency or injury at wages that are lower than the minimum wage applicable under section 6 of this act but not less than 50 per centum of such wages and which are commensurate with those paid nonhandicapped workers in industry in the vicinity for essentially the same type, quality and quantity of work. [Italics mine.]

Please note that the government itself admits that the law does, in fact, curtail "opportunities for employment," and so the law attempts to provide relief for those whose "productive capacity is impaired." However, the government does not recognize the fact that the absence of skills is also an "impairment" to employment. One who is otherwise physically normal and reasonably intelligent but without skills or training is as handicapped in terms of being employable as one with obvious physical and mental disabilities. But the law does not take this into consideration! Those provisions of the law which try to bring relief to those injured by it are bound with red tape. So, consequently, few actually benefit from them. For example, as of October 1, 1974, there were only 59 handicapped certificates in effect in New England. Obviously, most employers have no interest in becoming involved in bureaucratic red tape by filling out and waiting for a response to government form WH-222 (Rev. 12/72), entitled "Application for Handicapped Worker Certificate," nor do they care to subject themselves to additional government regulation and scrutiny. And, since these regulations stipulate that "every employer who employs a handicapped worker or trainee pursuant to these regulations shall keep, maintain, and have available for inspection by the Administrator or his authorized representatives, a copy of the certificate and all other records required under the applicable provisions of part 516 [recordkeeping regulation] of the chapter."

So, for all practical purposes, there is *no real relief* from what the government itself admits is a "curtailment of opportunities for employment" (a bureaucratic euphemism for "can't get hired") for the handicapped. However, this "curtailment of opportunity" extends not only to those who are physically and mentally handicapped, which is the only employment handicap officially recognized by the government, but to persons also handicapped by environment, by lack of skill and lack of training, by lack of motivation, and by marginal intelligence. *Just what constitutional right or expertise does the U.S. government have that empowers and justifies bureaucrats to establish and dictate arbitrary standards of employability*? The government has passed a law making it illegal to be employed unless one's productivity attains certain minimum standards—$111 for a 40-hour week. So, how does one acquire skills that might enable one's productivity to be worth $111 a week? The economic geniuses in Washington left that out . . . and government-sponsored "skill centers" *will not* provide the answer.

The Rationale Behind the "Minimum Wage" Law

Those who proposed, passed, and expanded the "minimum wage" law have basically accepted the Marxist thesis that capitalism "exploits" the working classes, and that the latter must be "protected" by state intervention. "Exploitation" of the laborer by private capitalism is a Marxist concept, and like most Marxist concepts is fallacious.

Now, what exactly is "exploitation"? According to Marx, it meant that employers withheld from the workers a substantial portion of their productivity, which Marx called the *surplus value of labor*. This surplus value was confiscated, according to Marx, from the worker by his employer, thus furnishing the basis for their *exploitation*. Marx knew nothing about manufacturing. Had he, he would have realized that the worker couldn't possibly receive, in wages, the total value of his production since the worker only supplied the direct labor. Others had to be compensated for their contribution to productivity for such items as the cost of rent, the cost of supplying the tools and other capital needs, the cost of insurance, warehousing, designing, research, the cost of selling the finished product, and the cost of the economic risk involved. In other words, there's a range of productive factors in addition to direct labor, but Marx naively recognized only one factor—*labor*.

In any case, given an economy where workers are allowed to move freely from any occupation and where capital is allowed to move freely from one industry to another, to assume that workers can be "exploited" when they are free to change jobs and/or to go into business for themselves, is to misunderstand the economics of employment.

Many individuals forget that initially man had to rely on his own resources to provide for himself and his family. Each man in essence was in business for himself as he foraged for food and other necessities for his family. This, of course, remains the fundamental economic option available to all, as well as each individual's primary opportunity for "employment." There are many who have chosen this route, from the peanut vendor, organ grinder, and umbrella repairman (vanishing breeds, I know) to the barber, insurance agent, shoe store proprietor, and physician. In connection with this, it must be self-evident that each individual must have the fundamental and unfettered right to work and pursue employment regardless of race, national origin, or religious, political, and economic beliefs. Therefore, no one should be compelled to join any particular religion, political party, or union as a prerequisite for employment.[1]

"Liberals" betray the principles their very label implies when they oppose "right to work" laws, which grant individuals the freedom to work without being coerced to join a union. If some workers have the right to unionize, others must have a comparable right *not* to be forced into a union. To justify the denial of one's fundamental right not to be coerced into unionism on the grounds that "since a worker receives the benefits of union negotiation he should, therefore, be compelled to join and support the union," is beside the point. Even if this statement were true,[2] such reasoning could serve to compel contributions to the Heart Fund on the basis that all stand to benefit from its research, or be used to force conversions to a state religion on the strength of an assertion that, since it is the state religion that makes possible the benefits flowing from the state economy,

[1]While all should have an unfettered *right to work* either for oneself or for others, one does not have a "right to a job." A "right to a job," regardless of how noble that sounds, does not assert a "right" but proclaims an "obligation," that some (exactly *who* we are not told) must supply jobs for others. Of course, no one has such an obligation since this would embody the principle that some are obligated to risk their own capital for the benefit of others. Exactly who, I wonder, feels so obligated? Certainly not, I suggest, those who assert this "right!" If it is therefore argued that it is society that must furnish the jobs, then it is socialism that is suggested.

[2]It could also be argued that militant unionism does not serve the long-run interests of the worker because in many cases there is a correlation between militant unionism and dwindling employment. The U.S. Maritime Union is a good example.

and, since all benefit from that economy, all must adopt and support the state religion. So, "liberals," who deny an individual his "right to work" while stoutly proclaiming his "right to a job," are denying an obvious right while asserting not a right but an obligation, which few are willing and able to fulfill—*the employment of others*.

All persons must realize that they are free to take a pail of water and a sponge and enter the window-washing or basement-cleaning business, but most individuals find that they will earn more if they work for an established business rather than strike out on their own.[1]

It is sometimes asserted that employees *must* work for a given employer and must accept substandard wages. But this argument does not face current economic and social realities. There are few areas in the country where there is only one available employer. If there is, and wages are truly substandard, employees will gradually leave the area while fewer potential employees will be attracted to the area, and eventually wages will have to be increased as the supply of potential workers is reduced. If a given employer is paying low wages relevant to his employees' productivity, he will, of course, be making exceptionally high profits. Other entrepreneurs will soon become aware of this profitable situation and become drawn into this area of productivity. Competition for the available supply of workers will soon force an increase in wages. To suggest that employers might formally conspire to hold down wages is to suggest that employers would risk criminally breaking the law—since, of course, it is a violation of the Sherman Antitrust Act to engage in such activity. (Moreover, the government would have every right to mete out severe punishment to employers guilty of such practices.) The operation of the law of supply and demand, and the force of competition, will deliver to the worker a wage commensurate with his productivity and do so without burdening society with the bureaucratic costs and the economic distortions caused by artificially determined wage rates.

Those politicians, therefore, who have imposed a minimum wage standard on the nation haven't the foggiest notion of how wages in a free economy are determined or how competition protects workers from "exploitation." Such a lack of understanding is, of course, understandable and forgiveable in the man in the street, for he can be presumed to be unfamiliar with the basic principles of economics. However, such ignorance is inexcusable in men who presume themselves fit to govern a nation supposedly dedicated to the FEAC system. Here is a simple example, therefore to show how wages are determined and to reveal the extent of the economic and social damage generated by the "minimum wage" law.

Suppose farmer Jones announced that he would allow anyone who wished to pick apples from his orchard, with the stipulation that the person leave him half of those picked. Suppose in response to this offer, one energetic fellow raced around

[1] This being the case, it's nonsensical to assert that one is being exploited by an employer to whom one has voluntarily turned and from whom one can freely leave.

and picked 400 apples, another less energetic fellow got only 300, one less able collected 200, while a blind person could only garner 60 and a crippled lad only 20.

These apple pickers would have left at the end of the day with 200, 150, 100, 30, and 10 apples respectively. We can further assume that if these individuals could have employed their time to more advantage they would have done so, as farmer Jones did not compel them to pick apples in his orchard in any way. For illustrative purposes, let's also assume that these individuals maintained the same level of production. Although the crippled lad was only able to earn 10 apples a day, this of course was better than earning nothing.

Now, given this illustration on productivity and wages, no rational person could accuse farmer Jones of exploiting any of these five persons. And, if workers were paid in *kind* directly in a portion of what they directly produced, our labor laws and much irresponsible trade unionism would never exist. But, payment in kind in a diversified and specialized economy is not only uneconomic, it's impossible. Nevertheless, the same forces and principles are at work when money wages are received, so we must grasp the underlying relationship between wages and productivity before the element of money is introduced.

Suppose farmer Jones established that the above apple pickers were selling their surplus apples (those they didn't wish to consume) for 20 cents each, and that they were also devoting considerable effort and time in doing so. Therefore, he makes the following proposition. At the end of each day he will give them 15 cents for each apple they earned (or 7½ cents for each apple picked) and he would assume the risk of selling the apples while they would be free to take either the apples or the money equivalent. Let's assume the workers agreed to this proposal, recognizing that even if they sold their apples to farmer Jones for less than they usually received, they at least were free of the effort required to sell them. Thus, if this effort were applied to picking additional apples, they would have the same amount if not more money in the end. Instead of leaving each day with apples for which they needed to find buyers, the pickers departed with $30, $22.50, $15, $4.50, and $1.50, respectively.

Now look at what happens when the pickers are paid in *money* wages rather than in *apple* wages. Socialists claim that farmer Jones is "exploiting" apple pickers and confiscating their "surplus value." He is accused of paying substandard wages. These cries and charges, of course, find sympathetic ears in Washington, where the politicians find it "intolerable" that farmer Jones is paying as low as $1.50 a day and enact legislation making it mandatory that pickers be paid a "living wage" of at least $1 per hour, or $8 for an eight-hour day. So, what does farmer Jones do when compelled to pay $8 per day for apple pickers? Will he pay these wages to those whose productivity to him is only worth $4.50 and $1.50? Of course not. He will have to let them go, and they and society will simply lose whatever productivity they were capable of contributing. Since by law they are now precluded from working, society must provide alternative schemes to care for them. Because whatever limited ability they had to provide for themselves has now been taken from them, they become dependent on charity. Of course, both the blind man and the crippled lad might have increased their ability so that in time they might have achieved the minimum standards of productivity set by the state in order to become employable—only now they have lost that opportunity.

Has the wage law helped the three workers who were already earning more than the minimum? Of course not. The wage law has done nothing but eliminate from the labor market those whose productive levels fall below the minimum level established by law as a condition for employment. To the extent that the law now makes employment unlawful for many individuals in society, charity (welfare) and crime must fill the void.[1]

Examples of how minimum wages destroy jobs, especially among the young and the most marginal members of society, are all around us. At age 14, I worked after school as a delivery boy in the Hill section of New Haven, Connecticut, for the National Food Store, a one-man grocery operation. For working from about 3:30 to 5:30 PM, five days a week, I earned $2.50. When I worked all day on Saturday, I received $5. The Hill section of New Haven was a blue-collar area. The year was 1942. There were probably six other similar grocery stores that employed delivery boys within a two-block radius and thus shopping for these blue-collar workers would, by present standards, seem almost luxurious. These people didn't have to take an evening off just to go grocery shopping. No, if they wished, all they had to do was telephone. I would jot down the order and deliver it on my bicycle. No minimum order was required. I would deliver a quart of milk if necessary, but no one would be so inconsiderate as to order only that. At that time, a number of my friends also worked as delivery boys. We were earning money while performing a public service that could only be done by inexpensive, marginal help. At that time, shut-ins, the elderly, and the handicapped had no difficulty getting the things they needed because there was an abundance of delivery boys.

Now look at the situation. Even if a small store wanted a delivery boy, this service cannot be economically offered at the prices firms are compelled to pay. Therefore delivery boys have virtually disappeared. As a consequence, shut-ins, the sick, and the elderly have a difficult time getting the things they need. For many years my mother traded with a store that made home deliveries. Its groceries cost more, but the service and convenience were worth the expense. Finally, the store's proprietor decided that the additional income generated by the expense of a delivery truck and driver was not justified and discontinued the service. When this happened, members of my family had to make special trips to secure groceries for my mother, who luckily had children able to shop for her. Such a problem, however, did not exist in the blue-collar section of New Haven when I, along with many others, was busy with my bicycle—and at no time did I feel "exploited."

Understanding the negative impact of the minimum wage law will go a long way toward explaining the vanishing delivery boy, the vanished Western Union

[1]It is no accident that America's crime rates and welfare rolls, even during "prosperous" times, have grown, responding to increases in the minimum wage. (The latter causes the former.)

messenger, the vanishing soda jerk, the vanished stock girl, the development of self-service shopping, and the changing patterns of so much of our economic life, not to mention the problems of youth in finding employment. My sister, for example, worked as a stock girl on Saturdays in a small but active New Haven dress shop for $2.[1] All women's shops in those days employed stock girls, who only hung up the coats and dresses as they were discarded by the salesladies who were thus free to concentrate on selling.

Not long ago, George, a friend of mine who operates a better-priced women's apparel shop, complained to me that he simply could not get good sales help. All his good salesladies were on in years, he said, and "when they go, I don't know how I'll replace them." I asked George if he employed any stock girls. He said, "Of course not, nobody does any more." In other words, the salesladies hung up their own garments. I pointed out to George that this was precisely why he could not find any good sales help. Salesladies learned to be salesladies while they served as stock girls. While hanging up garments they would listen, observe, and learn from the older, experienced salesladies, who would eventually let them "wait on trade." Thus, being a stock girl was good training for becoming a professional saleslady. I know this at firsthand, for I eventually graduated from delivering groceries to working in a women's apparel store. I retrieved garments from the alteration department, wrapped them, and collected any balances due. It was there I saw firsthand how stock girls learned to become salesladies.

Today, if an apparel shop wants a stock girl for an 8-hour day, it must pay a minimum of $16 or $18, including payroll taxes—far more than the $2 my sister earned in the early '40s. As a result, employers have stopped hiring stock girls, thereby eliminating the training grounds for good, professional sales help.

The minimum wage law makes it uneconomical to meet marginal economic needs with people; these needs are now filled by machines or eliminated. Automation, despite what many people believe, does not create unemployment, it simply fills the vacuum created by minimum wage laws and other increasing labor costs. Automatic elevators that replaced elevator operators because of their increasing wage demands are a good example of this.

Let me relate how I was able to witness firsthand how the "minimum wage" law destroyed employment. For years, I have run a "one-girl office"; however I had always routinely employed a high school girl who would work from around 3 to 5 P.M. The girl's basic duties were filing and getting out the day's mail. However, there were occasionally other tasks which would enable her to gain practical experience in such areas as typing and bookkeeping, which she was studying in school. Since the part-time girl theoretically worked ten hours a week, and since the minimum wage was then $1.25 an hour, the job paid $12.50 per week. I say "theoretically" worked 10 hours a week, because I didn't keep track of the actual hours and days these girls worked—what with their being late and absent due to holidays and illnesses, the actual hours worked per week were less than ten.

[1]She netted $1.98; two pennies were deducted for social security.

Maria, the particular girl working for me at this time, was absent more than usual, and would arrive often at 3:30 or 4 P.M., usually with some excuse for her tardiness. Although quite personable, Maria was not one of my better part-time girls—not one, anyway, that I would have rewarded with a raise.

It was during this time that I received a notice from the U.S. Department of Labor, informing me that my employees were subject to the new minimum wage of $1.60 per hour, meaning that I would have to pay Maria $16 for a ten-hour week. While I had always paid my part-time help the prevailing minimum wage, I had never felt that I was really subject to it. I, therefore, called the Labor Department and was duly informed that my office was indeed subject to the federal minimum wage law.

It annoyed me to think that the federal government was attempting to compel me to give an employee an unwarranted raise. If I compelled Maria to "punch in" and "punch out" and then tabulated the actual hours she worked on the basis of $1.60 per hour, I would probably arrive at a weekly wage somewhat less than I was paying her. However, I simply did not want to be bothered with this picayune task of keeping hourly and daily statistics on my part-time employee. While I reflected on this situation, Valerie, my full-time secretary, entered my office. She had only been with me a year and had proven so efficient that her salary had gone from $70 to $90 in one year. When I showed Valerie the circular from the Labor Department indicating that I would have to pay Maria $16 per week, Valerie replied, "Mr. Schiff, for $10 more a week I will stay an extra half hour and do my own filing and get out my own mail." This, of course, made economic sense, but by this time I had become somewhat fond of Maria despite her shortcomings, and did not want to fire her. I called Maria into my office. I asked her if she were happy with the job and salary. She said that she was. I then showed her the circular from the U.S. Labor Department, compelling me to pay her $16 for the work she was doing. I explained to her that the work was not worth $16 per week and so I might be forced to let her go. Her father happened to come to the office, and I discussed the situation with him. I told him that in my judgment, the government was unconstitutionally and unnecessarily interfering with Maria's right to contract for her services. Not only was she earning spending money, she was gaining valuable office experience which would help her when seeking full–time employment. I told him that I would furnish him with a statement indicating my willingness to maintain Maria as an employee at $12.50 per week, but not $16 per week. I suggested that he might take this up with the local office of the Labor Department or perhaps with the American Civil Liberties Union, assuming that the latter might finally become interested in defending the civil liberties of an average American. However, Maria's father didn't want to "start any trouble with the government" so her employment ended that week. I increased Valerie's salary by $10, she worked an extra half hour a day—and I never again resumed my practice of hiring part-time high school help.

Here was only one of the many jobs that was eliminated when the minimum wage was raised from $1.25 to $1.60 an hour. How many more jobs were eliminated when the minimum climbed to $2 cannot be readily determined, but they must have been considerable.

Here is another example of the loss of employment due to the "minimum wage" law. In the summer of 1967, New Haven was one of the cities that was struck by the outbreak of black rioting, so at the close of the following school year a campaign was launched to find employment for "inner-city" (black) youth. In this way it was hoped that the city might be "cooled" to avoid a repeat of the previous summer's rioting. At about this time, I was preparing to mail out some 3,000 pieces of mail, and I had been given a price of about $240 to cover the cost by a mailing service.

So, while driving to my office one morning, I heard a radio announcer make a strong plea that businessmen and others provide summer jobs for these youths. A representative of Community Progress, Inc., the agency in charge of the project, announced that "people are now at the phones ready to take your work orders. Students will be available to wash cars, clean attics and cellars" and do other similar types of jobs. The announcer told why it would be an act of good community spirit to help in the hiring of these students, who otherwise would be unemployed and on the city streets. As I listened to the announcer, I thought about the 3,000 pieces of mail that I had to get out. I thought that possibly three students might be able to do the job in two weeks. So if I paid each student $40 a week, I might get the job done for the same cost as I was prepared to pay a mailing service.

Wanting to help in the campaign to use these students, I called CPI upon arrival at my office. I informed CPI of my willingness to employ three students for two weeks. The initial reaction to my request was unabashed enthusiasm—"Oh, that's just wonderful." Then this reaction cooled, however, as the following exchange indicates:

"What type of work would this be, Mr. Schiff?"

"Stuffing envelopes, affixing postage, sealing and then sorting the envelopes. They will work in an air-conditioned office conveniently near the downtown area."

"That sounds just great, Mr. Schiff, how much will the job pay?"

"$40 per week," I replied.

"That's fine . . . ah . . . Mr. Schiff, how many hours will they be required to work?"

Our normal hours were usually 35 hours a week, nine to five with an hour for lunch, although we sometimes worked to 5:30, or 37½ hours. So, not knowing how long it would actually take to get the work done, I assumed that it might require the longer schedule, so I replied . . .

"37½ hours."

There was a slight pause, then the party continued.

"Mr. Schiff, the minimum wage is $1.60 an hour. If you want these students to work 37½ hours, you'll have to pay $60 per week."

"Well, the job is not worth that much, so I can't afford to pay that much," I replied.

"Well, I'm sorry, that's what you'll have to pay."

"You're mistaken, Miss," I replied, "I don't have to pay them anything."

I asked to speak to her supervisor and explained the problem to him—that if I were compelled to pay the students $60 per week, the job would cost me $360 (excluding payroll taxes) to get a job done that need only cost me $240. I explained that I didn't mind taking a chance on the students and undergoing the added inconvenience, but I was not prepared to pay 50 percent more for the privilege. The supervisor felt badly about not being able to place the students since he did have more students than job offers and my job seemed a good deal more pleasant than cleaning garages and basements. I inquired if there were any program that might qualify the students to work for a lesser rate than the minimum wage. He did not know of any. I asked him if, in his opinion, three students would be better off working 37½ hours for me for $40 or not working at all, perhaps getting into trouble in the street. He said that there was no doubt in his mind that they would be far better off working for me. He stated that he had the students that would want to do so, but that his hands were tied in that he could not send students out for less than the minimum wage. So unable to hire three black students, I hung up the phone and told my secretary to contact the letter service and have them pick up the material for the mailing.

On March 2, 1968, President Johnson's National Advisory Commission on Civil Disorders, otherwise known as the Kerner Commission, issued its report on the causes of the racial violence of the preceding summer. This report took seven months to prepare and God knows how much of the taxpayers' money, and ran to 1,400 pages. "White racism," the commission charged, was "essentially responsible for the explosive mixture" that existed in the black ghettos and caused the riots. Quoting from the official summary of the report issued on February 29, it was alleged that:

> Pervasive discrimination and segregation in *employment,* education, and housing have resulted in the continuing exclusion of great numbers of Negroes from the benefits of economic progress.
>
> Black in-migration and the white exodus have produced the massive and growing concentrations of impoverished negroes in our major cities, creating a growing crisis of deteriorating facilities and services and unmet human needs.
>
> In the black ghettos segregation and poverty converge on the young to destroy opportunity and enforce failure. Crime, drug addiction, dependency on welfare, and bitterness and resentment against society in general and white society in particular are the result.

Further, the report stated:

> Pervasive unemployment and underemployment are the most persistent and serious grievances in the Negro ghetto. They are inextricably linked to the problem of civil disorder.

Despite growing Federal expenditures for manpower development and training programs and sustained general economic prosperity and increasing demands for skilled workers, about two million—white and nonwhite—are permanently unemployed. About ten million are underemployed, of whom 6.5 million work full-time for wages below the poverty line.

The 500,000 hard-core unemployed in the central cities who lack a basic education and are unable to hold a steady job are made up in large part of Negro males between the ages of 18 and 25 . . . .

In other words, the Negro rioting was linked primarily to Negro unemployment and underemployment—and thus directly linked to the impact of the ''minimum wage'' law and not to ''white racism,'' as the report incorrectly asserts. How else can we account for the ''pervasive unemployment and underemployment'' within the ghettos which *at the same time,* according to the report, suffered from ''deteriorating facilities and services and unmet human needs''? What prevented all those unemployed from being employed fulfilling those ''unmet human needs?'' How could ''white racism'' have prevented the unemployed and underemployed form being employed alleviating the conditions which warranted employment right in the ghetto itself? Obviously, it was related to the lack of skills, which is directly related to the difficulties created by the minimum wage law in acquiring skills, especially for the most marginally employable.

It was tragic enough that the Kerner Commission did not uncover the true reason for such widespread Negro unemployment, but compounded its errors by blaming ''racist'' America. This revealed not only the commission's ignorance of economic forces, but its ignorance of social forces as well. For America obviously is not a ''racist'' society. Considering the substantially divergent backgrounds of our people, there is a substantial amount of harmony and cooperation. There is certainly less antagonism here than between the Catholics and Protestants in Ireland, the Turks and Greeks on Cyprus, between the different castes in India, and between the different tribes in Africa, just to offer a few examples. Many who have criticized us in the past for those racial problems that do arise have often come from countries possessing a far more homogeneous population and so could afford to assume a superior racial attitude.

The Commission made nearly 160 ''recommendations'' to answer the question of ''what can be done?'' Almost all such recommendations involved the spending of more federal funds and creating of more federal programs. Typical of the ''know-nothing'' character of these recommendations is this one:

Take immediate action to create 2 million new jobs over the next 3 years—one million in the public sector and one million in the private sector—to absorb the hard core unemployed and materially reduce the level of unemployment for all workers black and white. We propose 250,000 public sector and 300,000 private sector in the first year.

So, two million ''new jobs'' are to be created by a mere bureaucratic snap of the fingers, are they? Since it could require nearly $20,000 of capital for each "new job," no mention is, of course, made as to where all this capital is to come from. And how about the training for these "jobs"? Will these jobs be filled by people requiring no skills at all? And precisely what will be produced on these "jobs," and for whom?

Of course, such a statement as "take immediate action to create two million new jobs" is fashioned from the same bureaucratic ignorance that gave rise to the "minimum wage" law in the first place. Both are grounded in the philosophy that assumes that politicians can simply pass laws raising society's standard of living, and that government is the *creator* of national wealth, when in reality it is on balance the *consumer* and *destroyer* of national wealth.

When government appears to be helping a segment of the economy, it is simply because it takes from Peter to give to Paul (there usually being more Pauls voting than Peters). In the process, Peter loses both goods and incentive while Paul finds that since the government allows him to live off the efforts of Peter, his incentives are also reduced. Both Peter's and Paul's incentives are reduced, so they *both* produce less and total productivity drops. Meanwhile the politicians, who have thus contributed to this lowering in total productivity, must additionally be supported by the combined efforts of both Peter and Paul, since they make no economic contribution at all, thus lowering still further the standard of living that could have been achieved. The basic economic tragedy of the "minimum wage" is that it needlessly disrupts, interferes and, in many cases, prevents the transference of occupational skills from one generation to another. It prevents craftsmen from passing on their knowledge to those who are unskilled since it is impossible for skilled craftsmen to train people and also pay them significant wages at the same time.

Take, for example, the case of Morris Green, a first-class poster artist in New Haven, Connecticut. I would usually kid Morris about his having "golden hands," since he can pick up a brush and immediately letter in a multitude of styles. At one time, he had been responsible for all the "coming attraction" posters for the Loew's New England movie chain, when posters of this type played a distinctive role in the movie business. Whenever I would go to Morris' office studio, he would be swamped with work, so it would be "impossible" to get my work when I wanted it. However, Morris always managed to have it ready anyway. Since Morris always complained about being so busy, I asked him why he didn't hire an assistant. The reason he gave was, "if I got somebody good, I have to pay them an arm and a leg, and with what I would have to pay somebody who isn't good, I couldn't afford the time needed to correct him." So Morris, who could have used some help, worked alone, How beneficial it would have been, both for Morris and society, if some youngster could have, without all the bureaucratic red tape, simply been permitted to work under Morris' guidance for any salary that was acceptable to both. In lieu of this type of free private instruction by a superb craftsman, youngsters only have recourse to the inferior instruction provided by trade schools or have to pay personally for such training in private art schools.

How the Government Destroyed a Meaningful U.S. Apprenticeship System

It should be self-evident that a highly technical economy such as ours requires millions of skilled persons to build and maintain our homes, institutions, and factories; to build, operate, and maintain our various systems of transportation and communications; as well as to develop our natural resources and the capital equipment and the vast amount of consumer goods and services required by so vast a population accustomed to the world's highest standard of living. Yet page 2 of a handbook printed by the U.S. Department of Labor in 1971, *Apprenticeship Past and Present,* boasts, "There are now about a quarter million registered apprentices—an all-time high—in American industry."

The American population in 1970 was approximately 203 million, so this represented approximately an eighth of 1 percent of our total population that was actually enrolled in this program, learning the basic skills and trades upon which our industrial economy depends. In comparison we had, in 1970, 60.357 million individuals enrolled in schools, from nursery through college, or approximately 30 percent of our population. So while it is possible to run an industrial economy without psychologists, sociologists, history and philosophy majors, it is not possible to run it without tool-and-die men, plumbers, crews who can operate drilling rigs and string high-tension wires; yet we had less than half of 1 percent of those in school enrolled in our apprenticeship program. To put this figure into yet another perspective, it might be instructive to compare the number of apprentices in this program to the number of Americans busily studying the subject of sociology.

In 1970, U.S. colleges and universities awarded the following number of degrees in sociology:

Bachelor's degree in Sociology	30,848
Master degrees in Sociology	1,816
Doctorates in Sociology	534
Total	33,198

Thus, 33,198 degrees were awarded in sociology, not counting the related degrees awarded in such areas as social work, administration, and welfare.

Since the average period of apprenticeship is from 3 to 4 years, this would suggest (using an average of 3 years) that approximately 84,000 Americans completed their apprenticeship training in 1970. Thus it would appear that our economy for some obscure reason felt a need to turn out sociologists equivalent to 40 percent of all those being trained in 350 apprenticeable and essential occupations. Now do you see why it is such a problem to get a plumber? However, if you need a sociologist—you're in good shape!

One drawback to our apprenticeship system is that it is too formalized and bound with red tape. Figure 30 will reveal a chart from the U.S. Department of Labor's manual referred to earlier, showing the apprenticeship system for steamfitters and pipefitters. This is a far cry from the days when my grandfather made arrangements with a master carpenter for teaching a trade to my father.

Figure 30

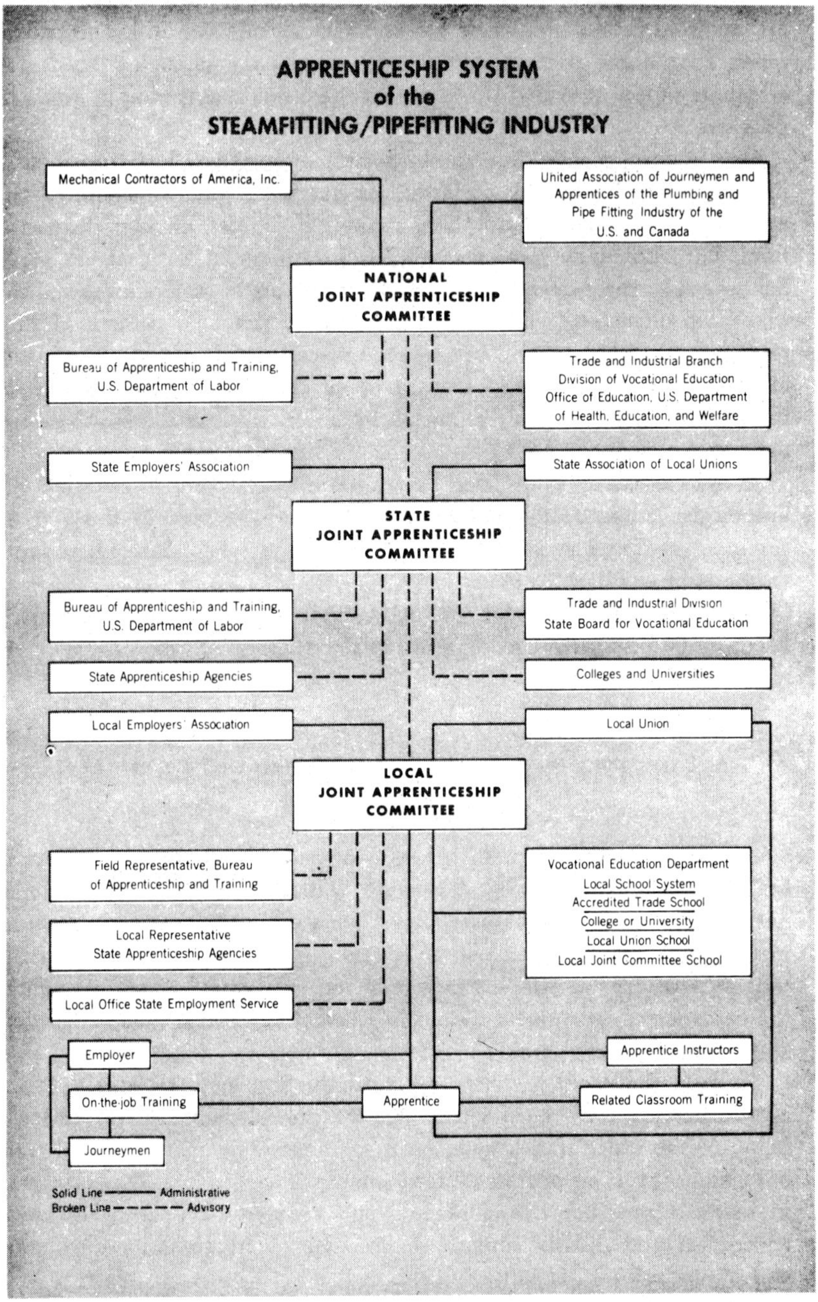
APPRENTICESHIP SYSTEM of the STEAMFITTING/PIPEFITTING INDUSTRY
Mechanical Contractors of America, Inc.
United Association of Journeymen and Apprentices of the Plumbing and Pipe Fitting Industry of the U.S. and Canada
NATIONAL JOINT APPRENTICESHIP COMMITTEE
Bureau of Apprenticeship and Training, U.S. Department of Labor
Trade and Industrial Branch Division of Vocational Education Office of Education, U.S. Department of Health, Education, and Welfare
State Employers' Association
State Association of Local Unions
STATE JOINT APPRENTICESHIP COMMITTEE
Bureau of Apprenticeship and Training, U.S. Department of Labor
Trade and Industrial Division State Board for Vocational Education
State Apprenticeship Agencies
Colleges and Universities
Local Employers' Association
Local Union
LOCAL JOINT APPRENTICESHIP COMMITTEE
Field Representative, Bureau of Apprenticeship and Training
Vocational Education Department
Local School System
Accredited Trade School
College or University
Local Union School
Local Joint Committee School
Local Representative State Apprenticeship Agencies
Local Office State Employment Service
Employer
Apprentice Instructors
On-the-job Training
Apprentice
Related Classroom Training
Journeymen
Solid Line Administrative
Broken Line Advisory

I am not advocating a return to the indentured apprenticeship system or a revival of the excesses that system perhaps encouraged. However, I do believe we must find the cause and solution for the deteriorating quality of American workmanship, our deteriorating productive capacity, and the consequential loss of our foreign and domestic markets.

Changes should be made in the U.S. apprenticeship program. An organized trade should not have control over the number of its own apprentices because of the conflict of interest it entails. Anyone should be free to teach any trade to anyone willing to learn. The proper regard for physical danger, and degree of difficulty, can be evaluated in terms of a person's physical and mental capabilities. To base qualifications *solely* on calendar age (as we now do) is to base them on standards determined solely in the interests of *bureaucratic* expediency and which have no relevance to actual needs, desires, or capacity. If we devoted some of the energy and money toward integrating our youth into the economy that we waste on "education," we would have more than enough personnel and money for this added occupational effort.

Time-and-a-Half after Forty Hours—Or How Uncle Sam Forces Two Jobs and Lowers the Incomes of Millions

Many workers, of course, cannot support their families on 40 hours a week. Yet many employers cannot economically provide them with more than 40 hours at the mandatory increased hourly rate. So employees have to seek part-time employment elsewhere and from employers who are not required to pay time-and-a-half wages. Thus, the time-and-a-half provision has spawned the phenomenon of "moonlighting"—the holding of more than one job. Employee A, for example, might work 40 hours for employer Y and 20 hours for employer Z, while employee B might work 40 hours for employer Z and 20 hours for employer Y. Both employees would, of course, be better off if they worked 60 hours at straight time for the same employer rather than working 60 hours at straight time for two employers with no compensation for the extra travel time required. But this is just the type of wasteful economic activity that politicians encourage while courting votes.

Can Trade Schools Really Teach Skills and Trades?

Not too long ago, a friend who operates a tool-and-die shop noted that in about ten years America will not have any good tool-and-die men. We simply are not producing or training any, he told me, or if we are, he was simply unaware of it. He then recalled how he had started out in a tool-and-die shop at Winchester's in the early thirties for 20 cents an hour. He was paid very little, but then his productivity was little since he was learning. However, from almost his first day he was given things to work on that were actually needed and would be used in a finished product. His work was carefully watched and supervised and as his skill and efficiency increased, he could look forward to receiving salary increases. In contrast to this, he pointed out that the high wages they had to pay today precluded him from training anyone in the same manner that he had been trained.

I then brought up the subject of trade schools, and asked if tool-and-die men were not being developed there. In his opinion, he said, there are very few first class tool-and-die men teaching in trade schools, "since if they were, they would be employed in some shop." (While I realize that there are exceptions to his statement, there still is, nevertheless, some truth in the saying that "those who can, do, and those who can't, teach.") Secondly, he pointed out, there is no real motivation in a trade school. Proficiency in trade school may result in a higher mark, but proficiency in a shop can result in higher pay—and the latter motivation is far stronger than the former. Also, when the students work on something in school, it is nothing that anyone really wants, "maybe a paperweight or a gift for your mother or girl friend, but rarely, as contrasted to shop work, anything that someone is expected to buy." This factor has an impact on motivation, concentration and diligence. "They also waste time," he said, "on other extraneous subjects that are unnecessary to becoming a good tool-and-die man."

I asked Frank how he would rank a tool-and-die graduate of our local trade school. Frank stated that during World War II the tool-and-die industry ran a training program for the local defense industries. In his opinion, a "good" graduate of our local trade school was the equivalent to what an average enrolee in that program achieved in six months, "Now," Frank explained, "it takes from five to six years to become a good tool-and-die man, so a graduate of a trade school is at 18 years of age only approximately six months into his craft. And at 18 he has developed a strong interest in girls and feels the need to make money, but he isn't remotely equipped to earn the money he needs and he is often reluctant, at this late date, to pay the price necessary to learn." He would have been much better off if he could have entered a private tool-and-die shop at 14 or 15, so that at 18 he would be close to becoming economically self-sufficient. Society would not have had to waste the money for his "training" in a trade school, and while he was learning a trade at no expense to either himself or society, he would have also been making an economic contribution to society—he would no longer have been making paperweights for mom and dad, but goods required by society.

How an Apprentice Relationship Instills Pride in Workmanship

Several years ago, my father did something that I don't think would be duplicated today by another trained American mechanic, though I am convinced that others trained like my father might have acted in a similar manner. After my father retired from active carpentry, he would occasionally work for a contractor who was the son of his former partner. It was on one such occasion that I came home earlier than usual and was surprised to find my father already home. When I inquired why he was home so early, my father simply indicated, without being specific, that he had had a "disagreement" with Irving Beer, the contractor, and so simply quit and came home. That evening, Irving Beer called to inquire about my father. "Irv, what happened?" I asked. "Your father is really a character," Irving replied, and then related the following story.

Beer had contracted to remodel a three-family house, converting it into six units, and my father was completing the trim on one of the rooms when he ran out of baseboard. When new baseboard was brought to him, it was a different size than what he had already nailed on. When he questioned this he was informed that it was "perfectly okay" to use this mismatched baseboard. My father, however, simply refused to use it. Coincidentally, the owner of the property happened to be inspecting the building and so both he and the contractor were now assuring my father that it was perfectly all right for him to nail up the wrong size baseboard —soon insisting that he do so. It was at that point that my father gathered up his tools and left.

My initial reaction, as I recall, was one of sheer amazement that my father could have been so stubborn. After all, if the owner didn't care whether he had a room trimmed with mismatched baseboard, why should my father? So after this conversation I sought out my father, hoping to point out to him why I thought his actions were unjustified. I found my father reading his newspaper in the living room. "Pa," I said, "I just finished speaking with Irving Beer; he told me why you left the job today." "So," my father replied, adjusting his glasses and continuing to concentrate on his newspaper. "Pa, if the owner of a building wants to pay you for nailing up different size baseboard, that's his business. Frankly, if he wanted you to nail the baseboard up the wall and across the ceiling, you should have done it. After all, he is paying you for your time and so you should give him what he wants." My father lowered his newspaper and with some annoyance said, "If he wants different size baseboard in a room, let him nail it up, I can't do it."

It wasn't until years later that I understood what my father had meant. It was that you could not pay him to do poor work—an attitude which, at that time, I did not even comprehend. Today, in America, it often seems that one cannot pay for any other kind.

For example, I recently accompanied a friend who was apartment hunting. In what might be described a luxury building, the one-bedroom apartment we were inspecting rented for $310 a month. When I walked into the kitchen, the floor for some reason seemed very busy and somewhat odd. It therefore attracted my attention, and I found myself staring at it until I discovered the reason. The floor had been finished in squares of vinyl tiles designed in a pebble pattern. They had been laid, however, without any concern for matching this pattern and so the floor generally gave the appearance of a checkerboard—except where tiles had *accidentally* been matched correctly, thus upsetting the checkerboard pattern established by the incorrectly laid tiles. It had been these tiles that had jolted my visual senses. Thus, it would appear that now we can't even get *good* bad workmanship.

The reason that one could not pay my father to do poor work was that he was a product of the European apprenticeship system, which had also been the American apprenticeship system until it was destroyed by government interference. My father had high standards of craftsmanship literally beaten into him, so that it was truly impossible for him to work in any other fashion.

All through my youth, I would hear countless stories of my father's apprenticeship to the husband of a second cousin in Hungary. How his father had taken him there as a boy of 12 from Galicia, in Poland. How he was poorly fed and poorly quartered. How he had run away and been returned. How he had spent his first year merely as a kitchen helper (this was how his tutor apparently secured household help for his wife). How he spent his second year learning how to make mouldings, finishing furniture, and sharpening tools. It is important to note that everything my father did or made was done directly for his tutor. If a tool was not sharpened just right, it would interfere with his teacher's work and so my father would soon discover his mentor's dissatisfaction by getting a crack on the head. He would be sure to get it right the next time. If my father polished a table destined for one of his teacher's customers and if the gloss was not perfect—"Idiot, you call that a finish?"—wham, again, over the head. He would be careful to get the gloss perfect the next time. While it is certainly true that my father was hit, poorly fed, and made to work for nothing, still by the age of 17 this cruel and oppressive teacher had turned a poor, unskilled youth into a knowledgeable and superb craftsman and given him the ability to support himself and a family any place in the world. Within days after my father's arrival in America at the age of 18, he was employed installing bar fixtures in New York City—productive, self-sufficient and confident of his future.

While I am certainly not advocating a return to the indentured apprenticeship system of the past, nor a revival of the type of excesses that system perhaps encouraged, still we must find the cause and a solution for the deteriorating quality of American workmanship, our deteriorating productive capacity, and the consequential loss of our foreign and domestic markets. If the old-style apprenticeship system produced child labor and corporal punishment, it also produced craftsmanship and pride in workmanship. We have, of course, eliminated child labor and corporal punishment, but what the public hasn't yet grasped is that in the process, we may have also eliminated good workmanship and an adequate labor force. There must be a better balance than the one we apparently struck. Would many of America's hardcore unemployed be better off today had they been exposed to my father's training, so that at age 17 they at least had a trade? No, they were forced to stay in public school until age 16, even encouraged to remain until 18, and were then cast out into the economy with little to show in academic terms for all those years, and possessing no employable skills. There is a Talmudic injunction that says, "He who does not teach his son a trade, teaches him to steal." It is apparent that America, influenced and encouraged by government, has been teaching many of its youth to steal.

10

How Unions Victimize the Worker

What's Wrong with Unions

American unionism is a proper subject for discussion in this book dealing with the monetary, economic, and social crimes of the U.S. government. Had unions never received the support of the U.S. government, they would not exert the destructive influence that they do today. Organized labor would not exist if the government subjected it to the same laws governing monopoly, extortion, intimidation, destruction of property, and physical force and violence that are routinely applied against other segments of society. The destructiveness of unionism can be blamed on those politicians who traded union votes and union money for national economic health, national strength, and national social and economic morality.

If the U.S. economy collapses, the biggest losers, apart from the retired, will be America's industrial and urban workers. Runaway inflation will wipe out their accumulated savings, which are almost always kept in such conservative dollar holdings as savings accounts, government bonds, credit unions, savings and loan associations, cash value life insurance, and public and private pensions. If this happens, a large share of the blame will rest squarely with America's labor "leaders." The American labor movement should be recognized for the destructive force it is. Next to the U.S. government, it is the most destructive force in the American economy.

Unionism's chief *economic* function now is to justify the salaries, expense allowances, and other prerogatives of its officials. Correctly understood, unions are simply another type of business, and like all businesses they function primarily for the benefit of those who control them. Unions differ from other businesses in that the federal government has granted them exceptional powers. Moreover, most union leaders have conned millions of their members and the American public into believing that they exist for the welfare of their membership and society. Like the Social Security system, American unionism has been relatively sacrosanct despite its shocking abuses. Like Social Security it is betraying those who believe in it. Unfortunately, rank-and-file union members are unaware of the nature of the betrayal.

Besides providing union officials with large salaries and offering organized crime a fertile area of activity, what functions does organized labor perform? (1) It promotes work rules that limit worker productivity and frustrate efficiency. (2) It compels the employment of unnecessary workers—"featherbedding." (3) It restricts entry into unionized crafts in order to create a labor monopoly condition that ups the price of unionized labor.

Let's examine how organized labor's promotion of these influences militates against the economic interests of the worker and the nation.

There are many, of course, who believe that a union serves its members by increasing wages and improving working conditions. Unfortunately, the union's publicized successes in achieving wage increases, often through the intimidating power of mass picketing and other lawless acts, obscure the actual long-term destruction of jobs and employment that such labor intimidation achieves. It should be apparent that wages and profits result from a working partnership of those who *supply the capital* and those who *supply the labor*. If a firm's efficiency is impaired, then its ability to sell the productivity of its labor force is also impaired, and so the very existence of that labor force is jeopardized. Despite this, however, we see many unions overtly reducing the productive capacity of workers, thereby unnecessarily lowering the competitive position of the very firms that the workers depend on for employment.

Increased productivity raises earnings and improves working conditions. By resisting improvements in productive methods, by restricting output, and by forcing the employment of unnecessary labor, unions reduce productivity and so reduce potential employee wages and benefits. But before treating these matters specifically, let's consider the real needs of both union and nonunion workers.

The average American worker will never be rich. There is simply not enough wealth to go around. Therefore, the average worker has an even greater stake than does an upper-income executive in a productive American economy; the worker's "good life" depends on the economy's ability to turn out an abundance of inexpensive goods and services.[1]

[1]An economy which turned out a profusion of inexpensive goods would reduce, to a great extent, the advantages and prerogatives of being rich. The American economy had the potential for producing that type of abundance, but it has been thwarted by the destructive policies of self-serving politicians and union "leaders."

If America produced houses as efficiently and inexpensively as possible, who would benefit the most? The rich? No, the rich can afford inefficient and wasteful construction, and the added cost hardly interferes with their lifestyle. The actual beneficiaries of a highly efficient construction industry would be the nation's workers; they would pay less money for housing and have more to spend on other needs. To the extent that painters' unions refuse to use rollers and employ spraying techniques, that bricklayers limit the number of bricks they will lay, and that other construction unions employ similar tactics, the higher the housing costs, to the particular disadvantage of the American worker. Thus, the bricklayer who lays fewer bricks, presumably to secure a higher wage for himself, pays higher prices for his necessities because other unions use the same tactics against him. Whatever advantage he thinks he gained is largely dissipated by the practices of all other unions.

It is true that if one or two unions "featherbedded" and limited their productivity, they could extract an economic advantage from society. When all unions do it, however, no one gains. All that has been achieved is that the unions have combined collectively to lower the nation's total productivity. Consequently, with less productivity to go around, the nation must suffer a lower standard of living —which must fall heaviest on the low-income and blue-collar worker. When unions, with government sanction and protection, force the railroads to employ unneeded firemen on diesels and compel the use of unnecessary crews, this increases transportation costs. These unnecessary costs are reflected in higher prices for everything that moves by rail, and they fall heaviest on the nation's workers. When the teamsters, through their awesome monopolistic power to paralyze the trucking industry, increase wages and benefits without increasing productivity, these increased costs raise the price of all goods that move by truck.

How and why did the worker allow the creation of a force so detrimental to his own economic interest? Unfortunately, most union members do not realize how unions actually work *against* their own welfare. The bricklayer, whose union restricts the number of bricks he can lay, can be persuaded that the union is protecting his employment since he believes that the union is apparently "stretching" the amount of available work. The bricklayer is making the wrong assumption. Actually, the union is unnecessarily increasing the cost of laying brick. This will automatically cause builders to lay less brick as they pursue more economic methods of construction, thereby reducing employment opportunities for bricklayers. Of course, this may be too complicated for the rank-and-file bricklayer to understand. All he can see is the *immediate effect* of limiting productivity, which he interprets as the union's contribution toward increasing his employment opportunities, when actually the union is destroying employment opportunities. The union, of course, tries to compensate for this shrinkage in employment by limiting those allowed to qualify for membership. Thus, relatively fewer workers are permitted to compete for the reduced amount of work available in order to maintain salary levels for those already in the union.

While there are other factors that cause drops in employment, excessive union wage and other demands play a key role. While some may suggest other reasons for the drop, in the area of maritime employment, for example, no other possibility exists. Because of the absence here of other economic forces, the maritime industry is a good demonstration of the causal relationship of union pressure and the reduction in total employment. Maritime unions increased the wages of their members so excessively that U.S. merchant ships could no longer compete with the ships of other nations. As a result, the U.S. merchant fleet has been drastically reduced, thereby reducing maritime employment.[1] And the railroad, still the most efficient method of transportation and once a valuable national asset, is tottering on bankruptcy, thanks in part to union featherbedding and thanks in part to government taxation and regulation.

The examples of how unions wipe out jobs are virtually endless. At one time, lathers—workers who nailed up the thin wooden strips that held the plaster in wall construction—had a strong union. However, as the lathers kept forcing up their wages, thereby increasing the cost of installing lathes, builders shifted to wire mesh, then to sheetrock, and finally eliminated the lathers.[2]

Americans often long for the Big Band Era, as if the reason for the current popularity of four- and six-piece combos can be traced to a change in musical tastes. What happened, though, was that the musicians' unions simply increased musicians' salaries to the point where it was no longer feasible to support the number of large bands. Here is another example of how unionism actually reduces the quality of life. Given the increases of capital and technological advances, it should be easier to afford the luxury of larger bands now than it was in the 1930s and 1940s. But it is actually more difficult. This, I suggest, is an example of economic regression, expanding GNP figures notwithstanding.

While most readers can probably cite other examples of union corruption that our government permits, even encourages, I wish to offer some examples I have experienced.

A friend of mine who was getting married asked me if I would take some 35mm pictures of the wedding with his camera. At the wedding, I chatted with the regular photographer who had been engaged. He casually mentioned that while he had no objection to my taking pictures, that if he wanted to, he could stop me from doing so. He said if the groom "wanted 35 mm, I could have arranged to have another

[1]For the first ten years of this century, the U.S. merchant fleet held steady at about 22 percent of the arriving and departing tonnage from American ports, moving to 51 percent right after World War I. For the next 20 years, this percentage held around 35 percent or better, climbing to 65 percent at the close of World War II. From the position of the world's preeminent merchant carrier in 1945, the United States has dropped to the point where less than 10 percent of arriving and departing tonnage moves on U.S. flagships—even with government subsidies. The fact that this percentage is less than half of what it was at the beginning of the century and a sixth of what it was in 1945 (when unionism was not a factor) suggests the type of increased economic stagnation that unions can cause.

[2]It might be argued that it was efficient building techniques that eliminated lathers. While this is undoubtedly true, it is also true that it was the *higher costs* of laying lathes that spurred the development of the techniques.

photographer here." *Technically*, I was apparently depriving another photographer from working. The photographer said, however, that since at least one photographer had been engaged, he would not object to my taking pictures. Intrigued by this logic, I asked, "Suppose the groom had a brother who was a good amateur photographer and decided to let him take all the wedding pictures instead of hiring a professional photographer?"

"He wouldn't have been allowed to take any pictures," the photographer replied.

"How could you stop him?"

"Well, a union inspector makes the rounds where weddings and parties of this type are held and if he saw a nonunion photographer taking pictures, he would call all union personnel off the job. That would be your waiters and musicians, so the wedding would be without music and for all intents and purposes without food. That would provide enough pressure to eliminate the nonunion photographer."

"But that was the groom's *brother,*" I insisted. "Certainly he must have the constitutional right to take pictures of his own brother's wedding?"

To this question, the photographer simply shrugged but was noncommittal. "By the way," I asked, "what studio do you work for?" He replied, "my own"—he was the *boss* and *owner*. Thus the photographer's "union" was in reality a "union" of bosses and not of employees, and thus was not a union but a guild. It had simply usurped the name union in order to practice the type of coercion that only unions can get away with.

Here's another example of union activity. I met a young chap who told me this story. Bill was a glazier employed by a New Haven glass company and was sent to install glass in the New York City area. Since this was out of the jurisdiction of the New Haven local, arrangements had to be made to hire a local glazier; apparently the rule was that one local man had to be engaged for every outside man brought in. Bill met the man as arranged, but was soon told by him that the size of the glass they were to install required the services of three men. Bill assured me that the glass could easily be installed by two men, as was done routinely in New Haven. He pointed this out to the local man, who was unmoved and insisted that the union be called to supply another man. Since Bill had no authority to hire another man, he called his company and they authorized the extra man. The local glazier then called his union. However, there were no other glaziers available. This being the case, the local glazier agreed to do the work with Bill (proving quite obviously that the additional man was not needed). A few days later, however, the New Haven firm received a bill from the New York union charging them for the services of a man that was never supplied and the New Haven firm paid it, not wishing to antagonize a union whose cooperation they might again need in the future. Now is this unionism? This is extortion plain and simple, and is quite characteristic of union practices in the New York City area.

My father, who had organized a carpenters' local and was a staunch union man, never expected wages for nothing. To him, unionism meant seeking an honest day's pay for an honest day's work. Today, many unions attempt to get a day's pay for a half-day's work or, as in the above case, a day's pay for no work at all—which, of course, is legalized stealing. Even granting that initially unions might have served some purpose in helping to eliminate some of the excesses of management, surely it must now be evident that the pendulum has swung far to the other side and it is now the unions that the American public needs protection against.

For another example, one day I was seated in the office of an individual who owned and operated a men's garment factory. We were discussing business conditions. When the subject of unions came up, he recounted the following incident. Lou explained that when a new garment was designed, a piece-work rate for the operators making the garment had to be established and approved by the union shop steward. The previous week Lou had determined that he would pay the operators 18 cents on a particular garment so he summoned the union steward to his office to agree on the price. However, the steward offered him the following proposition: "Lou, offer us 17 cents and we'll compromise for 17½ cents." So, Lou did just that. It was then made to appear that Lou had offered the operators 17 cents, but through the efforts of their union they would now receive 17½ cents. Because of their union, the operators would now receive a half-cent less per garment but would think that the union had secured them a half-cent more.

Do Public Employees Have a Right to Strike?

Over the last few years strikes by public employees have become commonplace, especially strikes by public school teachers. Public employees, of course, have no right to strike. As Calvin Coolidge, then governor of Massachusetts, aptly put it once regarding the Boston police strike in 1919: no public employee has a right to strike against the public anytime. This prohibition can be applied with equal force to all public employees, not just police.

Public employees who strike should, at the very least, lose all seniority status and tenure they might have earned, and their union and its officials should be heavily penalized. Public employees should be prohibited from striking because no balance of economic interests and economic forces exists as there is in a strike against a private business. When employees of a private business strike, they can be opposed by employers whose economic interest will be directly opposed to their demands, so at least a balance of economic forces is struck. The employers will weigh and judge the strikers' demands in terms of their economic reasonableness, by attempting to relate these demands to their impact on prices and profits.

No such economic balance exists when public employees strike. In essence, the public employees strike against themselves. They negotiate with public officials who may be beholden to them for votes and so may grant unwarranted wage concessions for fear of losing their votes and financial support at the next election. Consequently, there is no proper balance of economic interests when public employees strike. Also, since government is not a profit-making institution and since it does not sell its services on a voluntary basis (one is compelled to accept the services offered and pay the price they set), it may be impossible to judge whether the demands of public employees are economically reasonable.

The salaries of public employees, therefore, must be determined conscientiously, by objective deliberation by public officials, with due regard for the public's *capacity* to pay and its *other needs*. They cannot be determined by public employees threatening to cut off vital public services in an attempt to force a community to pay them not what they may be worth or what society can afford, but what they *demand*. Of course, no one *forces* anyone to become a public school teacher, a policeman, a fireman, or a sanitation worker. So, when individuals voluntarily enter these professions they must realize that they have simply surrendered their right to strike—there are, as we all know, other compensating benefits for being on the public payroll. If one feels that he must have the right to strike, then let him leave public employment and find employment in the private sector where his right to strike is secure. Public officials, therefore, who do not deal severely with striking public employees should themselves be severely dealt with by the voters.

What Direction Must Unions Now Take?

Given the current state of the economy, the pros and cons of unionism are meaningless. At stake is the issue of whether rioting, plundering, and bloodshed are going to spread across the land, especially in our large cities, bringing destruction to what many Americans, union and nonunion alike, have worked so hard to build. Faced with this prospect, I can't conceive of union leadership continuing its "business-as-usual" ways, since this can only bring financial disaster to their active and retired members and could so weaken the U.S. that we would be extremely vulnerable to an outside enemy attack. This, of course, is another reason why a current depression would be far more serious than the Great Depression—in 1929, the United States did not have to worry about a potential external threat. The real threat to every American worker and nonworker, union and nonunion member alike, is that runaway inflation will simply destroy what value U.S. "money" has left. This will, of course, destroy the values of all those pensions that unions have pushed so hard to install.

The people must save themselves and cannot expect the politicians or "union leaders" to do it. The way to avoid a repeat of the 1930s is to make the economy *more productive*. Each individual must be as productive as possible. Every union that has attempted to set limits on the productivity of its members and to cause the employment of unnecessary workers must reverse that policy. Restoring and increasing the dollar's purchasing value is the *only* way to prevent galloping inflation, for now the dollar is only as good as what it will buy. The more the dollar buys, the greater will be its value, and as the dollar buys more, the threat of runaway inflation will subside as will the possible destruction of all union pensions. *But only organized labor now has the power to make the U.S. dollar buy more,* [1] and the dollar will only buy more if Americans produce better and cheaper. This means that the unions, if they really care about their members and the nation's welfare, must begin reversing their traditional position, which has been to force Americans to work less efficiently and less productively. If organized labor does not do this, then union members must realize that when their savings accounts, government bonds, and union, company, and government pensions disappear in the ashes of runaway inflation, it will have been the fault largely of their own labor leaders, who in conjunction with politicians deliberately fanned the flames that turned them into paupers.

[1]Apart from the U.S. government, that is, but the government can no longer be relied upon.

11

The Energy Crisis– How the U.S. Government Planned It

America's energy crisis not only imperils our standard of living, it threatens the very independence of our foreign policy by exposing us to possible blackmail and intimidation by oil-producing nations. From 1970 through September 1973, crude oil imports into the United States doubled, while imports of refined products increased by 50 percent. As a result, U.S. dependence on foreign sources of crude and refined products climbed alarmingly from 23½ percent of domestic consumption in 1970 to nearly 36 percent for the same period of 1973.[1]

Such an increase in our dependence on foreign sources of energy, over whose continued supply we would have little control, has staggering national implications. However, realistic projections suggest that this trend will worsen. In 1972 a study by the Energy Economics Division of Chase Manhattan Bank found that:

> Clearly evident is a sharp decline in the self-suffiency of the United States in respect to its supply of oil. In 1970 the nation was capable of satisfying nearly 80 percent of its needs from domestic sources. But by 1985, it is not likely to be able to satisfy as much as half, *even with the production in Alaska included*.[2] [Italics mine.]

[1]Testifying before the U.S. Senate Finance Committee on February 4, 1974, John E. Swearingen, chairman of the board of the Standard Oil Company (Indiana), said that "it is disturbing to have imports of anything as vital to our economy as oil reaching even a 25 percent level. To see this reliance climb to the equivalent of *one barrel out of every three we consume*, as we did last year, should be enough to alarm every member of this committee and the constituents they represent."

[2]"Outlook for Energy in the United States to 1985," p.44.

This study also pointed out that the Middle East and Africa were the only realistic foreign sources that could satisfy our needs, concluding that the amounts from these areas would represent "nearly 40 percent of the nation's total supply of oil from all sources."

As early as 1970, the U.S. government was aware that this level of dependence on Arab oil was unacceptable. A report of the Cabinet Task Force on Oil Import Control found that in the interests of national security, petroleum imports from the Eastern Hemisphere should not exceed "an absolute maximum" of 10 percent of domestic demand.[1] What action did the U.S. government take to guard the nation from the conditions warned of in this report? Did it immediately launch a program to increase domestic supplies of oil and natural gas with the same vigor and intensity that it displayed in putting Americans on the moon? Hardly. As far as I can determine, the report did not change, by one iota, the government's policy of negligence.

To allow the United States to become dependent on unstable and antagonistic foreign governments for 40 percent of our oil needs is tantamount to us tying a collective noose around our necks, tossing the other end over a tree limb, and handing it to the Arabs. Even at this late hour, constructive steps can be taken to reverse our direction, but unfortunately the U.S. government is pursuing the same policies that led us into the disaster.

America's energy crisis can be blamed squarely on the U.S. government. Despite years of advance warnings, it did nothing to prevent the crisis. Disregarding the nation's real needs, it arranged priorities so that marginal and often wasteful economic projects received support while an obvious vital need, the development of the nation's domestic reserves of oil and natural gas, was ignored. But, as if to demonstrate conclusively its irresponsibility, the government instituted policies which not only hampered and penalized those developing the nation's energy resources, but increased the nation's energy requirements—even in the face of the looming crisis!

Here are some examples of how government helped to create the energy problems that now plague us.

1. In addition to causing many of our other problems, the destruction of U.S. currency by the government is the primary cause of the nation's energy problem. Despite what Americans have been led to believe, the price of oil has not been increased in the last few years—in reality, oil prices have remained relatively the same.

2. Our greater dependence on oil was accelerated by the federal highway program at a time when the nation's railroads were subjected to heavy taxes at all levels of government and forced by the federal government to submit to union featherbedding and other uneconomic labor practices. In many cases, it was

[1] "The Oil Import Question," Cabinet Task Force on Oil Import Controls (Washington, 1970), p. 98.

government encouragement, *government* planning, and *government* subsidies that shifted the nation from more to less efficient means of transportation.

3. Federal Power Commission regulations on natural gas prices distorted supply and demand relationships. Arbitrarily set low prices discouraged the development of greater supplies of natural gas while simultaneously encouraging its greater use. Thus, because the U.S. government set the price of natural gas unnecessarily low—now its price must be set unnecessarily high—some may be forced to go without it altogether. Had natural gas prices been allowed to move normally, they would have stimulated the development of greater supplies while simultaneously encouraging a more realistic appraisal of alternate forms of energy.

4. Emission controls enacted by Congress lowered automobile gas efficiency. In lieu of this (based upon our declining oil resources and increasing needs), American automobile manufacturers should have been required years ago to produce cars achieving greater gas economy.

5. In 1969 Congress passed a "tax reform" act which lowered the oil depletion allowance to 22 percent. A simple look at the oil and gas facts of life then would have shown that the depletion allowance should have been increased as a needed incentive for domestic development of these resources.

In short, U.S. policies have continually compounded past blunders.

The Fallacy Concerning "Higher" Oil Prices

Contrary to what the government and the media proclaim, oil prices over the last four years have actually not been increased at all.

On April 14, 1971, the day before the U.S. government repudiated its obligation to redeem Federal Reserve notes for gold, Middle East crude oil went for $2.33 a barrel. On December 12, 1974, when rates were set at $10.73, gold went for $179.75 an ounce. So, on April 14, 1971, when 35 U.S. dollars equaled an ounce of gold, an ounce of gold ($35÷$2.33) bought 15.02 barrels of oil. However on December 14, 1974 an ounce of gold bought 16.75 barrels of oil ($179.75÷$10.73) so that the price of oil had been reduced 11 percent in terms of gold, the only legitimate money measurement.[1] Had the U.S. government managed its fiscal affairs responsibly and held the value of a U.S. dollar at one thirty fifth of an ounce of gold, the price of oil in terms of dollars wouldn't have risen at all.

That the current high dollar price of oil can be blamed on the suspension of gold convertibility of the dollar is amply reflected in the statements of some oil-producing nations. On September 4, five weeks before the outbreak of the Arab-Israeli war, *Al Anwar*, a Beirut newspaper, quoted Libyan Premier Abdel

[1]True, the price of oil had increased relative to U.S. Federal Reserve notes and other national currencies, but it did so because the government had changed the nature of Federal Reserve notes from legitimate to illegitimate currency (from being convertible to nonconvertible), thereby reducing its value and the value of most other national currencies (the dollar being a reserve currency).

Salam Jalloud as saying "Libya will no longer accept payment in U.S. dollars," adding "the dollar has lost its value and we want a currency that is convertible to gold." In December 1973, the Shah of Iran said "We have no interest in hoarding paper money in banks if inflation makes it worthless."

Contrast these statements with the assurances of Senator Proxmire that "gold has long since abandoned its role as a metal for currency,"[1] and of Treasury Secretary Henry Fowler that it is not gold but "the strength and soundness of the American economy which stands behind the dollar,"[2] as they successfully campaigned in 1968 for the removal of gold backing from U.S. currency.

Before citing the other areas of government culpability, it should be recognized that America's developing energy problem was clearly evident as far back as 1950. But our government apparently did not wake up until the crisis exploded in the fall of 1973.

Figure 31 shows that in 1950 America's oil reserves started declining—the short increase in 1969 was a result of the Alaskan find. In 1949 domestic reserves equaled 13 years of the nation's needs, but by 1970 these reserves had fallen —to eight and a half years. Also, in 1970 total domestic oil production began a sharp decline, while total oil demand continued to rise. A collision course was, therefore, clearly evident.

Figure 32 suggests even a grimmer picture for natural gas. In 1947 America had a 40-year supply of natural gas; however, since then steady erosion of these supplies reduced this to a 13-year supply by 1970. We had steadily reduced the life of our reserves, despite the steady increase in total reserves, because of the vastly increased use of this source of energy—but in 1967, *even our total proven reserves began dropping*. Thus, another clearly evident energy crisis was in the making.

Figure 33 shows the number of wells drilled in the United States. There has been a rather obvious decline since 1956.

Figure 34 shows the decline in the number of drilling rigs in service in the United States and is indicative of a decline in the national interest and capacity for developing our own oil and natural gas resources. While in 1955, 2,686 rotary rigs were operating in the United States, only 1,028 were operating in 1970.

Now this information, I admit, comes from industry publications. So, some may feel that it is unfair to hold our congressmen and government officials responsible for information derived from technical and perhaps "biased" sources.[3] However, if only our political representatives had read some of our more popular newsmagazines, look at what they would have learned.

In its August 30, 1970, issue (three years before the Arab oil embargo of 1973), *Time* ran an article[4] entitled "The Energy Shortage Worsens," which stated that:

[1]Note A, Appendix C

[2]Note I, Appendix C

[3]A good deal of this information was compiled by the U.S. Bureau of Mines, but what use they made of it is a mystery.

[4]Reprinted by permission from TIME, The Weekly Newsmagazine; Copyright Time Inc.

Figure 31

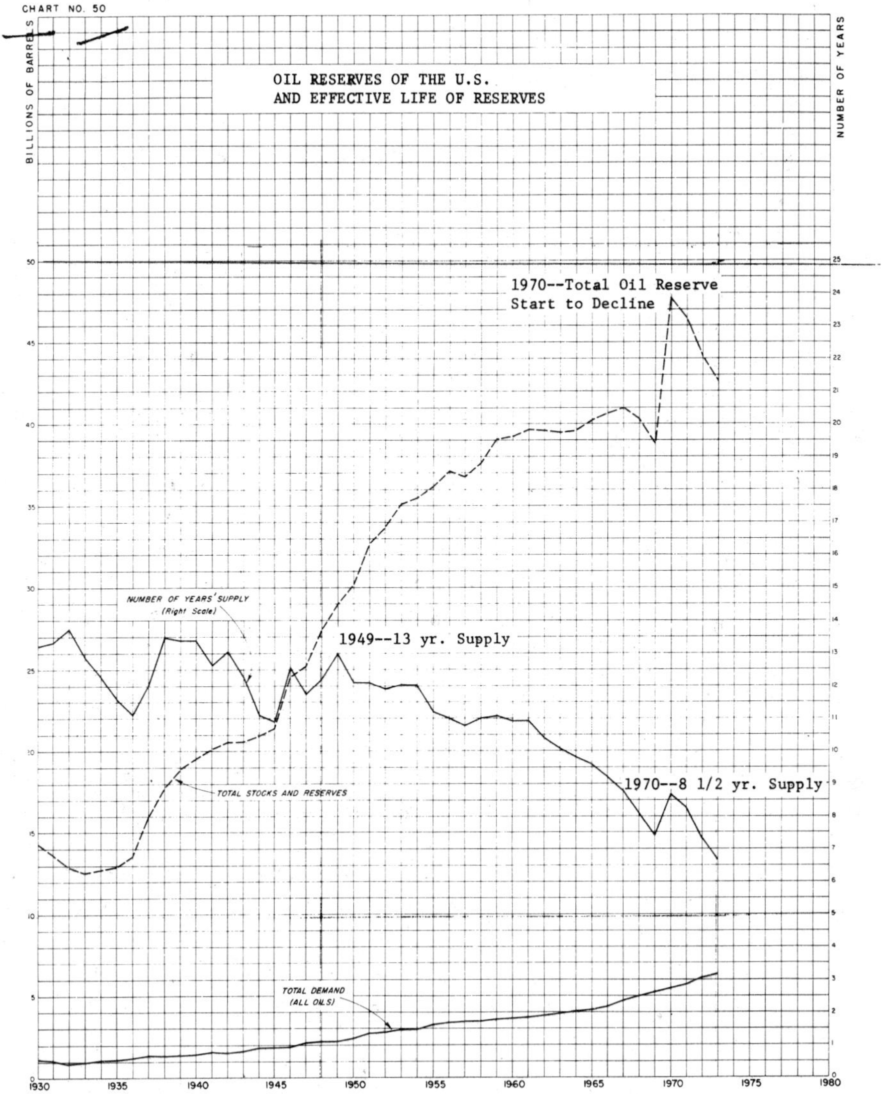

Source: "Twentieth Century Petroleum Statistics," 1974, DeGolyer and MacNaughton, Dallas, Texas

Figure 32

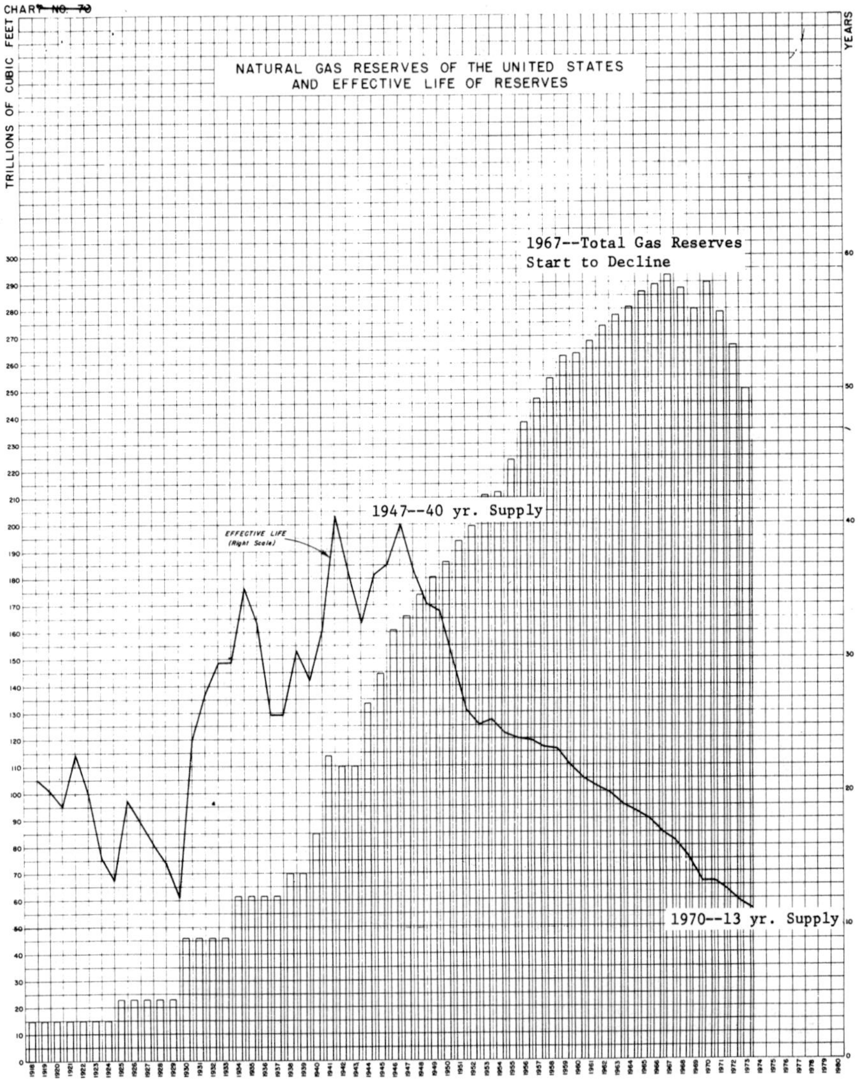

Source: "Twentieth Cantury Petroleum Statistics," 1974, DeGolyer and MacNaughton, Dallas, Texas

1972--12 yr. Supply

Figure 33

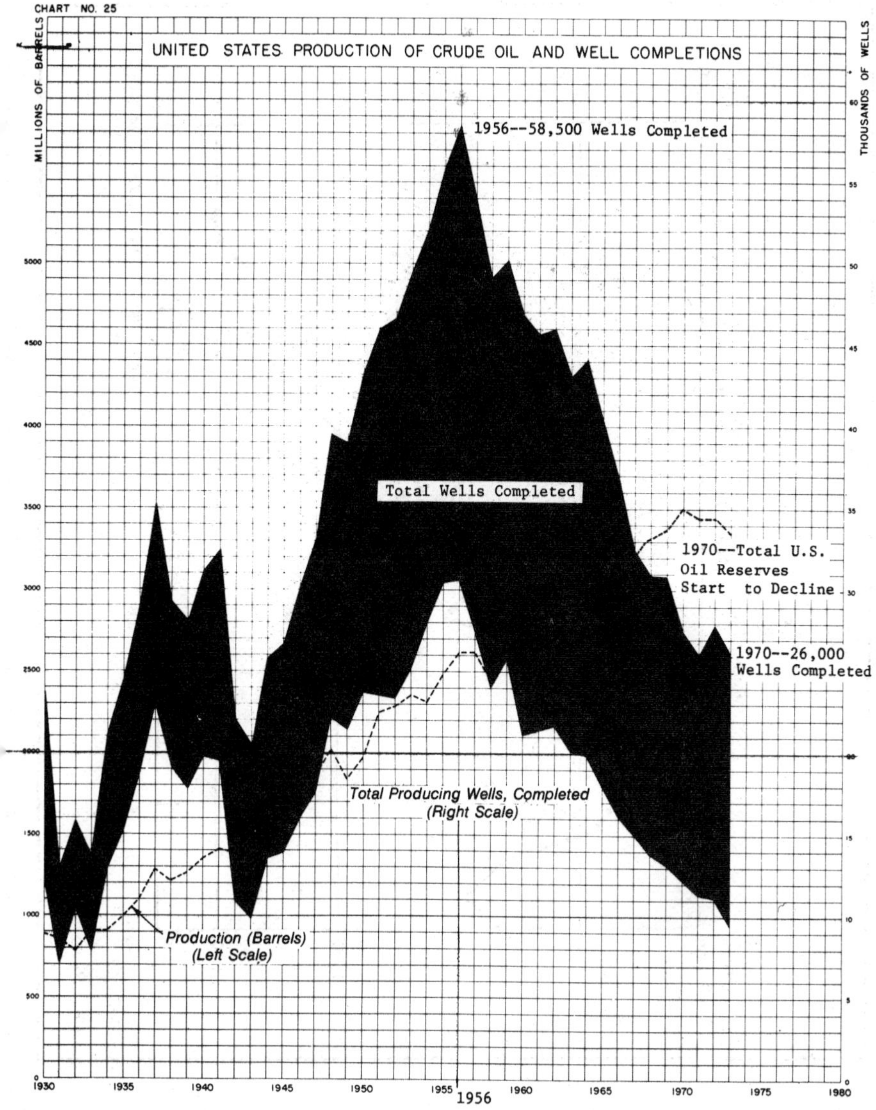
CHART NO. 25
UNITED STATES PRODUCTION OF CRUDE OIL AND WELL COMPLETIONS
MILLIONS OF BARRELS
THOUSANDS OF WELLS
1956--58,500 Wells Completed
Total Wells Completed
1970--Total U.S. Oil Reserves Start to Decline
1970--26,000 Wells Completed
Total Producing Wells, Completed (Right Scale)
Production (Barrels) (Left Scale)
1956
1930
1935
1940
1945
1950
1955
1960
1965
1970
1975
1980

Figure 34

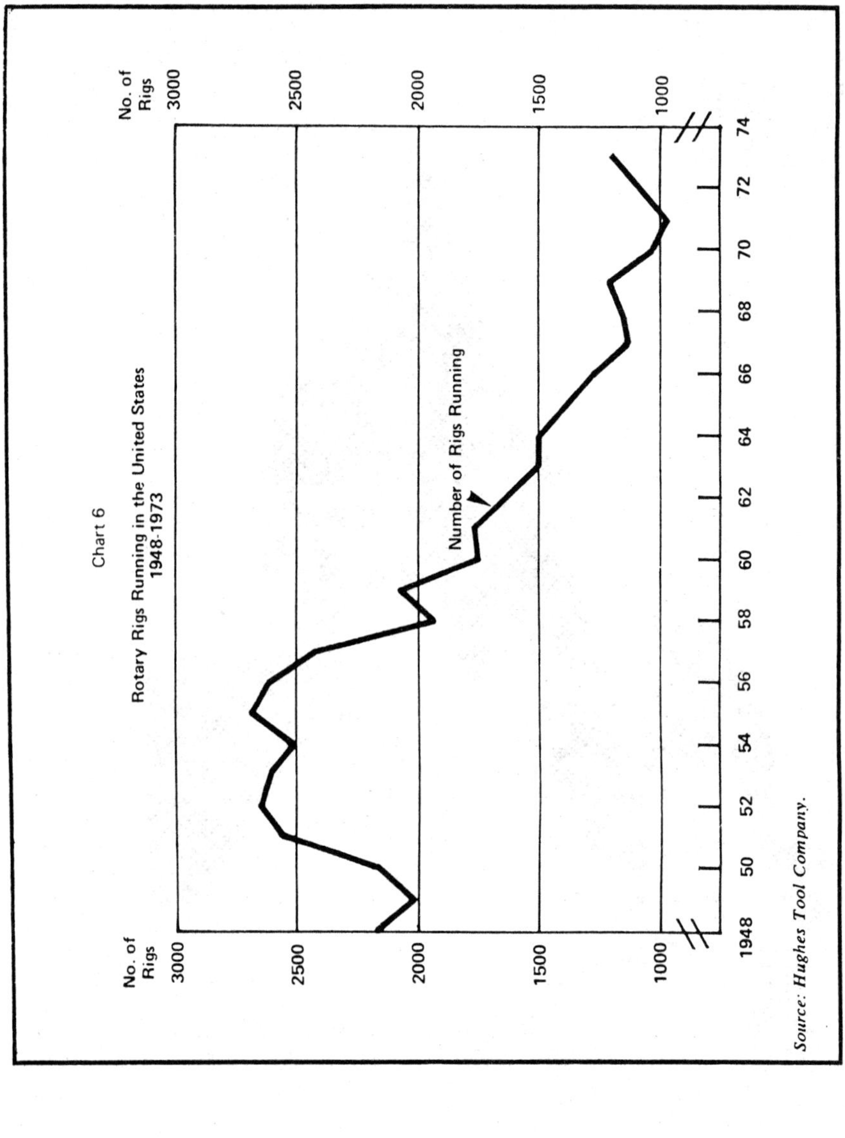

Source: Hughes Tool Company.

Incredible as it seems in the resource-rich U.S., this summer's discomfiting electric-power cutbacks are likely to be only a prelude to many more pervasive difficulties. Part of the industrial U.S. is running short of the main sources of energy—coal, fuel oil, and natural gas. Some forms of rationing have already been imposed, and more may be necessary if winter brings severe weather, strikes in crucial spots, pipeline breaks or new trouble in the Middle East. Though few if any residential consumers may be asked to curtail their use of fuel or power, there is a possibility of factory closings.

The article then cited instances across the land:

When the town of Braintree, Mass., sought bids recently for oil to run its generating plant for another year, none were submitted. Though there is plenty of natural gas available in the Southwest, the fuel has become so scarce on the East Coast that the Elizabethtown (N.J.) Gas Co. is turning away all new commercial and industrial customers. East Ohio Gas Co., which serves Cleveland and adjacent industrial centers, has turned down orders from steel, chemical and rubber companies for 27 billion cu. feet of gas. The company has also warned that a severe cold spell will cause a repetition of last winter's shortage, when local factories had to close temporarily to provide enough gas to heat homes, schools, and hospitals.

The Acute Phase. The fossil-fuel shortage, warns Chairman John N. Nassakis of the Federal Power Commission, is "the most acute phase of our developing energy crisis." . . . "Never before in peacetime have we faced such serious and widespread shortages of energy," says John Emerson, an economist and power expert for Chase Manhattan Bank. Many analysts believe the problems will be temporary, but some maintain that the energy gap may limit economic growth for years to come.

The article notes that, "incongruously, there is abundant fuel underground." Yet although "proved resources of natural gas have dwindled to an eleven-year supply," the Potential Gas Committee, a study group sponsored by the industry, calculates that the total amount of gas in the U.S., including Alaska, is 1,227 trillion cubic feet—*"enough to maintain production well into the next century."*

The article continued,

. . . exploration for new gas fields has declined sharply partly because investors do not consider the rate of return worth the high risk. The industry, with 40,190,000 commercial, industrial and residential customers, *blames the Federal Power Commission for holding down the price of natural gas to protect consumers*. [Italics mine.]

Perhaps John Q. Public can be excused for not understanding that an energy problem was mounting. He is not *paid* to tend to the overall needs of the American economy. But Congress and the President are; they should be anticipating and preventing such problems. Along these lines, allow me to offer yet another article published five-and-a-half years before the Arab oil embargo. This one is reprinted from *U. S. News and World Report*, January 15, 1968, issue.

Featuring a graph that showed that the drilling of exploratory wells in the United States *was down by 40 percent* between 1957 and 1967, the article also contained one showing how the demand for oil in the United States was soaring sharply, with the demand projected to increase by 99 percent by 1980.

> Now oil-industry executives see trends that cause them to doubt whether the industry can retain its ability to cope with fresh emergencies, or even to meet the coming growth in demand . . . .
>
> One reason is that the search for oil in the U.S. is declining at a time when demand is going up.
>
> The second is growing pressure to change tax laws in a way that, the industry says, will discourage oil discovery and development within the United States . . . .
>
> *The widening gap.* Over the past 10 years, demand for oil and gas in this country has risen about 44 percent. But proved reserves of those forms of energy have gone up only 15 percent . . . .
>
> "At the moment," one [oil] executive explains, "the U.S. is consuming about 12.7 million barrels of oil a day. By 1980, that demand will have risen to 17.5 or 18 million barrels a day. This takes into account the increasing use of other forms of energy, including nuclear power.
>
> "If that is the case—and it is the basis on which we are making our plans—we've got to discover in that interval *78 billion barrels of oil.*
>
> "By contrast, 81 billion barrels have been produced in the U.S. in the entire 108-year history of the oil business up to now."

Can this vast amount of new oil be found?

> "Yes," replies an industry economist. "The U.S. Geological Survey estimates there are still more than 300 billion barrels of oil waiting to be discovered in this country. The big problem is finding it."

The article then listed a "cluster of different but equally stubborn problems": (1) meeting energy demands that by 1980 will be 50 percent larger than in 1968, (2) counteracting a sharp drop in exploratory drilling for new oil reserves, (3) meeting a squeeze between rising production costs and relatively fixed selling prices, and (4) dealing with Congressional moves to change the depletion allowance for petroleum and other minerals that oil men contend is essential to spur further exploration.

One problem cited was the increased cost and greater risk involved in the pursuit of more domestic supplies of oil and gas. An oil company executive is quoted as saying:

> "All the low-cost oil and gas fields in this country already have been discovered," according to one oil-company president . . . "From here on, the risks and costs are to climb steadily higher. The essential requirement is a continuous and enormous flow of capital available to those who have the necessary combination of know-how and willingness to take risks."
>
> The average cost of drilling an oil well today is about $56,000—whether the venture is a success or a failure.

The article closed on this prophetic note:

> "If we learned one lesson from last summer's Middle East crisis," an oil authority recently declared, "it should be the need for maintaining a great measure of independence from foreign supplies that might be cut off without warning."
>
> Copyright 1968 U.S. News & World Report, Inc.

However, the article obviously gave the government far more credit than it deserved, since unfolding events demonstrated that the government had learned absolutely nothing from the 1967 crises.

One might have imagined that, at the very least, the government would have provided subsidies to those capable of developing domestic reserves of oil and gas. After all, if the government could at this very time pay farmers about $4 billion a year *not* to grow food, logic would dictate that it offer a *comparable amount* to those capable of finding oil and gas. However, our politicians thought it best to pay Americans not to produce something the country didn't need rather than pay others to produce something the country needed desperately.

How and Why the Government Forced an Increasing Energy Need on the Nation

We have already seen in connection with public education how the government promotes the growth of that which it controls and administers, regardless of the nation's real needs and demands. Obviously, we have too many students in school when it is apparent that more skilled persons are needed. So, also in the transportation industry, what the country needed was the preservation and modernization of its rail system—economically the more efficient method of transportation. Some statistics will show, however, how this vital national asset was allowed to deteriorate. In 1940 there were about 44,000 locomotives in service in the United States. By 1971, this had dwindled to about 29,000, while passenger cars shrunk from 38,000 in 1940 to under 9,000 in 1971. The U.S. rail system was permitted to deteriorate because it was in *private* hands, while the federal government sought to promote those areas of transportation that were in *public* hands. Efficiency and comparative national need had nothing to do with the massive federal highway program.[1]

So, because of the construction of thousands of miles of six-lane highways, more Americans and American merchandise must rely on autos and trucks than on

[1]Politicians strive to spend the public's money at every opportunity. Since the more they can spend, the more they can take in graft and kickbacks and the more power they can wield. A major TV network did a special on the federal highway program and concluded that at least 10 percent of the $25 billion-plus spent was skimmed off in graft and kickbacks.

the far more efficient and less polluting rail transportation. It is pointless to argue that Americans prefer to ride in their automobiles than ride on trains since they were never permitted to make a fair choice. Those using the railroads were taxed to help support *three levels of government* while those who rode the highways were *not similarly taxed*. Had the railroads been able to operate without this burden of taxation (as are the nationalized railroads of other countries) and had they not been compelled to hire unnecessary employees, they would have been able to provide rail service at far lower rates, in far more comfort, and with far better service and so would have had far greater appeal than the dilapidated and bankrupted system that confronts the public today. The public is unaware that it was the efforts of irresponsible government and irresponsible unionism that led to our rail system's moribund state. It has been the government's lavish subsidy to a public highway system at the expense of our private rail system that has now made the country far more dependent on oil than it ever needed to be.

Some of the same destructive forces were also at work in inhibiting and discouraging the growth of our privately operated urban transportation systems, which further encouraged dependence and reliance on uneconomic forms of auto transportation.

Before leaving the subject of automobiles, I should clarify a misconception concerning them—namely that much of America's prosperity depends on a high volume of auto sales. I don't know whether this misconception can be blamed on high-powered sales campaigns by the automobile industry or on governmental efforts to generate high but meaningless GNP figures. Often we are reminded that one out of every eight Americans "depends" on the automobile for employment—that 30 percent of all the glass, 20 percent of all steel, and 60 percent of all rubber we produce is used in the manufacture of automobiles—and carries the implication that if automobiles are not bought in sufficient quantity, many would become unemployed. If these statistics are right, then America is expending too much of its resources on a simple thing such as personal transportation, and automobiles are being used in a frightfully wasteful manner. If so many Americans were not employed wasting time and precious resources making and remaking automobiles that are junked every four or five years, these resources and this productive effort could be directed toward more worthwhile projects, such as (1) building up the nation's crumbling cities, (2) expanding the nation's rail and mass transportation systems, (3) expanding the nation's shipbuilding capacity, (4) developing a system of economical helicopter transportation, and (5) developing a rapid and reliable system of mail delivery.

How the Government Created the Natural Gas Shortage and Higher Gas Prices

On June 6, 1975, the Federal Power Commission announced a 19.78 percent shortage of gas needed to meet firm contracts through March 1976. Probable curtailments would be 45 percent greater than had existed for the prior twelve-month period ending April 1, 1975, but some carriers would experience even more drastic shortages. For example, the United Gas Pipe Line Company, serving the South Central and Southeastern states would face a shortage of 47.65 percent, while a 46.56 percent shortage was forecast for the Trunkline Gas Company, serving the North Central, Middle Atlantic, South Central, and Southeastern states. Curtailments of over 25 percent were projected for eight other pipeline carriers. Such drastic curtailments in contracted fuel agreements portend severe economic hardships for many firms, their employees, and their customers.

On June 30, 1975, the Federal Energy Administration ordered 25 utility companies to burn coal rather than oil or natural gas in 74 power plants. It also ordered 41 companies building new power plants to build them with coal-burning capabilities. The FEA hopes in this manner to save 64 million barrels of oil and 88 billion cubic feet of gas annually. Stating that these orders "are essential to encourage power plants to use coal," FEA Administrator Frank G. Zarb also noted that "American consumers are paying a dear price because of our increasing vulnerability and dependence on foreign oil (and lack of gas)." Zarb could have more accurately stated that "American consumers are paying dear oil prices and suffering a gas shortage because of the irresponsibility of Washington politicians." The American public little realizes that both problems can be blamed squarely on the U.S. government.

During the 1960s the average price of FPC-controlled interstate gas was 16.67 cents per 1,000 cubic feet.[1] To appreciate the amount of gas this is, an average family would not burn up this amount with a month's cooking. The fact that the family's monthly gas bill might be $6 or $7 was largely the result of refining charges, transportation charges, distribution charges, and taxes, while the actual producer received less than 16 cents for his trouble. That gives some idea of how low the FPC set the price of natural gas.

Of course, the availability of cheap fuel, priced below its fair market value, encouraged an unrealistic expansion in the demand for natural gas, so that by 1970 natural gas was industry's *most important* source of primary energy, supplying 49 percent of its total needs, with oil supplying 29 percent, and coal 22 percent.

At the same time the government's unrealistic price controls discouraged the development of additional natural gas reserves to balance this growing demand. The government's action in controlling the price of natural gas at an artificially low level, presumably in the interest of the consumer will, now, punish the consumer severely. The government's action in keeping natural gas prices artificially low can be likened to holding a basketball under water and when one's hand is removed the basketball bobs up. That is what is now happening to natural gas prices as the government is finally forced, as a result of the gas shortage it created, to remove its

[1]As late as 1973, it *averaged* 22.58 cents.

interfering hand from the ball of natural gas which it had for so long held under the water of a rising gas demand.

Had natural gas prices never been artificially controlled, increases in natural gas prices would have been slow, orderly, self-corrective. Price increases would have immediately created increased incentives for developing greater supplies, which would have then served to dampen further price increases, while increasing costs would have forced consumers to evaluate other fuels more realistically. Higher free-market prices would have acted, therefore, to reduce demand and increase supply, bringing supply and demand into balance at the most equitable price. If the U.S. government had never tried to control the price of natural gas, there would be no gas shortage today with all its dislocations and distortions.[1]

Emission Controls, Auto Safety Standards, and Other Such Government Meddling

Many of the nation's pollution problems can be traced to increased use of the automobile. Responsibility for this pollution rests with the federal government, which over the years has fostered and promoted this form of transportation. Over the last 40 years, America's more efficient forms of privately owned mass transportation should have been spared the destructive impact of irresponsible taxation, which routinely confiscated valuable capital needed for maintaining and improving service. Had this capital not been squandered by the federal government on wasteful and senseless projects having a lesser national priority than the maintenance of an efficient and modern mass transportation system, pollution would not have become a national problem.

Certainly by 1968 it should have been obvious to our political leaders that America could no longer afford gasoline-guzzlers from Detroit. But American politicians rarely save America from crises since they seldom act until the crises develop. It has now been proposed that automobile pollution standards be modified and deferred so that gas mileage might be improved by some 40 percent. Based upon all the evidence that was available, this should have been done at least five years ago, when the auto industry should have been required to produce cars achieving greater gas economy. If this had been done at that time, I doubt that today we would have to be concerned about an Arab oil boycott.

If, in this case, I appear inconsistent in accepting government interference, I am not. The primary duty of government is the defense of the nation. Adequate

[1]Current shortage of natural gas and its new unavoidable move to much higher prices will create hardships for those who were encouraged by the government to rely on a plentiful and cheap supply. Commenting on this folly, the Chase Manhattan's previously cited study noted that "as a result of the unnatural market conditions created by the price controls imposed on natural gas at the well, the consumers of all forms of energy have been living a fool's paradise. But the time has now run out."

supplies of energy are vital for that defense and enable the government to pursue a strong and independent foreign policy. Individual citizens cannot be expected to have either the knowledge or the ability to act responsibly to protect themselves and the nation from falling energy reserves. Only the government has the expertise and power to correct this situation. And if better gas economy would have materially helped our energy position, as it would, then the government, in my judgment, had every right to require it.

As far back as 1969, therefore, the U.S. government should have required that automobiles be engineered with increased gas efficiency. But incredibly, in the interests of reducing pollution (a condition largely created by the government itself), the government introduced requirements that *reduced* gas efficiency even further, thereby increasing the nation's dependence on imported oil. If the U.S. government thought emission controls were essential, then this should have been coupled with requirements that would have also reduced gas consumption. Autos might have been required to be made smaller and lighter to compensate for the loss of economy resulting from emission controls. But the government, in addition to emission controls, added requirements for new safety devices which additionally increased car weight and further increased gas consumption.

I have personally felt that while making automobiles safer is a worthy objective, at some point the law of diminishing returns sets in and the added cost and inconvenience may not be worth it. Life itself is a risk and many people are simply prepared to take risks that others are not. Elimination of risk costs money, and many would rather take the risk and pocket the saving. Short of compelling all citizens to drive around in Sherman tanks, how safe can government mandate automobiles to be? Should some be denied automotive transportation simply because they cannot afford the safest kind that bureaucrats can devise? Anyone like myself, who has owned a 1974 auto and was not mechanically inclined enough to disconnect the automatic seat belts must have, on more than one occasion, cursed those meddling bureaucrats who wouldn't let one move his car five feet without first buckling up. This was especially a lot of fun when one was making a number of short stops with children and packages.

I had always suspected that the reason the U.S. government did not require Detroit to produce automobiles with greater gas economy is that the government (as well as state and local governments) had a vested interest in inefficient automobiles—since this produces more in the way of gasoline taxes. According to *Platt's Oilgram Price Service,* the average tax on a gallon of gasoline in 1973 was approximately 12 cents. The U.S. government alone collected approximately $3½ billion in gasoline taxes, and this amount would obviously drop if Americans used less gas. I do not know that this was indeed the reason for the government's reluctance to require better gasoline mileage from Detroit—but since energy conservation was every bit as important (if not more so) as additional safety devices and pollution control, it certainly does seem suspicious.

The Lowering of the Depletion Allowance

As far back as 1968, based upon the wealth of statistics and readily available information plus the events surrounding the 1967 Arab-Israeli war, speedy development of domestic reserves of energy, especially oil and natural gas, became a national priority. To stimulate increased development of our own domestic sources of energy, the government could have subsidized the development of additional reserves, or encouraged the industry to increase its own development efforts based upon increased profit incentives. Profit incentives for the oil and gas industry could have been increased by either allowing prices to rise, thereby increasing profits, or allowing prices to remain the same but cutting taxes, in which case increasing profits would not be earned at the expense of consumers.

In 1969 the government could have spurred the domestic oil and gas industry had it raised the depletion allowance from 27½ percent to 35, 50, or even 100 percent, thereby allowing the industry to retain more profit while not increasing oil or gas prices.

Let us assume that the government recognized the peril of our falling oil and gas reserves and, wanting to reverse this trend as quickly as possible, simply provided that all those who invested in the development of domestic supplies of oil and gas would be permitted to recover tax-free income. Can the reader conceive of the additional capital that would have been diverted by the investing public and the major oil companies toward the development of America's oil and gas resources? I can only speculate, but I doubt whether America would now be having its current problems had this been done as late as 1969.

But what did the U.S. government do in the face of the impending crisis? It *reduced* the depletion allowance, thereby discouraging the development of domestic reserves. The decrease in drilling activity was thereby accelerated. But why, one might ask, would our government *reduce* incentives when there was such an obvious need to *increase* them? Well, the government felt that it needed the additional revenues that reducing the depletion allowance would provide. The government initially gained approximately $313 million[1] from this act, so now it had even more money to spend on its many "worthwhile" projects.

In 1970, the government spent approximately $11 billion on "aid to education" so this additional revenue financed three percent of that "aid." Our politicians in their infinite wisdom concluded that it was more important that the nation be provided with more sociologists, psychologists, philosophers and historians than more oil and gas.

In July 1973, the General Accounting Office charged the U.S. Department of Agriculture with unnecessarily paying out more than $300 million in export subsidies in connection with the Soviet wheat deal. So domestic drillers were

[1] "The Tax Burden on the Domestic Oil and Gas Industry," Petroleum Industry Research Foundation (New York, 1972), p.22.

additionally taxed in order to subsidize low-cost wheat ($1.63–$1.65 a bushel) for our communist friends.

Actually, by 1969 our energy position had become so shaky that the government could have, with complete justification, wiped out all income taxes paid by those finding oil and gas in order to stimulate increased development. Many Americans do not realize that about 75 percent of all domestic oil and gas wells are drilled by so-called independent producers, as contrasted to the major oil companies. There are about 4,000 such independents, whose prospects of raising drilling money from potential investors would have obviously soared if they could have offered investors "tax-free income" because of the depletion allowance being raised to 100 percent. Assuming we wiped out not only the revenue that might be lost as a result of the increase in the depletion allowance, but all *federal* income taxes,[1] what was really involved? Remember, for the sake of illustration, I am excusing *all* oil and gas *income* taxes; what the government had to do was merely excuse income taxes only on wells drilled *after* 1968. But I am willing to use an even larger figure in the interests of simplicity.

Figure 35 indicates the total amount the domestic oil and gas industry spent drilling domestic oil and gas wells, onshore and offshore. This has amounted to approximately $2½ billion per year. Obviously, if the oil and gas industry could have retained the $1.2 billion they paid in federal income taxes as well as the added capital that this tax inducement would have generated, a substantial boost would have been given to America's domestic oil and gas industry, which would have alleviated our current energy problems.

But, how badly would the nation have suffered had the federal government lost $1.2 billion in revenue? Federal receipts for 1969-73 averaged nearly $200 billion. Income taxes on oil and gas revenue thus amounted to only one-half of 1 percent of federal revenues. Could the government have squeezed this amount of fat out of its budget in order to create a powerful stimulus to make America self-sufficient in oil and gas? There is no question about that, since the budget was at least 25 percent fat already.

A report by the U.S. Senate Appropriations Committee revealed that foreign

[1]Figures supplied by the Petroleum Industry Research Foundation, Inc., show that the estimated domestic taxes of the U.S. petroleum industry were as follows:

	1970	**1971**	**1972**
Federal income taxes (in billions)	1.3	1.2	1.2
Other direct taxes	2.1	2.3	2.4
Total (excluding sales and excise)	3.4	3.5	3.6

The tax payments do not include the $10 billion-plus also paid in excise, state, and sales taxes. So even if federal income taxes were eliminated, there still should be a number of other industry taxes which would themselves increase with increased drilling activity.

Figure 35

ESTIMATED COSTS OF DRILLING AND EQUIPPING TOTAL WELLS IN THE UNITED STATES

(1) Year	(2) Total Wells Drilled	(3) Cost ($000's)	(4) Average Cost per Well (Dollars)
1959	49,563	2,651,096	53,489
1960	44,133	2,424,418	54,900
1961	43,988	2,398,163	54,518
1962	43,944	2,576,675	58,635
1963	41,853	2,302,864	55,023
1964	43,486	2,427,367	55,820
1965	39,596	2,401,437	60,648
1966	34,521	2,360,740	68,386
1967	31,538	2,299,178	72,902
1968	29,576	2,409,360	81,463
1969	29,481	2,610,671	88,554
1970	27,177	2,578,682	94,885
1971	25,040	2,371,491	94,708
1972	26,443	2,814,166	106,424

Authority: Joint Association Survey of the U.S. Oil and Gas Producing Industry

aid programs for fiscal 1973 would total $17.5 billion.[1] So our politicians considered it essential that America substantially weaken its energy position in order to fund a mere 6.8 percent of its global giveaway programs.

As the study by Chase Manhattan Bank's Energy Economics Division points out:

> In the fifteen years ranging from 1955 to 1970, the domestic petroleum industry spent a total of 68 billion dollars on its efforts to find more petroleum. And it drilled a total of 653 thousand wells. For its efforts, the industry found 50 billion barrels of crude oil, 10 billion barrels of other petroleum liquids, and 296 billion cubic feet of gas. In terms of energy value, the gas discovered was the equivalent of 88 percent of the amount of oil found. To have discovered enough oil and gas to satisfy all of the nation's needs during the period and also maintain a realistic inventory of proved reserves, the industry would have had to increase its drilling effort by 75 percent and spend an additional 50 billion dollars.[2]

[1]This amount (including the $7.3 billion loaned by the Export-Import Bank) was five times greater than the $3.12 billion supposedly authorized, prompting the report to state: "In truth, however, this [the formal appropriation] is but a relatively small segment of our total foreign aid package, and to unnecessarily fragment it is to belittle the very real burden which the American people are called upon to carry . . ." Senate Report No. 92-1231, p. 5.

[2]*Outlook for Energy in the United States to 1985*, p. 39.

America is in serious trouble today because an additional $50 billion was not spent developing our own energy resources. Over the last ten years, the federal government has routinely paid farmers about $3 billion a year *not* to grow food, while spending some $20 billion to reach the moon. Americans can take great satisfaction in knowing that, in lieu of spending money to provide the nation with sufficient quantities of energy, the government thought it best to spend the money fostering higher food prices and planting Old Glory on the moon.

Those Unconscionable Oil Profits

While I don't enjoy paying any more for a product than the next person, the political hue and cry in '73 following the increase in gas prices was just too much. It is true that America's oil companies increased their profits substantially in 1973. It is also true that most of these profits—more than 85 percent—were generated outside the United States, as Figure 36 shows.

Chase Manhattan's special petroleum report,[1] from which Figure 36 was taken, pointed out the reasons for these higher profits, not the least of which was that

> early in 1973 the dollar was devalued. And, in the process of the necessary conversion from various other currencies, dollars were automatically increased on the books of many petroleum companies. Thus, an action of U.S. government contributed directly and significantly to the growth of earnings of these companies.

Figure 36

COMPARISON OF PROFITS
30 Major Oil Companies*
1972-1973

Profits	1973	1972	Change from 1972: Millions of Dollars	Change from 1972: Percent
	Millions of Dollars			
United States	4354	3656	+ 698	+ 19.1
Rest of world	7368	3204	+4164	+130.0
Worldwide	11,722	6860	+4862	+ 70.9

*All but four of these being American organizations. However, the report noted in 1972 they (the four foreign corporations) were severely depressed. Because of the unusual development in 1973, the earnings of these four companies were much improved and that recovery alone accounted for more than one-third of the profit gain for the entire 30-company group.

[1]*The Profit Situation*, a Special Petroleum Report, Energy Economics Division, Chase Manhattan Bank, New York, April 1974.

Pointing out that "nearly one-fourth of the worldwide increase in profits can be attributed to devaluation alone," the report cited other factors that had contributed to the increased oil profits, such as the sharp increase in tanker profits. But what was unconscionable is that America's politicians conveyed the impression that the substantial increase in oil profits came out of the hide of the American public—which was obviously not the case. The following, however, illustrates rather forcefully the hypocrisy that abounds in the nation's capital and the double standards applied by legislators. Politicians obviously regard the bilking of billions upon billions from the public as perfectly proper when carried out by the government, but let a private concern *appear* to be earning additional profits and their righteous protests reach deafening proportions.

In a letter of July 12, 1973, to Roy Ash, Director of the Office of Management and Budget, and to Robert E. Hampton, Chairman of the Civil Service Commission, the General Accounting Office accused the Department of Labor's Bureau of Labor Statistics of violating "legislative pay principles" in a survey it conducted of salaries in private industry. This survey was used to determine pay scales for federal employees and the GAO claimed that the Bureau gave disproportionate weight to higher paying jobs. The GAO stated that this resulted in unwarranted pay increases which gave federal employees more than $250 extra annually and would cost the taxpayers at least *a billion dollars extra each year*.

Please note again Figure 36 which indicates the "unconscionable" 1973 oil profits earned by the 30 major oil companies whose activities are continually monitored by Chase Manhattan Bank. As indicated, only $698 million of their increased profits can be attributed to the domestic American market. This, as one can see, is substantially less than the billion dollars that was swindled from the American taxpayer by only one federal agency, namely the Department of Labor's Bureau of Labor Statistics. Thus, this one department of government conned the American public out of 40 percent more than the total increase in domestic oil profits as earned by the top 30 oil companies—which had been characterized by many politicians as "unconscionable." Naturally, there was no comparable display of righteous indignation regarding this far larger government ripoff of the American taxpayer.

In any event, suggestions that profits are "unconscionable" imply that they were earned unfairly, and of course, the only way that could have been done is if the oil companies had unfairly and oppressively overcharged their customers. Figure 37 shows the average price of gas in the U.S. since 1945. I am informed that the quality of today's gasoline is superior to that of 30 years ago; so, given a better grade of gas, the price of gasoline only increased 86 percent (column B) from 1945 to 1974. During the same period of time, the government increased the cost of first class mail from three to eight cents and the penny postcard to six cents while it reduced postal service in half. So, while the price of gasoline was going up 86 percent, the government was increasing the cost of first class mail approximately 300 percent and the postal card approximately 1,000 percent (adjusted for a 50

Figure 37

AVERAGE U.S. GASOLINE PRICES
1945-1974

Year	(a) Dealer Tank Wagon (ex. tax)	(b) Service Station (ex. tax)	(c) Service Station (incl. tax)
1974	30.53 cents	40.41 cents	52.41 cents
1973	19.48	26.88	38.82
1972	17.72	24.46	36.13
1971	18.11	25.20	36.43
1970	17.68	24.55	35.69
1969	17.11	23.85	34.84
1968	16.51	22.93	33.71
1967	16.31	22.55	33.16
1966	15.83	21.57	32.08
1965	15.38	20.70	31.15
1964	14.82	19.98	30.35
1963	15.22	20.11	30.42
1962	15.45	20.36	30.64
1961	15.80	20.53	30.76
1960	16.08	20.99	31.13
1955	16.18	21.42	29.07
1950	15.10	20.08	26.76
1945	10.33	14.48	20.50

Source: Platts Oilgram Price Service

percent reduction in services). Sharp increases in gasoline prices in 1974 were caused largely by having to pay for imported oil with a devalued dollar and thus were mostly the fault of the government and not the oil companies. Despite this, gasoline prices in 1974 were still only 179 percent greater[1] than 1945 prices while further increases in postal rates, ten cents for first class and eight cents for a postal card, meant that they had increased first class mail 460 percent and a postal card 1,400 percent in terms of their 1945 prices. Now, it is true that the U.S. postal service doesn't earn any "unconscionable profits." Personally, I would feel much better if it did, but who is obviously better serving the needs of the American consumer—the oil companies that have only increased their product by 179 percent (while the cost of most other commodities has increased 400 percent) while delivering a better product or the U.S. government which, though not making a profit, has merely raised the cost of its service some 460 and 1,400 percent?

It should, of course, be immaterial how much profit a corporation makes, the

[1]Total prices (*including taxes*) increased by only 156 percent (column C).

only important consideration being the price it charges, and the services it gives, relative to what is available in the marketplace. Should anyone really care if Henry Ford made millions in profits by capitalizing on an automobile shortage or if Thomas Edison made millions capitalizing on a lighting shortage? We are now confronted by politicians proclaiming that the oil industry will not be permitted to make undeserved profits by taking advantage of the current energy shortage. Nonsense!

The only way that the energy crisis can ever be licked is for the oil industry to hurry up and make as much profit as possible using, of course, these profits to drill even more oil and gas wells and to search for and develop alternate sources of energy. Huge expenditures of capital are required for such research and development and for drilling the number of oil and gas wells (and to pay for all the dry holes) that are necessary if our current shortages are to be overcome and if our dependency on foreign oil is to be reduced. These huge capital expenditures can *only* be generated by comparably huge profits. The nation must realize that if it wants a good deal more oil and gas, there must be room for profit in order to get the job done. If the government and the nation foolishly worry about how much profit the oil and gas industry is making, rather than worrying about the sufficiency of the nation's oil and gas reserves, then our energy problems will never be solved and the nation will be forced to settle down into a substantially lower standard of living embodying all kinds of domestic and global problems for a long time to come. Higher (after-tax!) oil and gas profits will mean increased supplies and lower prices while lower oil profits will mean decreased supplies and higher prices.

The Situation Today and What Must Be Done to End the Energy "Shortage"

The government recently spent approximately $5 million for an 800-page study by the Federal Energy Administration concerning methods to cope with the oil crisis. Like most government studies, it was a waste of the taxpayers' money. In the next few pages the reader will find the only possible solution to the nation's energy problem, and the government could have had it for considerably less than $5 million. If a shortage exists in a given commodity, there is only one of two ways to eliminate it: *increase* the supply of the commodity or *reduce* the demand for the commodity.

So far, almost all government efforts in connection with the oil shortage have concentrated on reducing demand. Rationing attempts to reduce demand, a tax on gasoline attempts to reduce demand, a tax on imported oil attempts to make it more expensive and again attempts to dampen demand. In short, all government efforts to relieve the energy shortage, aside from suggesting that navy petroleum reserves be opened, that there be a delay in more stringent emission controls, and that offshore leasing be expedited, have been concentrated on reducing the public's demand for energy. This, of course, requires very little imagination or creativity, requiring only that the public agree to accept a lower standard of living.

The American public and American industry, however, have developed certain energy needs, and to believe that the government can reduce the amount of energy needed without serious economic hardship and distortion is ludicrous. A two-car family, for example, living in the suburbs, may be totally dependent on automobile transportation. And certainly a ten-cent increase on a gallon of gasoline to discourage its use, as was proposed, would create a financial hardship as well as present some real practical problems. Consider the effect that this would have on those businesses that rely on auto traffic for their livelihood. Incidentally, the proposed increase of 10 cents per gallon is further proof that oil profits were not "unconscionable." To suggest that the government must increase the cost of gasoline to discourage its use is to suggest that the oil companies were selling gas too cheaply so as to overstimulate its use. So the government stepped in and forced an increase in prices. If gasoline prices were too cheap, how could oil profits have been "unconscionable"? The government has not yet offered a positive program for *increasing the supplies* of oil and gas. It would certainly help alleviate the energy shortage enormously if a way could be found to harness all the gas that is generated in the nation's capital and then channel it into the nation's power system. Lord knows how many cities that would light up. But since this may be years away from development, we must be more practical in our search to increase domestic supplies of energy.

The only way that supplies of oil and gas can be increased is if the profitability involved in their production is increased, and this is the only way that our dependence on foreign oil can be eliminated. We must simply start paying the price for all the years of government irresponsibility—and the sooner we start, the better. We will pay the price one way or another. In lieu of the $5-million, 800-page report on how to cope with the oil crisis, here is the answer in just 13 words: *The government has to get its hands off the oil and gas industry.*

What does this mean? First of all, it must remove all artificially and bureaucratically controlled prices. The government is still maintaining a ceiling of 43 cents per thousand cubic feet on natural gas. This must be decontrolled so that price of natural gas can seek its own realistic level.

Domestic oil prices must be decontrolled. Currently domestic oil prices are controlled at around $5.25 per barrel for old oil and decontrolled for new oil, which is bringing about $12.00 to $13.00 per barrel. So-called stripper wells, those pumping at the rate of ten barrels of oil a day or less, are also decontrolled. Thus, one is encouraged to allow a well that is capable of producing fifteen barrels of oil a day to produce only ten.

Ford's Energy Proposals

In essence, President Ford proposed in his 1975 State of the Union address to deregulate oil and gas prices, suspend stringent emission control standards, seek greater auto gas economy, and urge legislation to permit commercial development of naval reserves and the outer continental shelf. These are all admissions that these programs and provisions should have been adopted long ago. But the President's program again largely concentrates on reducing demand for energy while providing very little that would increase supplies of energy. Government plans for developing alternate supplies of energy are, in my opinion, just so much pie in the sky.

Deregulation of U.S. crude oil prices would mean that the price of about 60 percent of our crude oil would rise from around $5.25 a barrel to the prevailing world price of $11, while the price of natural gas would also be allowed to seek its *natural* level. Normally, higher prices for oil and gas would stimulate increased productivity but, incredibly, the American public is to be robbed of the stimulus by the government, since the government intends to levy a "windfall profits tax . . . to ensure that oil producers do not profit unduly." So it is the government and not the energy producers that is to profit from the energy shortage, to the tune of $30 billion—$18 billion from excise fees to be levied on oil and gas and $12 billion supposedly coming from the "windfall profits" tax.

President Ford claims that the government will return most of this revenue to the people in the form of tax cuts. In my judgment, if this program is ever adopted, a good deal of this revenue will simply be dissipated and wasted as it moves from the people to the bureaucrats.

The President's intention of levying a $3 tariff on imported oil and an additional tax of $2 on domestic oil would mean that oil prices would be higher in America than in the other parts of the world. What would this mean to our petro-chemical industry, which would thus be compelled to pay higher prices for raw materials than, say, their Japanese competitors? Could American producers of synthetics and other similar products requiring an oil base compete? In my judgment, artificially raising oil and natural gas prices above their natural levels and world levels is sheer lunacy. President Ford's proposal to levy a tax of 37 cents per 1,000 cubic feet of natural gas, in one fell swoop, is an act that would raise the price of natural gas by 250 percent over the long-controlled government price of 16 cents per m.c.f. and raise it 86 percent over the present controlled price of 43 cents[1] per m.c.f. This is in itself a clear indictment of the government's long-standing policy to control the price of natural gas.

Many of Ford's other proposals, such as his optimistic plans for developing 200 major nuclear power plants, 250 coal mines, and the "drilling of many thousands of new oil wells," as well as "the insulation of 18 million homes," are, as I have stated, just so much window dressing and hardly address themselves to the country's immediate energy problem. The tragic implication in President Ford's program is that it reveals the administration's lack of understanding of the substantial capital requirements and additional incentives that will be needed by the oil and gas industry to overcome an energy crisis caused by years of government neglect and economic and monetary stupidity. All the benefits that would inure to the

[1]Increased to 52 cents for new gas in January 1975.

industry and to the consumer by the deregulation of oil and gas and their higher prices are thus to be wiped out by the proposed $30 billion of new taxes levied on the industry. In all fairness to President Ford, however, it must be said that so far the Democrats have given no indication of offering anything that would be helpful either.

Stop Being Conned on This Vital Issue

In the months ahead, the American public will hear various energy programs offered by Republicans and Democrats, neither of whom will be seriously seeking a realistic solution of the country's energy problems, but will only be vying to find a "program" that will be most politically popular and for which they can claim credit. Since higher oil and gas prices are inevitable, politicians of both parties will, I am sure, be calling for "windfall-profit" taxes. The American public must not be taken in by such political pandering and should ask, what will the government do with any increased taxes taken from the oil and gas industry? Drill more oil and gas wells? Hasn't the public come to realize that the government is wasting enough of their money already? How much more is it to be allowed to waste? How will monies taken by the government from the oil and gas industry help solve our domestic energy shortage?

Should a citizen really care how much another might profit in undertaking to supply him with enough energy at reasonable prices to satisfy all his needs? Would he and the nation really be better off if they did not have enough oil and gas to meet their needs, as long as this prevented others from reaping large profits?

If the oil and gas industry were operated by the government like the space program, foreign aid, and education, we would probably be drilling for oil and gas in every state in the union, with a few crews looking for hydrocarbons on the moon, and with billions of our tax dollars spent in the effort. Fortunately it is private enterprise, not government, that is required to develop the nation's supplies of oil and gas. And to do the job, the oil and gas industry does not need a government subsidy. All it needs is for government to get off its back.

The depletion allowance should be increased to 100 percent. We need oil and gas so desperately we should be willing to let all those willing and capable of finding it have the bonus of tax-free income.[1]

We simply cannot afford to increase our dependence on foreign oil. The solution to our energy problem is well within our grasp if only the U.S. government will allow the powerful forces of free enterprise to operate, unencumbered by Washington's restraining and destructive influences.

[1]With the Tax Reduction Act of 1975 (effective March 29, 1975), the government further limited the depletion allowance, with increasing limitations continuing to 1984. Thus America's politicians, as if to underscore and flaunt their stupidity, decided to reduce incentives for developing the nation's critical supply of oil and gas when sanity demanded that incentives be increased.

12

The Uneconomists and the Science of "SIIGometrics"

If medical schools turned out doctors as competent as the economists turned out by our universities, Americans would undoubtedly have the highest death rate of any nation on earth. It's frightening how some economists who know nothing about economics acquire such awesome reputations.

Understand the poor economists' dilemma and you can understand their absurd ideas and economic nostrums. For example, suppose an individual with considerable medical training and a highly compelling urge to heal the sick discovered, after his huge investment in time and money, that the best way to cure the sick was to leave them alone—that is, not interfere with their bodies' normal recuperative powers.[1] To discover such a thing, after spending so much time and effort hoping to cure somebody, would be a terrible blow. Suppose that such an individual was now approached by another, seeking medical advice and treatment on the basis of all those years the former had spent training. It is understandable that some would be reluctant to say honestly, "My medical training has taught me that I am powerless to help you and that your own body is better equipped to help itself through the operation of powerful natural forces, than I am who can only employ weak artificial devices." How much, after all, could a doctor charge for advice like that?

This, in essence, is the position of most "economists." If they were taught

[1]This, of course, is not the case. I am making this assumption purely for illustration.

properly, they would have learned that an economy functions best if it is left alone, allowing free choice and competition to perform their miracles. Apparently Keynesian egos are such that they are not satisfied with only the intellectual pleasure derived from greater economic understanding and the financial rewards consonant with correct economic analysis. No, they have to *do* something. As economists, they lack the courage to admit that they are no better equipped than a high school dropout to increase society's normal rate of economic growth (in real terms).

In general, economic study[1] equips one to appreciate the economic order and to understand how untrammeled economic forces can provide higher standards of living (in real terms, not dollar terms). A competent economist sees the order, proportion, and reason for economic relationships. He understands the relative and absolute relationships between wages—for example, not only why a physician may earn four times what a barber earns, but why the former's salary is not $300,000 and the latter's not $75,000.[2]

The value of economic understanding today, however, is not in the intellectual and financial rewards it provides. No, its value is in exposing the "economists" who confuse the issues and compound our problems with their "economic" nostrums.

The President's "Economic" Summit

Need proof that American economics is an intellectual wasteland? Look at the front page of the *New York Times* of September 6, 1974. The headline, "Leading Economists Feel Federal Reserve Needs to Ease Monetary Policy," capsulized the main economic thrust of the opening days of President Ford's celebrated conference on inflation. He had summoned 28 of the nation's leading "economists" to a "summit conference" to help fashion what he had described as the nation's "battle plan against a common enemy—inflation."

According to the *Times* account,

> leading economists of widely differing philosophies approached unanimity today in concluding that the time had come for the Federal Reserve Board to ease its relentlessly tough monetary policy affecting money, credit, interest rates and indirectly the stock market. This was the major development at the first of a series of meetings called by President Ford to get ideas on dealing with the nation's economic problems, especially inflation.

[1]Those who refer to economics as the "dismal science" merely confuse the science with many of its practitioners.

[2]There their absolute salaries have changed, but their relative salaries have not. Is there a difference? If so, what is it? What might this tell you about all other wages earned by members of society? How high or low, in dollar terms, can relative wages go? What determines their absolute level at any moment? Are relative wages capable of rising forever? If so, what happens to the value of savings and debts expressed in these same dollar terms? If relative wages are incapable of soaring, what holds them, in absolute terms, to where they are?

That's clear evidence that America's leading economists don't know what they're about. Easing "monetary policy" and abandoning a "tough monetary policy" are euphemisms[1] and ways of saying gingerly "the government should generate more inflation."

President Ford did not need a special economic conference to learn about inflation or how to control it. Alan Greenspan, his economic adviser, could have told him with no fanfare and no difficulty that inflation originated in his Oval Office and on Capitol Hill. Fortunately, Greenspan and Treasury Secretary William Simon persuaded Ford to reject the conference's recommendations.

The conference's sole achievement was that it revealed the intellectual bankruptcy of the power structure of American economics. We shall soon deal with the conference's specific recommendations. But for now, the significance of the conference's suggestion that the government "ease monetary policy" in its battle against inflation must not be forgotten. As the reader will soon discern, Keynesian "economists" really have only one arrow in their economic quiver to use in battle—the arrow of inflation. Once they've shot that arrow, they're spent.

Over the last 40 years Americans have been conned into turning over the economic direction of the nation's economy to so-called Keynesian economists.[2] In short, Keynesians are nothing more than closet socialists. The New Deal, the Fair Deal, the New Frontier, the Great Society were all "covers" for the Keynesian penetration and assault on the U.S. economy.

During these years, Keynesians succeeded in gradually replacing the solid economic rock of honest money, hard work, thrift, and economic incentives on which American society had rested. In its place they substituted papier-mâché unmoney, wild spending, rewards for idleness, and the destruction of economic incentives. The economic rumblings and disturbances that we are now experiencing are merely the shock waves and tremors of an economic foundation that is beginning to give way. There is now simply too much papier-mâché and too little rock left to support us.

The Keynesian solution for any and all economic problems is simply to call for more inflation. That is it. That is the platform that supports all their understanding. Inflation is their god. Inflation is the key that unlocks for them all economic mystery. Keynesians, however, do have one ironclad rule. They never invoke the word "inflation" in vain. As a matter of fact, to the cult, inflation is so sacred it is seldom ever mentioned explicitly. Instead, they have developed a special language that permits them to teach inflation, preach inflation, and to supplicate for and in the name of inflation—all without ever having to utter its holy name!

To those of us who understand how the acid of inflation eats through savings,

[1]Examples of a "Modified SIIG-6" and a "Modified SIIG-5" See page 221.

[2]These "economists" are diciples of John Maynard Keynes (1883-1946). He taught that society's rate of economic growth could be increased by government influencing and manipulating the "money" supply and through increases in government economic and fiscal planning.

destroys thrift, corrodes ambition, and dissolves the very economic underpinning of society, inflation is no god. Inflation represents rather the distillation of all economic ignorance poured into a sterling silver chalice and offered to society as some sparkling, stimulative elixir, when in reality it is a concentration of economic knockout drops.

To help you understand and see through the strange incantations of the Keynesian order, I have prepared a small index of Keynesianisms. It will reveal how Keynesians invoke the spirit of their patron saint inflation without actually mentioning it by name.

The Schiff Index of Keynesianese Inflationary Terminology

SIIG-1[1] "Ease credit." This would enable the banking system to loan out more unmoney, thus "inflating" the unmoney supply.

SIIG-2 "Relax Credit." A variation of No. 1 above.

SIIG-3 "Loosen Credit." Another variation of No. 1 above.

SIIG-4 "Expand Credit." Another variation of No. 1 above.

SIIG-5 "Money is too tight." This implies, of course, that either Nos. 1, 2, 3, 4, or combination of all of them should be adopted.

SIIG-6 "Ease monetary controls." A suggestion that the Federal Reserve Board lower interest rates or lower reserve requirements in order to increase the amount of "unmoney" the banking system could loan out, in order to inflate the "unmoney" supply.

SIIG-7 "Relax monetary controls." Variation of No. 6.

SIIG-8 "Loosen Monetary Controls." Variation of No. 6.

I would interrupt my list at this point to indicate the infinite variety of the above that are possible, simply by employing modifying adverbs such as "a bit," "temporarily," "somewhat," as in "monetary controls should be eased *somewhat*." Inflationary intentions can also be disguised by the the use of such conservative sounding words as "move to" or "undertake"; e.g., "the Federal Reserve should immediately *undertake* to relax monetary controls" (notice the ring of respectability that has). Who would suspect that what was really being said was, "the Federal Reserve had better hurry and print up some more unmoney"?

SIIG-9 "Lower interest rates." The point of lowering interest rates is to make borrowing easier so that the "unmoney" supply can be further *inflated* by additional injections of borrowed "unmoney." Technically a variation of No. 1.

[1]Abbreviated SIIG for "Schiff Index of Inflationary Generators," with individual generators being referred to as SIIG-1, SIIG-2, etc.

SIIG-10 "Stimulate the economy." This involves calls that the federal government exercise its power and influence to expand inflation in one or more areas. It could use its influence to convince the Fed to lower interest rates (No. 9) and reduce reserve requirements (No. 6) while itself cutting taxes and increasing deficit spending (No. 13) or embarking on various government projects (Nos. 14, 15, and 16).

SIIG-11 "The economy needs an expanding supply of currency." This, of course, is getting pretty close to the no-no of calling inflation *inflation* and is stating, quite openly, that the economy "needs more inflation." This bit of Keynesianese was used by Treasury Secretary Fowler when he appeared before the Senate Committee on Banking and Currency urging that the U.S. switch from currency to unmoney.[1]

SIIG-12 "An expansion of note circulation." Actually a slight variation of No. 11 above, and used effectively by William McChesney Martin at the Senate hearing mentioned above, when he also urged Congress to convert U.S. currency to unmoney.[2]

SIIG-13 "A tax cut." When this is done as an anti-recession measure it is done to put more "purchasing power," that is, more "money," in the hands of the people, which is to "inflate" the unmoney supply. If, however, a tax cut were coupled with a comparable reduction in government spending, it would not be inflationary. So, whenever an economist or a politician calls for a tax cut without calling for a comparable cut in government spending, he is calling for *more* inflation.

SIIG-14 "Aid to depressed areas." This is to increase the amount of unmoney going into the depressed area so as to inflate its "unmoney" supply. Thus, inflation is suggested as a cure for falling productivity.

SIIG-15 "The creation of jobs by the federal government to aid the unemployed." The real purpose of all such jobs is *not* to increase society's supply of goods and services but to put more "unmoney" in the hands of the unemployed; therefore, increased levels of inflation is the method selected to help the unemployed.

SIIG-16 "Increases in unemployment insurance." Like the government's misuse of the term *insurance* in connection with the Social Security, the government, likewise misuses the term in connection with unemployment "insurance"—which, despite its alleged virtues, is nevertheless, simply another inflation generator—albeit a little more complicated. The levying of taxes on employers to pay for possible unemployment is an immediate, additional economic cost that must be either absorbed by lower profits (production reduced) or passed on to the consumer in terms of higher prices. In most cases, taxes thus collected are invested by the

[1]Note I, Appendix C.

[2]Note O, Appendix C.

state unemployment funds in U.S. debt obligations, which means the unmoney derived by this tax is sent to Washington and immediatedly spent on some silly government project. When benefits have to be paid, these government debt obligations must be redeemed, which means the federal government will, in all probability, simply crank out more unmoney to redeem its debt obligations. When this new unmoney is dispensed to those who are unemployed, new "purchasing power" is placed into the hands of those who are not themselves producing goods for market. We have thus reduced society's store of goods when the tax was collected, and increased society's supply of unmoney when benefits are paid. Both of these are inflationary.

The inflation caused by the payment of increased unemployment benefits, during a period of falling economic activity, must force prices up or prevent them from coming down. Falling prices during an economic slowdown would help those forced into unemployment; their savings would go that much further, while falling prices would serve as a self-correcting stimulant for a regeneration of buying as prices fell low enough. The present danger to the U.S. economy is that the U.S. government has shackled those self-correcting economic forces, which is why the economy is now suffering the worst of two worlds—inflation and recession—and why the government is powerless to help.

The best form of unemployment insurance is for the government to insure that a healthy nation has honest money and price stability—and if this were done, the very need for unemployment insurance would disappear. But since overall government activity is largely responsible for involuntary unemployment, the country is additionally and needlessly burdened by the distortions caused by unemployment "insurance."

SIIG-17 "Increases in federal spending" (on a variety of projects). Calls for an "increase" or "speed-up" in "government spending" are a catch-all inflationary category since they are used in various ways. The purpose of such programs is to inflate the unmoney supply by means of government spending.

While I only listed 17 SIIGs I do not mean to imply, by any means, that the list is complete. Regard this merely as your "starter list" of SIIGs. You should be able to find many more interesting examples in your daily newspaper. Sometimes they get very complicated and involved, but this list should get you through most of them. Once you get adept at spotting SIIGs you may want to start your own collection of unusual and interesting SIIGs. You might even consider trading them with your friends.

SIIGomastics is a game for the whole family. Who can find the most SIIGs on the front page of the newspaper? Or in the President's economic message to the nation? Or in any given magazine article? Audio-SIIG is played while listening to the radio or watching television. In Audio-SIIG, the first one to hear a SIIG shouts out "SIIG-SIIG," and is scored. Audio-SIIG can provide a lot of fast SIIG action, especially if, say, you were watching Walter Heller on "Meet the Press." In this age of economy, SIIGomastics can provide a good deal of inexpensive family entertainment.

For example, the February 17, 1975, issue of *Time* magazine would have provided an excellent opportunity to play an exciting game of SIIGomastics. In a feature article, the magazine presented the views of *Time*'s "Board of Economists." This board consisted of eight "economists," no less than two—Arthur Okun and Walter Heller—having served as chairman of the President's Council of Economic Advisers.

Would you believe that this five-columned article had *28 SIIGs?* Its caption, "Bigger Tax Cuts for Faster Recovery," immediately provided (since nowhere in the article was there a call for cuts in government spending) us with our very first SIIG as it recommended SIIG-13 as a basis for a faster recovery.

The second and third SIIGs were rather interesting, since the specific phraseology used actually combined the wording of SIIGs 4 and 6. The article stated that most of the members of the Board had "warned" in February 1974 that a "mild recession was coming" and had therefore "urged the government to switch to more expansive fiscal and monetary policies to alleviate the slump." Now while SIIG-4 is "expand credit" and SIIG-6 is "ease monetary controls," I used the "expand" of SIIG-4 and the "monetary" of SIIG-6, which now combined to give me "expand monetary" policies. This technically should be termed a "split altered SIIG-4 and -6" (altered since the word the article used was actually "expansive" and not "expand"). Since the sentence also threw in the word "fiscal," I considered its use as another variation of the word "monetary" and thus gave myself credit for two SIIGs.

Yale's Professor Triffin allowed me to garner my eighth and ninth SIIGs with this sentence. "Robert Triffin, too, favors greater stimulus, but he would also like to see greater emphasis on more selective anti-recession measures such as *bigger housing subsidies.*" [Italics mine.]

Now, the ninth SIIG, of course, I earned with "bigger housing subsidies," a clear-cut case of SIIG-17. This is such an obvious SIIG that any novice SIIGer should have had no trouble spotting it. What was, of course, slightly more challenging was getting the eighth SIIG. Previous to this sentence the article had been discussing what the article termed its "boldest suggestions," which were tax cuts of at least $25 billion that were favored by Board members Walter Heller and "tax specialist" Joseph Pechman. (This, incidentally, had provided me with my seventh SIIG.) Now, the wording "Robert Triffin, *too,* favors greater *stimulus* . . ." actually indicated his agreement with tax cuts previously suggested (however the statement is inconclusive as to whether Triffin was prepared to be as "bold" as were Heller or Pechman). So while the statement does not actually *state* that Triffin recommends a tax cut to stimulate the economy, it *implies* he does, because he agrees with a previously stated SIIG. This is an example of an ''inferred,'' ''implied,'' or ''dangling'' SIIG. Inferred, implied, and dangling SIIGs are the most fun because they're the most challenging.

The fourteenth and fifteenth SIIGs that I found are examples of a ''Double Extended Dipsy-Doodle SIIG'': (A) It's extended since it stretches to three paragraphs, (B) it's a ''dipsy-doodle'' SIIG because it is both for and against inflation at the same time; and (C) it contained two clear SIIGs. These SIIGs were contributed by another member of the panel, Robert Nathan, who, we are informed, is a ''Washington labor economist.'' Nathan stressed ''the need for a much more *expansive* program.'' Now, when economists of this sort use words like ''expansive'' and ''stimulative,'' they always, of course, are referring to the unmoney supply. It is the unmoney supply that is to be ''expanded'' and it is the ''expanded'' unmoney supply that is expected to provide the economic ''stimulation.'' This, then, is a combination of SIIGs 4 and 10.

What distressed Mr. Nathan, however, was the budget's projection of a ''full employment surplus'' which he felt was too ''restrictive.'' A real budgetary surplus has a restrictive influence on the money supply but a ''full employment budget'' is a make-believe surplus that doesn't really exist except in the surrealistic minds of politicians who dream them up. To believe, therefore, that Ford's full employment, make-believe budget surplus represents ''a very restrictive fiscal policy'' and does ''little to slow down inflation'' is to stand logic on its head.

Since all of Ford's actual budgets project huge deficits, they are ''expansive'' inflationary and not ''restrictive'' deflationary. So, when Nathan suggests that budgetary fantasy exerts more influence than does budgetary reality, he is merely admitting to being unable to differentiate fiction from fact.

He is *right*, of course, when he states that Ford's policy will do little to ''slow down inflation.'' Did he really expect projected deficits of $35 billion and $50 billion to slow it down? While Nathan obviously favors inflation (having just recommended an ''altered'' SIIG-4 and -6), his statement that Ford's policies do little to ''slow down inflation'' implies a sympathy on his part for desiring the rate of inflation to be slowed down. However, to be critical then of Ford's budgetary policies because they are *too restrictive* is again to be for inflation by recommending SIIG-5, which, of course, gave me my fifteenth SIIG.[1]

But the biggest clincher, however, that *Time*'s board of ''experts'' was confused came near the end of the article. *Time* reported that ''an overwhelming majority'' of the Board opposed the Ford administration's plan of increasing tariffs and taxes on oil because it felt that this would ''kick prices even higher'' and would add more than 2 percent to ''the consumer price index, which is now rising at an annual rate of 12 percent.''

[1]Technically, an ''altered SIIG-5.'' A true SIIG-5 is to suggest that ''money is too tight.'' To state that fiscal policy is *too restrictive* is another way of saying money is *too tight*.

From this one may conclude that the Board felt that a 12 percent rate of inflation was too high and that previous administrations should, therefore, have pursued far more deflationary policies. But *Time*'s Board contended "with few exceptions" that the bulk of the nation's economic troubles stemmed directly "from policy mistakes of both the Nixon and Ford administrations. The biggest miscalculation in the Board's view was the persistent pursuit of overly restrictive anti-inflation programs."[1]

This statement alone revealed the Board's true quality and character. I was able to capture my last SIIG, another SIIG-5, thereby closing out the article containing 27 SIIGs with this gem:

> On monetary policy the federal government is given low marks for its *stingy* money policies through much of the year. [Italics mine.]

Computing a SIIG-Quotient

The drift of the *Time* article had been revealed in the caption—the article's first SIIG. The article then merely repeated 27 times what had already been forcefully and clearly stated in the caption. Anyone reading the article, however, would have assumed that they were supposed to gather more information in the ensuing five columns than what could be picked up in its caption. Since they could not, they came away confused, thinking they must have missed something profound.

It is possible to evaluate an article's real economic value by its SIIG quotient. The *Time* article had a SIIG quotient of 142 percent. This is derived from the formula $\frac{S}{P} = Sq$, with S equaling the number of SIIGs, P equaling the number of paragraphs in the article, and Sq being the SIIG quotient. In the formula, the P is always expressed horizontally rather than vertically since its developer thought this lent it a little mathematical mystery.[2] Since the *Time* article contained 27 SIIGs

[1] So, Republican administrations which had been so irresponsible as to permit the inflationary rate to jump to 12 percent were now being criticized for pursuing programs that were "overly restrictive" and "anti-inflationary." Of course, these administrations were not solely responsible for this level of inflation; most of it had been generated in the two previous Democratic administrations—where Board members Okun and Heller exercised considerable influence.

With an admitted rate of inflation of 12 percent, one wonders what the rate would have been if these "restrictive anti-inflation programs" had not been adopted. The truth is that previous Republican administrations had *not* adopted anti-inflationary programs. That's why the rate of inflation worsened. It is also obvious that the majority of the panel, being Democrats, felt, out of partisan loyalty, a need to oppose Ford's oil suggestions on some ground. So on what ground did they oppose it? On the ground that it was "inflationary"—while at the same time being critical of both Ford and Nixon for not being *more inflationary*. A better example of doublethink would be hard to come by. Incidentally, SIIGers could have picked up a five-point penalty by counting the statement that our current difficulties were the result of an "overly restrictive anti-inflation program" as a SIIG. Remember, the *science* of SIIGometrics (not to be confused with the "game" of SIIGomastics) is concerned with uncovering and cataloguing disguised and hidden calls for inflation. This statement wasn't even disguised. It was blatant!

[2] In this regard, he was strongly influenced by that Keynesian offshoot—the unscience of econometrics.

in 19 paragraphs, it earned a fairly high SIIG rating. Nothing of any economic value can usually be extracted from any written material when its SIIG quotient goes above 49 percent.

Putting Your SIIG Knowledge to Work on the President's Press Secretary

A pristine example of a SIIG-16 was provided on January 30, 1975, when President Ford's press secretary, Ron Nessen, announced that some 2½ million veterans would receive their GI insurance dividends within the next 45 days instead of throughout the year. The Associated Press quoted Nessen as saying "The President feels that this action will distribute a substantial amount of cash at a time when it is needed to give a boost to consumer spending."

President Ford was thus duplicating what President Kennedy did in the early 1960s, paying GI dividends early in order to put "purchasing power" in the hands of the people. If one were to ask Nessen or any other bureaucrat, politician, or Keynesian how this inflationary act would differ in any economic sense from simply filling up the Strategic Air Command with freshly printed unmoney and flying low over the nation and releasing this "purchasing power" throughout the land, they would be stuck for an answer.

In their confusion to justify the former and not the latter they would say such an airlift (1) is impractical, (2) would not distribute the "new purchasing power" on a uniform or rational basis, and (3) might cause too many people to get trampled in a stampede set off by unmoney floating down from the sky.

The point is they simply could not draw an *economic distinction* between all their fancifully worded programs designed to "stimulate the economy" and the stimulative effect that showering the nation with new unmoney with the help of SAC might accomplish. And while in my judgment their objections are valid in a practical sense, they could be worked out. The SAC method of "stimulating the economy," after all, does offer one big advantage—it would be faster and could get the job done in one fell swoop.

On Becoming an Instant "Economist"—Keynesian-Style

Anyone can become an instant economic expert, Keynesian-style, if he will only learn to say "loosen credit" (or any other SIIG variation thereof) and in addition recommend the launching of at least one brand new government program. This is all there is to it. A parrot, of course, could be trained to say "loosen credit and start more federal programs." If one had been so trained and sent to any number of our past Presidents, it could have been placed on a perch in the Oval Office and the President's Council of Economic Advisers could have been dismissed. One adviser might have been retained simply to attend to the personal needs of the nation's new chief economist. Alan Greenspan is no Keynesian, but since the President obviously does not heed his advice, he might just as well be employing the parrot.

Just to show how this works, here might be a typical example: Suppose a city were sustaining an exceptionally high rate of juvenile unemployment and, because of this, juvenile crime was rising sharply. What advice might we expect from a Keynesian on how to cope with this problem? The Keynesian response would go something like the following:

(1) Government retraining programs should be immediately launched to raise the level of job skills of the unemployed youths in the area in order to render them more employable.

(2) Consideration should be given to the construction of a new multimillion-dollar "skill center," which could not only teach skills, but would provide additional employment opportunities during the period of its construction.

(3) An expanded program of federal projects might be considered whereby increased employment opportunities might be created in such areas as (a) weekly washing of U.S. post offices, court houses, and other federal buildings, whether they needed it or not, and, (b) matching federal grants for expanded programs of leaf-raking in municipal parks and for municipal street cleaning, whereby unemployed youths would be given job preference.

(4) The government might institute a program of educational grants whereby unemployed youths might be shunted off to colleges, thus at least lowering embarrassing unemployment statistics and relieving social pressures.

(5) The government might consider designating the city a disaster area, thereby qualifying it for low-cost federal loans. This should encourage more businesses to go into debt in order to expand and increase employment opportunities in the area—hopefully hiring unemployed juveniles.

Have you noticed how all these "programs" sound vaguely familiar? No matter how complicated, they always involve spending more federal monies.

Making This Type of Analysis and Proposing These Solutions Requires No Economic Understanding, Only a One-Track Imagination

Recommending the spending of money requires no intelligence or understanding. For example, if a friend is down in the dumps, tell him to snap out of it by taking a trip around the world. If your married daughter is unhappy with her home, tell her to get one with an Olympic-size pool in the backyard, a billiard room adjoining the library, and two bowling alleys in the basement. How could she be unhappy in a home like that? If your best friend confides in you that his son has few friends and feels insecure, tell him to get his son a new sports car, a new wardrobe, throw parties for him where he can invite all his peers to listen to the best rock band in town, and buy him a modest 32-foot sailboat. He will soon have plenty of friends and his self-confidence will improve immeasurably.

So, you see how easy it is to make recommendations requiring only the spending of money that sound as if they will really solve the problem. Keynesians find it so easy to recommend the spending of money because they don't really understand what money actually is. They don't know that the acquiring of legitimate money takes effort. Some years ago, when my son Peter was about six years old, he asked for a list of things. However, I quickly informed him that I would not be able to furnish them. When he asked why, I told him that I simply didn't have enough money to buy him all the things he wanted. He then asked why I couldn't go to the office and get the money. Peter, like all little children, did not understand the relationship between money and hard work, between money and effort. If one could indeed come by money as easily as dropping by the office and picking some up, it, of course, would not make sense not to buy everything one needed, nor would it make sense to establish a realistic order of economic priorities.

Keynesians are like little children when it comes to understanding money. In their view, money can be acquired with no more effort than it takes to run a government printing press—so why not spend money on anything and everything? Instead of telling daddy to run down to the office to "pick some up," they tell the government to run down and "pick some up" at the Federal Reserve.

Let us now consider the type of realistic economic advice that the city with the high juvenile unemployment rate should receive to help it solve its problems.

High unemployment is indicative that the city's youths are unemployable because of the high mandatory wages that are required by law, and because profits are too low in the area to provide the economic incentives for employers to hire more workers. Therefore, to create employment for juveniles in this area, we must eliminate artificial wage barriers interfering with employment and allow wages to adjust to their natural level based upon the forces of supply and demand, and increase profit potential in the area as a stimulus to employment. Some cooperation would, of course, be required from the federal government to implement this program, but long-term substantial employment can only be maintained by *eliminating* government influences.[1]

All Keynesian recommendations boil down to the same message: spend more money, generate more inflation. Look at the recommendations that emerged from President Ford's conference on inflation:

(1) That a cut in federal spending and the federal budget would not do very much very quickly to reduce the rate of inflation.[2]

(2) Some form of tax relief was recommended for low-income persons. (Here the conference recommended SIIG-13.)

(3) A program of public service employment for those who might lose jobs because of the economic slowdown was recommended. (SIIG-15 is recommended.)

(4) A "liberalizing" of the Federal Reserve's credit policy was deemed to be desirable. (The use of the word "liberalizing" is a variation of SIIG-1.)

[1]Property taxes and sales taxes might be lowered with corresponding cuts in government spending.

[2]This, of course, was the only major area where the battle *against* inflation could be fought.

(5) The conference also recommended maintaining a tough policy against the oil-producing nations, urging the government to develop greater domestic sources of energy and to institute strict conservation measures.[1]

(6) Reimposition of wage and price controls was opposed.[2]

So, 28 of the nation's leading "economists" offered not one concrete proposal for reducing inflation. But, then, what could the President have expected of a Keynesian-dominated conference?

In my opinion, Keynesians should not even be referred to as economists. For example, no bona fide economist would recommend that the government *expand* and *stimulate* the economy with *unmoney*. But "economists" such as Walter W. Heller, Paul A. Samuelson, John Kenneth Galbraith, Arthur M. Okun, Otto Eckstein, and Gardner Ackley do.

Who are the real economists? Well, there's Henry Hazlitt, whose *Economics in One Lesson* perhaps provides more information than can be gained by studying economics at Harvard. There's the prolific Murray Rothbard, professor of economics at the Polytechnic Institute of New York. There's the redoubtable, ever-popular Milton Friedman of the University of Chicago.[3] These are examples of contemporary American economists; however, the 1974 Austrian-born Nobel Prize winner, Frederick von Hayek, and New York University's towering Ludwig von Mises (1881-1973) are both sterling examples of legitimate economists. Unfortunately these men are characterized as belonging to the Austrian school of economics,[4] which is somewhat like saying that those who maintain that two and two are four belong to the "Austrian school of mathematics." And not to be overlooked are other individuals who have been warning the American public about the dangers inherent in Keynesian policies *vis-à-vis* the nation's monetary system. Among the best have been Franz Pick, editor of *Pick's Currency Yearbook,* Harry Schultz, editor of the influential *International Harry Schultz Letter,* and Harry Browne, author of *How You Can Profit from the Coming Devaluation* and *You Can Profit from a Monetary Crisis*. Organizations such as the Economist National Committee on Monetary Policy, the Foundation for Economic Education, and the American Institute for Economic Research, that have at times appeared to be but lonely voices in the wilderness, should be cited for their efforts and dogged determination to disseminate accurate economic information.

Henry Hazlitt's and Walter Heller's economic views are as different as cheese

[1]These recommendations required no particular economic training.

[2]This was about the only sensible recommendation, indicating that perhaps Keynesians had learned something from the dismal failures of Phases I-IV.

[3]I would fault Friedman only for his seeming unfamiliarity concerning the value and function of gold and his apparent willingness to accommodate to inflation by advocating indexing, and to entrust politicians with even limited but arbitrary monetary power.

[4]Though Milton Friedman is generally associated with the "Chicago" and "monetarist" schools.

and chalk. To say that they practice the same science is misleading. Many persons have been allowed to call themselves economists because the public has been duped into believing that since economics is a social science, it's not really a science and its truths are so relative that one economist's views are as valid as another's. Economic laws, however, are as dependable as those of physics and chemistry. Since a fundamental economic law is that prices are determined by supply and demand, an "economist" who suggests that prices are not determined this way but insists that they are determined by a "wage-price push" is comparable to a physicist who says "an apple when released from one's hand will fall skyward, not earthward."

Because it is *vital* that the public recognize the difference between *economists* and *uneconomists,* I set out to prove beyond question that the nation's most influential and vocal "economists" are in reality uneconomists.[1] Space, however, forces me to focus on only two—Paul Samuelson and Walter Heller.

Now, who am I, one might ask, to say that Paul A. Samuelson of M.I.T., Nobel Prize winner for economics, economic adviser to President John Kennedy, and author of the most widely used economic textbook, and Walter Heller of the University of Minnesota, chairman of the Council of Economic Advisers under Presidents Kennedy and Johnson, and past president of the American Economic Association are uneconomists? I say so because I find their economic understanding to be unsound, even unintelligible.

Why Study Economics at All

The reason for scientific study is that it provides a greater degree of accuracy when forecasting than could otherwise be achieved. For example, it was the sure knowledge provided by Gresham's Law[2] that guaranteed a profit to those who began hoarding silver coins when the government switched to the cupro-nickel kind. Those politicians having recourse to a Council of Economic Advisers who still maintained that cupro-coins would relieve a "coin shortage" were relying on economists who either (1) never heard of Gresham, (2) or if they had, didn't understand him, or (3) if they had, didn't believe him, or (4) had heard of him, believed him, understood him, but decided to lie about the reason cupro-coins were introduced into America's monetary system.

[1]For this task I had compiled SIIG analysis of many of their statements, writings, and testimonies before Congressional committees. This produced so much material, however, that when I correlated it, I had too much to ask my publisher to use and you to read. Boiling down the material I had on Paul Samuelson and Walter Heller, two of America's most celebrated uneconomists, required the elimination of much fascinating material such as Samuelson's task force study for President-elect Kennedy, "Prospects and Policies for the 1961 American Economy," and choice examples of SIIGoratory supplied by Heller's many Congressional appearances.

[2]"Bad money drives out good money."

My knowledge of economics enabled me to predict with remarkable accuracy the course of U.S. monetary policy when I testified before the U.S. Senate Committee on Banking and Currency on January 31, 1968. (My testimony is presented in Appendix B.) I will gladly pit my economic and monetary evaluations at that time against those made by Samuelson and Heller.

A Brief Analysis of My Testimony

I made nine accurate monetary predictions (Appendix B, Note A) to "What would be the effect of eliminating the 25 percent backing of Federal Reserve notes?" It would (1) aggravate our monetary imbalance and (2) increase the amount of gold losses. (3) Removing the gold reserve is inflationary. (4) Dollars can simply be run off a press and they would be. Prices would climb higher. (5) Price controls would be demanded, but (6) would do no good and gold would become scarcer. (7) Such a move would not be interpreted as strengthening the dollar since a dollar backed by nothing cannot be better than a dollar backed by something. Ultimately (8) we would lose two or three billion more, and then (9) hopefully, it would dawn [1] on someone that we dare not lose it all (and terminate the dollar's convertibility).

I challenge Samuelson and Heller to glean their testimonies and writings and produce *five* unhedged predictions *between them* that ever materialized.

A not atypical example of Heller's economic insight was his testimony before the Congressional Joint Economic Committee in July 1970. In his view, inflation was on the wane and so he urged the Nixon administration to stimulate the economy in an effort to avoid idleness and economic stagnation. While it was obvious to me in 1968 that if the U.S. government removed the gold cover we would be in for galloping inflation, heading right for an inflationary bust, Heller even into 1970 believed that inflation was apparently on the wane.

My testimony is also accurate in reflecting my adamant contention that the U.S. would do absolutely nothing to improve its deteriorating monetary position, which is stated in no uncertain terms in Appendix B, Note B:

> However, since no attempt will be made to correct the basic condition, we will simply end up losing more gold. If we lose an additional one billion (we lost 450 million in one week), this will be equivalent to a three billion dollar loss when we are compelled to devalue.

However, our losses will now be greater when we are finally compelled to "officially" devalue on a realistic basis. Since inflation was permitted to grow worse since 1968 (when I then estimated gold's value at $105 an ounce), we will be

[1] America lost approximately $2½ billion more before it "dawned" on the government to close the "gold window."

compelled to devalue at a substantially higher gold price. The nation's losses will thus be substantially greater than I originally predicted, due to the *stupidity* of public officials who continued to sell the people's gold at the ridiculously low price of $35.00 per ounce.

Now About Samuelson and Heller

Having used my testimony to demonstrate the analytical potential of *legitimate* economic knowledge and insight, let's revisit the world of the uneconomist.

My first exposure to Paul Samuelson was in 1958, when I used his textbook as part of an assigned course being given by the American College of Life Underwriters. Schooled in the principles of sound money, thrift, the importance of economic incentives, and the virtues of free enterprise, I was struck by his text's advocacy of unmoney, big government, the reduction of incentives, inflation, and many nonsensical propositions. Samuelson's *Economics: An Introductory Analysis* (3rd edition) was an affront to my economic training and insulted my intelligence.

In October that year I wrote the college expressing my shock and anger that the American College, supposedly the intellectual and professional arm of the life insurance industry, should use a text that represented an economic philosophy that seemingly embraced two conceptions which:

> 1. Countenance the systematic confiscation (by inflation) of funds that it [the insurance industry] is morally bound to protect, and 2. threaten heinous national consequence to personal thrift.[1]

Moreover, I argued that:

> If the college really believes in the economic philosophies that it espouses and encourages [as exemplified by Samuelson's text], then the life insurance industry is systematically, and with knowledge aforethought, guilty of a gigantic fraud to policyholders individually, and renders an economic disservice to the nation as a whole.

I suggested alternate texts which not only would be more accurate from the standpoint of economics but would reflect a far more responsible position as far as the financial interests of the industry's own policyholders were concerned.

I cited many of the errors and misleading statements liberally sprinkled throughout the text. For example, Samuelson states that if price increases could be held down to "less than 3 percent per year, such a mild inflation need not cause too great concern."[2] I pointed out that if this rate of inflation didn't bother Samuelson, it *would* bother those poor insurance and pension buyers and persons receiving

[1]For the sake of brevity, I have omitted tearing apart two of Samuelson's pet theories: the "paradox of thrift," and the "multiplier" concept, whereby society is able to spend itself rich.

[2]*Economics: An Introductory Analysis* (3rd ed.; New York: McGraw-Hill Book Co., 1958), p. 250.

proceeds under any fixed-dollar insurance settlement arrangement. Samuelson obviously would offer no objection to a rate of inflation of 2.9 percent that would compound to an inflation of 33 percent in ten years and to 77 percent in twenty years. Given a rate of inflation of 2.9 percent that Samuelson would accept, a 20-year $10,000 insurance endowment would lose 77 percent of its projected original value at maturity, while annuity and fixed-dollar recipients would by then receive only 23 percent of the purchasing power they had originally contracted for. I can only assume that inflation at this rate did not cause Samuelson great concern since he was smart enough himself not to invest in cash value life insurance and annuities. Given Samuelson's premise, therefore, I asked, is there really any point to cash values, pension planning, settlement options, or annuities? I could have also added—given a rate of inflation of 2.9 percent, is there any point to government bonds (which at that time paid only 3 percent) or any other fixed-dollar investment?

It was because of the influence of uneconomists such as Samuelson, having no ''great concern'' about an inflation rate of 2.9 percent, that the rate of inflation, along with interest rates, has soared to such staggering levels. Samuelson had overlooked, among other things, the fact that even with an inflationary rate as ''low'' as 2.9 percent, an investor would need to earn 7.9 percent to earn a legitimate, conservative return of 5 percent, just to compensate him for Samuelson's modest rate of inflation. Thus, interest rates would have to be 58 percent higher than necessary when using 5 percent as a basic rate of return.[1] However, since Samuelson favors all kinds of government services and is therefore not adverse to income taxes, for an investor to earn 7.9 percent, after a modest tax of 30 percent, he would need a minimum rate of return of 11.3 percent. So society must begin with a minimum interest rate of 11.3 percent in order to net a modest 5 percent for the use of one's capital and for taking a modest risk.

Given this modest rate of inflation and this modest tax bracket, what rate of return might an investor require to take a ''businessman's risk''? What would an equitable rate of return have to be, given a 10 percent rate of inflation and a 50 percent tax bracket?

Why did Samuelson say that an inflationary rate of less than 3 percent per year ''need not cause great concern''? From this can one conclude that a rate of 2.9 percent need not cause ''great concern,'' but a rate of inflation of 3.2 should? I wish he would explain the difference between an inflationary rate of 2.9 and 3.2 percent, or even 3.5 percent? How can he be so precise? I wonder what he would find to be concerned about in an inflationary rate of 3.9 or 4 percent that did not cause him great concern in inflation of 2.9 percent?

[1]Samuelson keeps assuming that savers and investors do not object to being swindled out of a portion of their yield by inflation. So he sees no relation between increases in inflation and increases in interest. This percentage would, of course, be higher for lower rates of interest and lower for higher rates of interest.

Although Samuelson might have modified or eliminated this statement in later editions, it does provide an excellent insight into his understanding of economics. He seems not to have the foggiest notion about the consequences of inflation, nor for that matter how Social Security was and is funded.

Of Social Security, he writes:

> A private insurance company would have to charge tens of thousands of dollars for such generous annuities and privileges. [p. 181]

So, in my letter to the American College, I argued:

> Is he not implying here that insurance companies are overcharging for their products, that one gets insurance bargains from the government, that ''tens of thousands of dollars of generous annuities and privileges'' can be produced out of thin air at no cost to anyone? These are ideas that we should be helping to dispel, not further! This sentence is then followed by another, which must be seen *to be believed*! It not only reveals the author's incomprehension of the Social Security System as such, but also demonstrates his total lack of understanding of the consequence of inflation, the inevitable result of all of his thinking.

The sentence I refer to is as follows:

> It is one of the great advantages of a pay-as-you-go Social Security System that it rests on the general tax capacity of the nation; if hyperinflation wiped out all private insurance and savings, Social Security could nonetheless start all over again, none the poorer.

Now, let's examine that gem. First of all, the implication that a ''pay-as-you-go'' Social Security System had an advantage over the supposed reserve method of Social Security ''funding'' implies that Samuelson accepts the ''reserve funding'' concept initially claimed for Social Security. There never was a legitimate Social Security reserve, so it has always been ''pay-as-you-go'' and has rested on the ''general tax capacity of the nation''—that is, unfunded and unsound. But the clue to Samuelson's understanding comes from his unabashed acceptance of ''hyperinflation'' that ''wiped out all private insurance and savings.'' Note how he takes such an obvious catastrophe in stride.

In my letter I countered:

> Is he suggesting here that the ''reserve system'' did *not* rest on the *sole* ''tax capacity of the nation''? In this hyperinflation, what are the *values* of the payments that the system contracted to make? Does he mean to imply that citizens forced to part with dear dollars for this ''insurance'' are none the poorer by being paid off in cheap or worthless paper; that a social security check of $108 which had been expected to buy food for a month is just as good as one of the same amount that can only be used to purchase a newspaper; that a capitalistic society is somehow no worse off even though all citizens have now been robbed of all their money savings?

> "Tax capacity of the nation"—what is the state of business in a hyperinflation? What good, therefore, this "tax capacity"? Of course, the big question is—why hyperinflation at all?

So here we have it altogether. Samuelson is unconcerned about a "mild inflation" of 2.9 percent or a "hyperinflation" which can wipe out "all private insurance and savings." In other words, he is just unconcerned about inflation at all.

My letter dealt at length with Samuelson's attitude and understanding of inflation. The following from that section of my letter shows that it was possible as far back as 1958 to predict the disastrous course that Keynesian thinking was taking.

> That we may have a reduced workweek and any more real purchasing power (in many cases this is illusory as many people hold down two jobs and in many families both parents are *forced* to work to keep their economic noses above water, and this despite the tremendous per capita increase in our capital equipment!) has been due to the fact that the momentum developed by the past generations of economic freedom has been able to force through the maze of government pauperizing policies *some* benefits. How much has been lost because of this filtering process staggers the imagination. Fortunately, those remaining economic freedoms that still survive have provided the pumping action necessary to save the ship of state from the havoc wrought by the army of politicians and "economists" busily boring holes in her keel. However, *the water is rising*—and at an accelerating rate!

Here I commented on Samuelson's understanding and characterization of wars as being "good times."

> On page 252, please read the paragraph surrounding the chart and notice where the high points of the paragraph are, then note this sentence "If prices rise in good times and don't fall in bad times . . ." Please note what Samuelson considers as "*good times*"—wars!
>
> This type of reasoning is why we have often been accused of fomenting wars and needing world tension for our prosperity. It should be obvious that wars are an *economic waste!* If, therefore, a process of economic reasoning can elevate this state to "good times," such reasoning must obviously damn the logic.
>
> To the extent that a society *seems* to derive some economic benefit from war, it is due to the increased national effort at such time which is directed toward research, invention, increasing efficiency, developing resources, building productive capacity, etc.—all accomplished by a severe curtailment of consumption (forced savings). The consumption goods that *are* produced, the weapons, ammunition, etc., are expended—and this is *total waste*. It is clear that any benefit that we derive from war is due to the complete harnessing of the nation (full employment in the true sense of the word—three shifts) to accomplish the above ends. These remain to function and benefit society after the war is over. However, if we wished to utilize the *same national effort in peacetime,* we could salvage this one economic advantage that wars do tend to thrust upon us. Samuelson's conclusions about wars being "good times" stem from the fact

> that during war time there is a huge surplus of (paper) money (due to people receiving payment for production which they cannot purchase). Since Samuelson confuses (paper) money with wealth he, therefore, logically concludes that these must be truly "good times."
>
> I have often wondered—how much real wealth and individual economic security could have been created had the American economy, operating *at the same capacity* and for the *same length of time* as it did during World War II and with the added manpower of the then armed forces, produced only useful civilian products? How many communities would have been left without adequate schools, hospitals, roads? How many families would have been left without ample clothing, housing, appliances? How much could have been stored for future consumption? For how many years after this huge "productive binge" could the economy have gone on one long collective vacation?

From the following examples, however, it will be observed that Samuelson's deficiencies as an economist are not secondary to his inadequacies as an investment adviser.

> United States Government Savings Bonds bought for $75 in 1944, paid $100 in 1954. But one hundred 1954 dollars had a lower purchasing power than did seventy-five 1944 dollars. [p. 249]

And

> A 3 percent yield for a perfectly safe, instantly redeemable [government] bond is a very great bargain. [p. 175]

In my letter to the college, I pointed out that Samuelson's ability to draw the latter conclusion on the basis of his former observation was obviously absurd and had to be indicative of either: "(1) an illogical mind that cannot even draw elementary conclusions from facts that it has already developed, (2) a willingness to compromise facts—maybe in this instance to spare the author from appearing unpatriotic if he had correctly assessed the investment worth of government bonds, and (3) an unwillingness to appraise objectively, if such treatment would in any way be prejudicial to the author's own preconceived conclusions or economic bias." I then pointed out that the obvious inference to be drawn from this information was that "the last line of that paragraph on page 175 must naturally be changed if it is to follow logically from the author's own facts to read: 'Since government bonds are not safe, neither is money nor bank accounts,' and if this trend is not stopped, can the collapse of level premium life insurance and pensions be far behind?"

Unfortunately, I was not able to dissuade the American College from using Samuelson's text and it has been continuously used by them in their program of economic studies. Apparently, the insurance industry was more concerned with promoting inflation, since inflation created an ever-expanding need for the purchase of more life insurance, even though, in the process, it destroyed the purchasing power of the billions of insurance savings that were entrusted to the industry and that the industry had a moral obligation to protect. Insurance and annuity contracts, in most cases, are sold on the basis of long-term fixed-dollar projections—projections that the insurance industry, based upon the philosophy promoted by the American College, should have known were misleading, if not unethical.

For a more recent sampling of Samuelson's economic wisdom, consider the following statement on inflation he gave on the Public Broadcasting System special, ''Inflation: The Money Merry-Go-Round,'' in October 1974.

> If you were ready to turn over the whole of the economy to the cruel forces of laissez faire, of supply and demand, and you didn't care whether at one time 10 percent of the population starved, whether at another time all the money, or a part of it went to a small fraction of the population, then certainly it would be the case that you'd have to scratch and get out and work or else you'd starve, and then it would be possible to control some aspects of modern creeping inflation. For example, under laissez faire, if you just kept a tight control on the money supply, then you couldn't have the hyperinflation that we had in Germany after World War I, or that many other countries have had or that Latin America has been having.
>
> But for most of us, that kind of a cure for inflation we would consider worse than the disease itself, because it means that a lot of kids go to bed at night hungry; it means a lot of rickets; it means a lot of inequality. And actually, it would mean, in the modern political context, blood in the streets and revolution.

This was Professor Samuelson's *entire* statement. It is hard to believe that it was delivered by one of America's foremost ''economists.'' I defy anyone not trained in Keynesianese to repeat what the professor really said to his national viewing audience. First of all, he states that if we didn't have inflation (remember that is the only arrow in his quiver), we would have starvation, a population racked with rickets, and ''blood in the streets.''

As Figure 11 already indicated, the American economy sustained almost no inflation for a period of over 100 years while absorbing millions upon millions of penniless immigrants, and did so without starvation, without rickets, and without blood in the streets. In the process, it also managed to create the highest standard of living in the world. Samuelson's statement also implies that the individual would have absolutely no protection against the ''cruel forces of laissez faire,'' which is, of course, nonsense. Apart from the natural protection offered by the forces of competition and economic self-interest, the citizen has the added protection of the government's antimonopoly powers as spelled out in the Sherman Antitrust Act. But what specifically are ''the cruel forces of laissez faire'' to which the professor alludes? The fact is that the economy would be free to produce what the public wanted rather than what politicians and bureaucrats decide they should have? As far as ''10 percent of our population starving,'' when has starvation ever been a problem in this country? My father tells of the first meal he had in this country when he arrived in 1902. Having very little money and unable to speak English, he ordered ten cents worth of Vurst (hot dogs). He claimed that this bought so many he couldn't finish them. Starvation indeed! Why, even in the depths of the Great Depression, the New Deal was notorious for destroying stocks of food that the "cruel forces of laissez faire" had apparently overproduced. Even Samuelson was aware of this since he wrote:

> In the early New Deal years the emphasis was on crop reduction and there was editorial weeping for the little pigs being killed and the crops aborted.[1]

Along these lines I have long felt that someone is lying about the Great Depression. Being born in 1928, I only dimly recall the early years of the Depression, but certainly remember from 1933 on, and our family had enough food and fuel. I have no memories of economic hardship although I lived in a working-class neighborhood. I realize, of course, that this was not true of other families, but whenever the subject of "depression" comes up, "liberal economists" are quick to cite the "starvation" in America after the "breakdown of capitalism" in 1929. Well, there certainly is a contradiction here. If there was starvation in America in the early '30s, why didn't the New Deal deliver the food it was destroying to the people who were starving?[2] The answer must be either (1) that no one actually starved in America *even* during the Great Depression and that any suggestion by Keynesians that they did is nonsense, or (2) if people were actually starving (or even going hungry) as a result of the Great Depression, then the Keynesians who recommended destroying food rather than supplying it to those going hungry were heartless brutes.

Either America's left-wing critics are wrong about the Great Depression or the cruelties of the New Deal have never been fully explored. If starvation and malnutrition were ever or have ever been a problem in this country, we can thank the successful efforts of Keynesians who have worked long and hard for farm price supports and restricted agricultural output. As even Samuelson noted:

> Even a flexible-price support program at 70 percent of parity has resulted in such tremendous production outpouring as to bring the emphasis back again to crop restriction, now in the *guise* of the Soil Bank . . . But with each cut in acres, the ingenuity of farmers in growing more per acre has shown that this too can only be a stop gap.[3] [Italics mine]

Who, therefore, tried to withhold food from the market in order to drive up food prices—the "cruel forces of laissez faire"? No, it has always been the forces of government planning supported by Keynesian theoreticians.

[1]*Economics: An Introductory Analysis* (4th ed.; New York: McGraw-Hill Book Co., 1958), p.417.

[2]Even if it had to use army trucks. I have even had Keynesians tell me that the reason the food didn't reach the people who were "starving" was because of a lack of transportation.

[3]*Economics: An Introductory Analysis* (4th ed.; New York: McGraw-Hill Book Co., 1958), p. 49.

Samuelson's inference that the alternative to Keynesian inflation would be an inflexible "tight control on the money supply" is an example of his willingness to take advantage of the public's unfamiliarity with how the U.S. monetary system really functions.

The primary reason for establishing the Federal Reserve System was to provide "elasticity" to the nation's supply of money substitutes, so that the supply of credit money substitutes could be expanded and contracted in response to realistic economic needs. The U.S. supply of credit money substitutes has never been required to be maintained under "tight control" as Samuelson infers. When a Keynesian economist such as Samuelson uses the expression "tight monetary controls," he means only that when the supply of money substitutes is being expanded at a 3 or 4 percent annual rate (even in the face of *falling* economic activity) rather than at some greater rate that he would prefer (say 6 or 7 percent). This constitutes "tight money!"[1]

Interestingly, Samuelson does recognize the danger of continuous inflation. He mentions the German hyperinflation following World War I. This hyperinflation ended on November 22, 1923, with the revaluation of one trillion old marks for one new gold mark—thereby wiping out the entire accumulated mark savings of the German people. What could be worse for America than a hyperinflation that would wipe out all dollar savings? A hyperinflation would transfer all wealth from creditors to debtors, and destroy all fixed-dollar assets, the principal form of saving for middle- and lower-income groups. So, what type of "inequality" would this create? Finally, Samuelson was not being candid with his audience by implying that a return to private free capitalism in the U.S. would mean that one would either have to "work or else you'd starve." Throughout our nation's history, there have always been charitable organizations, voluntarily supported by private individuals, which have stood ready to aid those in need. And, to my knowledge, no one has ever been allowed to die of hunger in America.

Moreover, Samuelson's reference to the possible need "to control some aspects of the modern creeping inflation" is less than honest. Since when can inflationary rates of 11 and 12 percent be properly termed "creeping"? And more specifically, how would Samuelson "control some aspects" of this "creeping

[1]To my knowledge, Samuelson has never called for a contraction in the supply of "money" substitutes when economic activity has contracted.

If the supply of "money" substitutes is expanded at a 6 percent rate when economic activity drops by 2 percent, then the expansion of the "money" supply is really 8 not 6 percent. This is the present predicament of the United States. The Fed continues to increase the supply of "money" substitutes even though economic activity has decreased. Therefore, it is increasing the relative supply of unmoney at a far higher percentage than claimed and is generating inflation at a greater intensity than it is willing to admit.

What Samuelson advocates is a constantly expanding supply of unmoney, responding not to the needs of business but to the insatiable needs of government and to the demands of Keynesians who are constantly urging that the unmoney supply be inflated in order to "stimulate" the economy. The latter presumption can only be held by someone with a distorted economic understanding.

inflation''? With price controls? So, despite the increasing hardships that inflation was inflicting on the nation, which had created the very need for the program on which he was interviewed, Samuelson couldn't utter a single unkind word for inflation, nor could he offer any reasonable suggestion as to how inflation might be reduced or contained.

Let's return again to that TV program, ''Inflation: The Money Merry-Go-Round,'' and consider the views of another top uneconomist—Walter Heller. When the panel was asked, ''Is inflation inherently good or bad or is it just something that we live with?'' Heller replied:

> I think that is the right question to start with, because we are in the realm of values. It's a question of how much we are willing to give up, on one hand, to subdue inflation on the other. And I think that is often lost sight of.
>
> You know, we make a devil of inflation and we're willing apparently to spend any amount of jobs, profits, output, financial stability, etc. to fight inflation.
>
> I would say that if our rate of inflation comes back down to 4 or 5 percent, and the rest of the world is inflating at 4 or 5 percent, that's something we can live with. I don't think we should try to live with double-digit inflation, [inflation above 10 percent] because it does have disturbing circumstances. And others, I am sure, will speak to that.

He was asked simply if inflation were ''inherently good or bad'' and avoided a direct answer. Even John Kenneth Galbraith noticed this. In response, to the moderator's question he declared:

> No, I think it's a bad thing and here I part company with my old friend Walter Heller who spent all of his life *fighting depressions and recessions* and wants to continue so. I would like to see him convert now to dealing with inflation, which can be done . . .'' [Italics mine.]

Galbraith continued by pointing out how damaging inflation could be and then suggested *combating it with price controls,*

Let's submit Heller's above statement to closer analysis. First of all, he suggests that we have to ''give up'' something to control inflation, which he suggests might be jobs, profits, output, and financial stability. In reality, those are among the things the economy would gain if it forfeited Keynesian-style inflation. Heller suggests that we could live with an inflation of 4 or 5 percent. This is absurd, since if one wished to earn a legitimate 5 percent interest on capital, that would mean rates of better than 10 percent, adjusting only for losses resulting from inflation, without making any adjustment for losses because of income taxes. Such a level of interest must necessarily stifle growth and economic expansion. Five percent inflation expropriates at least $35 billion a year from those who have unmoney in savings banks and savings and loan accounts, $10 billion a year from those who have cash value life insurance, and $15 billion a year from private government bond holders. Apparently Heller sees nothing wrong with fleecing the nation's savers of at least $60 billion a year through inflation, which would be an amount greater than is lost through all illegal and criminal activities in the United States.

Notice that Heller concedes that he doesn't think we should try to live with double-digit inflation (presumably we therefore could live with a 9 percent rate of inflation) because "it does have disturbing circumstances" which, he says, others "will speak to." He had previously noted that "if our rate of inflation comes back down to 4 or 5 percent . . ." but does not explain how or why double-digit inflation came into being.[1] Nor does he explain how this reduction in inflation is to come about. He only says "*if* the rate of inflation comes down."[2]

Heller, of course, admits that double-digit inflation has "disturbing circumstances." But what are those "circumstances," and how could they be disturbingly present in an inflation of 10 percent but mysteriously absent in an inflation of five percent?

Space limitations prevent me from covering many more of Professor Heller's statements before Congressional committees. However, to buttress my contention that Heller is an uneconomist, I shall focus on remarks he made in 1974 before the national convention of the American Economic Association as its outgoing president.

According to the Washington press service, Heller said

> the current recession could have been avoided if tax cuts[3] had been enacted last spring and if the Federal Reserve Board had not switched to a tight monetary policy in March and April.[4] The "drags" that higher oil prices put on the economy—by transferring 35 billion dollars in buying power from the U.S. to oil-producing countries, coupled with tight spending and monetary policies made the recession inevitable.[5]

Here's Professor Heller blaming the recession on a slight minimizing of inflationary forces, while inflation was soaring at better than 10 percent, with many prices increasing 50 and 100 percent per year, and on the higher paper prices of oil.[6] In all candor, I can never recall when Walter Heller was *not* calling for

[1]It was to a large extent the result of the fiscal and monetary policies of the Kennedy and Johnson administrations—policies that he helped to shape.

[2]If pressed for an answer, he might reply; "Why, by sacrificing ten vestal virgins to the god Inflation, and as its wrath is appeased, inflations of all kinds, including price-wage, wage-price, cost-push, push-pull, pop-up, pop-over, and ball and jack, will start to subside."

[3]Here he recommends a SIIG-13.

[4]Now he switches to a SIIG-5.

[5]Finishing up with an "extended" SIIG-5.

[6]Any housewife could have offered the observation that "higher" oil prices weren't doing the economy any particular good. Heller here overlooks any responsibility he might have had for the energy crisis while serving as chairman of the President's Council of Economic Advisers. Elements of the developing oil crisis were clearly visible during his tenure.

more inflation and/or placing the blame for some economic difficulty on the simple lessening of inflationary pressure.

GNP: The Big Bamboozle

Before leaving the subject of the uneconomists, some observations are in order regarding the gross national product (GNP), in which Keynesians and federal bureaucrats place great stock. In Keynesianese, an increasing GNP means economic prosperity and economic well-being; a falling GNP means economic stagnation, recession, and a declining standard of living. The Keynesians even have a subsect, "macroeconomists," who study national income figures with the religious zeal of cabalists, endlessly sifting through dollar statistics searching for the key to a healthier, happier, more prosperous economy.

I maintain that all statements suggesting that a higher gross national product or higher national income is indicative of an increased national prosperity are rubbish. Consider the following hypothetical example.

Suppose a tidal wave demolished the Florida Gold Coast from Miami Beach to Palm Beach, laying waste, in addition to those cities, portions of Fort Lauderdale, Pompano Beach, and Boca Raton. Let's say the cost of such destruction came to $2 billion. Let's say that the cost of cleaning up the debris alone came to $300 million. Obviously, the country has been made poorer by the destruction of $2 billion of real wealth—but is the dollar value of all this destruction subtracted from the gross national product? Of course not. Now, does the $300 million required for cleaning up the mess have any real economic value, and does it contribute toward increasing society's standard of living? Of course not. But that $300 million cleaning bill will go toward increasing the gross national product by $300 million, since all money received by all members of society finds its way into the GNP without any regard for its relative economic merit. Therefore, a tidal wave that caused $2 billion worth of destruction, leaving thousands homeless and hundreds dead and injured, increased the GNP by $300 million. There would be GNP losses, of course, but only to the extent of losses in *productivity* caused by the disruptiveness of the flood itself. To the extent that society was now forced to work to replace the destroyed properties, the GNP would be increased by another $2 billion—thus this holocaust would have generated a $2.3 billion increase in the GNP and would have contributed to the appearance of a higher standard of living as reflected by GNP statistics.[1]

Abundance Has the Tendency to Develop Lower GNP Figures Than Scarcity

Suppose U.S. farmers produced a thousand bushels of wheat having a value of $2 per bushel. The GNP value of this wheat would be $2,000. Suppose the following year favorable agricultural conditions enabled them to produce 3,000

[1]In addition, of course, government officials and Keynesians would have been quick to cite the added beneficial effects that the flood would have on unemployment in the area.

bushels of wheat. Such a dramatic increase in the supply of wheat might cause the price of wheat to drop as low as 50 cents per bushel, reflecting a GNP figure for the 3,000 bushels of $1,500. So, now our wheat production produces a lower GNP figure even though we have three times as much wheat.

A GNP of Zero Would Indicate the Highest Possible Standard of Living

It is important to recognize that all positive economic forces strive to produce lower prices and lower GNP figures. It is only because of government intervention that we in fact get higher prices and higher GNP figures. Let me illustrate. Assume that there was a massive horn of plenty in the center of every city (more horns in larger cities) and that all one had to do to get what he wanted was to go and pick it up. Obviously, in this situation, nobody would have to work, nothing would have to be produced, and consequently nothing would have any value. Nobody would buy or sell anything since one could get whatever he wanted for nothing.

By any economic yardstick, such a society would be well off, although its GNP would be zero. While the above state of economic nirvana is obviously unattainable, it certainly can serve as a worthy economic objective, but the higher the GNP, the farther we move from our goal. Correctly understood, therefore, all sensible economic activity—the striving to create capital, increases in economic efficiency, the development of more economical products—are essentially attempts by society to create more efficient "horns of plenty," and while we obviously have not developed the end product, we are nearing it. This can be judged by the variety of goods that can now be seen emerging from our factories (in effect "horns of plenty") as opposed to what flowed out of them ten, twenty, a hundred, or a thousand years ago. A good example of this is that in 1960 I bought a second-hand calculator for $300. It was heavy, bulky, and noisy. Today, calculators (emerging from our "horns of plenty") are smaller, lighter, more convenient, noiseless—and they sell for under $50.[1] That all prices and the GNP have not dropped in a similar manner, as they should according to sound economic theory, can be traced to the artificial inflationary forces generated by government and justified by America's uneconomists.

Inefficiency Will Generate Higher GNP Figures Than Will Efficiency

For example, suppose Economy A produced 10 million cars a year and junked 8 million. GNP figures will include in an index of Economy A's advancing standard of living the dollar value of the 10 million cars produced, while neglecting to deduct the comparable economic utility (not the dollar value which would be lower) of the cars that were scrapped. The net economic increase to society from the above productivity is only 2 million new cars plus only the *net increase in utility*[2] provided by the 8 million new cars that were produced to replace the 8

[1]And were it not for inflation, their prices would be lower still.

[2]Based on comparing *all* cars in terms of their *original* utility.

million cars that were scrapped. Suppose Economy B, manufacturing much better cars, produces 3 million cars, while scrapping only 300,000. The net addition of cars in Economy B is, therefore, 2.7 million cars versus 2 million for Economy A. GNP figures for Economy A, however, based on the production of 10 million cars, looks far more impressive than the figures for Economy B, which produced 3 million. Such figures would be misleading, however, since Economy B is generating a far greater overall increase in auto utility than Economy A, which, to a large extent, is merely spinning its economic wheels.

GNP Figures Artificially Distort Economic Value Since They Give Equal Weight to the Production of Capital and Consumer Goods

Generally speaking, the economy produces two types of goods—consumer goods and capital goods (sometimes referred to as instrumental goods). Instrumental goods are goods that are not wanted for themselves but are only produced to make other goods that are wanted for themselves alone. A factory is built, for example, not because anyone wants the factory, but for the products the factory can produce. The goal of economic production is to increase the amount of *consumer goods*, goods desired by the public for their personal use, enjoyment, and consumption. The fact that billions are spent on factories, post offices, office buildings, roads,[1] etc., in itself does not mean an increase in society's economic standard of living. The only figure that can be used as a measure of real economic progress is the amount of consumer goods that is produced on a per capita basis. The value of society's productive effort that went into making machinery, constructing factories, office buildings, dams, highways, etc. should *ultimately* be reflected in an increased flow of consumer goods generated by these capital investments. However, the cost of these capital and instrumental goods should not be included in GNP figures (as it now is) as an indication of an increasing standard of living, since their inclusion gives value to goods that are not wanted for themselves, and would also assign economic value to what may be only unnecessary, unneeded, and wasteful capital construction.[2]

For example, Economy A builds a $5 million factory capable of producing a million widgets having a GNP value of $1 million, so, Economy A's GNP reflects an increase of $6 million in terms of a year's widget production and the cost of the factory. Economy B, because of better design and efficiency, is able to build a factory for $3 million that is able to produce the same million widgets. So, because of increased efficiency, its GNP suffers in comparison to Economy A's by $2 million. Suppose further that Economy C spends $10 million for a widget factory which, after it is completed, is found to be unsuitable for making widgets and has

[1]If somebody, for example, invented an inexpensive jet back-pack, we wouldn't need so many expensive highways.

[2]The Soviet Union and the United States use this technique to convince their citizens that their nations are achieving higher standards of living.

to be abandoned. In that case, its GNP would go up by $10 million with its economy having absolutely nothing to show for this expenditure. So, its GNP should reflect a zero increase rather than the $10 million that would be reflected if its GNP were calculated as it is in the United States.

The danger of allowing capital goods as well as government armament production to be reflected in GNP figures is that it allows government, which has a vested interest in impressing us with higher GNP figures as both a reflection of increasing national prosperity and its successful management of the economy, to inflate and manipulate GNP figures with all manner of wasteful economic activity having no real bearing on consumption goods and the nation's prosperity. Expenditures on munitions assign a misleading value to armament production. In an economic sense, all armament production (with the exception of that produced for export and *sold*) is a total waste. All the bombs that were exploded in the Vietnam War obviously did not increase America's standard of living by one iota. Those American resources and productive efforts that were diverted and exploded wastefully in the air and on the ground in Vietnam might have been directed toward building up a part of America, but they weren't.

Not that armament production and the economic cost of war, even the Vietnam War, might not be worth the cost. But to include the cost of fighting a war in the GNP, which is then viewed and interpreted as an indication of national prosperity, is ludicrous. Doing so creates the illusion that wars are prosperous times (we had previously noted how Professor Samuelson was even fooled by it). It also conceals from the population the economic costs of war and leads many to think "we need a war for our prosperity," or "we need a war to get us moving again," or "a war will get us out of depression."

So, by including in the GNP instrumental production, armament production, and such wasteful government expenditures as unnecessary bureaucratic salaries, the government can inflate GNP totals so that the nation will be conned into thinking it is making economic progress when in reality it is sliding into an economic morass.

GNP Includes the Costs and Gives Value to a Variety of Services That Society Would Prefer to Do Without

Americans are now spending millions of dollars a year on private tax services just to compute their tax liabilities for the government. All fees collected by these private tax services, as well as all accounting and legal fees generated by tax considerations alone, go to increase the GNP. So, the more complicated and cumbersome our government can make its tax laws, which would compel more and more Americans to seek even more expensive tax and accounting services, the better the GNP looks.

For example, Americans spend over a billion dollars a year on burials. All money spent on funerals will, of course, go to increase the GNP. Since the GNP is interpreted as a reflection of economic prosperity, it, therefore, would illogically follow that the more money Americans spend on the ritual of *dying* the higher appears to be their standard of *living*. Obviously, if we had an increase in crime which would create an additional need for more policemen, jailers, and judges, all these salaries would also go to increase the GNP, while contributing absolutely nothing to raising society's real standard of living.

In 1972, Americans spent $83.4 billion or 7.5 percent of the GNP on medical health services while spending only $12 billion or 4.6 percent of the GNP for similar services in 1950. If one believes that the GNP adequately reflects our standard of living, then he believes that the sicker we are as a nation and the higher our national health and medical bills, the higher our standard of living as reflected by GNP totals.

Now, I am not saying that it is unimportant to have efficient and extensive medical facilities. I am saying that it is nonsense to consider payments for medical services, payments we would all rather avoid if we could, as an indication of an increasing standard of living . . . since, obviously, the sicker the population is, the greater will be the percentage of the GNP spent on medical treatment. Costs for medical care, like payments for instrumental goods, should not be included in the GNP since they interfere with accurately assessing real increases in the standard of living. Higher expenditures for medical services could mean that society was indeed bringing better medical treatment to more people, or it might mean that increasing social and economic pressures were forcing more people to seek more medical attention, and/or society was practicing a more uneconomic form of medicine. That this contributes toward higher medical costs cannot be denied. Medical research has succeeded, by the development of serums and new drugs, in eliminating many cases of infectious diseases such as poliomyelitis, smallpox, diphtheria, and whooping cough, and in reducing the prolonged treatment and disabling effects of diseases such as tuberculosis. At the same time, however, more care is now directed toward "stress ailments" and mental health problems to a large extent aggravated by economic pressures, pressures that are undoubtedly related to our extreme levels of taxation. By relieving productive citizens of much of what they produce, the wage earner is left with much less than he needs for supporting himself and his family. Thus, the U.S. government artificially increases financial anxieties, a key ingredient in stress ailment, and has thereby successfully generated an increase in the GNP by fostering the need for citizens to seek increased medical and psychiatric treatment.

If we do have an improved medical plant and a more comprehensive health service, this should result in a healthier population which would be reflected in positive medical *statistics* that have absolutely nothing to do with how many dollars the nation spends on health care. If we have a healthier population, we would have a healthier work force which would ultimately be reflected in the greater productivity of consumer goods and services (which is why payments for health care should be considered as an instrumental expenditure).

Of course, if we were all fortunate enough to not require any medical treatment ourselves, then we as a nation would save $83 billion a year. Why, then should we consider ourselves better off (according to positive impact on the GNP) because we are unfortunately compelled to spend so much for medical services no one really wants? The positive value of medical expenditures, removed from the GNP, would be revealed, for example, in statistical trends in other areas, which, as you will notice, have no paper dollar amounts attached to them. They would be reflected in such improving medical statistics as: (1) increases in life expectancy, (2) reduction in infant mortality, (3) reductions in the length of hospital stays, (4) reductions in the incidence of various ailments and diseases, and (5) reductions in time lost due to disabilities. Please note that better preventive medical programs would also reduce total medical expenditures, thus resulting in reducing GNP figures.

Expenditures for Education Should Be Considered an Instrumental Expenditure and Should Not Appear in GNP Figures

Along with medical expenditures that should not appear in the GNP are expenditures on education, since the slower we are to learn and/or the more incompetent our educational system, the more we might be compelled to spend on education, and thus the higher our GNP figures would appear because of both of these unfortunate conditions. If our educational system is worthwhile and efficient, its benefit to society will be revealed in the increasing quality of our national life—a falling crime rate, less delinquency, increasing levels of artistic achievement, a higher tempo of invention, and industrial innovation.

In 1950, Americans spent approximately $9 billion on public and private education or 3.4 percent of the GNP. In 1972, the country spent approximately $83 billion, or 8 percent of the GNP for education. During those 22 years, the U.S. increased the portion of economic effort going toward education by some 235 percent. Did anybody happen to notice any improvement in the quality of American life because of this substantially increased national effort going for "education"?

Despite this increased burden for "education," crime rose at an alarming rate. Since 1950, violent crime in the U.S. has risen at least 300 percent with no end in sight. In addition, welfare payments, despite a supposedly more educated and theoretically more self-reliant population, increased from approximately $5 billion in 1950 to $48 billion in 1972, or from 1.6 percent of the GNP to 4 percent of the GNP, which certainly suggests that Americans are not getting much for their "educational" dollar.

Removing some obvious uneconomic and instrumental expenditures from the 1971 GNP will reveal how misleading the GNP is as an indicator of national prosperity:

Gross National Product — 1971 (in billions)		$1,050
GNP value of defense spending	$ 71.6	
GNP value of medical expenses	75.6	
GNP value of educational expenses	76.3	
GNP value of non-residential construction	104.4	
Less total of listed instrumental expenditures		328
Net GNP less certain listed instrumental expenditures		$ 722

Recognize further that this figure of $722 billion does not make allowances for capital consumption (depreciation), and still contains a good deal of additional expenditures for instrumental and replacement goods and for wasteful and uneconomic productivity, prompting the question, "Will the real GNP figure reflecting society's true per capita increase in economic growth please stand up?"

As if all these aforementioned defects in the GNP weren't extensive enough, there are two other areas of distortion that should finally bury the GNP as being any real indication of meaningful economic growth—inflation and population growth.

All things being equal, inflation will increase the GNP by the amount of inflation. So 10 percent inflation could increase the GNP by 10 percent, without society having benefited economically. When the government initially announces gains in the GNP, it does so without making any adjustment for inflation. It generally does this later—in fine print. However, many will not understand the inflationary disclaimers and the government will probably lie anyway concerning the degree of deflationary adjustment. Thus, GNP figures, whether they are adjusted for inflation or not, are continually being artificially inflated by inflation.

The government never presents GNP figures on a per capita basis. As the country's population increases, naturally the GNP must increase (in terms of current economic activity and monetary policy) since more must be produced just to maintain the same per capita standard of living. When politicians trumpet, "there are more Americans now working than ever before," they should be reminded that there are now more Americans than ever before. So, such a boastful claim is meaningless. If the GNP goes up, but at a lesser rate than the increase in population, the country could still be experiencing a fall in its standard of living, and this would be true even if we *overlooked* any other consideration in connection with the GNP.

Please note Figure 38 as an indication of how such distortions work. At first glance, it might appear the GNP of the U.S. in 1972 had improved by more than 1,100 percent since 1929. That presumption would, of course, be entirely false, because on a per capita basis, the only meaningful basis by which the GNPs can be compared, the 1929 GNP could be the highest. Please note that after eliminating government purchases and adjusting 1929 figures upward for inflation and 1972 figures downward, the per capita GNP is about the same for all three years. However, since I suspect that far more instrumental and uneconomic goods were counted in 1971 and 1972, the per capita GNP in 1929 was probably higher in solid economic terms than in the latter years. Also, please note that I adjusted prices

Figure 38

HOW MEANINGFUL ARE GNP STATISTICS?

	1929	1971	1972
Gross national product (in billions)	$ 103.1	$1,055.5	$1,155.2
Less government purchases	8.5	234.3	255.0
Net civilian purchases	$ 94.6	$ 821.2	$ 900.2
Inflation adjustment	Plus 400%		Less 6%
Civilian GNP adjusted to 1971 prices	$ 473.0	$ 821.2	$ 849.2
U.S. population (in millions)	121.7	207.0	208.8
Per capita value of GNP	$3,886.0	$3,967.0	$4,067.0

Source: 1975 U.S. Statistical Abstract Table Nos. 2 and 598.

between 1929 and 1972 by 400 percent. The official CPI index would only be 150 percent (from 48.5 to 122.3 percent) but such figures are outright nonsense as can be easily seen by perusing old newspapers (especially the real estate sections), catalogues, menus, etc. It should also be noted that I based my 1972 deflation adjustment by 6 percent. The official CPI inflationary rate was approximately 3 percent. Therefore, I used 6 percent for the reasons already stated.

In the light of all the above, of what significance is the GNP as a measure of economic well-being? The answer, of course, is that it has no significance—it is misleading and meaningless. However, the GNP does have a value to two segments of society: the government, and the uneconomists. Because of their efforts, the country in an economic sense has been led to believe that black is white and fiction is fact.

Why Are We All Working?

Before leaving the question of GNP, and why an increasing GNP cannot be a reflection of an improving living standard, the reader must reflect on exactly what it is that human beings actually want and what they seek to accomplish. I personally do not believe that most Americans work for work's sake. Some people, I know, do. I, unfortunately, work to earn enough money to permit me to do the things I really want to do. Certainly, if some Americans had a choice of working, in the traditional sense, or not working, they would choose not to work or to work a good deal less. Many Americans, I am sure, would prefer to spend more of their time fishing, hunting, pursuing their hobbies, playing with their children, engaging in independent study, cultivating their talents, listening to music, hiking, writing poetry, playing chess, making love, camping, surfing, or just being able to relax around the house and not having to jump out of bed when an alarm clock says so. All these activities, valued by most Americans, *would not* (with the minor exception of the relatively small amount of material goods that might be required for these activities) *increase the GNP!* As a matter of fact, to the extent that more and more Americans were fortunate enough to be able to engage in more of these activities, this would result in a lowering of the GNP, insanely reflecting a reduction in our standard of living as more Americans were able to do all the things that they really wanted to do. It should be recognized that if an American went to the hospital for a heart transplant, the GNP would go up. But if he were to lounge in a hammock in his backyard, sipping a martini while enjoying a good book or a ball game on TV, the GNP would drop!

The government's vested interest in the GNP is that the latter creates jobs for bureaucrats who can be occupied compiling and interpreting all the useless statistics that are required for all those meaningless government indexes. It also creates a number of unnecessary departments and agencies to be staffed with political appointees. Artificially inflated and meaningless GNP figures can also be effectively used by any administration to convince the American public that they are economically better off than they really are, or to convince them that they are less worse off than they really are.

However, the government has a far more profound reason in selling GNP figures to the country, and that is its vested interest in making sure that those who do work, work as much as possible, even if *uneconomically*.

When World War II ended, many American servicemen observed the spectacle of the U.S. not only abandoning materials, but intentionally destroying usable equipment.[1]

The government, remember, lives on the productive efforts of others; it takes a piece out of every economic transaction. Everytime someone is paid, something is sold, something is produced, or something is transferred, the government is there with its hand out for a piece of the action. If the people of the country simply decided to relax, enjoy life, and produce less, the government would suffer a reduction in revenue. Like an individual denied water, politicians and bureaucrats would literally die of monetary thirst. The government, therefore, must whip American producers into feverish activity, or else how could they pay themselves? Thus, through inflation, confiscatory taxes, and the creation of needless economic activity, it keeps confiscating from society's producers the increased leisure that science, technology, and productive progress could normally be expected to bring, and therefore keeps forcing society's workers to work even harder so that their activity can be taxed in order to provide cushy jobs for those who are a part of the political bureaucratic complex, and to support those whom the government decides need not produce at all.

[1]A relative of mine, stationed in the Philippines when the war ended, told me of seeing jeeps and bulldozers sent over cliffs into the Pacific Ocean. Another relative of mine, returning from the Pacific on a destroyer, told me of expensive electronic equipment dumped over the side. He was involved in electronics, and could have used some of the equipment. But neither he nor anyone else was permitted to salvage any of it.

Uneconomists, of course, find merit in the GNP since it provides them with more confusing material on which to build hours of expensive economic instruction. Since they now can develop complicated charts labeled gross national product, net national product, national income, total personal income, and disposable income, they are more able to confuse their students, in particular, and society, in general, into believing that they really know what they are talking about, and that they know something about the subject of economics.

The Marshall Plan that followed World War II, and most other U.S. foreign aid programs, were designed (apart from serving to provide more jobs for the political-bureaucratic complex) to compel the American worker to not only support himself, but to support all sorts of people around the globe. It was this work and this effort that U.S. politicians wanted to tax. So, those vast American global give-away programs were not motivated by government altruism; they were designed to create jobs for politicians and bureaucrats as well as to force economic activity on the nation's workers—activity that it needed to tax for its own self-serving purposes.

The National Income—And Behold, A New Economic Indicator, The National Cost

A term Keynesians like to use interchangeably with the GNP is "national income." The government periodically proudly announces an increase in the national income as if this also were indicative of an increasing national prosperity, while Keynesians maintain that "an increase in national income may induce a higher level of net investment" (quoted from Samuelson text cited earlier, 3rd edition, page 236).

Now, the entire fallacy that an increasing national income is an indication of increasing prosperity or that it will necessarily increase net investment, as Samuelson implies, can be noted by the simple substitution of one word in this index. Since "income" to one member of society is merely a "cost" to another member,[1] the national income is equal to the national cost.[2] As the national income goes up, so does the national cost. What reception, therefore, would a government spokesman receive if he brought the following good news to the nation: "The government wishes happily to announce that the latest statistics reveal that there has been a significant increase in the national cost."

If you would not be thrilled over the prospect of an increasing national cost, it is only because you lack the *intelligence* of an *un*economist.

[1]To illustrate this, the *income* that a barber has for cutting my hair is my *cost* for getting my hair cut. Obviously, what is income to him, is cost to me. This holds true for rent, wages, and interest.

[2]National cost is not an officially recognized economic index but is merely my own creation. It is, nevertheless, as valid an index as the national income and to compile one, simply take any index labeled national income and substitute "cost" for "income." You have my permission.

13

The Decline of U.S. Economic Power— How the Government and the Federal Reserve Arranged It

If one had to select a year when the seeds of America's economic undoing were sown, it would be 1913, when the Sixteenth Amendment became part of the U.S. Constitution and the Federal Reserve Act became a reality. In that pivotal year Americans unwittingly gave the federal government the means to plunder both their productivity and their savings.

On July 12, 1909, Congress submitted the Sixteenth Amendment—enabling the U.S. government to "lay and collect taxes on incomes from whatever source"—to the states for ratification. On February 25, 1913, the Secretary of State announced that the amendment had passed by more than the necessary three-fourths. Only Connecticut, Florida, Rhode Island, and Utah had the foresight to reject it.

The U.S. electorate was tricked into voting for it because it was presented to them as a "soak-the-rich" scheme. The income tax, its backers insisted, would only affect the "wealthy"—and even they would feel its effects only slightly.[1] Clearly, therefore, there has been a breach by the federal government of the taxing power initially conveyed to it, which required a constitutional amendment. Since current levels of taxation go far beyond anything that consenting voters contemplated, there was, in legal parlance, no "meeting of the minds," and hence no contract binding the Sixteenth Amendment to the citizens of this republic can now be assumed.[2] At the very least, current tax law—given its confiscatory rate structure, its all-inclusiveness, its complexity, plus the costly administrative and time-consuming burdens it imposes on us all—flagrantly violates the spirit and intent of the Sixteenth Amendment, if not actually being unconstitutional itself.

How the Supply of Credit Currency Is Expanded

Creation of the Federal Reserve System enabled the government to abolish legitimate currency and substitute unmoney in its place. This allowed the government to use inflation to rob its own creditors while shifting wealth, unconstitutionally, from one economic class to another. To understand how and why the federal government was able to employ the Federal Reserve System to plunder the country's economy, more must be known about bank notes—a credit money substitute.[3]

Suppose A arrived in town and planned on staying at an inn. However, on arrival he discovered he neglected to take along his supply of money, and so had no money to pay for a room. Fortunately, while contemplating this embarrassing state, he spies B, an old college roommate, explains his plight to him, and asks for a loan. B, wishing to help out his old friend, unfortunately discovers that he too has neglected to bring any money.

"What inn had you planned to stay at?" asks B.

"Why, the Steprite Inn," replied A.

[1]The original law was contained in 14 pages. Today it wanders to over 1,500—which no one person can comprehend, thereby making a mockery out of the principle that "a citizen is presumed to know the law." The original law levied a delicate tax of 1 percent, graduated as follows: 2 percent on $20,000-$50,000, 3 percent on $50,000-$75,000, 4 percent on $75,000-$100,000, 5 percent on $100,000-$250,000, 6 percent on $250,000-$500,000, and 7 percent thereafter. In addition to providing the usual business and personal deductions, it provided a personal exemption of $3,000 plus an additional $1,000 for married taxpayers. The government's CPI index climbed from 29.7 to 136.2 between 1913 and 1974, or by 358 percent. Obviously, therefore prices rose at least 700 percent, Simple calculation in current dollars will reveal why Americans thought that they were giving the government the power to tax only the very wealthy. Statistics confirm this. In 1916, only 362,970 Americans out of a population of 102 million paid taxes—or less than 4/10 of one percent. Would the amendment have carried if voters thought the government wanted to substantially tax the incomes of better than 50 percent of the population, as it now does?

[2]Let us now put it to the test, honestly.

[3]We have already covered the subject of real money (which exists as a commodity, valued within a trading area) to money substitutes, such as warehouse receipts for money (gold and silver, "currency" certificates). Now we shall consider "credit money substitutes" which are, like gold and silver certificates, a risky "money substitute."

"Well, fortunately, the owner is a good friend of mine and he will recognize my signature. So, I will give you a note that will take care of the room." B writes out a note for A stating, "I, B, will pay to bearer on demand $50." B, of course, places his signature on the note which will be recognized by the owner of the Steprite Inn.

So, while A has no real money, he takes this note (a substitute for money) with him to the Steprite Inn and, sure enough, the owner recognizes B's signature and accepts this money substitute in lieu of real money. The owner accepts this money substitute because he has full faith and trust in B to honor his money substitute with real money. This money substitute, created by the stroke of a pen and whose value is based solely upon the honor and integrity of its maker to exchange the money substitute for real money, serves as effectively as money itself, if not more so.

Let's further suppose that before the inn owner is able to present his note for redemption, his food supplier makes a $50 delivery. However, the inn owner, unfortunately, has nothing in the till but B's note. Since the food supplier also knows B, he willingly accepts B's demand note in lieu of $50. On the way back to the warehouse, the food supplier's truck breaks down and so he pulls into a garage for repair. The garage owner reminds the food dealer that he has a bill outstanding on which he would like some payment. The food supplier points out that at that moment he has no money but that he does have B's money substitute. The garage owner willingly accepts B's note for $50 and credits the food merchant's bill accordingly. Since B is in the auto parts business, the garage owner knows he can easily have B's note exchanged for real money or credited to his own outstanding account with B.

In the above example, we have seen how approximately $200 worth of economic activity was conducted with $50 worth of a money substitute. From this illustration we can draw some rather basic economic conclusions.

(1) *Sound* credit currency—a money substitute—can serve an economy as effectively as it is served by real money and more conservative money substitutes, such as warehouse receipts (gold and silver certificates).

(2) When B created his IOU, he, in fact, "expanded" the "money" supply (lumping money and money substitutes together, which is what most monetary statistics do anyway). This did not require the services or the help of government or the Federal Reserve System. Note that *citizens* are perfectly capable of "expanding" the "money" supply to meet their own legitimate economic needs.

(3) U.S. government claims, therefore, that there was not enough gold to support world trade and that Special Drawing Rights (SDRs) or "paper gold" had to be created to support an expansion of world trade were, therefore, so much hypocritical nonsense. Private commercial traders were perfectly capable of expanding the quantity of money substitutes necessary to support any given amount of world trade. SDRs were only a new type of international unmoney developed to serve the wasteful international monetary needs of the U.S. govern-

ment (and those governments that the U.S. could intimidate into accepting them) in the same manner that the U.S. had pushed unmoney on the American economy for wasteful domestic needs.

(4) It can also be observed that it is not an expanding supply of money substitutes that stimulates business. It is business activity that stimulates the need for additional money substitutes. Money substitutes (Federal Reserve notes) "expanded" in order to "stimulate the economy" do not "stimulate the economy"; they inflate the quantity of money substitutes, thereby artificially upping prices. A free economy can generate, expand, and provide for its own money substitutes, providing government merely furnishes the economy with a sound money base—something the U.S. government has done poorly since 1934 and not at all since 1968.

Readers must continually remember that "money substitutes" have no intrinsic value themselves, but are merely promises to pay the bearer real money. In most instances, they are accepted almost as readily as money itself. However, it must be remembered that they are not money!

A typical example of how the word "money" is misleadingly used can be noted in this revealing excerpt from an article by Representative Wright Patman, the long-time and powerful chairman of the House Banking and Currency Committee and the former chairman of the Joint Economic Committee:

> The [Open Market] Committee determines the volume of bank reserves and the nation's *money supply*, primarily by instructing the New York Federal Reserve Bank to buy or sell securities in the open market. When the New York Bank buys, it adds to reserves and increases the *money supply*. When it sells, reserves and money supply fall.[1] [Italics mine.]

In the last 25 years, the Fed *has never* increased the nation's money supply. On the contrary, it was instrumental in reducing the money supply by causing a sharp outflow of money (gold and silver) from the American monetary system. Correctly, the word *unmoney*, or at the very least currency, should be substituted wherever Patman incorrectly uses the word "money." Then, again, Representative Patman never has understood money, currency, or credit or their respective functions. Incidentally, Patman suggests removing control of the Fed from the hands of the bankers and placing it in the hands of Congress by redeeming the stock that the

> . . . area banks own in the Federal Reserve District Banks and allowing the Federal Reserve Board, appointed by the President of the United States with the advice and consent of the Senate, to manage the nation's money.[2]

[1] "What's Wrong with the Federal Reserve and What to Do about It," *American Bar Association Journal*, February 1975, p. 179.

[2] Ibid., p. 180

Politicians have already demonstrated their financial incompetence by destroying the nation's money and currency supply and by plunging the nation into debt to the tune of $5 trillion. So Patman's recommendation for improving the management of the "nation's money" is as sound as his use of the word "money." The Fed need not be changed or amended; it need only be abolished.

The reason that Federal Reserve notes originally stated "redeemable in lawful money" was to distinguish them (currency) from the real money for which they could be redeemed. However, returning to our illustration of B's IOU, the problem with issuing personal money substitutes is that not everybody can be expected to recognize their legitimacy, therefore their value in commerce would be limited. Banks, given their financial position and their corporate character, were the logical community agencies to issue a more acceptable and useful money substitute—the bank note. Banks, therefore, assumed the important economic function of substituting their superior credit position for the credit of others.

The Importance of "Note" Currency

Arnie T. Preneur has an excellent idea for manufacturing a new type of teapot. He determines that he could manufacture and sell 1,000 of a new and improved model for $5, grossing $5,000. He estimates his costs as follows:

Labor	$1,200
Material	1,000
Overhead	1,000
Selling Costs	500
	$3,700

This leaves him a profit of $1,300. Arnie has only one problem—no money. He, of course, could ask his employees to accept IOUs in place of real wages until he could sell his teapots, at which time he would honor them. Employees, however, generally do not subscribe to propositions like this, because even if they believed that he was going to build a super teapot and be in a position to honor his personal notes, they in turn would have to convince their grocers, landlords, and all their creditors of this as well. No, they would have to be paid in something more substantial than Arnie's notes. Never having been in business before, suppliers would also be reluctant to ship Arnie merchandise on credit, since they could not be certain whether he would be in business the week after the merchandise was shipped. Arnie had also exhausted his friends and relatives as a source of funds and so it would appear that society was to be denied the better teapot that Arnie could provide. At long last, Arnie calls on the local bank. Sheldon Smiley, the bank's president, likes Arnie's teapot design, is impressed with Arnie's enthusiasm, his presentation, his apparent honesty and business ability. In short, he feels that Arnie might indeed have a really hot teapot. Smiley also feels that this might very well be the beginning of a teapot empire; and if so, it would not only provide the bank with a new and substantial client, but would, by increasing employment in the area, spawn a number of smaller bank accounts. So, Smiley agrees to loan Arnie the $3,700 to cover the cost of producing a thousand teapots. It is estimated that the time necessary to produce and sell the teapots will be six months, so the loan is set up to run six months at 10 percent interest. Therefore, Arnie has another cost to absorb, that of $185 in interest, which in reality, is the cost of buying the bank's credit in place of his own.[1]

Arnie gives the bank his note for $3,700 plus a few family heirlooms as added security and leaves the bank with $3,700 worth of the bank's *notes*. Prior to the Federal Reserve System, private banks issued their own bank notes. (See Figure 39.) The point is, now Arnie can pay for what he needs with the bank's IOUs which will be far more acceptable than his own. He has substituted the bank's strong credit position for his weak credit position. When Arnie pays his personal bills with the bank's notes, some of these notes will find their way back to the bank for redemption in real money, some will be deposited in the bank and held on account, and some will continue to circulate like real money.

Let us now assume that Arnie, as planned, sells his thousand teapots in six months and pays off his loan. For purposes of simplicity and illustration, let us assume that Arnie sold his teapots for real money (gold), with which he paid off his note (obviously the bank would have also accepted bona fide notes drawn on other banks). Once the bank receives payment of his $3,700 in real money, it is fully prepared to redeem the IOUs it had created when granting the loan. Now, assuming all of the bank's IOUs (notes) find their way back to the bank for redemption, they will leave circulation as the bank redeems them for real money.

Ultimately, after the economic activity of creating a thousand teapots has subsided, all credit-money substitutes created to handle the transaction will have been withdrawn from circulation, therefore causing no inflationary pressure. It is important to note what has occurred. The total currency supply had been inflated by $3,700 to accommodate the economic activity required to produce a thousand teapots.[2] After the teapots were produced and sold, the extra money substitutes (notes) came out of circulation. Before the inflation of the currency supply, the community had $5,000 worth of gold (real money) but no teapots. As a result of the

[1]The social justification and value of the bank's credit charge of $185 (which now must be absorbed by society in either the cost of the goods it buys or by a reduction in profits) will be found in the total economic savings that it contributes to society. The economic effort involved in Arnie's having to convince every possible creditor (and they in turn their creditors) of the safety of his personal notes, plus his less-efficient redemption capability, would be far more costly in economic terms than his one trip to the bank to convince one man of his credit-worthiness. And, from a social and economic standpoint, the banker is in a much better position by training and experience to evaluate Arnie's credit than would other members of the community.

[2]Credit was expanded to *produce* teapots, not just to *purchase* them.

Figure 39

PRIVATE BANK NOTES

An unissued bank note of the City Bank of New Haven. Federal Reserve notes were designed to replace this type of credit currency.

currency inflation and *subsequent deflation*[1] (contraction), the community still has \$5,000 worth of gold *plus the added wealth represented by the thousand teapots*. Real money (gold) had merely been shifted from those who now own the teapots to those who had a hand in producing them—labor, \$1,200; suppliers, \$1,000; those who provided overhead services, \$1,000; salesmen, \$500; the bank, \$185; and for Arnie T. Prenuer, who put it all together, risking even his prized family heirlooms, \$1,115. Notice that the supply of real money was not increased to accommodate this increase in economic activity. Bank and personal notes and all money substitutes were withdrawn from circulation, leaving society with real wealth (gold) and its new supply of teapots.

This is an example of the economic and proper use of credit currency. If credit currency were not made available to Arnie T. Preneur, better teapots might not have been produced and society would have been the loser.

The Federal Reserve Act[2]

One of the problems with the old bank note system, claimed proponents of the Federal Reserve System, was that all kinds of bank notes circulated. A note issued by a California bank might make its way to New York where a potential recipient might not know that the particular bank had, in the interim, folded. So, to an extent, we return to the old problem—how good is the money substitute? Credit techniques developed, of course, by which the credit standing of hundreds of the nation's banks might be checked. But this again proved time consuming, and errors might still be made. In other words, there were still problems in determining the legitimacy and the value of note currency. It was therefore proposed and adopted that the creation of bank note currency be centralized in a national banking system. This system was envisioned as a private banking system and not a part of the federal government, theoretically owned and operated by those member banks within the system.

The way the system was designed to operate was that when Arnie T. Preneur went to his bank for a loan, the bank, instead of issuing to him its own notes, would take Arnie's note to the Federal Bank within the district, and there rediscount Arnie's note—earning the difference between the interest it would be charged by the Fed Bank and the interest[3] it would then charge Arnie. All banks would now

[1]This is what is meant by an "elastic" currency supply. In the absence of this type of elasticity, changes in the volume of trade will cause changes in price levels, commonly known as "inflation" and "deflation."

[2]Its full title reads as follows: "An act to provide for the establishment of Federal Reserve banks, to furnish an elastic currency, to afford means of rediscounting commercial paper, to establish a more effective supervision of banking in the United States, and for other purposes."

[3] Technically not an interest charge, but merely a charge for credit. Commercial banks' proper function is to supply short-term credit. Investment bankers arrange capital loans which earn interest.

issue a uniform bank note rather than the conglomeration of bank notes that previously circulated within the system. That, of course, made pretty good sense. I might have been in favor of the act myself—had I not already learned that the politician will find a way to corrupt anything, no matter how good it sounds. And, this is what happened to the Federal Reserve System, as unfolding events demonstrate.

The original Federal Reserve Act required that all Federal Reserve notes issued by the system would have to be backed by 100 percent "commercial paper" and 40 percent gold. So, using Arnie T. Preneur's loan as an example, before Arnie could be issued $3,700 in Federal Reserve notes, the Federal Reserve Bank needed to have at least $1,480 in gold on hand with which to immediately honor any notes presented to it for redemption in connection with his loan, besides having Arnie's note for $3,700 as additional collateral. Obviously, this provided a good deal of safety for Federal Reserve notes.

We didn't mention it earlier, but Arnie's original bank had its own gold reserve with which to redeem those notes which might be presented to it for redemption before Arnie made any payment on his original note. That bank might have been less conservative than the Federal Reserve Bank, having only 25 or 30 percent of a gold reserve against its personal outstanding notes. Since many of the country's banks collapsed as a result of the Panic of 1907 (which had created demands that reforms in the banking system be instituted, which ultimately led to the Federal Reserve Act), a gold reserve of 40 percent was undoubtedly a higher gold reserve than many banks normally maintained. Federal Reserve notes thus provided a greater degree of safety and dependability than had bank notes. Bank failures were primarily caused by banks extending far more credit than their liquid gold positions realistically allowed. The lower the percentage of gold reserves to notes, the riskier and more vulnerable a bank's position, so, the reserve requirements of Federal Reserve notes presumably would provide the nation with bank notes of the highest quality.

With this in mind, let us see how the Federal Reserve System, which was created to provide a greater degree of safety as well as elasticity to America's monetary system, has fulfilled that responsibility.

Please note Figure 40, which shows the assets and liabilities of the Federal Reserve System as of December 31, 1971. You will note that, as of that date, the Federal Reserve had issued $53.819 billion of Federal Reserve notes (a sorry money substitute that Americans have been brainwashed into believing is actually money). Now, what was the main asset backing these notes? Why $70.804 billion of "U.S. government securities," a euphemism for U.S. government IOUs. How much private commercial paper did the Fed have? Why only $.3 billion worth. So, the Fed only had approximately four-tenths of 1 percent of the type of assets which the Act had originally envisioned would supply the backing for Federal Reserve notes; almost all the backing for Federal Reserve notes consisted of governnent IOUs—a type of collateral never authorized in the original Act.

Figure 40

A COMPARISON OF CURRENTLY HELD FED "ASSETS" VS. ASSETS REQUIRED UNDER ORIGINAL ACT AS OF DECEMBER 31, 1971

FED LIABILITIES (In Billions)		ASSETS ORIGINALLY REQUIRED (To Support Fed's Note and Deposit Liabilities)	
		Gold (In Billions)	Commercial Paper (In Billions)
Federal Reserve notes	$53.819	21.528 (40%)	53.819 (100%)
Deposits	31.101	10.885 (35%)	— 0 —
Total assets (etc.)		32.413	53.819
Actual assets on hand (a & b)		9.875 (a)	.300 (b)
Shortage—In terms of the act's original requirements		22.538	53.519
Percentage increase needed to bring assets *up to act's original standards*		228%	17,840%

FED ASSETS ACTUALLY HELD DECEMBER 31, 1971

U.S. government securities		$70.804	(The government always refers to its IOUs as a "security" which is slightly misleading.)
Gold certificate reserves	(a)	$ 9.875	
Special drawing rights		$ .400	(International unmoney)
Cash and collection items		$12.148	
Loans and acceptances	(b)	$ .300	
Other assets		$ 1.068	

Source: 1975 U.S. Statistical Abstract, Table 719

"Monetizing government debt," which means simply creating money substitutes out of government debt, can now be clearly understood. The Federal Reserve simply created unmoney out of the federal government's willingness to go into debt, and so a banking system, which had been originally envisioned as a means for rediscounting commercial paper, simply degenerated into an agency for printing unmoney for the federal government.

Moreover, in this situation it makes no economic sense whatsoever for the U.S. government to seek or pay for bank credit. As we have already noted, the purpose of bank credit is to substitute the weak credit standing of the borrower for the stronger credit position of the bank, while the economic justification for its credit charge is for saving society the trouble of passing on the borrower's credit-worthiness. Therefore, why does the U.S. government have to substitute the credit of the Fed for its own credit? Don't we all know who the federal government is? Wouldn't we trust the U.S. government to pay its bills? Do the government's direct creditors worry about it going out of business or skipping town, and thus prefer being creditors of the Fed rather than of the federal government? How does the Fed pass on the credit-worthiness of the federal government anyway? Does it run a credit check and an inspection report? Does it ask the federal government for a financial statement?

If the Fed does not investigate the credit-worthiness of the federal government, what is the economic justification for the interest[1] it charges the government and for which we are all taxed? In case you're still confused—there is no justification, economic or otherwise. Federal Reserve notes being backed by U.S. notes is simply a monetary sham, designed by politicians to hide the printing-press nature of American unmoney.

What happened to the gold backing requirement for Federal Reserve notes? As already explained, the Federal Reserve Act of 1913 required 40 percent gold backing (35 percent was required against deposits) in addition to 100 percent commercial paper backing for Federal Reserve notes. In 1945, gold backing for deposits was dropped. In 1968, gold backing for Federal Reserve notes was also eliminated and so they became no better than the poorest quality bank notes they were designed to replace.

In terms of the Federal Reserve Act of 1913, what assets should the Fed have had in order to support its liabilities as of December 31, 1971? This is found in Figure 40. So, as of then, the Fed would only have had to increase its gold position about 228 percent and its commercial paper by 17,840 percent in order to meet the standards set by the original Act.

It is just possible that the Federal Reserve Act, which set out to protect holders of bank notes and deposits from losses resulting from overextensions by individual banks, might have inadvertently combined all banks into a system that now appears to be as overextended as any one bank could possibly be! Certainly no *individual* bank, prior to the establishment of the Federal Reserve Act, would have loaned out bank notes or created deposits with *less* collateral than the Federal Reserve System. So, just where does this leave John Q. Public?

Few people realize that the original Federal Reserve Act did not authorize the issuance of Federal Reserve notes backed by government bonds. The reason for this was simple. If U.S. bonds could be used as collateral for Federal Reserve notes, government bonds might be used to expand the currency supply for other than commercial purposes, which would then (1) rob the System of its elasticity, and (2) convert it to a paper-money machine of the federal government. However, the Federal Reserve Act was amended to allow the Fed to back its notes with government bonds as well as commercial paper. History, therefore, has proven that the Act's original disallowance of government bonds as acceptable collateral was well founded.

[1]The Fed is supposed to return to the U.S. Treasury all earnings in excess of its own high and unnecessary expenses.

Why a Federal Reserve System at All?

American taxpayers may now ask: What is the legitimate purpose of the Fed in terms of why it was originally created? Consider the following:

1. The elasticity that Federal Reserve notes were supposed to give to the currency supply has been destroyed, since America's supply of Federal Reserve notes is being continuously expanded and never contracted.

2. Instead of being an agency for the "rediscounting of commercial paper," the Fed has become an agency for monetizing the expanding debt of the U.S. government, resulting in continuous inflation.

3. Since the conservative reserve requirements, which were originally established for Federal Reserve notes to ensure their unquestioned integrity, have now all been abandoned (requiring absolutely no money backing whatsoever), Federal Reserve notes are no better than the poorest quality bank notes they were created to replace.

Today Federal Reserve notes perform none of the three major monetary duties for which they were created.

How an Economy Grows

Comprehending the extent of the economic damage that our politicians and their economic handmaids, the Keynesians, have caused our country requires a greater understanding of such concepts as savings, capital, credit, and investment —how they are created, how they are divided, how they grow, and how they are destroyed.

Since capital is the difference between a higher and lower standard of living, the more capital society has and can generate, the greater will its output and standard of living be (or the less it has to work to get the same output). In other words, capital can either be applied to increase society's supply of goods or its supply of leisure. Creation of capital is the difference between a primitive economy and an advancing economy, and it is in the understanding of how capital is created, encouraged, and destroyed that one discovers why societies advance, stagnate, or crumble. It is the vast destruction of capital in the United States, destruction that was and is promoted by government, that explains and accounts for America's bleak economic prospect (to put it mildly).

Capital,[1] correctly understood, is the tool that increases the productivity of man's two hands, his ten fingers, his two legs, and the muscles of his back. When man first fashioned a stick to knock fruit out of a tree to avoid climbing and picking the fruit with his bare hands, he might have employed the first piece of capital equipment. The difference between a primitive and an advanced society is the difference in their store of capital equipment. Here are some principles that will

[1]Capital is also used to refer to the total supply of one's savings, which can be invested or loaned.

explain where society's supply of capital goods comes from, and how this supply relates to savings, credit, and investment.

(1) Capital must either come from savings or self-sacrifice.

(2) All savings come from underconsumption and self-sacrifice.

(3) All investment capital comes from society's limited store of savings.

(4) Economic progress can only come by increasing society's amount of capital or the efficiency with which it employs its capital. Therefore, it can be seen that all economic progress comes from savings and underconsumption. (The government and uneconomists would have you believe it comes from consumer spending and putting "money in circulation.")

(5) Economic uses of credit[1] and savings will continually propel society to ever-greater levels of prosperity, limited only by the availability of natural resources and the application of human ingenuity.

(6) Economic breakdowns, such as "recessions" and "depressions," are unnatural economic conditions and are breakdowns in the System resulting from government artificially interfering with natural economic forces.

(7) While to many persons the word "credit," like "air," appears to have a formless existence, it nevertheless exists in terms just as concrete as so many barrels of oil. Therefore, as society would not normally waste its limited supply of oil, so too should society not knowingly waste its limited supply of credit.

(8) That which encourages a wasteful use of the nation's limited supply of savings and credit contributes to the lowering of America's standard of living. It will thus be shown that since the Federal Reserve System and the federal government have shamefully plundered and squandered our economy's limited supply of savings and credit, they have substantially weakened our economy and thus have contributed to the reduction of the nation's standard of living while increasing its vulnerability to foreign aggression and intimidation.

Let me try to put these principles into more concrete terms.

All Capital Must Come from Self-Sacrifice or Savings (Underconsumption)

Let us suppose three men, Able, Baker, and Charlie, lived on an island. Each day they fished for food. The only way they knew how to catch fish was with their bare hands, and each day they managed to catch one fish. Each consumed his fish the day it was caught, thereby enabling him to survive to the next day to catch another fish. In this society, therefore, there are no savings, no credit, no investment; all that is produced is consumed.[2]

Let us suppose that one night, Able, lying on his bed of leaves and staring up into the star-studded sky, is suddenly struck with a thought that there must be more to life than simply catching fish each day with one's bare hands. An idea starts to

[1]When I use the word "credit," I refer to commercial bank credit, not trade credit.

[2]This according to Keynesians would be a highly desirable condition since it would create a marginal propensity to consume of 100 percent -- a "multiplier" of infinity!

form in his mind; if he had a conical-shaped instrument through which water might pass, but not fish (later he and his friends would label this a "net"), it might increase his ability to catch fish. All night he thought about how this conical instrument might be constructed. He visualized that it would have to be fashioned out of vine and flexible twigs which he would have to search for. He realized that it might take him a day or so to find the right material to make his net—time he normally devoted to fishing. He further realized that if he spent this time building his "net," he would have no time to fish, and would, therefore, go hungry. If he wanted to build the net, he would have to sacrifice by not eating for at least one day (thereby he would have to underconsume one fish), with no guarantee, of course, that the net would even work. But this was the risk he would have to take. Believing the sacrifice and the risk to be worth it, he spent the whole of the next day building his net, while Baker and Charlie spent their time fishing and eating. That evening, while Baker and Charlie were sound asleep, Able finds that he is unable to sleep thanks to the pangs of hunger; however, his hunger pangs are mitigated somewhat by the excitement of contemplating fishing the next day with his new net.

With the help of his net, Able indeed catches two fish on that very first day, and is thus relieved of having to fish the following day. Since Able is now no longer required to spend every day fishing for food, he can now devote time to building a better shelter, fashioning tools, and cultivating the soil. Here we see that since the island society had no store of savings, the island's first piece of capital equipment was derived solely from Able's willingness to deny himself food for one day. Without a supply of savings, capital can only be created by a reduction in consumption. In Able's case this meant creating capital by extreme personal sacrifice.

All Savings Must Come from Underconsumption

Soon, of course, Able's companions realized that they too could benefit from his net. They, therefore, asked Able if they might use it. Able, remembering the hunger pangs, the risk, and self-sacrifice he had undergone to acquire his net, is reluctant to simply hand it over, so he suggests to them that they simply do as he did, and make nets of their own. He'll give them his idea, but not his net.

But, let us suppose that they point out to Able that (1) they are not capable of making the same self-sacrifice that he did, and (2) there would be no guarantee that they would be able to fashion their nets as quickly as he did. So they propose to Able that he simply loan them some of his surplus fish while they make their nets, a loan which they will then repay from the increased productivity that their new nets would provide. Able asks Baker and Charlie why he should risk loaning them any fish since, if their net project should fail, he would be out of his savings—thus he has nothing to gain and everything to lose with such a loan. Considering this a legitimate objection, Baker and Charlie huddle and then offer Able the following proposition. They agree that there would be no economic advantage to him if he merely loaned them his supply of savings which they could possibly lose. So, to balance his possibility of loss, they offer him this possibility of gain. For each fish that Able loans to them, they will repay him with two. Therefore, if he loans them four fish and their net project succeeds, as in all probability it will, he would receive four additional fish—fish that he would acquire for performing no work at all! (So, now we see how capital can work in place of an individual.)

Baker & Charlie, in the meanwhile, had reasoned that the "interest" payment to Able of four extra fish would not in reality cost them anything, since it would have been derived solely out of the increased productivity made possible by Able's savings. Because of this, Baker & Charlie can acquire their capital without any personal sacrifice, since they have been assured of one fish a day while they construct their capital, and both can enjoy a fish a day while repaying Able his principal and interest. Thus, we see how Able's self-sacrifice in constructing the island's first piece of capital equipment not only benefited him but his community.

By now, Able has learned the art of smoking fish (as a result of his being able to employ the time his capital had created) and agrees to this suggestion. He, therefore, proceeds to catch two fish a day for four days. By the fourth day he has saved four fish that he did not consume. He also elected to work everyday. In any case, as a result of work, underconsumption, prudence, thrift, and what have you, he now has four smoked fish which constitute the island's total stock of savings. What might Able do with these savings?

In deciding this question, Able reasons as follows:

(1) He simply might hold onto his savings, and while they would not "grow," they would always be available to him as a possible source of nourishment, should he not desire or be able to fish.

(2) He could indulge himself and consume all of his savings.

(3) He might loan out his four fish to Baker and Charlie, and if they successfully build their nets, he would be repaid with eight fish, thereby increasing his savings by four, which would not have required additional effort on his part. However, he would risk losing what he had already saved if their net project failed.

(4) However, another possibility struck Able. Instead of loaning Baker and Charlie the consumption goods they required to sustain themselves while they built a capital good, he could use his fish to sustain himself while he built two more nets. He might invest his savings of consumption goods into increasing his own stock of capital goods. He could consume two fish while spending two days making two more nets, at the end of which time he would have decreased his savings by two fish while increasing his capital stock to three nets. He could then offer to rent the nets to Baker and Charlie for half a fish a day. They certainly would be agreeable to that since, with his net, they would catch two fish per day, and even after paying him his half-fish, they would still be 50 percent better off. So, actually, the rental fee would not cost them anything. Since his rental income from both nets would be a fish a day, Able reasoned he would never be required to fish again. He could retire. Why, in one month's time, his two nets would have earned him 30 more

fish, while, by loaning Baker and Charlie four fish with which to build their nets, he only stood to earn four more.

Therefore, reasoned Able, it would be wiser to invest my savings in making more nets for myself rather than loaning my savings so that others can make nets for themselves. Having decided to build two more nets, he is suddenly struck by another thought. Suppose after using my nets for two days and acquiring a savings of a fish each, Baker and Charlie decide to use their savings to support themselves in order to construct nets of their own. If they succeeded, I would now only receive the equivalent of two fish after having invested two from my savings. Able must, therefore, decide on whether it would be more advantageous to loan out four fish with a reasonable assurance of securing eight, or to invest his two fish with the potential of receiving far more than eight but with the possibility of only recovering two and being left with some excess net capacity. In any case, he has only (as society only has) five things he can do with his savings. He can save what he has saved, consume what he has saved, loan out what he has saved, invest what he has saved, or try a combination of all four.

What he does will be based upon the relative risk and profit rewards and his personal economic needs. It is apparent, however, that since it is Able who has created the island's total stock of savings, and since only he stands to lose directly if these savings are wasted, then only he has the moral and equitable right to decide how these savings should be employed.[1]

In any case, we now have proof of the other half of the proposition that capital can only come from saving and self-sacrifice. When Able constructed his net, society had no savings. So, capital could only come from his personal self-sacrifice. Baker and Charlie, however, can now sustain themselves on Able's supply of savings. Their economic fortunes must now be improved regardless of whether Able chooses to invest his savings in more nets for himself or whether he elects to use his savings to supply them with the credit they need in order to build their own. This should illustrate how wealth in a community, regardless of who has legal title to it, benefits the *entire* community. Please note that the only way Able's wealth can increase is if he makes this wealth available to other members of the community. In this case, he would have to make an arrangement whereby his personal savings would benefit others in order for his savings to financially benefit himself. Without employing his wealth for the economic benefit of others, it cannot grow. It can only stay the same (option 1) or diminish (option 2). Thus, it can be seen that one of the noble attributes of private capitalism is that it forces those who may only be motivated by personal gain to elevate the living standards of others, if only to achieve their own economic goals.

[1]Please note that when government extends credit and guarantees debt, it merely loans out the savings belonging to others. And this credit is extended not for economic reasons, that is, to benefit those who have saved, but is usually loaned out for political reasons, simply to benefit the loan's recipient.

Regardless, therefore, of whatever choice Able makes, employment of his capital to enrich himself must also enrich Baker and Charlie and enable them to acquire a source of capital which will eventually enable the community to generate the equivalent of three extra fish a day, assuming they employed the same amount of effort they expended before.

If Able, Baker, and Charlie now fish for a full week, they would have acquired enough savings collectively at the end of that first week to devote a week's effort on another larger capital project. They might employ one week to make a large fish trap capable of trapping fish on a continuous basis. This would relieve them of the task of fishing three and four days a week, leaving them only the task of gathering the number of fish they desired to consume each day. Assuming, therefore, that they did not choose to use the free time thus created to build any additional capital or to pursue any more consumption goods, they would have accomplished the following: where once, without capital, the three spent all day simply working to catch one fish, they now enjoy a day's leisure and all the fish they can eat. Periodically, of course, they are required to inspect and repair their trap. Short of a natural disaster destroying or damaging their capital (their trap), there need be no breakdown in their economy. In modern economic terms, short of a storm destroying their net, they need not suffer any recessions or depressions.

Similarly, in economic terms, only natural disasters such as an earthquake, a drought, a tidal wave, or a flood can create economic hardship and disrupt a community's economic life. When we find economic hardship, such as the case of a recession or depression, in the absence of external physical forces, then it has been brought about by man. In the final analysis, recessions and depressions are nothing more than the consequences of destructive, *unnatural* economic interference, usually caused by nonproductive politicians meddling in the *natural* economic order. Governments, throughout history, have been organized political and social forces designed to steal to a greater or lesser degree the productivity of some for the benefit of others.[1] This negative economic force ultimately leads to a breakdown of incentives, a breakdown of productivity, and a breakdown of the economy, depending upon the degree of destructive force that the government is allowed to exert. In the absence of the negative economic interference of governments, a society's standard of living would continuously increase without any economic breakdown. Its economic welfare would be limited only by its natural resources and the intelligence, the industry, and the thrift of its population. Business cycles, recessions, depressions, and inflation are *man-made* economic phenomena and are *unnatural* economic conditions—always predictable, always avoidable.

[1]For a greater understanding of this statement, I urge you to read *The Mainspring of Human Progress,* Henry Grady Weaver (Irvington-on-Hudson, N.Y.: Foundation for Economic Education).

Consumer Credit Versus Commercial Credit

As we already know, commercial credit (credit extended to increase society's supply of consumer goods, as represented by the loan to Arnie T. Preneur), or a capital loan as represented by the loan to Baker and Charlie, will ultimately increase society's supply of consumer goods, out of which will come additional savings, which in turn will generate increases in investment capital, which in turn will generate even more consumer goods in an ever-increasing ability for the economy to generate more consumer goods or more leisure. Consumer credit,[1] on the other hand, as will be illustrated, wastes credit (less credit is now available for commercial purposes) and thereby reduces society's ability to generate increases in consumption goods, thereby lowering society's standard of living. Using credit to finance consumption (such as automobiles, clothing, vacations, meals in restaurants, appliances) is uneconomical and wasteful and contributes toward lowering a nation's standard of living.

Many people are under the impression that consumer credit permits the purchase of goods that otherwise would go unpurchased, thus simultaneously benefiting the consumer and "stimulating" the economy. However, this is not so. As we shall see, loans made for consumption purposes are an uneconomic use of savings and bank credit, which ultimately reduce the amount of consumer goods coming to market, and raise price levels. But more specifically, consumer credit simply permits higher prices to be charged for goods and services.

For example, suppose the government outlawed bank credit to finance automobile purchases. If one wanted a car, he had to pay cash for it. I would venture to say that most automobile sales in the United States are financed, so if buyers were compelled to pay cash, no doubt automobile sales would drop drastically. Prices of autos in showrooms and on sales lots would have to be slashed so they could be sold for cash at any price. As car prices dropped, automobile manufacturers could no longer afford to pay the same level of wages nor the same prices for supplies. Consequently, their suppliers and labor force would have to cut their prices if they wanted to sell their supplies and their labor. These suppliers, in turn, would have to compel their labor forces and their suppliers to roll back prices and this would work its way back to the raw materials themselves.

Labor, of course, would not suffer by its falling wages since prices would fall back at least to the same extent, making smaller paychecks buy as much or more than before. Workers would fall into lower tax brackets, therefore they would have relatively more after-tax income to spend on lower-priced goods. Ultimately, the same number of cars, if not more, would be sold for cash than were sold on credit. Prices would simply have adjusted to the same *relative* levels as before, but absolute prices in terms of currency would have shifted downward, reflecting a

[1]When created by a commercial bank.

lower price structure dependent on cash purchases rather than a high price structure supported by the availability of consumer credit.

Older and retired citizens, living on fixed incomes and savings, would be helped by this downward shift in the price structure; their savings would buy more. More could now afford a car at these lower cash prices than before when they had to pay both a higher price and finance charges. This fact alone would increase the total number of cars sold.

The only segment of society that would suffer, apart from overextended speculators and debtors, would be society's most overextended debtor and biggest spendthrift—the United States government. Since government tax revenues would fall, the government would have trouble meeting its payrolls and paying off its $5 trillion of funded and unfunded debts.

Now the reader can understand why the government encourages consumer credit—not to benefit the consumer, but to benefit itself.

For example, suppose that when Baker and Charlie first approached Able for credit so they could make their own nets (intending to repay him out of the increased productivity made possible by the loan itself), they had instead suggested that they wanted a "vacation loan." They suggested to Able that they were tired of fishing everyday, so why couldn't Able loan them two fish so they could lie on the beach and relax for a day or so. When Able inquired how they would repay the loan, since they were now consuming all they produced, they replied that they would work that much harder in the future, possibly even going without eating "one or two days" in order to repay him. Able pointed out that they were perfectly capable of doing that now in order to finance their vacation—what need therefore had they to borrow from him? Further, Able pointed out, since they would be required to pay him two fish for every one they borrowed, they would have to go fishless for four days in order to finance their two-day vacation, while without borrowing they would have to go fishless for only two days to finance it.

Able, therefore, pointed out how they would compound their problems further by asking him for a loan and pointed out to them that "Whatever pleasure my savings might furnish you with now will only increase your misery later. Without receiving a loan from me, you are perfectly capable of giving yourself a one-day vacation now by only underconsuming one day. In order, therefore, to help you economically," said Able, "I have to deny your loan, which would only economically benefit me and economically burden you." This might be the basis for the saying "the rich get richer, the poor get poorer," and if there is any truth in this saying, it is probably because of the promotion and use of consumer credit.

Consumer credit, even granted to those who want it, obviously hurts them more than it helps them. Here we have seen an example of how society's total stock of loanable and investable funds is limited by its total stock of savings, and why bank credit extended for uneconomic purposes reduces the amount of credit available for economic purposes.

Society's total supply of credit is limited by its total supply of wealth. Obviously, Able cannot loan out nor grant credit for more than four fish. If he issued to Baker and Charlie a paper instrument agreeing to provide them immediately with five, ten, or twenty fish, this would not "expand credit"—he would simply be lying about the amount of credit (fish) he could immediately deliver. Therefore, it is nonsense to talk about the Fed "expanding," "easing," or "relaxing" credit. Since society's total stock of savings and credit is fixed by its real worth, it can only be expanded by the producers and savers of the country, and not by the Fed or the federal government. By guaranteeing, extending, or "expanding" loans and credit, the Fed and the federal government merely inflate the supply of paper credit instruments beyond the economy's true capacity to deliver real, liquid wealth, or surreptitiously invade society's limited stock of credit and savings and drain it off into less economic areas, usually based on political and uneconomic considerations. In either of the above cases, the efforts by the Fed and the federal government will weaken America's economic strength, which will in turn lower our standard of living and impair our ability to defend ourselves from foreign aggression and pursue a strong foreign policy.

Let's return to Able, Baker, and Charlie for a moment. Let us assume that Able again had rejected Baker and Charlie's request for a loan to finance consumption, but a week later, because of a storm or sickness, Baker and Charlie are unable to fish. In this case, not having consumption goods is now a matter of life or death for them. In this instance, Able's store of savings could now help Baker and Charlie in this dire emergency. While Able, and rightly so, felt no great compassion to loan out his savings (the result of his self-sacrifice and underconsumption) so that Baker and Charlie could simply lie on the beach watching sea gulls, he would, I am sure, loan to them a portion of his savings if it were a matter of life or death. So, the existence of Able's store of savings is protection for both Baker and Charlie, even though it remains in the sole and legal custody of Able.

Let us use an exaggerated example of how unwise consumption loans can destroy an entire society. Suppose that Able makes Baker and Charlie that needless consumption loan, and before Able can rebuild his savings, a storm developed, making it impossible for all three to fish. Since the community now has no savings to fall back on, theoretically Able, Baker, and Charlie could now perish from hunger. If the community's stock of savings hadn't been needlessly wasted, it might have carried them through the storm. While the storm raged, making it impossible for the community to work (fish), they could have obviously gotten by on less food per day, since they were not expending any energy in working. In this manner, each man might have survived on one-fourth fish a day, and Able's savings would have allowed the community to survive for five days. Since consumption during this period would have dropped from one fish a day to one-fourth fish a day, we could say a recession or depression had set in. While this would indeed be true, it should be noted that such a reduction in consumption was caused by external forces over which the community had no control. It must, therefore, be noted that a reduction in the quantity of consumption goods that is not caused by external forces is, in every case, caused unnecessarily by individuals and governments interfering with natural and creative economic forces.

One thing should be noted here. Not all investments or capital loans work out, and they could bring about a reduction and a waste of society's store of savings. Able might have loaned Baker and Charlie his savings to build their nets, but despite their good intentions they might have failed. Society would then be out Able's four fish as surely as if they had been dissipated by consumption loans. Likewise, Able's decision to invest his savings into constructing additional nets could have been wasted. He could have failed to find the material, the nets might have failed to work, or conceivably Baker and Charlie might have irrationally refused to use them. In this case, except for replacement purposes, he would derive no economic benefit from his investment. So, while all investments and loans for capital creation may not pan out, society must keep trying. Investments and commercial loans that succeed help compensate for those that fail, and it is this "net" success ratio that elevates society's standard of living. Since society's savings are limited, so is the amount available for investment and loans. Therefore, we may draw these conclusions: 1. Loans for consumption purposes reduce the amount of funds available to finance both capital projects and the production of additional consumer goods, and therefore can only lower society's standard of living and its economic security. 2. Government programs encouraging loans to poor-quality and high-risk applicants, thus developing a higher degree of capital failure, waste society's savings in the same way as the granting of consumer credit.[1]

When the federal government and/or Keynesians talk about "expanding credit" or "loosening credit," they mean, in all cases, using society's limited amount of savings in an increasingly wasteful and uneconomic manner for either consumption loans or compelling society to make unwise and wasteful commercial loans. Since neither the U.S. government nor the Fed has any "savings," how can either "expand," "guarantee," or "loosen" credit? With what store of savings can it meet such guarantees? Through its manipulation of the "independent" Federal Reserve Board, the government gains access to society's savings which it then proceeds to wantonly dissipate by assigning it (based on political not economic considerations) to support consumption purchases or to finance marginal and unnecessary commercial projects.

Let us take note of another situation which should be introduced in connection with the island's ability to generate savings. Let us suppose, for example, that while Able was negotiating with Baker and Charlie about their consumer loan (a loan he would wisely turn down, more for their sake than for his), Franklin Dee, the island's bully, showed up. Hearing the discussion, Franklin might have simply

[1]Overlooking government "bond" sales themselves, which obviously waste much of society's limited supply of savings.

said to Able, "Now listen, you old skin flint, you have four fish that you don't really need, so why don't you loan them to these guys?" With this he gives Able's fish to Baker and Charlie, saying, "Here, enjoy. If you can, you might consider paying Able back."

Since Franklin Dee is much bigger than Able, there is not very much Able can do about it. However, since he now finds that his savings are not really "safe," and since they can apparently be confiscated by the bully, Franklin, at any time, Able is now less motivated to save and hence society's store of savings will be reduced. In essence, it can be demonstrated that the Federal Reserve's influence on the banking system is (in only a slightly more complicated manner than was just demonstrated by Franklin Dee) to: (1) waste savings by encouraging the uneconomic uses of credit, and (2) discourage savings by reducing if not eliminating completely the rewards of thrift.

Let us now move from our simple economic society to a more complicated one and see how the same economic rules apply. Assume that there are now a number of Ables on our island, all fishing with their own nets. We can now, of course, recognize that the ability of all of these islanders to enjoy the advantages of their nets was due to Able's initial willingness to create capital through his own personal self-sacrifice. However, as the islanders were able to increase their own supplies of fish, they simply did not have the necessary facilities for storage, and while they would have liked to have seen their savings grow by loans and investments, individual producers had neither time nor training to judge the merit of business propositions offered them. So one of their number, an honest and wise member of the island community, Max Goodbank, built a storage facility for the island's fish savings. It should be noted that, while the island now produced other commodities (the island's population now consisted of chair makers, mat makers, wheelbarrow makers, road builders, umbrella makers, wagon makers, wagon pullers, etc.), they still upheld the island tradition of consuming a fish a day. The islanders also used fish as their medium of exchange: all merchandise and wages were quoted in terms of so many fish. Since each person on the island consumed a fish a day, the island's price structure was related to their daily consumption of fish.[1] All production on the island was quoted in terms of fish, loans were negotiated in fish,

[1]Using gold, however, as a medium of exchange, society's price structure is tied to the "work effort" required to mine and refine one ounce of gold. When processed gold was valued at $35 per ounce, the price of a loaf of bread could never, for example, rise to $35 since the value of the "work effort" required to produce a loaf of bread was considerably less than the value of the "work effort" required to produce an ounce of gold (three tons of earth, in all likelihood, would have to be processed to recover an ounce of gold, or many hours would have to be spent "panning" for it). Thus, the "work effort" involved in producing an ounce of gold was the "feet and inches" by which all other "work effort" was priced, related and measured. However, with unmoney serving as the medium of exchange, society's price structure is not anchored to any "work effort" at all. Thus, prices are free to float upward like a hot-air balloon into the economic firmament. A loaf of bread could now conceivably cost $35, or even $35,000.

and savings were maintained in fish (let us assume that each fish is uniform in size and quality).[1]

When the Ables of the island underconsumed, thereby generating additional savings which they deposited with Mr. Goodbank, Mr. Goodbank acknowledged these deposits by giving each saver a paper receipt for his fish deposit, such as ''Mr. I. M. Able, deposited ten fish on January 1, 1975.'' Now those requiring consumption goods (fish) in order to finance a capital project needed only see Mr. Goodbank, custodian of all the island's savings, rather than having to visit individually all the Ables on the island.

No one desiring savings merely for their own consumption needs would call on Mr. Goodbank. Mr. Goodbank was a banker of integrity, and he would never approve a consumption loan. Mr. Goodbank had far too much concern for savers, borrowers, and the community to finance this type of uneconomic activity (supporting the overconsumption of some with the underconsumption of others).

In the event of a dire emergency, poor health, loss of employment, or what have you, some may have desperately needed consumer credit. In this case, Mr. Goodbank had compassion. As a matter of fact, as a consequence of his managing the economic affairs of the island so well, the island's store of capital and consequently its supply of fish savings had risen steadily. As a result of this increased wealth, Mr. Goodbank created a special fund for such purposes. Convinced that, due to unfortunate circumstances, one, through no fault of his own, was in need of a consumption loan and was not making such a request simply because he was unwilling to work or too undisciplined to save, he would make loans out of this contingency fund. If borrowers are able to repay these loans, fine. If not, in Goodbank's judgment, he would not have impaired the amount of savings available for essential island projects.

Several generations have now passed since the original I. M. Able made his personal sacrifice and created the island's first piece of capital equipment. The island's economic and social progress began at that point. With the development by Mr. Goodbank of his facility for storing the island's fish and his being made responsible for preserving and loaning out the island's supply of savings, the island continued to prosper. You will note that investment decisions as opposed to loan decisions continued to be made individually. Soon, however, islanders who wanted to take the greater risks for the potentially greater rewards that investment capital offered, risks that Mr. Goodbank was not prepared to take on their behalf, began to pool their risk capital and entrusted it to a fellow named Manny Fund. So, Manny Fund invested that portion of the island's savings for those islanders willing

[1]Since fish are obviously not uniform in size and quality, they are less suitable for use as money than gold, for example, which can be expressed in exact size and quality. However, since fish have *intrinsic value,* they would serve the purpose of money far better than Federal Reserve notes, which are worthless.

to take larger risks for potentially higher returns, while Goodbank was entrusted with capital growth through more conservative forms of investment.

As the island's savings continued to increase, the island's ability to undertake increasingly larger capital projects by the prudent use of its supply of savings continued to grow. The island was now capable of undertaking such vast capital projects as the building of a new water system, which brought water directly into the homes of all the islanders in contrast to the islanders' traditional practice of having to draw water out of their mountain stream. This project enabled the islanders to live much further from their source of water than they had hitherto been able to do, since now they were relieved of having to haul water a great distance. Also, a reservoir system was constructed that would retain water, which could then be available to the island community in the event of a severe drought. The island had suffered a severe drought only a few years previously which had caused considerable amount of economic hardship. The point is that it required some 250 islanders working two years to construct the water system. Fortunately, the island had acquired such a supply of fish that those required to work on the project could be supplied with their consumption needs throughout this period.

The island's ability to save had reached the point where capital projects of this magnitude could now be undertaken. We have seen how at one time the island did not have enough savings to support even a day's capital construction by one man, and how it advanced to where it could support a capital investment requiring two men working two days, and how it then was able to support a capital project requiring three men working one week, and now it could support a capital investment requiring 250 men working two years. The water works project required an investment by the savers of the community of 182,500 fish, a lot of fish to lose if the project failed. But the islanders considered that if the project succeeded it would pay for itself in the years ahead. The considerable amount of uneconomic time the islanders now had to devote to drawing and transporting water could be more productively used making more consumer goods and developing new capital projects.

So, as the island continued to prosper, it appears that the economics of prosperity and disaster became more complicated. This, of course, is not true. The economics of prosperity and disaster have not changed one iota from when Able, Baker, and Charlie existed on the island with one net among them.

What has happened is that the direct relationship between self-sacrifice, savings, credit, investment, economic incentive, and social and economic progress have become more difficult to follow. Society's economic agencies and economic terminology have become more complicated, while economic relationships have remained as uncomplicated as when Able first handed Baker and Charlie four fish so that they could build their own nets.

In time, the island organized a government primarily to protect the islander's life and property. As the islanders prospered, they acquired quantities of personal property, the legal ownership to which at times was in doubt. Also, as the islanders prospered, trade developed and the need to enforce contracts between tradesmen became a matter of economic welfare and economic concern for the entire community. Too, the increase in leisure time, made possible by the increasing ease by which islanders could satisfy their basic consumption needs, led to a certain amount of idleness which was used by some to harass and prey upon the other more productive members of the community. Personal disputes and crimes of passion had long been settled by the islanders in a direct and personal manner, wherein the aggrieved islander would enlist friends and relatives in order to redress supposed wrongs committed to them. For these reasons, and because of increased affluence, the community was now able to maintain an official court of arbitration and establish a constabulary composed of the biggest men on the island to maintain domestic tranquility. The constabulary quickly discouraged those islanders who thought they could intimidate others by either force or violence. A senate was elected whose function was to select and oversee the judges and the constabulary. The salaries for the full-time judges and full-time constables, as well as the expenses for the 12 senators, of course, had to be paid. While the judges and constables received full-time salaries, the senators received token salaries since it was considered an honor to serve on this body—the community's recognition of a man's integrity, intelligence, and productive ability. The islanders decided to underwrite these expenses with a voluntary tax. All who thought the new system of government was a good idea and wanted to, would vote for the senators, and would at the same time contribute five fish. No one was compelled to pay the tax but if one wanted to have a say in how the government was to be run he was merely expected to help defray its costs. At the time the government was established, it was considered important to have responsible and concerned people voting in order to ensure the election of the most responsible members of the community. It was felt that those who were willing to pay five fish in order to vote might attribute some value and importance to their vote and would, therefore, exercise their right to vote more responsibly. If a vote cost nothing, it was worth nothing, so the community had initially reasoned. Those that had formed the government attempted to fashion an electorate in which the quality of the voter counted more than the quantity of voters. Given a population, for example, of 10,000, it was considered better to have senators selected by 1,000 interested, informed, responsible citizens than by perhaps the full 10,000, the majority of whom might be uninterested, irresponsible, and uninformed.

The islanders did not even establish an age criteria for voting. Since youth on the island started to work at an early age, they became responsible at an early age, so that a fourteen year old who was prepared to contribute five fish toward the cost of government was given a voice in selecting that government in place of an older man who was not interested or unwilling to support the cost of government. Naturally, everyone, whether he supported the government or not, whether he voted or not, automatically received the same benefits. The new government did establish a greater degree of domestic tranquility, provided greater safety for all, whether one voted or not or paid taxes or not. The court system, by expediting and enforcing contracts among tradesmen, facilitated trade which further increased the division of labor, increasing economic benefits for all. Justice was dispensed equally to those who paid taxes and to those who didn't. In other words, those that voted and paid taxes could gain no special advantage, economic or otherwise, over those that didn't—they were simply five fish poorer.

Why, therefore, might one decide to vote and pay his taxes? He might vote and sacrifice five fish out of a feeling of regard for his civic duty which others might not feel, in much the same way that men who are responsible donate to charity if they are able, while others do not. Most of the responsible members of the island's community elected to pay their fish tax because of their desire to ensure themselves that the most uncorruptible men in the community served as senators, and out of the recognition that five fish was a cheap price to pay for economic and social justice. Some of the island inhabitants, of course, would not have given one fish to promote economic and social justice let alone five; so, fortunately, they did not have a voice in the island's government.

In a few generations, the political complexion of the island changed. In a burst of democratic spirit, everyone on the island was given the vote. Senators were now highly paid individuals, so that their positions were now desired more for the money than for the honor, with senators now spending much of their own money just to get the position. Getting elected and staying in office cost so much that senators became more concerned with dispensing favors than with dispensing justice. Dispensing favors won votes; dispensing justice didn't.

While the island still had a court system that theoretically dispensed justice, the quality of justice had suffered because of the judges that the senators were now appointing, though some decent judges still remained. The senators had created a number of administrative courts to handle all the new laws that they had passed and these administrative courts functioned outside the regular legal system and were controlled directly by the senate itself. As a result, the power and influence of the senate was now far greater than what was originally contemplated.

Franklin Dee V, the chief senator at this point in time, was a direct descendant of the island's original bully. He won reelection to the senate time after time because of the favors that so many of the islanders thought he did for them (while all the time he was doing favors for them with their own money and overcharging them to boot).

Now, Franklin was forever looking for ways to ingratiate himself with the island voters to ensure for himself even more votes at the next election. While reflecting on this problem, it struck him that he had heard that the new director of the bank, Seymour Goodbank, a direct descendent of Max Goodbank, the bank's founder, had been rejecting a number of requests for commercial and consumption loans, thereby creating a certain amount of dissatisfaction among those denied access to the community's store of savings. Franklin, therefore, got the senate to pass a law enabling the senate itself to make commercial loans and even emergency consumption loans that the bank had refused to approve when, in the senate's opinion, such loans were in society's interest. Thus, the senate, in reality, could now make loans and invade the community's limited supply of savings for projects and for purposes that had been rejected by those in the community who had the necessary training and expertise with which to judge them.

Franklin and his cohorts had learned that increasing government "favors" and "government benefits" meant increased taxes. (Payment of taxes had become compulsory when everyone was given the right to vote.) What really hurt, however, was when they discovered that taxes had to be increased by more than these "benefits." Provision had to be made for all the extra cost of government overhead—so providing more popular government benefits required raising unpopular taxes, a seemingly self-defeating task. But, using "Franklin Reserve notes" as a method to bribe voters was more practical and more compatible with the new character of the senate. It was decided that the government would make loans by issuing borrowers this new type of currency, Franklin Reserve notes. The recipient would simply take a Franklin Reserve note to the bank and use it to withdraw part of the community's supply of savings. In other words, a saver's claim to fish that he had worked for and subsequently deposited, as evidenced by his deposit book,[1] was no better claim to his productivity than what could be withdrawn with Franklin Reserve notes. Thus, the government provided producers and nonproducers alike with the same democratic access to the community's store of savings.

In other words, a saver's claim to fish he deposited with the bank was no different than the person's to whom the government issued Franklin Reserve notes, and the bank and the community could not in a practical sense differentiate between them.

The senators found it difficult to decline any potential voter wanting a consumer or a commercial loan of questionable merit. All they had to do was authorize more Franklin Reserve notes. Naturally, the senate issued a substantial amount of

[1]In the interests of simplicity, I have lumped time (savings) and demand (checking) deposits together in one bank while they should, as in the U.S. banking system, be kept separately. Savings banks store savings; commercial banks store credit.

A savings passbook indicates the amount of savings that one has in the bank. A savings bank is not a storehouse for savings, it is where savings are put to work and made available to society, usually in the form of long-term mortgages, which develop a cash flow that becomes available to meet the current withdrawal needs of the depositors. Since savings deposits are expected to be left in the bank over a long period of time, so that they can work for the depositors, they are called *time deposits*. Time deposits earn interest and should show a continual growth pattern as the community increases its store of savings.

Commercial banks, however, store credit, not savings or money. As a result, credit earns no interest; it only needs to be available for spending purposes. So, such checking accounts are referred to as *demand deposits* and earn no interest. Naturally, the savings departments and certificates of deposits issued by commercial banks are characteristic of mutual savings banks. However, these functions are incidental to the real purpose of commercial banks, which should be to serve as a source of short-term commercial credit.

these money substitutes. The senators found that they could even increase their own salaries and expense allowances and hire more assistants by paying them in the same money substitutes which they could now create. They and their cronies and a whole army of similar nonproducers went in droves to the bank, withdrawing the savings of society's producers.

When the idea for a Franklin Reserve System was first proposed to Mr. Goodbank, he vigorously opposed it because he recognized that such a system could be a corrupting influence on the community's ability to generate savings. Certain safeguards, therefore, were written into the law to meet Goodbank's objections, and assurances were given that the senators would wield their credit power judiciously. All in all, Goodbank's power could not match that of the senate or the naïveté of the voters, so the senate passed the law.

After the law became a reality, it was soon amended to remove any restrictive provisions. Assurances concerning the government's responsible use of its credit power were quickly forgotten. At the end of the first year, therefore, a good deal more fish flowed out of the bank because of the number of Franklin Reserve notes that were presented for redemption in relation to the amount of fish deposited in the bank by the island's producers. Therefore, instead of the producers having a profit to show for their savings, Mr. Goodbank discovered that he could now only return nine fish for every ten deposited. This was terrible. Mr. Goodbank realized that obviously it was now pointless for the islanders to use the bank as a depository for their savings.

Introduction of Franklin Reserve notes into the island's money system betrayed the purpose for which the bank had been created. Mr. Goodbank had simply miscalculated the extent to which the senate would abuse its notemaking authority. He had not anticipated that they would be so irresponsible and consume so much of the island's stock of savings. While he had assumed that Franklin Reserve notes might retard the island's rate of savings, he had not figured that they would actually reverse it. Goodbank, shaken by this discovery, sent word to Franklin Dee requesting a meeting immediately. He was prepared to explain to Franklin Dee and the other senators that continued use of Franklin Reserve notes must cease; that the number of nonproducers now withdrawing from society's stock of savings had reached a point where savings were actually lower now than they were at the start of the year. A meeting was, therefore, arranged between Goodbank and the entire senate.

"I fear," said Mr. Goodbank, "that when the savers of the island learn that they can now only withdraw fewer fish from the bank than they deposited, they will cease using the bank. They will withdraw all their savings, and they and the community will lose all the economic benefits that we jointly derive from the bank. The producers will start storing their fish at home, in which case I don't see how we can efficiently raise sufficient capital to maintain the capital equipment we now rely on, much less raise capital for new projects."

He was thinking of the waterworks, which had been greatly expanded. Many islanders now lived far from the main source of water as viaducts transported water to all parts of the island. The system now required 150 workers just to maintain it. This required that they be supplied with at least 54,750 fish a year (150x 365—the islanders, despite their added wealth, still maintained their tradition of eating only one fish a day). If workers stopped bringing fish into the central bank, there would be no way that those who maintained the waterworks could be supplied with fish. If these workers abandoned their jobs to fish on their own, the water system would cease to function, causing all kinds of economic havoc. This, then, was the economic chaos Mr. Goodbank envisioned as a result of any additional issuance of Franklin Reserve notes.

"Once the savers on the island realize that they are losing their savings by storing them in my bank, they will stop saving. You will then see our whole economy disintegrate before your very eyes! It will be like watching an earthquake in slow motion," he shouted.

"Don't get so excited," said Franklin Dee, casting a knowing glance toward his fellow senators. "Why should the savers have to know that their savings are shrinking and not growing?"

"Why should they have to know?" exclaimed Goodbank. "Why, it's now the beginning of December and in several weeks, I will have to report to all savers the interest earned per ten fish left in the bank for a full year. My preliminary estimates show that it will be eight to nine fish for every ten, instead of the usual twelve and thirteen, and you say 'why should they have to know?'"

"Suppose I told you," said Franklin, leaning forward a little, "that I and the other senators had anticipated this very problem. We are prepared to deal with it in a most satisfactory manner. We have been secretly collecting discarded fish skins and discarded fish heads and tails and have developed a process whereby we can take the innards of a fish and shape around it the empty carcass of another so that we have two fish that look genuine."

Amazed by such a proposition, Goodbank could only respond, "Surely, Franklin, you must be kidding."

"On the contrary," replied Franklin, "we are quite serious." So saying, he motioned to the two men who had been sitting at the far corner of the room. They moved to a table next to Mr. Goodbank and unrolled the contents of a carefully wrapped package. Fascinated, Goodbank stared at its strange contents—one dried fish and the skeletal remains of another. Using sharp knives, the men quickly removed some of the insides of the dried fish and shaped around them the skin of the hollowed carcass and then, with the aid of a special "fish glue," fastened on the tail and the head. Then they repeatedly shaped and trimmed each fish, finally plunging the two fish in a brine solution. The solution contained some added fish glue which firmed both the meat and the skin of both fish, drawing them together into a firm unit. In less than a minute the "fish" were taken from the pot, dried, and placed on a mat before Goodbank.

"Well, what do you think?" asked Franklin.

Goodbank could only stare at the two fish in amazement. Incredible, he thought. They have really done it. Realizing, of course, that he could not go along with such a scheme, but curious as to how they would answer the questions that now crossed his mind, he probed further.

"Well," said Goodbank, "I wouldn't have thought it possible. Both fish look amazingly like the real thing. But I am sure that when the islanders compare them directly to regular fish, they will spot the fraud, and so your scheme is bound to fail."

"We've thought about that," said Franklin. "Tomorrow we shall pass a law making it illegal for anyone to eat fish taken directly from the sea. We shall announce that we have discovered a certain amount of contamination in fish taken from the sea and so they have to be officially decontaminated. All fish, therefore, have to be turned in for official fish which have gone through our special decontamination process. This will also help explain the somewhat altered look of official fish if anyone happens to notice. After this decree, any islander caught storing, selling, or eating 'potentially contaminated' unofficial fish will be punished, fined, and imprisoned."

"All very good," said Goodbank, "but such a scheme is going to require a number of discarded fish skins and discarded fish heads and tails. Where will these come from? I notice that the skins that you used were in good condition, but normally they are torn apart and mangled and would be completely useless for your purposes."

"We thought of that," said Franklin. "We decided to levy a tax in fish carcasses as well as fish. Each citizen will be required to pay a tax of 365 fish carcasses a year in addition to his regular fish tax. We will simply announce that the state must now dispose of all fish due to the possibility of environmental contamination if fish are not disposed of properly. We will also announce that our disposal process requires that the bone structure of eaten fish as well as their head and tail sections be in reasonably good shape in order to go through our disposal equipment. No one will get credit for fish that are returned in poor carcass condition. We feel that the islanders will not seriously object to this tax since we are levying it in something that they would discard anyway. They may be somewhat annoyed at having to eat a little more carefully, but when we explain that we are doing it to protect their health and the island's environment, I'm sure that they will be convinced that it is well worth the added inconvenience."

Good God, thought Goodbank, they really have thought this out, and as crazy as it first appeared, they really might pull it off at that—at least initially. "But wait," he said, "this scheme cannot possibly work in the long run. Sooner or later, the island's supply of real fish must be reduced to where there would not be enough fish to support consumption requirements for capital replacement and growth, and the whole economic structure of the island must eventually collapse."

"We know that," said Senator Richard Trickson, "but meanwhile it will hold together until the next election, and we can worry about it then."

"Meanwhile," said Senator Lyndon B. Swanson, "this will solve your immediate problem, and we can produce enough official fish with what you already have stored so that you can announce that this year's fish interest will provide eleven fish for every ten saved.''[1]

There was a silence in the room as all the senators awaited Goodbank's answer, all realizing that they would need the banker's cooperation in order to pull off this swindle. For the government to be able to steal the people's savings after they have been deposited in the bank for safe keeping required that the government control the bank by placing it in the hands of men lacking intelligence or integrity—or both. After a moment or two, another senator, young Jack Kassidy, somewhat annoyed with Goodbank's silence, said, ''Well, what will it be, Seymour?''

''We've thought through all possible contingencies,'' said Senator Hubert Humpty, known as ''Chubby'' to his colleagues. ''Nothing will go wrong—at least not immediately. Why,'' he said laughingly, ''this scheme will enable us to establish a Great Island Society.'' This brought on some good-natured laughter from the other senators, which reduced some of the mounting tension.

With this, Goodbank exploded. ''Of course, I will not go along with this swindle, since fraud and deceit are simply not part of my makeup; however, dishonesty is apparently one trait you senators have in common. Obviously, if the lot of you had any integrity, you'd never have been elected in the first place. But more important, I love this island, its people, and its traditions, and I will not see it wrecked in order to provide myself with some temporary financial gain. I have enough economic sense to know that what you propose would not merely deprive the islanders of their savings, but would eventually deprive them of their lives—lives that are now dependent on a store of capital equipment that in turn is dependent upon and must be maintained out of a flow of savings. You are not just rank-and-file swindlers and thieves, you are worse! You are nothing but a pack of murderers, whether you realize it or not. You will not get away with this scheme for I am closing the bank. I will tell the island savers that they will be better off keeping their savings at home. This will certainly cause extreme economic hardship, but at least this will save the island from the fate that you are planning for it.''

''Well, Goodbank,'' said Franklin Dee, ''sorry you feel that way about it. Some senators suggested that it would be pointless to ask you for your cooperation, but we felt we would offer you the proposition anyway since it would make matters so much simpler. In any case, Seymour, you offer us no choice.''

So saying, Franklin signaled two guards by the door, who positioned themselves on either side of the banker. Seymour now realized what the senators had in store for him. He was now infuriated with himself for not having the good sense to have kept quiet at least until he left the meeting. He simply had not reckoned that the senators would actually stoop to this.

''Take him away, and send in Chesley Bartin,'' said Franklin Dee. Chesley

[1]This would be comparable to our eloquent banking fraternity waxing enthusiastic about how savings ''grow'' in their banks at six percent interest while inflation is shrinking principal and interest by ten percent—leaving even ''sophisticated'' Americans with less ''fish'' than they started with.

Bartin had been waiting in the outer office. He had been told to expect that something big might happen to him tonight and as he passed Goodbank leaving the senate chambers, flanked by two guards, he guessed what it might be.

The senators had anticipated that if they could not get Goodbank's cooperation for their plan, they would have to appoint a new man to run the bank. After having discussed several possibilities, they decided on Chesley Bartin. Chesley had acquired a certain amount of fame working for Manny Fund in connection with his mutual investment trust. He had made some good investment decisions and had a reputation for making money for investors. Presumably, therefore, he could make money for savers and instill the same kind of confidence in the bank that Goodbank had been able to create.

The senators explained the bank's problems to Bartin, who indicated that he had expected these problems to develop the moment he got wind of the Franklin Reserve note scheme. He was, of course, flabbergasted by the disclosure of ''official fish'' and the operation that had been performed for Goodbank was now repeated for him. He quickly agreed to front for the bank. The meeting adjourned after toasts were made all around.

The next day, the islanders were saddened to learn of the death of Seymour Goodbank. He apparently suffered a stroke while fishing—at least that was the opinion of those who found him after his body had been washed ashore. He was buried with full civic honors befitting one who had served the community long and well. Franklin Dee delivered the eulogy, and announced that because of the importance of Mr. Goodbank's position, a hurried meeting had been held that very morning, and it had been decided that Chesley Bartin succeed the ''late and lamented'' banker. After the services, a contingent of senators acting as pallbearers carried Goodbank's coffin through the streets, now lined with silent and respectful mourners, to the island cemetery where he was to be buried alongside his honest and industrious forebears. How could the islanders have known as they watched their senators solemnly lowering Goodbank into the ground that not only they were burying Seymour, but they were also burying the island's tradition for honest banking.

Franklin Dee's plan worked; the islanders never suspected the dishonest relationship between their senators and their banker. The size of official fish became smaller and smaller, the islanders little realizing that their fish money had less and less food value. When official fish reached the point where they were approximately half the size of normal fish, the islanders were, of course, eating two fish a day to give them the same food value that they had hitherto gotten from one fish. Prices, which had been geared to the islanders' daily fish consumption, were now, of course, approximately double what they were before Franklin Reserve notes were first introduced. The islanders, however, could not account for this mysterious rise in prices. Walter Hickel, a local fish merchant and the island's part-time economist, attributed the inflation to a ''cost-price-fish-push'' and was quoted as saying, ''If price increases could be held down to about a half a belly a year, that would, in fact, stimulate the economy.'' The government maintained that price increases were simply indicative of the island's increasing prosperity. That as a result of this the islanders were demanding more, were willing to spend more and had become more wasteful—why the island's consumption of fish was far greater now than ever before. Islanders, the government was quick to point out, were now consuming an average of two fish a day where their fathers and grandfathers before them had traditionally eaten only one. So, inflation was merely the price they had to pay for their higher standard of living.

Of course, when official fish reached the point where they were only a third the size of normal fish, prices were 200 percent greater than what they were before Franklin Reserve notes began to circulate. Before it even reached this point, however, other laws had to be passed by the government in order to support, buttress, and legalize its own criminal and economically destructive activities. When official fish had lost 15 to 20 percent of their size, the government passed a law that all fishermen had to fish wearing blinders. The population was informed that the government had discovered that natural fish cast a ray that caused a rare blood disease that could be transmitted by inheritance, posing a problem for the entire island's population. The blinders only had to be worn while fishermen hauled in their nets, at which point, trained and equipped "fishing coordinators" would take over, emptying their nets, and crediting them for the number of fish caught. The new government fishing regulations also provided that fishing could now only be performed in groups of not less than ten, and only during officially prescribed fishing hours, in order to make efficient use of the government's "fishing coordinators"; after all, the government explained, the specially developed protective goggles, with which fish coordinators were outfitted, could not be economically provided to all fishermen. So, fishermen were required to sit idly in their small boats and wait for the government's "fishing coordinator" to haul in their nets.

The government had, of course, explained that all these new fishing regulations and the island's "fishing coordinators" had been developed in order for the government to "promote the general welfare" of the island as provided in the island's constitution. However, not all the island's productive fishermen were foolish enough to be taken in by the government's new "fishing regulations." Some fishermen had detected the fraud and had withdrawn their official fish from the bank, deciding to forego the fraudulent "interest payments." They also stopped bringing their fish to the bank and stored them at home. This violated the law, but more and more fishermen were now violating the law in order to retain more of what they produced.

Other productive fishermen, initially unaware of the deception, became suspicious. More and more fishermen removed their blinders and began comparing normal fish with the "official" fish. They, of course could do this only outside the surveillance of the "fishing coordinators." As time went by, fewer fish found their way into official channels. A black market in legitimate fish developed. Soon the government dispatched search parties to seek out hidden catches of real fish.

In the original law prohibiting the storing of natural fish, the government had stated that natural fish could no longer be stored on the island. However, the act failed to specify that islanders could not store fish on some of the outlying islands. So islanders began fishing off the outer islands and depositing these fish in the honest banks on the other islands. Some islanders at great risk[1] began transporting fish to these other islands and depositing them in foreign banks.

Initially, the government expanded the law, making it illegal for islanders to store natural fish on any other island. Later, it outlawed the transportation of fish to other islands.[2] In promulgating these new regulations, the government claimed it did so to prevent the smuggling of fish from the island by corrupt "fishing coordinators" who, the government claimed, were taking illegal fish bribes by allowing fishermen to *look* at the fish they caught. The government explained that apparently fishermen had now developed a mysterious sexual attraction for the fish that they had for so long been allowed to catch but not allowed to see or touch. Some fish coordinators, the government maintained, were taking advantage of this unfortunate condition and allowing fishermen (for a stiff price) to actually look at and stroke their catch, thus endangering the entire island community. It was, the government asserted, to catch these culprits and to prevent such practices that the government was now implementing its "Foreign Island Fish Control Regulation No. 91-508."[3]

Well, as official fish got smaller and smaller, it made more economic sense for real producers to spend more time just to hide one real fish from the authorities than to spend their time catching seven fish that they were compelled to exchange for seven Franklin fish notes, which were now good for seven teeny-weeny official fish. Other government regulations also interfered more and more with the job of producing fish, so now even fewer fish were being turned into the fish bank. As fewer fish were turned into the fish bank and to Manny Fund for investment, capital building projects were discontinued. Those workers who had left fishing to develop new skills in order to work on the capital projects required by the island soon found themselves unemployed. Since official fish now were so small, each islander had to consume approximately seven official fish a day to get the same nutritive value of one natural fish. Prices were now 600 percent higher than they

[1]Since there were now patrol boats searching for "smugglers" trying to store their fish with honest banks on other islands.

[2]There was, therefore, a similarity between this and U.S. Executive Orders 10905 and 11037 issued January 14, 1961, and July 2, 1962, which banned all American residents and corporations from buying and storing gold overseas.

[3]By a strange coincidence, this is the same regulation number attached to the U.S.'s "Financial Recordkeeping and Currency and Foreign Transactions Act of 1970," effective July 1, 1972. This act attempts to control the amount of dollars leaving the country, one requirement of the act providing that ". . . All persons transporting, mailing or shipping from the U.S. to a foreign country, or receiving from out of the U.S. currency or bearer instruments in amounts in excess of $5,000 to report such transactions to Customs."

The government claimed that the "issuance of these regulations is a further step in major efforts directed toward frustrating organized crime and white-collar criminal elements who use secret filing accounts to conceal substantive violations of drug smuggling, securities and gambling laws, as well as the untaxed incomes generated from these and other illegal activities." The government, in other

were before Franklin Reserve notes were introduced. Since prices were now so high, islanders were forced to use more of their savings on necessities, leaving less available for buying other types of consumer goods.

As employment declined, both in the production of capital and consumer goods, unrest increased in the island community. Therefore, to keep unemployed islanders happy (remember, they were voters), the senate created "unemployment insurance." More Franklin fish notes were printed and given to those who were unemployed so that they could go to the bank and withdraw the island's dwindling stock of stored fish at an even faster rate. Official fish now became so small that no longer could any productive fisherman be fooled into exchanging natural fish for "official" fish. Many now didn't even bother to fish at all, since by this time they had managed to secrete for themselves and their families enough fish to last them a long time.

With no new fish coming into the bank, the bank quickly exhausted its supply of legitimate fish, and so had nothing with which to stuff its ample supply of empty fish skins. All the bank had, at this point,were piles of empty fish carcasses while the islanders held plenty of Franklin Reserve notes and bank deposit books indicating that they were entitled to fish which the bank no longer possessed.

At the very end, Chesley Bartin was in the cage himself, trying desperately to find one teeny-weeny fish that had some meat on it, when he was presented with a ten-fish Franklin Reserve note. Not finding any fish at all, in desperation he handed to the holder of the ten-fish note the skeletal remains of ten fish saying, "Here, see what you can pick off of these bones." With that, he ordered the bank cleared, locked the front door, and hung up a hastily made sign that read "Closed, Bank Holiday."

Chesley ran over to the senate building to inform Franklin Dee that the jig was apparently up. The bank was officially out of both *genuine* and *official* fish. Franklin Dee summoned all of the senators to the senate chamber. Crowds were forming in the streets, chanting, "We want jobs, we want jobs," "Open the Bank," "We need money, we need money."

Meanwhile, in the senate chambers, all was glum.

words, would have you believe that smugglers, gamblers, criminal elements, and those already engaged in "illegal activities"—and who are thus already violating U.S. law—are going to report their illegal currency activities to the U.S. government in compliance with these regulations. These criminal elements will, of course, violate these currency laws in the same manner that they now violate other U.S. laws. You will, of course, note that the U.S. government's rationale in imposing these and other currency laws which seek to interfere with a citizen's right to save and store money and unmoney where and how he chooses is cut from the same lying, bureaucratic double-talk as Franklin Dee's "fish rays" and his sexy fish. No, these regulations are not aimed at criminals. They are aimed at America's law-abiding citizens and designed to keep them from seeking more honest foreign currencies in which to store their savings—while providing the government with a list of law-abiding Americans who might have a store of foreign currency capable of being confiscated by taxation should American unmoney go the way of the 1923 German mark. In this case, those Americans who had the intelligence and foresight to store their savings in stronger foreign countries will, in all probability, now be characterized by the government as unpatriotic foreign-currency speculators, who should have their "dishonest gains" taxed away by government by the imposition of an "Excess Profits Tax Covering Ill-Gotten Gains due to Foreign Currency Speculation."

"What can we do now?" said young Jack Kassidy, always eager to explore new frontiers.

"Let's get some economic advice, quickly," said Lyndon B. Swanson. "Get Walter Hickel and Paul Sibling in here at once."

So saying, a guard was dispatched to bring the senate's economic advisers. When they arrived, they were immediately asked by Senator Hubert Humpty, "So, what's your economic advice now?"

With this, a rock came sailing through the balcony window making the mob's chants of "We want jobs, we want jobs" even more audible and more ominous.

"Expand credit," said Walter Hickel.

"Lower taxes," said Paul Sibling.

"Expand credit?" repeated Franklin Dee incredulously. "We have expanded credit as far as it can go. There is absolutely nothing left to expand with. And, how can we lower taxes? There is nothing left in which taxes can be paid. Come on boys, you'll have to do better than that," demanded Franklin.

"Expand credit," repeated Walter Hickel.

"Lower taxes," repeated Paul Sibling.

Angered by these repetitive suggestions, Franklin stood up and menacingly confronted his two economists.

"Look, what do you want from them?" said Richard Trickson. "That's all the economics these birds know."

"That's right, I forgot about that," said Franklin Dee. "Look," turning to the guard that had brought the economists in, "put these two birds back on their perches. There are still some crackers left in their box, see that they get them. I think those may be the last of them, though there still may be some sunflower seeds in a jar on the window sill in their office. If so," he said to the guards, "fill up their cups and see that they get some water. In any case, I don't think that we will be needing them any longer."

With this, the guard turned and departed, one economist perched on each arm. As they were transported from the room, the birds continued to cackle. "Expand credit," squawked Walter. "Lower taxes," cackled Paul, as another rock crashed through the window.

"Well, what are we going to do?" asked a troubled Senator Jack Kassidy.

"What can we do?" answered Franklin Dee. "All we ever did was steal the people's store of savings to finance our various projects. But now that there are no more savings to steal, we can't provide any more government benefits."

"I don't understand you," said Senator Kassidy, "why can't we simply create jobs for all those unemployed people?"

"Look," said Hubert Humpty, "if we really knew how to create employment, we would be in business for ourselves and not in government."

"But," persisted Senator Kassidy, "I don't understand why we can't create the jobs like we always have. Like the time Franklin Dee launched that project where we were able to employ 150 people washing the rocks on the beach. Why can't we put people to work washing more rocks? I'm sure that they must be just as dirty.''

Richard Trickson now turned to young Senator Kassidy. ''You mean, even at this late date, you still don't know what's been going on? We never created jobs, we never extended credit, we never expanded credit, like Franklin Dee said. All we ever did was to steal the community store of savings with Franklin Reserve notes and provide the people with goodies stolen from the proceeds of their own savings. For a long time the suckers were too dumb to understand what was going on. Now, however, all of the island's producers are wise to our little scheme, so they refuse to put any more savings in the bank. Since there is nothing left to steal, we are, therefore, economically powerless.''

''Yes,'' agreed Senator William Poxfire, ''as long as there were some extra savings that we could siphon with Franklin Reserve notes, we looked pretty good. But now we're all through.''

''But doesn't the government have any money?'' persisted Jack Kassidy.

''Of course not,'' said Hubert, ''the only money we had is what we taxed and stole from the people. Now that the people are broke, we're broke.''

''Well, if the government has no money,'' said Jack, ''how are we going to pay off all those bonds that we sold to the people by telling them to 'Invest in the Island' and the notes we gave to the bank in exchange for all those Franklin Reserve notes that we distributed?''

''That's the point,'' said Franklin Dee. ''Old Chesley here knew that we never had any intention of paying him or his bank for all the credit they gave us. Neither he nor anybody else will ever get paid because there's nothing to pay the debt off in.''

''I guess it's every man for himself,'' said Senator Poxfire.

With this, the chanting of the mob for jobs got louder and louder.

''The people still don't understand,'' said Lyndon B. Swanson. ''Even at this late date they think we really have the power to help them.''

And another rock crashed through a window.

''Maybe I have,'' said Franklin Dee. ''Somebody will have to talk to them or they will burn the place down.'' So saying, Franklin Dee walked out on the balcony of the senate building. When the crowd saw him, the chanting died down. However, some individuals continued to shout and expletives were hurled up at him from the crowd.

''We want jobs, Franklin Dee.'' Another shrill voice called out, ''The bank is closed, Franklin Dee, what's the government going to do now?''

With this, Franklin Dee held out his hands to silence the crowd and then uttered the only honest words of his entire political career. ''My friends,'' he said, ''I think the time has now come for all of us to begin fishing—and quickly.''

14

The Solution to America's Economic and Social Problems

They that can give up essential liberty to obtain a little temporary safety deserve neither liberty nor safety.
—Benjamin Franklin

The January 27, 1975, cover of *Newsweek* pictured a beleaguered President Ford in knight's armor, battling a fierce, three-headed, fire-breathing dragon labeled inflation, depression, and energy.

The *Miami Herald* of December 18, 1974, carried the following headline: "How Four Forces Imperil Man's Future." The article painted a bleak picture. France's President Giscard d'Estaing was quoted as saying that "the four horsemen of the . . . modern apocalypse—energy, food, population and finances," now threaten mankind. The article went on to state that the nation's 23,000-mile interstate highway could become virtually useless. Former Interior Secretary Stewart Udall, termed "one of the nation's leading independent energy experts," was quoted as saying that our highway system "may very well be used primarily . . . for trains and bicycling." The article even quoted Secretary of State Henry Kissinger: "If current economic trends continue, we face further and further mounting world-wide shortages, unemployment, poverty, and shortages." Now, the amazing thing about these gloomy forecasts is that no one put his finger on the *real* problem or even offered any practical solutions.

Since America is potentially a wealthy country, with an array of natural resources and the world's most efficient farm population, solving its economic problems will be relatively easy, compared to those of countries like Japan and the Soviet Union. Solving America's current economic problems is simple, providing the underlying cause is properly understood.

A Worker, Is a Worker, Is a Worker . . . Or Is He?

Does it make sense to talk about *full* employment without caring about the *economic nature* of that employment? If farm A employs ten persons, nine producing and one counting, and farm B employs ten, two producing and eight counting, do we have in fact, ten equally employed people on farms A and B (assuming the same productive efficiencies)? Suppose those employed on farm A decided that they no longer needed the services of one of their producers, so, in essence, one member of farm A became "unemployed" while farm B still boasted of "full employment." Where, in fact, is the greater amount of "unemployment," on farm A or farm B? Sad to say, of course, farm B is the good ol' U.S.A.

When President Ford stated in his first State of the Union message that

> there were 59 million Americans employed at the start of 1949, now there are more than 85 million Americans who have jobs. And in comparable dollar terms, the average income of the average American family has doubled in the past 26 years,

he was misleading the public.

Figure 41 is a chart from the President's own 1975 economic report. Note A indicates that the average gross weekly wages for private nonagricultural workers in 1949 was $50.24, while in 1974, Note B, it was $154.45. Adjusting for taxes, however, these amounts become $49.74 and $134.37 respectively, Notes C and D.

These figures simply adjust for taxes and Social Security (for a worker and three dependents). We must now adjust for inflation. Since the United States has experienced an inflation of at least 300 percent since 1949 (a hot dog then was still 10 cents, while a Coke, a cup of coffee, an ice cream cone, two Hostess cupcakes, and a subway ride were all still 5 cents—what are they today?), adjusting the $49.74 for 300 percent inflation would give 1949 workers $198.96 of comparable 1974 purchasing power, or about 48 percent *more* purchasing power than the average 1974 worker.

Even using the table's own figures,[1] Note E shows spendable after-tax income for the 1949 worker in 1967 dollars as $69.66, while for 1974 (Note F) it is only

[1]These figures do not adequately reflect the degree of inflation since the official CPI only shows price increases of 105 percent between June 1949 and June 1974 (71.5 to 146.9)—and since the Table adjusts the "tax bite" for a worker and *three dependents*, it minimizes the greater negative disparity for single taxpayers and those with fewer dependents.

Figure 41

TABLE C–31.—*Average weekly earnings in selected private nonagricultural industries, 1947–74*

[For production or nonsupervisory workers]

Year or month	Average gross weekly earnings					Average spendable weekly earnings, total private nonagricultural			
	Total private nonagricultural		Manufacturing	Contract construction	Retail trade	Amount		Percent change from preceding period	
	Current dollars	1967 dollars	Current dollars			Current dollars	1967 dollars	Current dollars	1967 dollars
1947	$45.58	$68.13	$49.17	$58.87	$33.77	$44.64	$66.73		
1948	49.00	67.96	53.12	65.27	36.22	48.51	67.28	8.7	0.8
1949	50.24	70.36	53.88	67.56	38.42	49.74	69.66	2.5	3.5
1950	A 53.13	73.69	58.32	69.68	39.71	C 52.04	72.18	4.6	3.6
1951	57.86	74.37	63.34	76.96	42.82	55.79	E 71.71	7.2	−.7
1952	60.65	76.29	67.16	82.86	43.38	57.87	72.79	3.7	1.5
1953	63.76	79.60	70.47	86.41	45.36	60.31	75.29	4.2	3.4
1954	64.52	80.15	70.49	88.91	47.04	60.85	75.59	.9	.4
1955	67.72	84.44	75.70	90.90	48.75	63.41	79.06	4.2	4.6
1956	70.74	86.90	78.78	96.38	50.18	65.82	80.86	3.8	2.3
1957	73.33	86.99	81.59	100.27	52.20	67.71	80.32	2.9	−.7
1958	75.08	86.70	82.71	103.78	54.10	69.11	79.80	2.1	−.6
1959	78.78	90.24	88.26	108.41	56.15	71.86	82.31	4.0	3.1
1960	80.67	90.95	89.72	113.04	57.76	72.96	82.25	1.5	−.1
1961	82.60	92.19	92.34	118.08	58.66	74.48	83.13	2.1	1.1
1962	85.91	94.82	96.56	122.47	60.96	76.99	84.98	3.4	2.2
1963	88.46	96.47	99.63	127.19	62.66	78.56	85.67	2.0	.8
1964	91.33	98.31	102.97	132.06	64.75	82.57	88.88	5.1	3.7
1965	95.06	100.59	107.53	138.38	66.61	86.30	91.32	4.5	2.7
1966	98.82	101.67	112.34	146.26	68.57	88.66	91.21	2.7	−.1
1967	101.84	101.84	114.90	154.95	70.95	90.86	90.86	2.5	−.4
1968	107.73	103.39	122.51	164.49	74.95	95.28	91.44	4.9	.6
1969	114.61	104.38	129.51	181.54	78.66	99.99	91.07	4.9	−.4
1970	119.46	102.72	133.73	195.45	82.47	104.61	89.95	4.6	−1.2
1971	B 127.28	104.93	142.44	211.67	86.61	112.41	92.67	7.5	3.0
1972	136.16	108.67	154.69	222.51	90.99	D 121.09	F 96.64	7.7	4.3
1973	145.43	109.26	165.65	236.06	95.57	127.41	95.73	5.2	−.9
1974 p	154.45	104.57	176.00	248.71	101.04	134.37	90.97	5.5	−5.0

$90.97 for an "official improvement" of only 30 percent, which is still a far cry from the President's implication that there was an improvement of 100 percent.

Now, the President misled the nation by stating that it was the "*income* of the average American *family*" that had "doubled," not *wages* that had doubled, which, I am sure, was the impression his listeners received. That the income of the average family may have increased to a greater extent than the average wages was the result of factors other than gains in productivity. Forty percent more married women are working today to supplement family income than in 1949. More Americans are forced to hold down two or more jobs. Yet, despite all this additional work, the income of the average family obviously has not doubled "in comparable dollar terms," as the President contended.

The President gave the impression that more than 85 million American workers were economically employed in 1974. He did not say "economically" employed (politicians never make this distinction), only "employed . . . who have jobs."

However, the implication is that there were more than 85 million Americans working to supply the necessary goods and services required by 212 million Americans. Or that about 40 percent of America's population is being effectively employed in supporting themselves and the other 60 percent who are not working.

If this were true, that would not be a bad percentage. If it were true that 40 percent of our population were *economically* employed, America would not now have an energy shortage, a balance of payment problem, a depreciating currency, and a weakening diplomatic and military posture. But the sad fact is that only 16 percent[1] of our population (and now probably less), only 16 out of every 100, are working to produce all the country's material needs for food, fuel, clothing, construction, utilities, and transportation services. In other words, *84 Americans out of every 100 produce nothing that they themselves require in the way of food, fuel, or implements for their comfort and survival.* It can truly be said that never in recorded history has so much been produced for so many by so few.

U.S. Government, Inc.

In order for Americans to proceed with a program to correct the nation's economic and social ills, it is essential to realize that the United States government *is* the problem. Think it unpatriotic to be so antagonistic toward our government? Then, you still have your blinders on and haven't recognized what our government is all about. Allow me to enlighten you.

U.S. Government, Inc., is just another big American business like General Motors or Exxon, only much larger and much less efficient. GM manufactures and sells automobiles, and Exxon processes and sells petroleum products. But U.S. Government, Inc., mainly sells services. Some of these services include national defense, crime protection, administration of justice, provision of a "dependable" currency supply, "delivery" of the mail, education, and research, to name a few. U.S. Government, Inc., differs from most businesses in that it (1) is nonprofit,[2] (2) is largely unregulated by either law or competition, (3) is a monopoly, and (4) can compel us to buy its services, regardless of how unnecessary, overpriced, and destructive they might be.

[1]An examination of U.S. "employment" statistics will reveal that of the "more than 85 million Americans" who, according to the President, had "jobs," only 35 million (or approximately 16 percent of the U.S. population) were employed in manufacturing, mining, construction, transportation, utilities and agriculture (1975 Economic Report of the President, p. 282). The rest were employed in service and distribution occupations and 14.599 million were employed by government. Now I'll grant that accountants, lawyers, school teachers, police and firemen, bank tellers, economists, guidance counselors, financial planners, PR men, human resource coordinators, stock brokers, union organizers, and tap dancers have a place. But the question is—how big? At some point continued proliferation of these occupations *reduces* society's ability to deliver sufficient quantities of food, clothing, shelter and fuel—the main objective of a sensibly run industrial economy.

[2]Only as far as the taxpayers are concerned.

So, while America's largest, most powerful corporation is unchecked, few individuals and organizations have the wherewithal to challenge its illegal activities.[1] Agencies and officials of U.S. Government, Inc., routinely make claims that would result in stiff fines and imprisonment if attempted by private individuals. U.S. Government, Inc., presents its debt position by declaring its funded liabilities, while neglecting to divulge publicly its unfunded and contingent liabilities. U.S. Government, Inc., calls what the Federal Reserve System prints "money" when it is actually *unmoney*. U.S. Government, Inc., insists on labeling the tokens produced by the U.S. Treasury as money, while if any American manufacturer so mislabeled his merchandise, he would be prosecuted for fraud by an outraged government. U.S. Government, Inc., forces Americans to participate in a chain letter called Social Security which will bring tragic losses to many while benefiting, in comparison, only a handful. U.S. Government, Inc., claims it sells "savings" bonds. These "certificates of guaranteed confiscation"[2] are not bonds in the economic sense. Anyone in the private sector who implied that straight commercial paper was actually a bond would surely violate some SEC regulation. Bonds are floated to create capital goods from whose increased productivity the interest and principal of the bond can be paid. No reputable investment banker would sell a commercial bond whose proceeds would be used to meet the operating needs of the borrower. But this is the case with U.S. Government, Inc., "bonds." The government uses the money it raises to pay operating expenses—or to refinance maturing debt—and creates little capital with the proceeds from which the bond's future interest and principal can be paid. In reality, U.S. Government, Inc., "bonds" are only "prepaid tax receipts" of various interest and maturity dates, not "freedom shares," or "investments in America."[3]

Now, in order for Americans to move as expeditiously as possible to correct the nation's problems—it is imperative that we understand that the present administration and the U.S. Congress will be of no help in solving those problems. The country must stop looking to official Washington for economic and social solutions. One of the first priorities should be the recruiting of citizens behind a program that seeks to reduce the domestic economic power and influence of U.S. Government, Inc. U.S. Government, Inc., cannot be expected to relinquish its power and influence voluntarily. So, responsible and patriotic citizens must organize and *force* it to do so.

[1]For example, its criminal prohibition depriving individuals of the appreciated value of silver they owned in coin form.

[2]*Pick's Currency Yearbook* —1972, p. 28.

[3]In my opinion, U.S. Government, Inc., uses this phraseology to trick "bond" buyers into thinking that owning a U.S. "Savings Bond" is comparable to owning a *share* of stock. If a registered security salesman were to infer that a *bond* was a share, he would probably lose his security license. Also, to imply that those who pay taxes in advance are "investing in America" is misleading. If one wishes to "invest in America" he can do so only by investing directly in U.S. industry and commerce.

Since the American people do not have responsible economic leadership, a national convention must be convened with delegates drawn from all productive elements of society—trade unions, manufacturing and agricultural organizations, national professional associations and societies—to formulate a program for our national recovery.[1]

Developing the Right Attitude for Bureaucracy-Pruning

To do the job right, Americans have to begin ridding themselves of double-think—for example, such expressions as "federal aid to education," "federal revenue sharing," and "federal insurance." The painful fact is that the federal government is not endowed with any independent wealth for "aiding" education or anything else. Nor does U.S. Government, Inc., have an independent "revenue" to share with local governments.

Whatever the federal government "gives" in benefits, it first "takes" away in taxes. However, it must add, to whatever it takes, the additional nonproductive overhead costs of government collection and administrative services. Ironically, what has contributed substantially to the growth of government is the statists'—advocates for increased government—skillful use of language. "Federal aid to education" is an impossibility. The government has no income that it does not first take away from citizens, and in the end citizens have much less money to spend on education. When all federal "aid" programs are analyzed properly, it becomes apparent that they destroy far more than they create.

1900-1930 Versus 1945-1975

Undoubtedly many believe that it would be disastrous for America to scrap the many laws and bureaucratic agencies created since 1930. But let's look at the facts.

Visualize America at the turn of the century—76 million people still living largely in the horse-and-buggy age. Now picture the nation 30 years later—the transformation is astounding (even given the depression)!

America has gone from the horse and buggy to the automobile and air travel. Electric lights now illuminate the streets. Telephone communication binds the nation with instant communication. The development and mass distribution of such things as radios, phonographs, and motion pictures have literally transformed America, creating living standards that could scarcely have been imagined when the century opened. All the while the nation absorbed 19 million largely penniless immigrants—*a fourth* of its 1900 population!

Visualize the U.S. at the close of World War II—in 1945. Now look ahead thirty years to 1975. What kind of a transformation do you see? With the exception of a few TV sets around the house and air conditioning, how has America

[1]Ultimately, something will have to be done with the electoral process. As constituted, it guarantees that a majority of those elected to high public office are largely unfit to lead the nation.

changed? Well, if you overlook the sharp increase in working mothers, moonlighting, crime, drug addiction, and urban blight, the deterioration of our mass urban transportation systems and postal service, the bankrupt state of the nation's railroads, airlines, many municipalities *and the federal government*—things have changed very little. It should also be noted that during this period America absorbed only 8½ million immigrants—or only 6 percent of its 1945 population. In which era then was there greater economic and human progress? Since it is clear that the nation sustained greater progress without the federal ("progressive") laws and the hundreds of bureaucratic agencies they spawned—why should we be reluctant or fearful about eliminating them?

Wielding the Axe

As we begin scaling down U.S. Government, Inc., all enlisted in this crusade should keep the following in mind:

1. The U.S. government is so bloated with fat that regardless of where you bury your axe, you'll not hit anything that is vital for the preservation and protection of the United States of America.

2. Since U.S. Government, Inc., is already bankrupt, there's nothing you can do to make its financial position any worse.[1]

3. Those Americans who join the crusade to scale the government down to a manageable size will be helping to increase the nation's ultimate military strength, raise the country's standard of living, and restore solvency.

The only federal agencies that the country probably needs are the Defense Department, the Justice Department, and vastly reduced Treasury and State Departments. Most everything else the federal government does, the people could do better and cheaper for themselves.[2] Unfortunately, the functions of these four departments must remain in bureaucratic hands since I do not see how the country could conveniently contract them out—however, I am willing to maintain an open mind on this. By removing most other duties from U.S. Government, Inc. (and lowering the nation's tax bill accordingly), the increase in the national wealth

[1]Not only have government's debts grown enormously but their average maturity has been drastically compressed. In 1946, the interest-bearing portion of its debt had an average maturity of nine years and one month, while by December 1974, it was shortened to two years, eleven months. See 1975 Economic Report of the President, page 334.

[2]By this I do not necessarily mean on an individual basis, but individually and through organizing private facilities to provide many of the same services now ineptly provided by government.

It never ceases to amaze me how people can suggest that an activity such as a health insurance program be turned over to the government, when the government has yet to demonstrate it can do *anything* right. What prompts people to suggest it should do more? U.S. Government, Inc., has yet to demonstrate that it can efficiently deliver the nation's mail or provide the nation with currency that will maintain its value. Let U.S. Government, Inc., demonstrate that it can perform these *two* relatively simple tasks before it presumes to have the ability to perform any other.

would be so overwhelming that we could afford the luxury of overpaying the government in connection with administering these four necessary departments.

The subject of where the federal government should be cut is so vast that I shall merely content myself with broad areas and suggest some general guidelines. Reductions in overall government spending must be made in two general areas: the direct cost of government itself, and government transfer payments.

Government Statisticians. First of all, we can begin with all governnent statistical gathering services and agencies. We don't need them. Most government statistics are biased, anyway, and used merely for propaganda purposes. The government itself admits that despite its mountains of statistics, it was not able to foresee the oil crisis, double-digit inflation, or even the recession. So, what good were all the statistics? They merely provide jobs for thousands of unnecessary government statisticians, statistical interpreters, and those engaged in disseminating the stuff. With the government out of the statistic-gathering business, those industries needing statistics previously compiled by government can hire those discharged and pay them with revenue saved as a result of lower taxes.

Government Economists. Any bureaucrat with the title of economist should be discharged immediately. The state of the economy is proof that the nation has not benefited an iota by the hundreds of economists and the thousands of research assistants, secretaries, and typists who support them. They can all go, and that includes the President's Council of Economic Advisers—founded in 1946.[1]

Department of Agriculture. The Agriculture Department had done little for the nation's consumers except increase their food bills. To appreciate how vast and wasteful this department is, the following table will show the department's expenditures relative to the entire net national product of the agricultural industry including forestry and fisheries.

	1960	1965	1970	1972
		(In billions)		
Net agricultural product—U.S.	$15.3	$17.4	$20.0	$24.4
Expenditures of U.S. Dept. of Agriculture	$ 5.4	$ 7.3	$ 8.3	$10.9
Expenditures as a percent of U.S. agriculture	35%	42%	42%	45%

Average Agricultural Department expenditures as a percentage of the net agricultural product for the years shown equals 41%.

Source: U.S. Department of Agriculture

[1]The country somehow made it to 1946 without such a body. The Council's mere existence implies that the President of the United States actually receives and acts upon sound economic advice. The nation should no longer suffer the cost of such deception.

Government Regulatory Bodies. Much of government activity has to do with regulation of industry and commerce. The public believes that government regulates industry for the benefit of the consumer, while actually business is regulated to protect existing businesses and, in many cases, to protect inefficient businesses from efficient businesses—at the expense of the consumer. Even the present administration admits that "most governmental regulation is now concerned with the regulation of competition rather than with the regulation of monopoly"[1] and that

> governments also regulate product and input standards. For example, in the case of drugs, the costs of regulation include not only the direct cost of testing (borne by the FDA [Food and Drug Administration] and private drug manufacturers) but also its side effects: fewer new drugs and delays in the introduction of those drugs which ultimately get to the market. In 1962 Congress amended the Food, Drug, and Cosmetic Act of 1938 to require that new drugs be proved effective as well as safe. Since then, the rate of introduction of new drugs has fallen more than 50 percent and the average testing period has more than doubled. Moreover, it is not clear that the average efficacy of drugs introduced after 1962 is any higher than that of drugs previously introduced. One recent study estimates that the 1962 drug amendments cost consumers on balance, between $300 million and $400 million during 1970.[2]

So, while assessing the value of FDA by contemplating the comfort it provides by guaranteeing the nation only gets drugs tested to the highest medical standards possible, we should also be aware of discomfort many are compelled to sustain by being denied drugs whose market potential might preclude the exhaustive and expensive testing required by FDA. For example, the average cost of testing a new drug has soared from $1.3 million at the time of the 1962 amendments to around $25 million today. Yet despite these astronomic increases, the government admits that the FDA can not show that the U.S. has any more efficacious drugs than it had before or that exist in other advanced countries. However, the public is denied the healing and comfort potential of many drugs. The question is not so simple as how many lives the FDA saves by requiring the more thorough testing of drugs, but how many lives it saves in relation to how many lives are lost because individuals are denied drugs that simply may not be able to meet unnecessary FDA standards. It should also be recognized that no major drug firm would consider marketing a drug it has not tested to its satisfaction, regardless of the FDA, since marketing a harmful drug would subject the firm to lawsuits which could bankrupt it.

The Interstate Commerce Commission is another regulatory agency that should be abolished. As the *Economic Report of the President* noted this year: "In surface transportation alone, one study puts the cost of regulations at between $4 billion and $9 billion annually."[3] So, apart from the direct costs of government

[1]*Economic Report of the President, 1975*, p. 151.

[2]*Ibid.*, p. 158.

[3]*Ibid.*, p. 159.

—the taxes we all pay—there are indirect costs which, in this case, are estimated at between $4 billion and $9 billion annually. Here is a more detailed explanation of how the ICC promotes waste in surface transportation:

> In the public sector, federal policies, regulations, subsidies, import quotas, tariffs, and price supports pose innumerable obstacles to a smoothly running market economy. For example, because of Interstate Commerce Commission regulations, a truck, after carrying goods from one city to another, may be required to return empty. Partly as a result of other ICC rules, railroad cars travel about 50 percent of their mileage with no freight.[1]

In sum, the ICC was created after the railroads were built in order to regulate them, but it merely presided over their demise. Without ICC regulation the railroads prospered; with it the railroads have all but vanished.

I would padlock the Securities and Exchange Commission (SEC) because U.S. Government, Inc., itself swindles so extensively through phony bonds, phony money, and phony financial reports that it adds insult to injury to suffer the hypocrisy of a government agency designed to protect the public from fraud; besides, the SEC costs more than it saves. Even with it, the public still gets swindled—witness Equity Funding, Pennsylvania Railroad, Homestake Oil, and King Resources, all multi-million-dollar fiascos. Still, legitimate promoters are required to spend substantial sums in order to comply with all the SEC regulations—costs which are then *passed on to the public*. Promoters who cannot afford such costs, legal and otherwise, must modify or abandon their projects. How many worthwhile projects are thus penalized will never be known. I am confident, however, that the entire cost of the SEC, direct and *indirect*, exceeds the *net amount* it saves by way of stock frauds.

Moving along with our axe, I would get rid of every government public relations man. I would close every U.S.I.A. office.[2] We should not have to "sell ourselves" to other peoples and governments. If our country were run right, we wouldn't need to.

Is it vital that the U.S. government print and distribute books and pamphlets such as the following ones listed in the Government Printing Office's spring 1975 catalog?

Teenagers' Guide to Babysitting
What Happened to Mushrooms?
If You're Coloring Your Hair
Toys in the Making

[1]*Interim Report of the Joint Economic Committee,* Congress of the United States, September 21, 1974, p. 29.

[2]See Eugene V. Castle, *Billions, Blunders and Baloney* (New York: Devin-Adair Company, 1955).

Here are examples of government "research" uncovered by the National Taxpayers Union:

Study of the impact of rural road construction in Poland. Cost: $85,000.

Study of teaching mothers how to play with their children. Cost: $576,969.

Study of wild boars in Pakistan. Cost: $35,000.

A dictionary on witchcraft. Cost: $46,089.

Study of American and Indian whistling ducks. Cost: $5,000.

Study of bisexual Polish frogs. Cost: $6,000.

Grant to Central College in Iowa dealing with "enhancement of cognitive abilities and self-image of freshmen women." Cost: $22,470.

Reducing Government Transfer Payments: Unrealistic Promises from Irresponsible Politicians

Government transfer payments are transfers of money from citizen Y to citizen Z. They are monies collected by the government which are not used to pay for normal government operations, but are deposited momentarily in its checking account to be forwarded by the government to recipients who will receive a check drawn on the funds. Transfer payments include interest payments on the national debt, agriculture subsidies, Social Security payments, welfare payments, veterans' pensions, and pensions for retired government employees.

In 1929 government transfer payments of $1.5 billion, were less than .2 percent of the net national product. By 1974 these payments had grown to $139.8 billion, or 11 percent of the net national product, for a relative increase in economic terms of 5,400 percent. To put this increase in another perspective, in 1929, personal income from rent, dividends, and interest was more than 1,100 percent greater ($18.4 billion) than transfer payments. Yet by 1974 transfer payments ($139.8 billion) had increased to where such income only exceeded transfer payments by 17 percent[1]

Let's examine the largest components of government transfer payments for 1976. Some were for the following.

Social Security	$74.4 billion
Federal employee retirement and disability payments	7.9 billion
Unemployment insurance	18.2 billion
Public assistance and other income supplements	18.4 billion
Veterans' pensions	7.7 billion
	$126.6 billion, or

36 percent of the budgeted outlays for fiscal 1976.

[1] While by 1976, transfer payments actually overtook and exceeded these income payments by $10 billion. See Figure 42 on page 327.

Putting this $126.6 billion in economic terms will reveal the extent of the government's madness since the government fully intends to reward those who will produce nothing in fiscal 1976 with about all of the wealth produced in 1972[1] by the following industries:

Agriculture, forestry, and fisheries		$ 37.5 billion
Mining (including petroleum and natural gas)		18.2 billion
Transportation		45.8 billion
Communication		28.5 billion
	TOTAL	$130.0 billion

Are Such Expanding Levels of Transfer Payments Realistic?

There is simply no way that our economy can continue to honor such generous commitments, expecially since they are contributing to our falling productivity. However, veterans will understandably take offense at my suggestion that by awarding them pensions, the government is transferring purchasing power to those who "themselves produce nothing." They will claim, and justifiably so, that they gave "30 years of service to the country in payment for those benefits," so how dare I suggest they are receiving payment for producing nothing? Social Security recipients will also bristle at my suggestion that they receive payments for "producing nothing." Retired government employees, likewise, will point out that not only did they "pay" for their retirement benefits with years of loyal service but that they also contributed their own money toward their retirement pensions.

Well, I certainly sympathize with these groups, but sympathy cannot be permitted to override reason, and emotionalism cannot alter facts I did not create. If the nation wishes to continue deceiving itself concerning its ability to support vast numbers of nonproductive citizens, the result will be economic disaster. Certain painful facts must be faced, and veterans, Social Security recipients, and retired government workers as well as all others must start becoming realistic.

Consider, for example, the Social Security claimant who maintains he is entitled to Social Security payments because he "paid in" for 35 years. While it is true he "paid in" for 35 years, the tragedy is that over those years, the government stole his contributions and did not invest them so that payment to him of a current annuity is not financially possible. He must realize that our politicians have dissipated all past "Social Security contributions."

Retired government workers must also realize that there are no "trust funds" from which their pension benefits can be paid. Their pension contributions were never "invested" by the government, but were continuously *spent* on numerous federal projects. They are thus in no different position than employees of a private concern, confronted by the unpleasant fact that their employer has run off with the assets in their pension fund.

[1]The last year shown in the *U.S. Statistical Abstract* for 1975.

Who Is Liable for Political Irresponsibility?

In the final analysis it boils down to this: Is the nation's current generation of producers (especially those in their twenties), who are themselves struggling with families and careers, liable for the unrealistic economic promises of past generations of irresponsible politicians? Did politicians long gone have the right to indenture unborn generations of Americans to the service of other Americans, simply to make good on their irresponsible campaign promises?

The answer is obvious—No! And the bitter price that must now be paid for this fiscal folly must be borne by those Americans who bought the promises—not the nation's young men and women who had nothing whatever to do with it. Americans now reaching 65 were not at age 20 saddled with the burden of having to support a large retired, disabled, and dependent population—and twenty-year-old Americans are entitled to the same consideration. So, where do we go from here?

Deflating the Transfer Payments Bubble

Once the nation realizes that Social Security is defunct, it can begin to handle the consequences more intelligently.

The first thing that has to be done is to institute a realistic "needs" test for future Social Security payments. There are some citizens who might have no other source of income and who would be destitute without Social Security payments, while obviously there are others, (retired millionaires, for instance) who also receive Social Security, but who could survive without it. Between these two extremes there will be degrees of need, which must be evaluated in determining the levels of Social Security payments, taking into consideration age, financial circumstances, health, and one's employment potential.

The fact that one paid Social Security taxes in the past cannot now determine the receipt of such payments in the future. If it makes citizens feel any better, they should simply regard their past Social Security taxes as merely an indication of a prior higher ordinary tax rate (which is precisely what it was), while all those who are currently receiving "benefits" should regard such "benefits" as welfare checks. Thus, a taxpayer who thought he was paying a Social Security tax of 5 percent while being in a 25 percent tax bracket, was really in a 30 percent bracket and paying these taxes, so that the U.S. government could make welfare payments to many citizens who were far wealthier than the taxpayer.

Since Social Security is "financed" on the same basis as welfare, welfare standards obviously must apply. Future Social Security "benefits" will have to be based on need. The country has no other alternative.

It is not necessary at this time for me to attempt to outline in detail a program for reforming Social Security. I will, however, suggest a brief outline for such a program:

1. A needs test, as I have suggested, will have to be immediately instituted.

2. The Social Security tax itself would be abolished and regular tax rates adjusted accordingly.

3. No Social Security recipient should be penalized because of the receipt of earned income.

4. A sliding scale of reduced future benefits should be projected over the next ten years for those otherwise eligible for current benefits. This would enable future Social Security claimants to plan their retirement more realistically. Obviously, the farther an individual is from 65, the more time he has to adjust to the phasing out of the program.

5. A target date must be established for the official termination of the entire program—say, December 31, 1987. This would allow for gradual phasing out, enabling and encouraging individuals to seek more dependable sources of support for their later years than mere political promises.

A needs test would bar Social Security "benefits" to many now receiving them. However, before such individuals despair over losing their Social Security "benefits," they should recognize that, actually, they were not receiving any "benefits" in the first place. For example, suppose a retired widow or widower with approximately $50,000 in cash assets, such as CDs, bonds, and savings accounts, received the maximum Social Security monthly benefit of approximately $300 a month, or $3,600 a year. During 1974, the inflationary activities of the government (both in increasing the money supply and interfering with the production of goods) were responsible for at least an 18 percent rate of inflation (official figures of 12.2 percent notwithstanding). This rate of inflation would have caused a loss in this individual's liquid savings of $9,000. Therefore, the inflation generated by the government so that it could make unrealistic Social Security payments would have *cost* this individual $5,400. Furthermore, if the above individual had income from a private pension or annuity of $400 monthly, or $4,800 annually, the government, through its inflationary activities, would have reduced the value of these annuity payments by an *additional* $864. It should be further recognized that stock values plummeted in 1974 largely because of government economic and monetary policies and the high taxes paid by corporations. So in addition to the above dollar assets, if the individual started 1974 with stock worth $50,000, he would have suffered stock losses (conservatively estimated) of at least 15 percent or $7,500, as a result of unstable market conditions caused by government economic and fiscal policy. In addition, inflationary losses applied to its year-end value of another 18 percent would have yielded additional losses of $7,650. So this individual would have suffered inflationary tax losses of $16,650 and additional government-related equity losses of $7,500 for a total government-related loss of $25,014 sustained by him in order to receive $3,900 from the government. Obviously, such individuals cannot afford such government "benefits"—they are *too expensive*. It is apparent that this person, like others who apply these same financial adjustments to their own asset portfolios, would discover that he is getting nothing from government in the way of real purchasing power through Social Security. So by eliminating Society Security payments, we eliminate *nothing*, while if we do not quickly eliminate such payments in an orderly fashion, they will be eliminated *anyway* (in my judgment, in from three to five years), in an atmosphere of financial and social chaos with recipients losing a good deal more than merely paper checks.

So, by simultaneously scaling down Social Security and cutting out government and government waste, we will be restoring to the nation's retired citizens a good deal that is now being taken from them.

Much of the same reasoning will, of course, apply to persons receiving any "income payments" from the government. Many now receiving such payments are losing far more because of the shrinkage in the purchasing power of their other assets than they are gaining by way of their government "pensions." So, even if they were to lose a portion or all of these promised government "benefits," they would be gaining far more than they would be losing.

In addition, and I feel it bears repeating, those who feel that they are "entitled" to government pensions must keep in mind that if all those who feel similarly "entitled" insist on pressing their claims, they will succeed in forcing the financial collapse of U.S. Government, Inc., and will thereby create (for themselves and the rest of the economy) a situation where they will not only end up losing their pensions anyway, but in the process also lose their accumulated savings, the value of their private pensions, the value of their bonds, and a substantial portion of the value of their common stock.

Getting the Government Out of the Welfare Business

While I have suggested subjecting all government "pensions" (transfer payments) to a needs test and treating all such payments no differently than ordinary welfare payments, the government must also be phased out of the welfare business. Welfare payments must also be given a time span—say, ten years. This will provide the time for those now receiving welfare to attempt to develop the necessary skills to become self-supporting. Many people have not bothered to become self-supporting because U.S. Government, Inc., makes it convenient for them to rely on it for support. Not only will many welfare recipients be on notice that government programs will be terminated, but government welfare workers will be on notice that they should seek more useful employment. As of now, of course, the government's bureaucracy has a vested interest in maintaining welfare—maintaining their jobs. Many bureaucrats assigned to the Department of Health, Education and Welfare would not relish a program that would enable the nation's increasing number of welfare recipients to find useful employment since this would eliminate substantial numbers of HEW employees. This is another reason why HEW consistently minimizes the extent of welfare abuses, when actually the abuses are rampant.

However, before anyone accuses me of having no compassion for the nation's "disadvantaged," let me say that these people would be far better off without welfare programs. Reductions in welfare and corresponding reductions in government taxation and other forms of government economic interference would raise the nation's standard of living, thereby eliminating in most cases the need for welfare. With the government no longer able to restrict food production, food prices would drop, thereby enabling the nation's "disadvantaged" to feed themselves far more economically. Then, perhaps, they would not be "disadvantaged." Those unable to find employment and on welfare will find it far easier to find jobs with the increasing employment opportunities that would suddenly be available as a result of the sharp reduction in government taxation that hitherto drastically curtailed employment opportunities.

For hard-core cases there still would be all types of private charity. With sharp reductions in spending for government welfare programs, these funds would remain in the private sector and a good portion would find its way to private charities, both religious and nonsectarian. Americans have always been charitable, so the thought that a prosperous nation would allow other more unfortunate Americans to "starve" or to be without necessities in the midst of plenty is simply too ludicrous to comment upon.

It might be helpful to point out that prior to 1932 Americans had no significant public welfare programs and no one starved despite the huge burden of immigrant absorption. To assert, therefore, that such would be the case today would demonstrate not only ignorance of America's economic history and traditions, but indicate a failure to recognize our improved economic potential due to striking advances in technology and overall economic efficiency which makes such a possibility more remote. Certainly the danger to those now on welfare in this situation involves less risk than confronted those who headed west in covered wagons to face all kinds of dangers and an uncertain future. Should they have been met by government "case workers" after crossing the Missouri? Lord knows, they were without "adequate housing," without jobs, and probably their hospitalization insurance had lapsed. Obviously, government "case workers" would have been a *big help* in settling the West.

No, I'm afraid that government bureaucrats and addlebrained social scientists have hoodwinked the American public into believing that there are vast numbers of Americans that cannot sustain themselves without the aid of the federal government.

Another reason government has to be driven out of the charity business is the tendency of politicians to appeal to voters on a "here's something-for-nothing" basis. The attitude that all too many Americans have, which has largely been cultivated by the government itself, is that individuals have a legal right to be supported. Such a belief can no longer be tolerated by a nation wishing to be free, strong, and prosperous.

Less Government + More Producers = National Prosperity (−G +MP = NP) —The Formula for National Prosperity

The basic economic problem facing the nation is not the energy problem or the employment problem, or even inflation: we have too much government and too few producers. By simply attacking the former problem, the latter problem will correct itself and most of our other economic and social problems will vanish.

Reducing the size and the cost of government will restore incentives and the economy will expand, blossom, and grow as the economic employment of the nation's land, labor, and capital is thus increased. Industries that are now languishing due to high interest rates and the inability to raise capital will find interest rates dropping as money ceases to fall in value as government-created inflation is brought to an end. The numerous individuals weaned away from economic employment by a multiplicity of government welfare programs will begin adding their productivity into the common pot, thus increasing the community's store of goods and services, which will now swell. The nation's standard of living will begin to float upward on a rising tide of increased productivity.

Therefore, the battle plan to restore America's economic health is simply one of reducing government, government taxes, personnel, and its economic and social influences. Government again must be returned to the role of simply serving the modest needs of the people and not, as now is the case, the people serving the gargantuan needs of government. The country must insist that government immediately stop its current futile attempt to fight our "recession," since unless the government's power and influence are reduced, the current recession will become a permanent depression. It should also be noted that all government efforts to "stimulate the economy" out of the recession are doomed to failure and will only compound our economic problems.

The vaunted 1974 and 1975 tax cuts are out-and-out frauds and will not save the nation's taxpayers a dime. For example, if a family who had been promised a $200 tax rebate simply has a total of $5,000 in accumulated savings, in either stocks, bonds, life insurance reserves, or annuity and pension values, the government's antirecession measures, like the tax-rebate gimmick, will add at least 5 percent to the nation's level of inflation. Thus, the above family that is being told that it is getting a $200 tax "rebate" will simply have $250 stolen from its assets to pay for it. Actually, the government's tax rebate is nothing more than the government's returning to taxpayers a portion of their own looted savings.

The public should also guard against government propaganda claiming success in controlling and overcoming inflation—the cause of our recession. It should be noted that even if the rate of inflation is reported to have dropped to, say, 8 percent, enabling the government to claim that inflation has subsided from the 1974 rate of 12.2 percent, this would be inaccurate and misleading. The reason is that there has been a continued slowdown in the nation's economic activity with rising unemployment and falling productivity, factors which should have forced prices *down* substantially. In the absence of government inflationary pressure, such economic forces might have forced prices down by 15 percent. Such a sharp drop in prices would not be that severe but would have simply returned prices to 1973 levels. So, a reported rate of inflation of 8 percent in reality, might be hiding a rate of *23 percent, a rate much higher than 1974's!*

In the absence of any concerted government program to reduce its own size, citizens can disregard any optimistic government claims concerning the state of the economy or the rate of inflation.

The Practical Side of Saving the Country and What Each Citizen Can Do

Americans must simply concentrate all of their efforts in only one direction and should not allow themselves to be sidetracked—they must constantly exert pressure to deflate the government, compelling it to start the task of figuring out where the $100 billion of excess "federal air" is to come from. Nothing else is of any economic importance.

Along with performing this cost-cutting operation on itself, the government must immediately do another thing—it must abolish all laws that arbitrarily attempt to set wage rates, and it must also remove all barriers standing in the way of increased productivity. The first order of business should be to eliminate minimum wages, since they accomplish absolutely no good whatever. Scrapping minimum wage laws will immediately open avenues of employment for America's unemployed, and unemployment levels will begin to drop. In line with this, arbitrary wage scales, such as mandatory time-and-a-half provisions, should also be thrown out, leaving employers and employees free to determine wages acceptable to each. To save time, of course, the entire 1938 Fair Labor Standards Act and all of its amendments could be scrapped.

In addition, all union contracts that seek to limit productivity, prevent the use of labor-saving devices, or require the arbitrary employment of unnecessary personnel must be declared illegal and void, and union officials found guilty of pressing such practices on employers should be subject to arrest and prosecution for extortion.

All of these measures are, of course, directed toward increasing America's overall productivity, since it is only by increasing productivity that the dollar can be saved, inflation arrested, jobs restored, and all private savings and pensions rescued from what otherwise will be *a financial disaster*.

U. S. "Savings Bonds" Revolt. Denying funds to the federal government can contribute substantially toward saving the nation. I have already pointed out why ownership and purchase of "savings bonds" are a poor investment both for the individual and the nation. For one thing, the government takes from bondholders far more each year by way of inflation than the government pays them in interest, while the purchase of the bond itself diverts capital from worthwhile economic projects in the private sector to government, where it is largely wasted. This waste of capital that government ''bond'' purchases produce forces a lower standard of living on the nation.

I have always felt that if the government's creditors, its bondholders, could ever organize, they, like the creditors of any faltering business, could force fiscal reform on the government by threatening bond redemptions if the government didn't cease its spendthrift ways. Suppose the owners of $60 billion worth of U.S. savings bonds tried to restore some of the stolen purchasing power in the following manner: a committee of government bondholders could forward a note to the government demanding, for example, that unless 10 percent of the personnel of, say, the Agriculture, Labor, and HEW departments were slashed ''within 90 days,'' the bondholders would ''within 15 days demand payment of our bonds.'' I believe that such concerted action by government bondholders might halt falling government bond values while halting skyrocketing government costs.

Such a program would not be that difficult to organize. Bondholders wishing to participate in such a program need only drop a card to a duly organized committee. It would not even be necessary for participants to indicate the amount of bonds they own. However, once the committee determined about how many people had joined to force fiscal responsibility on the government, they could then act. The committee could determine a reasonable degree of government rollback which would be acceptable to all participating government creditors and send the following message to the government:

> We wish to see evidence that at least 10,000 government employees have been released from government service by September 1, or on September 15 all savings bonds in Connecticut, Texas, Wisconsin, Alabama, and Ohio will be presented for redemption.

In this way, the creditors of U.S. Government, Inc., like the creditors of any mismanaged corporation, might exercise some fiscal control. I would urge all readers who may have discovered the *real* value of government ''savings bonds'' not to run out and cash them. There should be no disorganized, individual cashing since this would serve no constructive national purpose. However, if bondholders would organize the threat of mass cashing, it would serve a national purpose since it might force the government to institute a program which would not only restore value to the bonds held by government creditors, but bring economies that would benefit all Americans whether they were bondholders or not. So, hold on to your bonds for a while. You have lost so much purchasing power that further losses will not be of any consequence, while probably these losses could be restored, and in the process help the country.

Lets Have a Tax Revolt

Scattered throughout America, small bands of patriots have been engaged in a growing tax revolt. Often fighting alone, they have been waging what amounts to every American's war against U.S. Government, Inc. They have suffered casualties, but they have also won battles. It has been estimated that thousands of Americans, using tactics and strategies developed by the tax rebels, no longer pay federal income taxes.

Tax rebels are independent and proud; they understand the literal meaning of freedom and liberty and mean to hold on to it. They refuse to be dictated to by unproductive bureaucrats. They have discovered that they have to be their own lawyers and have become experts on constitutional law and legal proceedings. They share their information and their experience with others. They even have their own publications.[1]

Here are some of their arguments against the Internal Revenue Service.

Form 1040 Violates a Citizen's Right against Self-Incrimination. Tax rebels regard the IRS form 1040 as a "confession sheet" which citizens must sign "under penalty of perjury," thereby enabling the IRS to use such information against them in future criminal proceedings. Tax rebels clearly see this as a violation of the Fifth Amendment guarantee of the right against self-incrimination, claiming that they are under no obligation to sign any form that may be used against them. Many insist that they will only provide the government with the information requested if government officials first grant to them immunity from criminal prosecution. To tax rebels, this appears to be a reasonable request since the government routinely gives such immunity to criminals and politicians from whom it wants possible incriminating information. Thus, tax rebels see no reason why the same protection should not be extended to law abiding and productive citizens.

Tax rebels insist that the Sixteenth Amendment, which gave Congress the right "to lay and collect taxes," a mere four-line amendment, did not automatically abrogate every other line and right secured to Americans by the same Constitution. They believe that the Constitution was primarily established to protect the lives, property, and privacy of Americans, and that the Sixteenth Amendment, given current tax rates and the manner it is enforced, attempts to destroy all the rights which are secured by the Fourth, Fifth, Sixth, Seventh, Eighth, Ninth, Tenth, and Thirteenth amendments.

In refusing to testify against themselves, tax rebels rely heavily on the Miranda decision.[2] In this landmark case, the U.S. Supreme Court overturned the conviction of Ernesto A. Miranda, an individual who had confessed to a crime while in official custody. On reversing his conviction, the Court enunciated some principles in connection with self-incrimination which tax rebels find comforting. For example, the Supreme Court held that

> the Fifth Amendment privilege is available outside of criminal court proceedings and serves to protect persons in all settings in which their freedom of action is curtailed from being compelled to incriminate themselves.

[1]TRUE, Box 424, Altadena, CA. 91001; TAX STRIKE NEWS, P.O.Box 1089, Porterville, CA. 93257; *Also* Rene Baxter's FREEDOM FIGHTER, Box 204, Trail, OR. 97541; and Bill Drexler's PATRIOT NEWS, P.O.Box 22569, San Diego, CA. 92112

[2]*Miranda vs. State of Arizona,* 86 S.Ct. 1602 (1966). Reproduced with permission from volume 86, *Supreme Court Reporter,* copyright© 1967 West Publishing Co.

Tax rebels assert that this ruling can be applied to citizens to avoid incrimination by completing "under penalty of perjury" form 1040. They also view many IRS procedures as void.

The high court also held in *Miranda* that

> where rights secured by the Constitution are involved, there can be no rule-making or legislation which would abrogate them

and that the

> government seeking to punish an individual must produce evidence against him by its own independent labors, rather than by the cruel, simple expedient of compelling it from his own mouth.

Moreover,

> the privilege against self-incrimination is fulfilled only when a person is guaranteed the right to remain silent unless he chooses to speak in unfettered exercise of his own will.

Tax rebels also contend that the income tax violates both the Thirteenth Amendment and Article 1, Section 9, clause 8 of the U.S. Constitution. The Thirteenth Amendment's abolition of slavery and involuntary servitude did not only, they assert, abolish such relationships between individuals but denied such a relationship to the state as well. As pointed out in Chapter 7, our level of taxation attempts to reduce all productive citizens to peons in the service of the state. Tax rebels claim that the Thirteenth Amendment protects Americans from such bondage.

Article 1, Section 9, Clause 8, prohibits the government from conferring any "title of nobility." Tax rebels interpret this as an injunction prohibiting the government from establishing a "privileged" class of citizens as distinguished from a "discriminated" class. Thus, they claim that all government cash subsidies violate this clause. By taking money from some citizens for the exclusive benefit of other citizens, the government is, in fact, setting up two classes of citizens. One class, a "nobility" if you will, is to be "served" and "maintained" at the expense of the other class—clearly unconstitutional. A related consideration that some tax rebels cite is the attempt throughout the Constitution of maintaining and asserting that we were to be a nation of free and equal citizens. However, tax rebels maintain that the tax structure establishes inequality among citizens. If all citizens are equal, they say, and have an equal right to vote, one citizen cannot use that vote to compel another citizen to support him. Thus they claim that if citizen A must support citizen B, then obviously A and B are not equal and should, therefore, not have the same privileges of citizenship. Citizen B has no right (to vote) to compel A to support him; so, if B chooses to take advantage of public welfare, he must forfeit his privilege to vote, while if he wishes to exercise his voting privilege, he must surrender his claim to public welfare. A citizen cannot claim both a right to vote and a right to be supported.

All voting citizens, rebels feel, must be free and equal, but they are not if one is compelled to support himself and the other voter.

Protecting Yourself from the IRS

Not all Americans have the courage, tenacity, spirit, knowledge, and patriotism to lock horns with the IRS as did that gallant lady from Connecticut, Miss Vivian Kellems. She demonstrated that it is possible to defy the IRS and win. Despite the fact that millions of Americans, like little lambs, dutifully transport all their personal records to the IRS when requested, Miss Kellems refused, claiming this violated her rights against self-incrimination. *And she prevailed*![1]

Despite such clearcut victories, the IRS will, when it can, ride roughshod over the constitutional rights of Americans. A series of articles on this subject by John Downes appeared in *Readers' Digest*. One entitled "Tyranny in the Internal Revenue Service" appeared in the August 1967 issue.

To protect themselves against such IRS tactics, tax rebels rely on the Fifth Amendment and on Sections 241 and 242 of the U.S. Criminal Code. These latter sections provide up to $10,000 in fines and 10 years imprisonment if "two or more persons conspire to injure, oppress, threaten, or intimidate any citizen in the free exercise of enjoyment of any right or privilege secured to him by the Constitution of Laws of the United States."

Since tax rebels feel that their constitutional rights are infringed by the IRS, they threaten government officials who "threaten or intimidate" them with personal lawsuits as provided by these sections. If the IRS insists on pressing its claim, tax rebels say, let the government haul them into court and there before a jury prove that their constitutional rights are not being violated. In such cases the jury will decide their penalty. Rebels point out that as long as they haven't signed a 1040 form under "penalty of perjury" they cannot be charged with that crime —the charge customarily leveled by the IRS against citizens who cooperated in their own entrapment. Rebels can only be charged with the "willful failure" to pay taxes, which becomes a question for a jury to dispose of.

Would a reasoned explanation by a taxpayer that he could not complete a return, since in so doing he would not only be surrendering constitutional rights but would also be contributing to perpetuating a government inadvertently bent on destroying the nation, be a "willful failure" to pay taxes? Some might suggest that it is one's

[1]In a letter dated April 1, 1970, to Federal Judge Robert Zampano of New Haven, Assistant Attorney General J. M. Walker stated: "We are of opinion that Miss Kellems has properly pleaded the Fifth Amendment privilege against self-incrimination as to her personal records." As a consequence, he added, the government "would withdraw our request for enforcement of these summonses." Commenting on her victory, Miss Kellems was quoted by the AP as saying, "No longer can the IRS arrogantly demand a taxpayer's books and papers. I have pleaded the Fifth Amendment, go thou and do likewise."

patriotic duty under such circumstances not to. Since all veterans took an oath to defend the Constitution from "all enemies domestic and foreign," to subsidize (through taxation) violations of the Constitution would be to break that sworn oath! Can such rebels convince juries of Americans that under these circumstances they did not "willfully fail" to complete a return but were conscientiously attempting to protect not only their liberties but the jury's as well? This is the legal risk that tax rebels are apparently willing to take. Also as all readers know now, no one earns any money in America, but only noninterest-bearing, irredeemable notes of a private agency, a Federal Reserve Bank, which are worthless on their face. The Internal Revenue Code states that the receipt of notes does not constitute taxable income—*only their fair market value*. Since the fair market value of Federal Reserve notes cannot be determined (since they are only quoted in like notes), tax rebels say they have no taxable income!

Are Social Security Taxes Now Unconstitutional?

In addition to all of the above, Section 151, of *American Jurisprudence*, 2nd edition, volume 16, states:

> Constitutionality of federal legislation is to be determined by the manner in which the enactment works in its practical application.[1] A statute fair upon its face may be shown to be void and unenforceable on account of its actual operation.[2]

This clearly establishes the unlawful nature of Social Security. Since the intent of Social Security was to establish a degree of financial security for retired Americans, and since it can now be demonstrated that the program will not do this but instead will create financial hardship, then the act in "actual operation" is clearly opposite of its legislative intent and therefore unconstitutional. Certainly individuals under age 30 can cite the *1975 Report of the Advisory Council on Social Security* to substantiate their contention that they will not receive promised benefits.

Even this report admitted in findings, which were themselves cited as being overly optimistic, by the Senate Finance Committee (p. 125) that Social Security might run into difficulty by the year 2005, "when pressures might well develop to increase the retirement age beyond age 65" (p.63). So, even based on optimistic government projections, it is doubtful those 35 and under will receive the retirement benefits promised.

Of course, in my opinion, the system cannot last more than *five years* in its present form, if that, while the existence of its huge unfunded liability should support anyone's claim that the plan is a fraud and will not deliver the benefits promised, thus making it and the taxes levied to support it unconstitutional.

[1]*Communist Parties* v. *Subversive Activities Control Board,* 367 U.S. 1, 6L ed 2d 625, 81 S Cp 1357, reh den 368 U.S. 871, 7L 3e 2d 72, 82 S Cp 20.

[2]*Great Northern R.* v. *Washington,* 300 U.S. 154, 81 L ed 573, 57 S Ct 397 reh den 300 U.S. 686, 81 L ed 888, 57 S Ct 504.

Can a Government that Violates the Law Compel Others to Obey It?

My contribution to the tax revolt might be in uncovering the way the government willfully violates Section 404 of Public Law 89-809, a law designed to protect citizens fiscally from the government, and the manner in which it hides and misleads the public concerning the extent of the public debt. If the government wishes to prosecute rebels for their "willful failure" to file form 1040, the federal government must enter court with clean hands. But how can it?

It seems to me that tax rebels are now free to argue that if the government does not feel obliged to account to the people as the law requires concerning the debts it is accumulating in the public's behalf, then the public itself is free to adopt the same attitude—it is not obligated to account to the government. Ours is a nation of laws and not of men. So, when the government places itself above the law, by violating and neglecting a law whose purpose is to protect taxpayers from fiscal abuses by the government, then all government fiscal power and authority itself becomes unlawful and unconstitutional.

In writing this book I hoped to present an economic and monetary insight coupled with an understanding of how the U.S. government works, in order to change economic and political thinking. Those of us who believe in the virtues and economic benefits that flow from less government and more personal freedom can certainly, at this time, use a lot more help from our fellow Americans.

I know there are many Americans with a good deal of human compassion and political energy who call themselves, or consider themselves, "liberals." Tragically, their compassion and enthusiasm have been misdirected; they have been directed toward promoting the omnipotent state, the antithesis of liberty —sometimes called the welfare state. To "liberals," I say don't despair. We all make mistakes. I suggest you look into a more humane political-economic philosophy -- libertarianism.[1] You'll find its ideology much closer to what you *really* believe -- if, that is, you really believe in personal liberty.

Remember: America has only *one* problem—*too much government*! If we all begin concentrating on ways to get rid of that problem, then all of our other problems will vanish. We will then move into an era of technological and material achievement that will make the progress America made during the first third of the twentieth century look sluggish at best.

The American productive giant can achieve miracles, but only if freed of the shackles of government regulations. Americans today find themselves before an awesome crossroad. One road leads to the promised land, the other leads to economic and social tragedy of gigantic proportions. The choice is still ours.

[1]For information on libertarianism contact: Foundation for Economic Education, Irvington-on-Hudson, N.Y. 10533

Appendix A

INVESTMENTS

Due to my background in investments and insurance, the publisher felt that my book should logically contain recommendations in these areas. This presented me with an uncomfortable dilemma, however, since such recommendations would have to be made on the premise that America is heading for economic collapse, while my book was written on the assumption that such a catastrophe can be averted. So in making these recommendations I am forced to assume that Americans (during their Bicentennial celebration honoring their courageous revolutionary forebears) passively permitted politicians and bureaucrats to continue their destructive assault on the American economy—which must lead to economic and social chaos.

A Glimpse at America's Economic Future—Assuming Americans Fail in Throttling Their Government

Assuming that productive citizens do not immediately launch an open rebellion in response to politicians creating budget deficits of $58 billion for fiscal 1975 and $96.5 billion for fiscal 1976, such outrageous deficits will fan the flames of inflation to new and awesome heights. Soon the government will be forced to admit "official" levels of inflation exceeding 15 and 20 percent. Inflation at these "official" levels will consume savings at such a ferocious rate that savings, and therefore investment capital, will start to shrivel up, driving interest rates to new and dizzy heights. Even at these heights, however, it will be impossible to fool anyone any longer concerning phony "interest" yields. Capital will cease being "saved" and "loaned." Without a continuing supply of new capital the operation of many businesses will come to a halt. Business failures and unemployment will accelerate. Both of these developments will cause tax revenues to drop, generating even larger fiscal deficits. So the government will print unmoney at a faster rate to compensate for falling revenues and to pay for the new programs launched to "fight the recession." Soon the government, like the sorcerer's apprentice, will be caught up in a monetary nightmare printing unmoney at an ever faster pace until it succeeds in utterly destroying the trading value of the nation's unmoney supply.

The "Investment" Picture

Given this economic scenario you can begin focusing on what will be the best investment strategy for you. Since in the long run all "fixed dollar" investments[1] will become relatively worthless, basing one's financial future on them will prove disastrous. However, while in the long run it makes little difference whether bonds are rated AAA or BB, since runaway inflation will destroy them all equally, in the short run some bonds, due to outright default, will become worthless quicker than others. For example, debtors like the City of New York might be forced into bankruptcy before inflation affords them the opportunity of paying off their creditors in cheap and worthless paper.

The Importance of Timing

Since runaway inflation has the effect of wiping out debts (debtors gain access to a vast supply of feverishly printed but worthless "money" in which to pay off their debts), it makes good sense to go into debt to acquire real wealth—houses, land, automobiles, equipment, gold, etc. Individuals, for example, would profit, in my judgment, if they mortgaged or remortgaged their homes to invest in gold. Since gold will be increasing in relative dollar value[2] the mortgage note can eventually be paid off with a few ounces of gold (or a small fraction thereof) so purchased.

This is not to suggest that the rise in the price of gold will proceed in a straight line. All of the government's monetary, economic and political power, as well as its extensive propaganda machinery, will be enlisted in a constant battle to drive its price down–and, in the short run the government will indeed enjoy some tempor-

[1]Such as cash, savings accounts, bonds, cash reserves of life insurance, annuities, pensions, and other types of cash receivables.

[2]As will gasoline, soda pop, and jockey shorts. It is wrong, therefore, to suggest—as some do—that "since gold has already risen from $35 to $150 an ounce, it is foolish to expect it to go up further." Just because a cup of coffee has gone from five cents to a quarter, can it not go to thirty or forty cents or even a dollar? On the contrary, the fact that our politicians could produce such dramatic price increases during periods of relative economic strength (and cheap energy) is an indication of the prices they will produce during a period of economic weakness (and high energy costs). It can further be assumed that political interference will grow more irresponsible and more destructive as politicians are confronted by their own failures. Blinded by their egos, ignorance, and mounting frustration, they will attempt even more idiotic schemes in attempting to convince voters that they are "trying to do something" to fight the "inflation and recession."

ary successes. But in the absence of any fundamental change in the nation's monetary, fiscal, and economic direction, simply regard any major retreat in the price of gold as an unexpected buying opportunity.

A Word of Caution

Leverage—using borrowed money to increase profit—introduces another risk: debt. You should be relatively certain that you can manage this debt through the economic pinch that will precede runaway inflation. A realistic evaluation of your assets and the size and dependability of your income should be considered in order to balance opportunities for leverage with safety.

What About Life Insurance?

I had previously noted how the life insurance industry cooperated in selling out its insureds. It should have long ago adamantly refused to purchase government bonds unless the government halted its inflationary practices, while simultaneously employing its vast resources to inform the public how their insurance assets were being systematically looted by government monetary policies. Such a program would have stopped inflation dead in its tracks. The industry, however, elected to promote inflation due to the favorable effect it had on sales.

Similarly, this industry was the logical source to expose Social Security for the "insurance" fraud it was, and the disaster it was destined to be. Again, however, the insurance industry chose instead to exploit Social Security for its own purposes. How many were first approached by an insurance agent on the following basis? "Hello, Mr. Prospect? My name is Fred Grooper of Aquarius Life. Were you aware, sir, that in the event of your death your widow could lose thousands of dollars of valuable Social Security benefits if you did not make provisions to insure them against loss?" In this manner, Social Security was used to sell billions of dollars of insurance. It was the best salesman the industry ever had.

With this record it may not be wise to rely on the industry to help you fashion an insurance program that intelligently reflects today's economic realities.

Since at any given age there are numerous policies that can be purchased, the industry generally pushes those generating higher commissions and higher premiums while buyers are better served by those developing smaller commissions and premiums. In such a conflict, the industry wins nine times out of ten. To ensure an easy victory the industry developed a language that few not trained in actuarial science can penetrate. For example, "whole life" insurance is a combination of *decreasing term insurance and an increasing cash endowment* (a combination of the two providing a level death benefit) but is sold on the basis that it is "permanent insurance. The only "permanent insurance" the industry sells -renewable term[1]-

[1]It is "permanent" since the insured is able to *renew* the amount of insurance originally applied for (which is not reduced by an accumulation of mortality overpayments called "cash value") for the life of the contract, generally to age 70—which is beyond the period for which most insurance is required.

is labeled "temporary insurance."[1]

Thus, by incorrectly glorifying one and maligning the other, the insurance industry hopes to sell more whole life than term, since whole life generates more immediate cash flow and commissions per $1,000.

What Type of Life Insurance Should You Own?

Today the main purpose of life insurance should be *to insure* (as with auto, fire, and theft policies) and not to serve as a "savings" vehicle. Since it is pointless to project future dollar values, you should try to get as much current death protection for the least outlay while tying up little of your own cash. This means that all forms of cash value insurance should be replaced by term—one to five year renewable, and/or decreasing term. As far as practical your insurance should be stripped of all cash. The techniques for this are to:

(1) Cash in existing policies, especially those that are "paid up," and apply for new term insurance or

(2) Borrow out cash values and maintain the "net insurance" with premium loans, and

(3) Keep policies in force with "extended term" options.

What precisely is the best arrangement for you depends on a number of factors such as your state of health, tax bracket, insurance needs, other assets, and existing policies. Many Americans now pay substantial premiums but are inadequately insured. It is not necessary, however, to spend a lot of money for insurance. For example, $100,000 of decreasing term is $287 at age 35,[2] $604 at age 45,[2] and $1,092 at age 55.[3]

In comparing these premiums to whole life you will have to adjust for its cash value. For example, if you are paying $200 for a $10,000 policy which has a current cash value of $1,000, you may incorrectly assume that you are paying $200 for $10,000 of insurance. Actually you only have $9,000 (the face of the policy less the cash value), while your premium is $200 *plus the loss of interest on $1,000*. If you can earn at least 5 percent[4] after taxes on your tied-up cash, then

[1]The insurance departments of most states cooperate fully in this deception by throwing their full bureaucratic weight into helping the industry preserve high premium insurance. Most consider it quite proper for an agent to replace term insurance with "permanent," but frown on them for replacing "permanent" with term. In the latter case the agent is made to complete lengthy "replacement forms" which project cash and dividend values for 20 yrs. and longer. Though these replacement forms are less than useless, they can delay an application. Therefore, insurance commissioners who require them should be held personally liable for losses (due to death or impairment to insurability) that result because coverage was needlessly delayed.

[2]20-year decreasing term, $75,000 of insurance remaining at the beginning of the sixth policy year. Issued by Old Security Life Insurance Company, Kansas City, Mo.

[3]10-year decreasing term, $55,000 of insurance remaining at the beginning of the sixth policy year.

[4]You could easily earn 8 percent by investing directly in Triple A bonds, which is what the insurance companies do anyway.

your insurance cost is $250 (less any premium refunds you receive on participating policies). So, while you might think you are paying $200 for $10,000 of insurance, you are in reality paying $250[1] for $9,000.

All things considered, you should seek competent professional help if your insurance portfolio needs substantial overhauling, and while good insurance advice may be hard to come by, it is not impossible to find. In interviewing a prospective agent you might ask him what he thinks of term insurance. If he says "it's okay for temporary needs," or if he talks "permanent insurance" or your "retirement needs" or "insurance guarantees" and projects future "cash values," get rid of him and look for someone else. The public itself shares some of the blame for the amount of poor insurance advice it gets. For example, if after a lengthy analysis a conscientious agent recommended that one needed no more insurance and in addition offered to rearrange the existing insurance to save $350 in premiums and $30,000 in estate taxes and then submitted a bill for $250 for services rendered—a typical American would turn hostile. We all have come to expect insurance agents to work for nothing and to be paid only if they sell us something. If, in the above example, the agent was motivated by an overdue note at the bank and so used his persuasive selling skills into talking this individual into needlessly spending $600 more for insurance, he would earn $350. By giving good advice, however, he earns nothing but a pat on the head and hopefully a few "leads." The best way to assure yourself of good insurance advice may be to contract with a knowledgeable professional to go over your insurance for a fee. Any commissions that might result if new insurance were indicated could be applied against this fee. But at least the agent will be assured that he will be paid for his time, so he may respond like a counselor, not a salesman. Unless you pay a fee for services, in most cases you will not get an insurance "adviser," "counselor," "planner," or "consultant." You will get—a salesman.

In conclusion, I would like to point out that while "whole life" is generally misrepresented by the industry, it was nevertheless a remarkable financial instrument which for many years served its owners and the nation well. Thousands of agents working night and day in good weather and bad used it to sell thrift and self-reliance and to teach financial responsibility in the kitchens and parlors of the nation. Their salesmanship and hard work helped to generate a stream of capital which flowed into the American economy, raising the living standards of all while strengthening the financial position of the insured and his family. There is nothing intrinsically wrong with whole life insurance; it was the short-sighted greed of the insurance industry that permitted it to allow the government to destroy its economic usefulness—along with the economic usefulness of all annuities, pensions, and long-term fixed-dollar financial planning.

[1] True, a good portion of this will be accumulating in your reserve, but death or runaway inflation makes such a consideration unimportant.

The Stock Market—Or Let's Give the Wheel Another Spin

As inflation destroyed fixed dollar investments, so taxes destroyed stocks as a serious investment vehicle. Does it really make sense to invest in businesses that are *already* nationalized? While legitimate stock investment was quietly passing from the American scene, speculation (the financial term for gambling) was quietly ushered in.[1]

A few years ago, while addressing some 20 brokers of a major New York Stock Exchange firm at their Hartford, Connecticut, office, I asked: "What would you recommend to a client who called today looking for a good investment?" Immediately several hands shot up and the name of a common stock was suggested. "What does it yield?" I inquired. "About 2 percent," came the reply. "Well," I asked, "why would you recommend an investment paying 2 percent when one can get 5 percent from a bank, with no risk?" Confused by my strange reasoning the startled broker replied incredulously, "But money in the bank can't grow while this stock can go up 20 to 30 percent or even double." "Therefore," I replied, "you recommend that stock based on the sheer speculation that its *market price* will go up and not down."

"A good investment," I continued, "should deliver a better than average return to compensate for the risks of stock ownership while offering the promise that an increasing yield might cause its market price to rise also. With this criteria in mind would someone please offer me an *investment* and not a speculation?" Not a hand now went up, and after awaiting in complete silence for about 10 seconds, I proceeded with my talk.

According to the August 4, 1975, issue of *Barron's* its high-grade bond portfolio was yielding 8.61 percent while the Dow Jones Industrial common stocks were yielding 4.69 percent. Since stocks should provide a return of at least 2 to 3 percent more than high grade bonds, the Dow Jones would have to drop almost 60 percent before stock prices realistically reflected stock yields. When you *think* about it, does it make sense to permit stockbrokers but not bookmakers? Why should the less affluent be barred from calling a bookmaker and placing a bet on say, "Showboat running in the fifth at Hialeah," while the more affluent can call a broker and place a bet on say, "Polaroid running on the New York Stock Exchange"? What confuses most people is the impressive array of gadgetry in a typical brokerage office: electronic quote boards, the chattering wire service, TV-style stock analysis machines, shelves of research reports, dignified furniture and decor, all creating an image that there is more going on than mere "tulip trading."[2] If we would only legalize *all forms of gambling*, brokerage offices

[1]After all, the brokerage community still had to make a living.

[2]I urge you to read up on the "tulip craze" that seized Holland during the period 1623-27 when trading in tulips sent prices to dizzying heights. An account of this interesting phenomena can be found in Charles Mackay's *Extraordinary Popular Delusions and the Madness of Crowds*, published by Noonday Press.

could also have slot machines, blackjack, and crap tables, and maybe even a $2 window. At least then they would project a more honest image.

The only stocks that I recommend the average American own (as investments) would be gold and silver stocks. If I were forced to recommend others I would limit myself to those in natural resources, principally oil and coal. Another consideration for stock ownership might be stock in companies with large amounts of bonded debt which runaway inflation will wipe out, thus delivering all their assets free and clear to the common stockholders. However, they should reasonably be expected to manage this debt through the preceding economic crunch. If not, they could default, thus wiping out the interests of the common stockholders in favor of the bond holders. Public utilities and producers of necessities (inelastic goods) might be candidates for stock ownership based on these considerations.

What Can You Invest In?

The financial hurricane that is brewing can blow away claims to wealth[1] and paper assets whose values are supported only by nonexistent profits—it cannot blow away *real wealth*. That is why food and gold are now better investments than stocks and bonds.

Gold's value is not based on another's solvency nor on political promises. Its value is intrinsic—it is not a *claim* to wealth, it *is* wealth. Its value has been increasing for over 2,000 years while billions and billions of paper assets have turned to dust. Gold represents a haven in which savings can be stored in times of financial danger, its owners knowing full well that when the storm has passed it will emerge not only with its value undiminished but enhanced. All those who take seriously the statements of U.S. monetary officials that gold will be "phased out" of the world's monetary system are victims of a propaganda effort that even Paul Goebbels would not have attempted. Not only will gold not be "phased out," but its importance will increase after the "bloodbath of paper currencies" that the world is destined to experience.

Ways of Owning Gold

You can take ownership of gold in three ways—bullion, coins, and through the ownership of gold stock. There is really no point in owning bullion unless one intends to store substantial amounts, and even then I would prefer coins. Coins make more sense than one, two, five, or ten ounce bars. For one thing, the premium that one pays for coins is not substantially higher than what one pays on bars, yet coins deliver gold in a much more convenient and negotiable form. Coins

[1]Claims to wealth are exactly what "fixed dollar investments" are. One who owns dollars (or a future claim to dollars) owns no wealth—only "claims to wealth" which he hopes will be honored (for food, clothing, gold, etc.) in the future. Inflation, however, erodes these claims, while runaway inflation destroys them completely.

are more liquid, with a market made through numerous coin dealers, employing teletype machines. Their price is supported by their bullion content, their numismatic value, and their value as pieces of finished jewelry. If, on the other hand, one wanted to convert a ten-ounce gold bar into food, clothing, and shelter, one might have to sell it first to a processor, giving the government the opportunity to claim that one had a "taxable gain." If, on the other hand, one had a comparable amount in coins, these could be traded *directly* for goods, as needed, and so would not develop a comparable "taxable gain." A good deal of gold and silver transactions are conducted on a cash basis (and without benefit of Social Security numbers) and thus constitute one of the few types of investments affording privacy and anonymity.[1]

COMPARATIVE PRICES OF GOLD COINS AND BULLION AS OF AUGUST 1, 1975

Closing Gold Price $167.70*

	Price	Premium
Austrian 100 coronae	$ 170.65	3.8 percent
Austrain 20 coronae	35.00	7.0 percent
South African krugerrand	176.20	5.0 percent
Mexican 50 pesos	219.65	8.6 percent
British sovereigns	51.30	30.0 percent
US Double Eagles	252.50	56.0 percent
10 ounce bar	1,764.00	5.0 percent
1 kilo bar	5,635.00	4.0 percent

*Prices furnished by Monex International, Ltd.

For convenience in trading, I recommend the ownership of smaller denominations of coins. Despite their added premium, they will prove more convenient for shopping than will large gold coins, thus saving you money (notice how I can now use that word correctly) in the long run.

You should also have a supply of silver coins, since you wouldn't want to shop

[1]After a monetary collapse, the government will need to rebuild its gold supply in order to furnish the country with honest, dependable currency. Since it will not be able to replace unmoney with more unmoney, it will seek to nationalize gold at artificially low prices, as before. In 1934, the government demanded that citizens turn in gold for $20 per ounce and then announced that its value was $35. I suggest that a similar swindle is now in the cards. I feel that holders of bullion will be less able to find ways to defy the government than will holders of coins. For forty-one years, Americans were not allowed to own gold—then suddenly in 1975 they acquired the "right." Do you think the government suddenly changed its policies for reasons of justice and equity? No, a more practical reason suggests itself.

Since the government is stuck with the fiction that gold is only worth $42.20 an ounce, the government cannot acquire more gold. Who would sell gold at such a ridiculous price? Yet the government is barred from paying a higher price since, to do so, would constitute another devaluation of the dollar—which the government does not wish to do *at this time*. (When it devalues again, it will be a whopper!) So, the government now graciously permits Americans to do what it cannot itself do—acquire gold, gold which it can later confiscate in order to repair all of the monetary damage it has committed.

for corn and potatoes even with smaller gold coins. Remember, when U.S. money finally reaches a trading value commensurate with its intrinsic value, you will need various forms of wealth for trading purposes. Historically, gold and silver have proven to be the type of wealth best suited for this purpose. Further on I will suggest others.

Some Thoughts on Acquiring Gold

It is not my purpose to detail at length how one's investment portfolio can be most efficiently arranged. There are books devoted to this one subject, while additional books have been written treating only one specific investment of a well-planned portfolio.[1] However, in purchasing gold coins, there is a risk of getting coins that are not genuine. Therefore, you should only deal with established firms and should not purchase your coins from traveling salesmen or think that you will acquire them at a bargain at some foreign flea market or bazaar.

Some individuals may feel that they cannot invest in gold coins because they need "income." For example, let's assume that one has $100,000 invested in bonds yielding 8 percent (6 percent after taxes) and so feels that he cannot invest in gold and give up $6,000 of net income. This individual could cash in his bonds and put approximately $18,000 in the bank and $82,000 in gold coins. He could then draw out approximately $6,000 per year (more, including interest) from the bank, which will be comparable to receiving his bond interest. If the price of gold should double within the next three years—a distinct possibility—$82,000 of gold coins would appreciate to $164,000, while the individual still enjoyed the same income he would have received on his bonds. However, if the price of gold only went up 22 percent in the next three years, his principal would be restored. And such an increase in the price of gold is not an unreasonable expectation. So, in this instance, the individual secured the income he needed while ensuring that the bulk of his capital would not be wiped out during a difficult economic period.

Gold Stock

The ownership of stock in gold mining companies offers advantages and disadvantages over the direct ownership of gold. The physical ownership of gold requires the exercise of far more care than does the ownership of stock certificates. In the event that you have to travel, perhaps leave the country, transporting stock certificates might prove more convenient and safer than traveling with a large physical quantity of gold.

Sharply increasing gold prices will increase both the value of gold and gold

[1]For example: *How To Invest in Gold Coins* and *How To Invest in Gold Stocks and Avoid the Pitfalls* by Donald J. Hoppe, *How You Can Profit from the Coming Devaluation*, by Harry Browne, *Panics & Crashes and How You Can Make Money Out of Them* by Harry Schultz, *How the Experts Buy and Sell Gold Bullion, Gold Stocks and Gold Coins* by James Sinclair and Harry Schultz and *Getting Rich in Commodities, Currencies or Coins–Before or During the Next Depression* by Robert Vichas.

stock. However, the government could nationalize gold (as previously explained), thus denying to the holders of gold (at least those who turned it in) the full benefit of its price rise or its value in the "new money" that will be created. However, holders of stock will benefit in the rise in its price through the dollar's final devaluation and will see the values of their stock expressed at their full gold value in the "new money."

On the other hand, those who own gold outright "have it" and can use their ingenuity to devise ways to thwart the government in its attempts to deprive them of its full value. Those who own stock could find that the profits generated by increased gold prices might be taxed away at their source by both the United States and foreign countries. In addition, those who own gold feel that a breakdown in communications (postal, and even the stock market itself) might interfere with the receipt of dividends and conversion of stocks to other values.

The solution to these contingencies is to diversify your holdings to give you flexibility and safety based on considering all possible contingencies and how you will deal with them.

How To Purchase Gold Stocks

Gold stocks are traded on the New York Stock Exchange, the American Exchange, and on the Over-the-Counter Market. Popular New York Stock Exchange gold stocks are Homestake, the largest American gold mine; Campbell Red Lake, and Dome, Canadian gold stocks; and ASA (American South African) which is a popular "closed-end" fund of South African gold stocks.

The richest gold mines are in South Africa and individual South African shares are traded on the over-the-counter market. The yield on South African gold shares averaged approximately 10½ percent as of August 1, 1975, compared to yields of approximately 2.7, 2.3, and 3 percent for Homestake, Dome, and Campbell Red Lake.

One of the best ways to acquire a diversified position of gold stocks is through two open-end mutual funds specializing in gold stocks. The oldest and largest, International Investors, Inc., has the best growth record of all mutual funds over the last ten years. The younger fund, Research Capital, is ably managed by the Franklin Research, Inc. The advantage of acquiring a portfolio of gold stocks through an "open-end" mutual fund rather than through one which is a "closed-end" fund is generally overlooked.

The price that one pays to purchase a "closed-end" fund is based upon supply and demand and not directly on its asset value. The price that one pays for an "open-end" fund, however, is based directly on its asset value plus a sales charge (known as "the load"), while its shares are liquidated by selling them back *to the fund* and at their "asset value." In actual practice this means that one acquires shares of either International Investors or Research Capital at asset value plus 8¾ percent,[1] out of which will come the salesmen's commissions. Closed-end funds,

[1]For purchases under $25,000. For larger purchases, lesser charges apply.

on the other hand, usually trade at a discount—that is, they sell *below* their asset value. For example, the August 2, 1975, issue of *Barron's* reported the average discount of thirty-one listed "closed-end" funds (omitting ASA) as 22 percent. However, ASA was selling at a *premium* of *42½ percent*! (Two others were also selling at a premium.) This meant that those purchasing a gold portfolio through ASA and the New York Stock Exchange paid 42½ percent (plus brokerage commissions) above asset value, while those who bought the open-end portfolios paid a premium of only 8¾ percent or less. That's not all, however. In my judgment, after the golds have peaked and there is no particular incentive to get into them, ASA will revert to acting in a way "closed-end" funds customarily act, and that is to sell at a discount. The discount could be 22 percent (the largest discount reported in that issue of *Barron's* was Diebold Venture Capital, selling at 55.7 percent below asset value), while investors liquidating open-end shares are assured of getting asset value.

So, for the long haul, for those planning to hold their gold shares to the end of the monetary battle, an open-end fund would appear to offer more value than a closed-end. ASA, in my judgment, is an excellent trading stock and a stock which can be utilized for assets that need to be liquid while still offering the protection of a gold investment.

In addition to gold, silver will provide its owner with a dependable store of value. In the past, U.S. politicians augmented the world's supply by depleting ours. With this huge hoard gone, silver should remain, for years to come, an asset in short supply.

Storing Your Gold and Silver

Many people store their precious metals in bank vaults, while others for many reasons want theirs under their immediate control. They secrete their gold and silver in all sorts of places, from burying it in the back yard to hiding it in a hollowed-out bed post. It is not too difficult to secrete large dollar values of gold, since it concentrates a good deal of wealth in a small area. Not too long ago, I met with a woman who had easily placed $4,000 in common gold coins in her change purse.[1]

You will have to decide the proper balance, based upon how much is involved and your storage facilities. I would keep some in a vault and some where I could get at it directly. I can, however, sympathize with those who, for reasons of estate taxes, the dangers of nationalization, and because of the possibility of social and economic unrest, want to keep it all securely and secretly buried in their cellar.

Other Investments

Currently, one of the best investments is food.

With savings deposits earning only 5 percent (before taxes) and with food costs

[1]This consisted of two fifty-coin rolls of the Austrian 20 coronae—which occupied as much space as two comparable rolls of dimes.

rising better than 10 percent annually, does it pay to store savings in the bank or in the pantry? Why keep money in the bank when you can use it to purchase food which will be increasing in value faster than your money will "grow" in a bank? Naturally such purchases would be limited to foods with a longer shelf life and the availability of storage space. But, all things considered both from the survival and investment point of view, investing in food makes good sense.

Naturally, your larder won't be set up to provide you with gourmet-style fare, but it should be able to provide you with at least one nourishing daily meal for at least six months to a year.[1] Items with shorter shelf life can be rotated periodically (all of this is very time consuming and terribly uneconomic, but this is the price we have to pay when politicians are allowed to destroy our money supply.)

Along with food, you might wish to store vitamins, drugs, toilet articles, and a variety of items that you continuously use. Food and other commodities can also be relied upon to serve as money. Remember, the Romans used salt and American colonists used pins. So, in certain circumstances, these items, along with such things as razor blades, cigars, and cigarettes (if they can be stored properly) could increase in value even more than gold and silver and could become extremely valuable as trading items.

For many, storing food and goods also means storing water and purification equipment (or at least knowing of an alternate water supply to the public system), guns, ammunition, seeds, fuel, lighting equipment, alternative power sources, and methods of transportation which are not dependent on large quantities of fuel. Many are organizing "retreats" where they can be separated from centers of population and live on a self-sustaining basis for a considerable length of time.

Other suitable investments and stores of value might be the direct ownership of land, real estate, oil and gas resources, diamonds, paintings, antiques, and other foreign currencies—however, space does not permit me to enlarge my remarks into these areas. One thing that I will mention, however, is that individuals in the better than 50 percent tax bracket should look into "leveraged" investments which can be designed to generate tax write-offs of two and four times one's original investment, thus saving the investor more in taxes than he invested. This does not constitute a "loophole" since tax liabilities will only have been postponed and subject to "recapture" at a later date. By that time, in my judgment, future tax liabilities can be paid in cheap currency, while, if current tax savings are invested in gold, they will have appreciated substantially by then.

As I stated previously, in making investment suggestions I have not attempted

[1]While I am no nutritionist, these foods might consist of dehydrated soups, milk, potatoes, eggs, spaghetti, beans, sardines, oil, bullion cubes, spices, evaporated milk, etc. There are firns that specialize in planning and packaging dehydrated and survival foods. Most of them are located in Utah, since Morman's routinely store the year's supply of food. Also see Howard Ruff, *Famine and Survival in America* (Alamo, Ca.: Target Publishing, 1974).

to pinpoint specific investments since personal situations vary and investment opportunities can change. I merely wished to lay down certain principles and areas of investment which can apply at all times for all individuals. For specific investment information, you might explore some "hard money" investment market letters. However, a suggested investment portfolio might be as follows, recognizing that suggestions like this do not take into consideration specific needs and exceptions.

	$100,000	$15,000
Dehydrated Foods and Miscellaneous Supplies	$ 5,000	1,000
Miscellaneous Gold and Silver		5,000
Miscellaneous Gold Coins	$25,000	
Two Bags of Silver ($2,000 Face)	$ 7,000	
Gold Stock	$40,000	6,000
Miscellaneous Cash, Stocks, and Bonds.	$23,000	3,000
	$100,000	$15,000

In conclusion, may I say that I took no great pleasure in making these "investment" recommendations. No one has ever given investment advice with more hope that it prove wrong. Since I am a firm believer in the FEAC system, I realize how important it is that our financial institutions, banks, insurance companies, and stock exchanges be active and have the confidence of the people. It is vital for our welfare that these agencies channel the nation's savings into commerce and industry. If *all* Americans suddenly turned against these institutions and began storing their savings only in real wealth, our economy would collapse.

Based on current trends, however, I would have made these recommendations to a personal client. I can hardly offer different advice here. It could be argued that advice suitable for a few may not be suitable for many—that if one were sitting in a crowded theatre, and saw a fire that others did not see, one might quietly whisper to a few friends, "Look this place is on fire, we had better leave." If, on the other hand, one wished to warn everybody equally by announcing, "The theatre is on fire," he could set off a stampede in which most would be trampled anyway. Ideally he should be able to say, "Ladies and gentlemen, there is a small fire in the rear of the theatre. However, it will be a simple matter to put it out. All I need is ten volunteers, then we can all go back to enjoying the movie." This is somewhat the position I feel myself to be in. If enough people run for the exits converting their dollar savings into "hard assets," we could all get trampled in the economic stampede. We can't, therefore, lose our heads. Asset conversions should be made slowly while closely watching economic and political trends. It is important that you help in changing the nation's political and economic direction since, in the final analysis, that will be your best investment.

Federal Transfer Payments to Persons
(Robbing From Peter to Pay Paul)

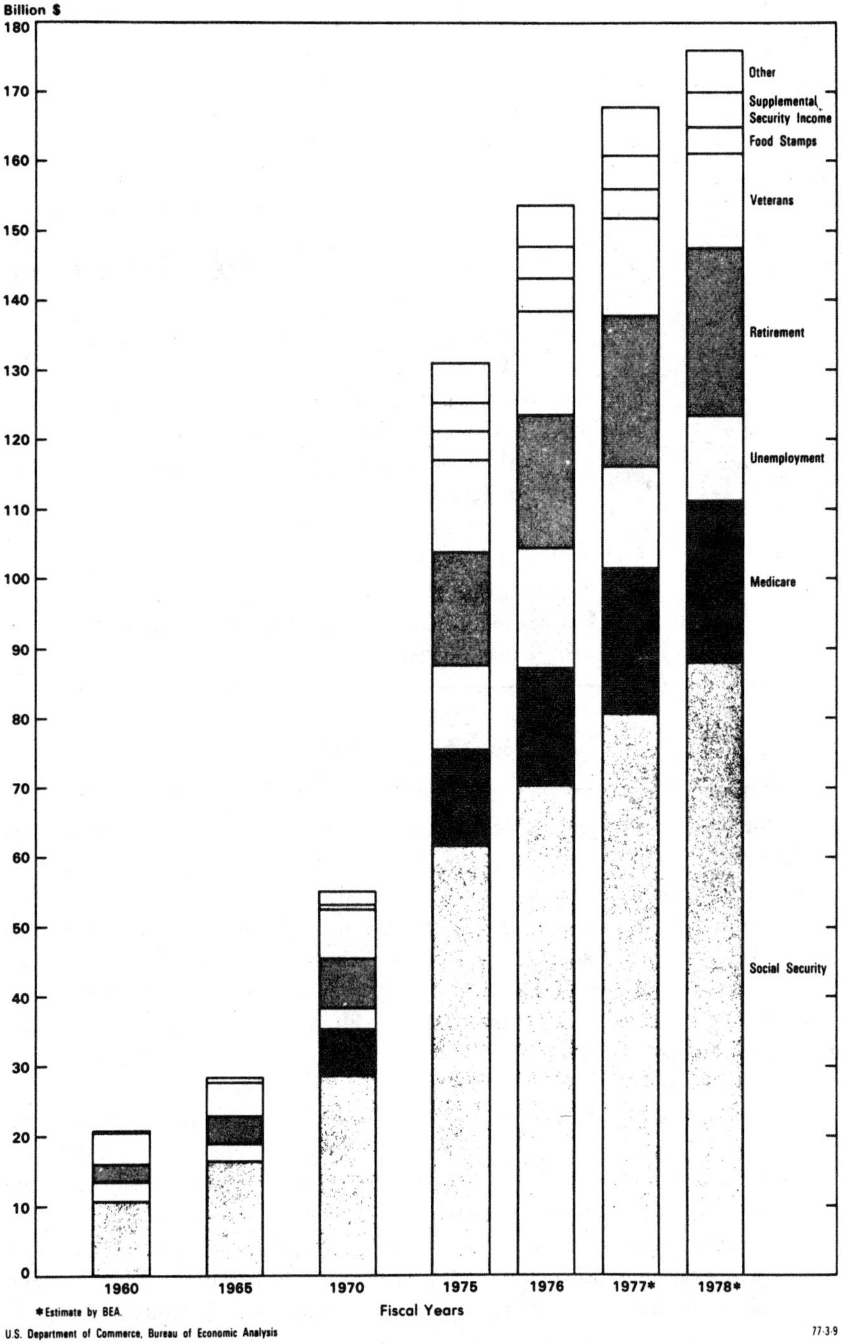

Figure 42

Appendix B

The Testimony of
Irwin A. Schiff
as submitted to
The Committee on Banking and Currency
United States Senate
Nineteenth Congress
Second Session
on
S. 1307, S. 2815, and S. 2857
Relating to Repeal of the Gold Reserve Requirements
for United States Currency

January 30 and 31, 1968
(Pages 136, 137, 138, 139, 140)

Of all the learned gentlemen offering testimony concerning the removal of gold backing from U.S. Reserve notes, I don't think any of them actually makes a living selling U.S. money. Since I do (I sell it for future delivery), I believe that I have a better working knowledge of the subject and how it affects my customers than do many who only have an academic or theoretical knowledge. Government witnesses, of course, will not be able to shed any light on the subject at all since, if they could, the United States would not now find itself in the monetary crisis which has necessitated these hearings.

When a widow asks me if she should take the proceeds of a life insurance policy in cash or as an annuity for life, I am not being asked any mere theoretical question, but upon my advice and judgment rests the possible welfare or deprivation of a small family unit. When a newly married man asks my advice as to the type of insurance he should buy, he is, in reality, asking me to express my opinion concerning the future purchasing power of the U.S. dollar since, if I were to advise him to purchase an endowment at 65 policy, I would be advising him to send money ahead so that it could be spent some 30 years hence. Obviously, if I am to sleep comfortably at night, I had better know something about U.S. money and the subject of inflation when I am called upon for this type of advice. Since I believe that a man should know his product, I have spent a good deal of time studying and learning about U.S. money, which leads directly into a study of U.S. monetary policy over the past 30 years. Any impartial study of this subject can only lead to the inescapable conclusion that there are many government officials who, by all laws of justice, should now be behind bars. Since a program of monetary inflation has been the direct result of U.S. monetary policy, and since inflation robs a citizen just as effectively as a bandit who cleans out his safe, there seems to be no reason why one is hunted down, tried, and jailed while the other is allowed to freely walk the streets of Washington, D.C. The success that the U.S. government has enjoyed in escaping the blame for inflation has been possible only because of the widespread ignorance of the subject on the part of the private citizen. This ignorance is so widespread that, in the past, American presidents have been able to accuse American companies of contributing to inflation when they have increased prices and have labeled as inflationary, union wage agreements. Such accusations were, of course, sheer bunk!

Price increases are the direct and unavoidable result of monetary pressure caused by "inflating" the money supply. The word inflation, of course, even means to blow up as a balloon . . . to inflate. The United States government has consistently, over the past 30 years, permitted this "blowing up" of supplies of money and credit. It has permitted direct issuance of Federal Reserve notes backed by U.S. government bonds which, in effect, is the printing of money . . . the most naked inflationary device. This manner of issuance of Federal Reserve notes was never envisioned when the Federal Reserve System was created. It was, in fact, specifically prohibited. It has also encouraged low interest rates, low reserve requirements, and has, by guaranteeing debt, made consumer credit much easier. All of these devices have permitted prices to rise. One has only to look into the yearly increase in Federal Reserve notes to understand where all of the inflation is coming from. It is, of course, possible to blame the vast amount of monetary ignorance, which apparently exists in the nation's capital, to the tremendous influence exerted by the Keynesian school of economics, as represented by Heller, Samuelson, Galbraith, and Keyserling, etc. Their whole economic mumbo-jumbo (they like to use the term "compensatory fiscal management") can be reduced to their simple remedy for overcoming all economic ills—create more money and more bureaucracy.

Neither space nor time, of course, will permit me to treat in depth many of the points I am attempting to cover but these concepts of "cost-push inflation" can be dispensed with quite quickly. This "theory" does no more than redefine inflation in its own terms and answers nothing. Since inflation results in higher "costs" and all such costs are themselves "prices" (the price for labor, the price for raw materials, etc.), to explain inflation as "cost-push" is to say that "prices rise because prices rise." Apart from being sheer double talk, this "theory" flies in the face of fundamental economic law which is that costs have nothing to do with price but that "price is determined by supply and demand." The lay public can be forgiven, of course, for not understanding this, but such ignorance is unforgiveable in anyone presuming to call himself an economist. Costs will, of course, affect supply, which will then have an affect on price but costs in themselves have nothing to do with price. So, how could there be any such thing as "cost-push inflation"?

All of our inflation (price increases) has been the direct result of government monetary policy and it has permitted the government to get its revenues through a program of inflation rather than by taxation. I would suggest that, since the government was given the power to collect revenue by direct taxation but not the power to collect it by inflation, all government inflationary practices must be unconstitutional.

Inflation has permitted the government to appear to be delivering vast amounts of government benefits which would have otherwise required even higher levels of taxation and it has allowed the government to retire its debts, not by programs of bond redemption, but by inflating them away. I will not even attempt to offer figures showing the amount of the taxpayers' loss, but it runs into the billions, far more than was ever lost by bank robberies or bank failures. Suffice it to say that figures were just released showing that prices rose last year by 3 percent. Since the funded national debt is approximately $350 billion (forgetting all other dollar accumulations), this enabled the government to "retire" $10 billion of its bonded debt. But to define inflation in terms of American price levels is to continually understate it, because it hides the beneficial effects of increased productivity —prices have risen despite increased efficiency, etc. However, to see the full effect of our monetary inflation, we should compare prices of items that cannot be manufactured . . . the cost of a haircut, daily rates in our hospitals, the cost of a doctor's house call (if it is even available), the cost of a violin lesson. If these costs are compared, it will be readily apparent that all government figures which purport to indicate the level of inflation *actually understate it*.

The reason that I have spent so much time on the subject of inflation is that a thorough understanding of it is essential in understanding the monetary crisis now facing the nation, and an understanding of inflation is essential if this crisis is to be solved.

That the current administration does not understand the problem or how to solve it is obvious, since they now propose removing gold backing of Federal Reserve notes. That such a ludicrous proposal can be made is indicative that federal mismanagement of our monetary system has simply brought us to the end of the line, inflationwise. The bubble of U.S. monetary inflation cannot be blown up any further and I simply wish to prevent political hot air from bursting it completely (as happened in Germany in 1923), since this would have the effect of making me a party to the swindle because such a step would victimize all those little people to whom I have sold cash-value life insurance and annuities over the years.

Now to our immediate problem: Why does America face a balance of payments crisis, and why has our economy been hemorrhaging gold over the last eight years? The answer to both of these questions is really quite simple. America's money managers have simply allowed our inflation to reach such levels that our internal price structure is out of whack with (1) the 1932 price of gold, which is $35 per ounce, and (2) world prices generally.

It should be obvious that there would be a shortage of anything that had to be sold at its 1932 price. If bakers were allowed to sell rolls only at their 1932 price of 15 cents a dozen, there would be a roll shortage. If cars could only be sold at their 1932 price, would anyone on this committee be surprised if this resulted in a car shortage? There would be a shortage of anything today if its sale were dependent on its 1932 price. In order to obtain an ounce of gold ($35), approximately three tons of ore have to be processed. Can members of this committee conceive of processing three tons of anything today for $35? Since gold can still be purchased at its 1932 price, it has become relatively much cheaper and has, thus, become more common while carat ratios have risen.

Why buy costume jewelry when gold is so cheap?

It would have been possible, even given our irredeemable paper money, to have controlled inflation, if the government monetary experts understood how to manage irredeemable money. Money which cannot be redeemed and is, therefore, on its face, worthless, can be given scarcity value. The question is how do you know if you are oversupplying the irredeemable paper—that's easy. When shortages in the one controlled price (in this case gold) start to develop, this would immediately indicate that too much paper has been issued and deflation would be called for. (Given gold's fixed price, as all other prices started to rise, less gold could be mined, more gold would be used. Gold reserves would dwindle, etc.) The fact that our monetary managers have been blind to these signs, especially over the last eight years, is an indication of just how incompetent they are; and if they could permit the inflation that we have experienced *despite gold backing*—what kind of inflation could they produce *with no gold backing at all*?

Our government keeps insisting that our gold losses are the result of our balance of payments deficits. This is like blaming an ailment on a high temperature. The temperature is merely indicative of an underlying ailment that requires attention. The fact that we have a gold loss, and a balance of payments problem, are both indicative of an underlying economic malady, and it is this malady that must be corrected if the patient is to survive.

As inflation has given the U.S. a gold problem, it has also given us our balance of payments problem. Inflation has simply priced much of what we produce out of world markets and has simply lost for America the economic edge in areas where we traditionally had comparative and real advantages. It was not too long ago that imported items were generally regarded as being more expensive. This even gave them a snob appeal. One need only walk into any discount store and see that the cheap items are all imported—from Japanese nails and sporting goods, to British shoes, Italian knits, and, yes, to even foreign vacations. The fact that we still export a lot (though much of it in areas that other nations simply cannot compete in) does not disprove the fact that we have an inflated price structure relevant to the rest of the world. Since it is increasingly easier to sell in America and more difficult to export, foreigners will be able to earn dollars easily, which they will have a tendency to convert and buy from us our one cheap commodity, which still can be purchased at its 1932 price—gold.

This now brings us to understanding how our gold and balance of payments problem can be solved. It can only be solved in one of two ways: We must either deflate our price structure to bring it more in line with 1932 prices, or we must bring *up* the 1932 price of gold to a more realistic 1968 price. *In two words, we must now choose between deflation or devaluation*. What the Administration now proposes is, of course, to do absolutely nothing to correct our underlying monetary problem. It, in fact, proposes to do something even worse than nothing—and that is to do precisely the wrong thing and that is to make matters worse—but I will get to that later.

Let us now examine the consequences that will flow from electing one or the other (or as England is now doing, a little of both) of our choices.

Consequences of Deflation

Deflation, of course, represents the most honest solution to our monetary problem and would offer the best long-term solution to our economy and future economic growth. For these reasons, of course, it will not be adopted, but let's examine it anyway. A good dose of deflation would restore to the savers of America a good portion of what has been robbed from them through inflation. Bonds, savings accounts, insurance, etc. would all be worth more.

American merchandise would become more competitive while foreign merchandise would become more expensive. Foreign travel would automatically be curtailed without the necessity of imposing travel restrictions, while travel to the states would be encouraged without the need of travel subsidies which has been proposed. Since mining costs would now be lower, more gold would be mined and since the relative price of gold would have been increased, less gold would be used for nonmonetary purposes and our gold reserves would increase. Our gold drain would stop. Would there be some painful economic consequences? Of course. For one thing, government tax revenues would drop drastically. (It would be relatively easy for all segments of the economy to adjust to lower prices *except* the government because no one has such huge debts or such a built in, high payroll. Because of drastic cuts in government revenue, vast government projects would have to be cut or dropped entirely. I told you that this offered the best long-term solution for the country.) The government would have to admit that it could not pay such lavish social security benefits and these would have to be cut. (But smaller checks would also buy more.) Government pensions would have to be cut, and the government might even have to honestly repudiate some of its funded and unfunded debt. But those who had any portion of this debt would not be hurt that much because their fewer dollars would also go further. Equity owners, especially speculators, would get hurt the most. As equity prices fell, the margin buyer (who is never poor) might be wiped out. But that was the chance he took when he played the market. Now equity owners don't take much of a chance since they are aided by government inflationary policies. Lots of people now on the dole would have to find useful work. Since minimum wage laws would now have to go, there would be no "hard core" unemployment problem. People would start taking pride in their work and start learning skills and trades. Keynesians would have to start looking for honest employment—in short, America would be on the road back to a sane, free-enterprise economy and our socialist nightmare would be over.

Now, let's turn to devaluation.

Devaluation, of course, attempts to bring the gold price up to a more realistic price. This readjustment in the gold price is the direct consequence of the action of the government's allowing the inflation in the first place. Since 1968, prices are at least three times what they were in 1932. *This would indicate gold would have to be revalued realistically at about $105 per ounce.* This price would pull a lot of gold out of the ground that cannot be pulled at $35 per ounce. At $105 per ounce, gold would regain its comparative value and would be used less extensively for nonmonetary purposes. Devaluation would make imports more expensive while it would make American products cheaper in world markets. This is not to claim any real economic or trading benefits from devaluation, which are usually claimed for it by politicians when they are compelled to devalue (they make it sound like a shrewd monetary move to distract from the bankruptcy it really is). Devaluation compels the citizens of a country to export more wealth for the same amount of imports and hence are made poorer because of it. So, in effect, devaluation would solve our gold drain (temporarily) and our balance of payments problem (temporarily). Would a devaluation result in some painful consequences? You bet it would. For one thing, devaluation, which is nothing more than a repudiation of debt (in our present circumstances, a repudiation of our external debt) is simply a government's complicated way of declaring bankruptcy. It is, of course, embarrassing for a country, like an individual, to admit that it cannot manage itself fiscally. Well, America couldn't, so we might as well admit it. Central bankers around the world know it anyway.

We would, of course, prove to the world that Charles de Gaulle was the smart one for getting his gold out when he did. Should a devaluation occur, de Gaulle, who is estimated to have carted off some $6 billion of U.S. gold, would have ended up with gold worth $18 billion. The total American loss since the gold drain started, which has seen our gold level go from $24.6 billion down to about $11 billion, would total a loss of (after devaluation) about $30 billion. Of course, all of this is going to make de Gaulle look good, but that's because de Gaulle understands the U.S. money position more thoroughly than our own money managers. Our trouble is that he understands it too well. It has become increasingly apparent that America is looking for a scapegoat to our problems and we have blamed de Gaulle and his so-called attacks on the dollar. He, of course, is merely a creditor who is interested in getting back something of value and is simply proving that he is a much better Frenchman by protecting French interests than Johnson is an American by not protecting American interests. If we are looking for somebody to blame, why don't we blame those responsible for permitting de Gaulle to get into the position he is now in rather than to blame the man himself? Devaluation, of course, will not really solve any of our problems—but will simply prevent matters from getting worse. Our basic economic problems only can be solved if we replace our present monetary managers and reduce the size and scope of our bureaucracy.

Since there is no question that we will be compelled to devalue either now or later, and since devaluation really doesn't solve any of the nations's underlying monetary problems but only makes an adjustment for past monetary mistakes, we will then be off again on a new round of inflation. The dollar would simply be following in the footsteps of the old French franc which, in its years between 1914 and 1958 shrank to 1/180th of its former self.

To recap our present monetary position, only two choices are possible—either devaluation or deflation. Both courses of action will be painful and will hurt many segments of our economy (as inflation has hurt, but nobody in government seems to care about that). But this is the price that America must now pay for 30 years of monetary mismanagement. Now we pay the piper for all our welfarism, New Dealism, New Frontierism, and Great Societyism.

There was one other monetary ploy that might have enabled America to avoid either of these painful monetary corrections and that was to somehow convince the world to inflate their economies to match ours. This, of course, was what all that talk of "shortage of international liquidity" and "paper gold" was all about. Well, of course, the world's responsible monetary managers, especially in Europe, simply cannot be sold that bill of goods. The fact is that there is not now, nor could there ever be, a shortage of international liquidity. All world trade is basically a system of barter. A nation that has iron will find a way of trading with a nation that possesses coal, and prices will simply be adjusted to whatever monetary reserves happen to be available. If world prices were reduced 50 percent, this would have the effect of doubling present world liquidity if world liquidity is important—which it isn't. Increasing liquidity is important if you are basing your economy on ever-increasing levels of inflation, which is what the U.S. has been doing. The reason that Europe will not allow us to continue to export our inflation to them is that they have experienced the painful consequences inflation offers. They fear inflation, while we fear only depression or deflation.[1]

What would be the effect of eliminating the 25 percent backing of Federal Reserve notes?

The above, for the following reasons, would simply aggravate our monetary imbalance further and would simply increase the amount of our gold losses. For

[1]In retrospect, I obviously misjudged the leverage that the U.S could exert in pressuring Europe to accept increasing levels of the U.S.-engendered inflation. I also erred (because of their past calamitous monetary experiences) in crediting European politicians with greater monetary wisdom and judgment than was warranted. As I have since discovered, in general, politicians are politicians and it is sheer naïveté to assume that, as a class, those of one democratic country will prove significantly more responsible in these matters than those of another.

one thing, removing the gold reserve is inflationary. Dollars can simply be run off a press and they would be. Prices would climb higher and higher (price controls would be demanded but would do no good) and gold would get scarcer and scarcer. Such a move would not be interpreted as strengthening the dollar since a dollar backed by nothing cannot be better than a dollar backed by something. Ultimately, we would lose two or three billion more and then hopefully it would dawn on somebody that we dare not lose it all. In this instance, U.S. dollars would not go the way of the French franc, but the way of the German mark . . . when a dollar went from being worth 40,000 marks to 4 trillion 2 billion in eleven months. On November 22, 1923, the price for one match was 900 million marks. Stabilization took place the next day on the basis of 1 trillion marks equalling one gold mark.

Removal of the gold reserve is nothing more than a bribe offered to our external creditors at the expense of the domestic holders of U.S. dollars. It can be likened to a situation where one about to be placed in bankruptcy prevails upon his maiden aunt to loan him some $2000 of her egg money. He then asks his creditors that if he pays them $2000, would they hold off their bankruptcy proceedings. Since his creditors realize that they would get very little anyway, they really have nothing to lose. Therefore, they accept the $2000 and permit him to continue. Since he has no intention of correcting the way he operates, he continues on his merry ways and ends up eventually in bankruptcy anyway. All that he succeeded in doing is unnecessarily losing his aunt's $2000. Removal of the gold cover is to take gold, which was to be for the protection of American citizens, and make it available to European creditors. *However, since no attempt will be made to correct the basic conditions, we will simply end up losing more of our gold. If we lose an additional $1 billion (we lost $450 million in one week), this will be the equivalent of a $3-billion loss when we are compelled to devalue.* Note B

Since it is considered a criminal act to water stock, why should it be considered any less criminal to water money or fritter money away. As a result of this action, additional billions would be lost, so every legislator who contributes to this loss should be held criminally or civilly liable. The gold reserve or the interest penalties required if the reserve drops below 25 percent cannot be dispensed with simply to appease the whims of politicians. The situation is analogous to the construction of a boiler and its safety valve. Given the passage of time, nobody remains who apparently understands how a boiler operates. Suddenly, steam starts to pour out of the valve and since the sound of escaping steam is annoying those now responsible for operating the boiler, they simply shut the valve. This is exactly the situation we stand in with respect to the further issuance of Federal Reserve notes—the reserve requirement can be regarded as the safety valve.

The Federal Reserve System might have been built by people who understood how a monetary system should work—*but the only people who are left to operate it apparently do not; so a lot of people figure to get hurt in the monetary explosion.*

(Whereupon, at 11:45 A.M., the committee was adjourned, to be reconvened at 10:00 A.M., Thursday, February 1, 1968.)

Appendix C

Direct Excerpts from Testimony
Presented to The Committee on Banking and Currency
United States Senate
19th Congress 2nd Session
On S. 1307, S. 2815, and S. 2857
Relating to Repeal of the Gold Reserve Requirements
for United States Currency

The following excerpts are from the testimony of William Proxmire, U.S. Senator from the state of Wisconsin and chairman of the Joint Economic Committee; Henry H. Fowler, Secretary of the Treasury; and William McChesney Martin, Jr., Chairman of the Board, Federal Reserve System, are important in that they demonstrate how dangerous and foolhardy it is to trust and allow economic and monetary decisions to be made by government ''experts.'' Here were three of the most influential people who shaped U.S. monetary policy and their testimony reveals that they knew little concerning monetary matters. Their testimony reveals that they were unfamiliar with

1. the value and role of gold,
2. the requirements of a sound money system,
3. the function of the U.S. gold stock, and
4. how to preserve confidence in the U.S. dollar.

Not only were these gentlemen mistaken on their assessment of these four issues, but, as my testimony revealed, the truth was clearly there for all to see—*but they were blind to it.* If government "experts" can be so completely inept in their understanding of a problem for which they are held out as "experts," dare we entrust them with problems that are complicated?

On the Value and Role of Gold [Italics and comments in parentheses are mine throughout]

According To Senator Proxmire:

A) Page 24 . . . "*Gold has long since abandoned its role as a metal for currency.* The entitlement of Americans to hold gold in monetary form was removed about 35 years ago. The function of gold as a reserve against notes in circulation is no longer that of assuring the convertibility of these notes. *Thus, as an active reserve, gold is an anachronism.*" (Let Senator Proxmire tell that to the OPEC nations!)

B) Page 24 . . . "There is indeed a restraint on the expansion of liabilities by such a requirement. *But it would be meaningless and irrational to control the U.S. money supply by the vagaries of the gold reserve.*" (What else, Senator, would you use to control the supply of money substitutes? Political hot air?)

C) Page 26 . . . "*The international strength of the dollar will be enhanced by the visible availability of all our gold stock.*" (Was it?)

D) Page 26 . . . "*The gold reserve requirement should be removed. It is as simple as that. For the strength of the dollar will be found to rest not in an arithmetical calculation, but in the quality of the management of the money supply.* This is what we in Congress should support—a Federal Reserve System that makes good judgments and stands publicly answerable for them. The Banking and Currency Committee and the Joint Economic Committee have not hesitated to call the Federal Reserve Board to task for its mistakes. *We shall find security in this discipline—not in a phony discipline arbitraily applied by a stock of gold.*" (The country will find monetary discipline in the Fed and not in real money? Proxmire is hallucinating. He should be compelled to explain why the dollar has a lower international value today, since it is now controlled by "quality . . . management," than it had in 1968 when it was only *partially* controlled by that "phony discipline," gold.)

E) Page 26 . . . "*We shall have fewer foreign demands for gold, not more,* if we offer *no room for doubt about our determination to make available all our monetary gold for the sole purpose on which it is usable.*" (Did we in fact have fewer? Then why were we eventually compelled to devalue again . . . and again . . . and again?)

The Chairman: "Thank you, Senator Proxmire. Let me just ask this question bearing upon the very last statement that you made. Isn't the fear of foreign governments and people that the dollar will not be defended the cause of a good bit of the gold-buying rush?"

Senator Proxmire: "I think that is true, Mr. Chairman, because *there isn't any rationality at all in buying gold* unless one assumes that the dollar will not be defended, that it will be devalued.

"Because gold yields no interest at a time when interest rates are extremely high. *And those who invest in gold are foregoing an excellent return,* and in a period of inflation in all the countries in the world *they are sure to lose much of the value of what they invest* unless the dollar is not to be defended." (Investors who have held, not speculated, have only made about 500 percent in 7 years.)

The Chairman: "And your argument is that to remove the gold reserve requirement would be one way of showing our determination to defend the dollar?"

Senator Proxmire: "Absolutely, I think it would make it clear that the Congress intends to support the President's position to defend the dollar, *and that we mean business when we say it will be held at $35 an ounce.*"

F) Page 28 . . . Senator McGee: "I would like to rephrase Senator McIntyre's question because of the kind of mail we get on this.

"What will this proposal do to Fort Knox? I mean this puts it in two words from the standpoint of the man in the street. And I think for the record, if you addressed yourself to that, it would be very helpful then in response."

Senator Proxmire: *"Well, it would seem to me that this proposal would do nothing to Fort Knox. It would not reduce the gold holdings by a single ounce* ." (It did not reduce it by a "single ounce," but by some 70 million ounces.)

G) Page 29 . . . "And I think this will make it clear we are going to use all of our gold to defend the dollar. *We aren't going to devalue. And this should strengthen the dollar's position and reduce the demand for gold.*

"In fact, I might modify my answer to your first question by saying this legislation, *if it has any effect, might very well result in less of an outflow of gold from Fort Knox.*"

According to Secretary Fowler:

H) Page 34 . . . "Second, there should be no doubt whatsoever that our total gold stock is available to insure the free international convertibility between the dollar and gold at the fixed price of $35 an ounce." (Here our Secretary of the Treasury is saying that a paper money substitute need not be backed by money!)

"Third, the world knows as a fact that the *strength of the dollar depends upon the strength of the U.S. economy rather than upon a legal 25 percent reserve* requirement against Federal Reserve notes, and it is clearly appropriate for this fact now to be recognized in legislation."

I) Page 35 . . . "Today the strength of the dollar is not a function of this legal tie to gold—a tie which is only applicable to one portion of our total money supply, Federal Reserve notes. *The value of the dollar–whether it be in the form of a bank balance, a coin, or 'folding money'–is dependent on the quantity and quality of goods and services which it can purchase.*

"It is the strength and soundness of the American economy which stands behind the dollar. Balanced growth at home and a strong competitive position internationally give the dollar we use as everyday pocket money its strength.

"An expanding U.S. economy needs an expanding supply of currency. Our main form of currency is Federal Reserve notes."

(This is all meaningless oratory. So what is the dollar's value today? Can you find SIIG-11?)

J) Page 3 . . . "We cannot afford to permit an *outmoded provision of our law to impinge on the Nation's supply of pocket money."*

(Is it outmoded to have money backing for money substitutes?)

K) Page 36 . . . "First, we must continue the longstanding U.S. policy of maintaining *the gold-dollar relationship at $35 an ounce. This must not be open to question,* and the best way to make continuation of that policy crystal clear is to free our entire gold stock for that purpose.

"Second, we must assure that the U. S. economy grows in an environment of cost and price stability through enactment of the *anti-inflation tax* and through *expenditure controls and appropriate monetary policy."*

(First create unmoney and then enact taxes and legislation to fight it.)

L) Page 36 . . . "Our policy of maintaining the fixed relationship between gold and the dollar at $35 an ounce for legitimate monetary purposes is one of the reasons why virtually all countries hold dollars in their reserves and why many of them hold very large amounts of dollars. In addition, of course, *countries hold dollars because unlike gold they can invest them in interest-earning assets."* (Those that held dollars, of course, got burned. They would have been wiser, as was de Gaulle, to take our gold when they could get it at the bargain price of $35 per ounce.)

M) Page 37 . . . "Thus, legislative action on the cover requirement, by making it clear to the world that the Congress as well as the executive branch are committing our total gold stock to international use, *is necessary to maintain confidence in the dollar."*

According to Mr. Martin:

N) Page 39 . . . "Removal of this requirement would in no way reduce our determination to preserve the soundness of the dollar. To achieve our goals both domestically and internationally we must pursue sound and equitable fiscal and monetary policies. Whatever discipline gold imposes in this connection makes itself felt from the fact of *a decline in the gold stock rather than from the existence of a reserve requirement, and this will continue to be the case."* (Our gold stock had been declining for 13 years. What *"discipline"* did it impose?)

O) Page 39 . . . "Convertibility of the dollar into gold at a fixed price—$35 an ounce—*is a keystone of the international monetary system* and is a fundamental reason why foreign monetary authorities are willing to hold dollar reserves. The role of the dollar as the major international reserve currency, together with the readiness of private foreign organizations and individuals to hold dollar assets, *places the dollar in a unique position in international commerce and finance*. Prompt enactment of legislation to remove the gold cover requirement would *reaffirm to the world the convertibility of the dollar. At the same time it would meet the long-run requirements for an expansion in note circulation commensurate with steady growth in the economy*.'' (Since the dollar is no longer convertible, what is now the ''keystone'' of the ''international monetary system''? Can you find SIIG-12?)

O-1) Page 44 . . . ''As a standard, gold is like feet and inches and yards and ought not to change. I don't know what the price of gold as a commodity in the world would be today. I personally happen to think it would be considerably less than $35 an ounce.''

P) Page 46 . . . Senator Proxmire: ''I would like to ask, apropos of a question Senator Bennett asked: Isn't it true, in view of the fact that estimated gold production outside of the USSR, which is substantial there, is 1.5 billion, 1.4 billion, perhaps a little more than that, and that the nonmonetary uses are $500 million, that absent monetary use for gold, the price of gold would be very likely to drop?

''If production exceeds demand, under these circumstances we have been taught in economics courses that the expection is, as you implied, *that the price would go down*.''

Mr. Martin: ''*That is my judgment, Senator, definitely*.''

(Here is Senator Proxmire inferring and Martin agreeing that the price of gold would go down!)

On the Need to Remove the Gold Reserve Requirement So That the Government Could Be Free to Produce Unmoney

According to Senator Proxmire:

Q) also B), Page 24 . . :''But it would be meaningless and irrational to control the U.S. money supply by the vagaries of the gold reserve.''

R) also C),''For the strength of the dollar will be found to rest not in an arithmetical calculation but in the quality of the management of the money supply.'' (It was the quality of that management that had already produced the gold drain, silver drain, inflation and the need for these hearings.)

S) See (I)

According to Mr. Martin:

T) Page 39 . . . The Chairman: ''I want to ask you a question based on the last paragraph of your statement which I think is rather important and significant. That is, '*Convertibility of the dollar into gold at a fixed price—$35 an ounce—is a keystone of the international monetary system* and is a fundamental reason why foreign monetary authorities are willing to hold dollar reserves.'

"Now, will the removal of this gold-reserve requirement change that in any way?"

Mr. Martin: "*Quite the reverse. In my judgment,* it will strengthen it."

The Chairman: "In other words, it does not take it away. It makes available a larger supply of gold from which they may expect to be able to exchange their dollars for gold, doesn't it?"

Mr. Martin: "That is right. That is the basis of what we call the gold exchange today."

On Preserving the Strength, Acceptability, and Character of the U.S. Dollar

According to Senator Proxmire:

U) Page 26 . . . "I believe, indeed, that the best way to insure the safety and stability of the dollar in the international system is to declare our intention to defend it. That is the purpose of the President's balance-of-payments program. It will be assisted by the action proposed in this bill.

"*We shall have fewer foreign demands for gold*, not more, if we offer no room for doubt about our determination to make available all our monetary gold for the sole purpose in which it is usable."

V) See F).

W) Page 29 . . . "*I think it is most helpful that the Federal Reserve has taken the emphatic position they have taken in advance of the President,* because the Federal Reserve is recognized I think throughout the country, in the business community and elsewhere, as a group of very responsible, *highly competent people who understand the situation. This is their business.*

"And it is the unanimous position, as I understand, on the part of the Federal Reserve. And I think that should give the business community and the country itself great confidence—that this isn't a position simply taken by the President or by Members of Congress. *It is one taken by the most responsible and competent money managers that we have.*"

According to Secretary Fowler:

X) Page 35 . . . "We Americans have not used gold as a domestic currency since 1934. Gold belongs in a nation's international reserves. The dollar serves as a reserve currency to the world; the U.S. gold supply is available to convert dollars held by national monetary authorities at a fixed price. *As such, it is one cornerstone—and a very main cornerstone—of our international monetary system.*

"Removal of this requirement is also of key importance from the viewpoint of the role of the dollar and of gold in the international monetary system."

Y) Page 37 . . . "In conclusion, I urge the committee to consider and act promptly on the gold cover legislation before you in order that, domestically, we can continue *to be assured that the Federal Reserve will be able to supply appropriate amounts of currency to meet the needs of our growing economy for cash, and in order that* our policy of maintaining the gold-dollar relationship—one of the major elements of *confidence in the dollar* and the international monetary system—*will not be open to question*.''

(Find SIIG-11. As Fowler predicted—confidence in the dollar is not now ''open to question,'' simply because there is so little confidence in it that needs questioning.)

According to Mr. Martin:

Z) Page 39 . . . ''Prompt enactment of legislation to remove the gold cover requirement *would reaffirm to the world the convertibility of the dollar*. At the same time it would meet the long-run requirements *for an expansion in note circulation commensurate with steady growth in the economy*.'' (Can you find SIIG-12?)

Within months after this legislation was passed there were runs on the dollar in Europe. Americans, for the first time, suffered the indignities of finding American currency less than acceptable. The dollar's convertibility ended on April 15, 1971, with the dollar being devalued on December 18, 1972, and on February 2, 1973, and the dollar has grown steadily weaker on the international market ever since. Yet look at the rosy picture U.S. monetary ''experts'' were painting if only the dollar's domestic link with gold were terminated. Incredibly, these gentlemen were advocating the production of US *unmoney* to replace U.S. *currency* on the assumption that such domestically worthless unmoney could accomplish a monetary miracle. In essence, they were telling the American public they could, in a monetary sense, fashion a ''silk purse out of a sow's ear.''

ADDENDUM

After 250 review copies of *The Biggest Con* were sent out to the media in March, 1976, I sat back to await the explosion I thought must surely follow a disclosure that the Federal government fraudulently reports only 10 percent of its debts.

However, not until July 7th did a major financial news source offer any comment. On that day, the Wall Street Journal stated in a lead editorial captioned "In Hock To The Hilt" that my calculation showing the national debt approximately equal to all of the nation's real wealth, was "hard to refute." Despite the obvious ominous implications in this, coming as it did from such a respected and influential newspaper, the only media reaction to it came from Time-Life's syndicated TV financial news supplement, "Money News Inserts," who filmed a 40 minute interview concerning my charges; however, it took the producer over a month to get a responsible government official to view the film.

Finally, Assistant Secretary of the Treasury, Robert Gerard, was assigned the task of viewing and responding to it. In his filmed reply, seen by over 10,000,000 Americans on over 50 TV stations around the country, he said:

> "There is a lot of substance to Mr. Schiff's concern. Clearly the public and the government is not aware enough, not in enough control of the commitments that are being made in the public's behalf."

I was nonplused when I heard this since how could the public be "aware enough" when the government deliberately keeps it in the dark concerning government expenditures and liabilities?

But, Gerard avoided answering my main charge. I would have sought a direct answer to the question:

> "Which figure more accurately reflects the government's debt — $5 trillion, as I allege, or $500 billion, as the government alleges?"

Figure 43

Summary Statement of Liabilities and Other Financial Commitments of the United States Government as of June 30, 1974 — Continued (In Millions)

Section	Description	Maximum theoretical measure of contingency
IV.	Contingencies:	
	Government guarantees, insuring private lenders against losses (Schedule 8)	$159,754
	Insurance commitments (Schedule 9)	1,040,805
	Actuarial status of annuity programs (Schedule 10)	*
	Unadjudicated claims (Schedule 11)	7,333
	International commitments (Schedule 12)	9,788
	Other contingencies not included above (Schedule 13)	19,165

Note: The data presented in this report were compiled from reports submitted by the agencies in accordance with Department Circular No. 966, Revised, dated December 20, 1972, and Treasury Fiscal Requirements Manual Transmittal Letter No. 95. In several instances incomplete data have been submitted by certain agencies since their accounting systems have not yet been developed to the point where they are able to provide the required information. In other instances the data furnished were on the basis of estimates by the reporting agencies.

* Because the various annuity programs have been computed on different actuarial bases, a total has not been computed. Details of individual programs are given in schedule 10.

Although Gerard avoided answering this directly, he obliquely conceded that my figure was the correct one.

Updating the "Public Debt"

On page 88, I stated the government's claim that is was "...not possible to compute a total" in connection with the government pension liabilities was "sheer rubbish." So, I wrote Secretary of the Treasury William Simon, and demanded to know "what the current unfunded liabilities of all the government's trust funds are — in total!"

In a letter dated November 12, 1974, Mr. Gustavo Mercanti of the Treasury Department responded:

> "In regard to annuity programs, there is nothing to prevent us from adding up the net liabilities of all of the systems, *even though they are not on a uniform basis.* As of June 30, 1973, this total was $578,035 million." (emphasis mine)

Thus, even though all government Summary Statements, to and including fiscal 1973, claim that totals "could not be calculated," here Mercanti unabashedly admits that such claims were indeed false and *supplies the missing total.*

So, after I called the government's attention to its ludicrous claim, it stopped *making* it — and switched to making another. Figure 43 is page 3 of the 1974 Summary of Government Liabilities. Note how the old claim was changed to:

> "Because the various annuity programs have been computed on different actuarial bases, *a total has not been computed.*" (emphasis mine)

This false claim also appears in the 1975 and 1976 reports, while the three missing totals were $1.717, $2.593 and $4.638 trillion respectively and were given to me (because I specifically asked for them) with the reports themselves. Figure 44 is the letter I received with the 1976 report.

All the above totals, of course, understate government liabilities due to the fictitious interest assumption. A more realistic picture of government liabilities as of September 30, 1976 will be found in Figure 45 which shows government bonded and statutory debt at $8.603 trillion, somewhat higher than the $634 billion debt the government claimed. The government now reports only 8 percent of its debts as opposed to reporting 10 percent in fiscal 1973, as shown in Figure 15.

DEPARTMENT OF THE TREASURY
FISCAL SERVICE
BUREAU OF GOVERNMENT FINANCIAL OPERATIONS
WASHINGTON, D.C. 20226

IN REPLYING QUOTE:
GFO-SRB

MAR 23 1977

Mr. Irwin A. Schiff, C.L.U.
P. O. Box 5303
Hamden, Connecticut 06518

Dear Mr. Schiff:

In response to your letter of March 15, we are enclosing a copy of a Statement of Liabilities and Other Financial Commitments of the United States Government as of September 30, 1976.

A statement for the fiscal year 1976 was not prepared due to the change in the fiscal year to October 1 through September 30, commencing with the fiscal year 1977 (October 1, 1976, through September 30, 1977).

The total actuarial deficit of the annuity programs shown in Schedule 10 (pages 22-24) amounted to $4,638,727 million. This is the total of the amounts reported by the various agencies.

These annuity programs are computed on various actuarial bases, so a total has not been included in the statement.

Very truly yours,

Daisy P. Burley
Manager, Special Reporting Branch

Enclosure

Keep Freedom in Your Future With U.S. Savings Bonds

Figure 44

Figure 45

SECTION
IV

THE ONLY HONEST SUMMARY OF LIABILITIES AND OTHER FINANCIAL COMMITMENTS OF THE U.S. GOVERNMENT AS OF 9-30-76
As prepared by Irwin A. Schiff
From Information Assumed to be Accurate

DESCRIPTION	REASONABLE MEASURE OF TAXPAYERS' LIABILITY (IN BILLIONS)
Contingencies	
Government guarantees, insuring private lenders against losses (Schedule 8)	
An assumption of a 10 percent loss on $190.6 billion of debt guarantees	$ 19.0
Insurance commitments (Schedule 9)	
An assumption of a 5 percent loss on $1,629.1 billion of face commitments	$ 81.4
Actuarial status of annuity programs (Schedule 10)	
This figure disregards (with the exception of TVA retirement calculations) all government bonds held (approximately $103 billion) and eliminates any interest assumptions, since "reserves" are nonexistent. In essence, therefore, this figure reflects the total amount of future taxes required to pay future benefits for those covered as of September 30, 1976	$ 7,652.0
Unadjusted claims (Schedule 11)	
Assume 50 percent liability on $14.01 billion	$ 7.0
International commitments (Schedule 12)	
Assume 100 percent liability	$ 10.2
Other contingencies not included above (Schedule 13)	
Assume 90 percent liability since one item alone is $23.8 billion and appears to be a definite obligation	$ 25.9
Total of contingent and unfunded liabilities (i.e. Statutory debt)	$ 7,795.5
Other debts owing to the public and International Monetary Fund	
As shown in Section 1 as $559.7 and Section 11 as $248.3 (omit Section 111)	$ 808.0
Total debt of the U.S.: Funded, unfunded and contingent (bonded & statutory)	$ 8,603.5
That is	$ 8,603,500,000,000.00
As of 9/30/76, the government implied that the total U.S. debt was	$ 634,702,000,000.00

THUS, AS OF THE DATE OF THE REPORT, THE U.S. GOVERNMENT ONLY ADMITTED TO DEBTS OF APPROXIMATELY 8 PERCENT OF WHAT IT ACTUALLY OWED AND SO FAR NOT ONE GOVERNMENT OFFICIAL HAS BEEN CRIMINALLY INDICTED!

A Doubling of Social Security Liabilities

The 1976 statement admitted Social Security liabilities of $4.148 trillion, which, when adjusted to eliminate the interest assumption, brought Social Security liabilities alone to about $6.8 trillion, *which is a sum far greater than the combined total of all the nation's real wealth.* Who will seriously suggest that such a staggering liability can be paid off in meaningful purchasing power?

After finishing this addendum and only days before turning it over to the printers, President Carter proposed sharply higher Social Security taxes to keep the System from going broke, and stated that unless the Administration's proposals were adopted, the money in the OASDI Trust Fund would "run out in 1983." What Carter should have told the American public is that the System is already broke and that the "trust funds" are a mirage. Undoubtedly, the "running out of money in the early 1980's" bit is used to give the public a false sense of security by implying that "trust fund" deficiencies can be corrected with some slight increases in taxes.

In addition, Carter's attempt to soften the blow of higher Social Security taxes by implying that they would be paid largely by "employers" is, of course, ridiculous since, as already explained, *all* Social Security taxes are paid by employees since they are an indirect labor cost. So, all new Social Security taxes will come directly out of the hide of the American worker-consumer no matter how politicians attempt to disguise it. The fact is that no amount of tax increases can make the Social Security System viable, since the amount of taxes required to do so would themselves collapse the economy and terminate the government's ability to collect any taxes at all.

As explained on page 302, the Social Security "chain letter" has simply run out of chain, and this must be recognized before politicians are allowed to do even more damage to our economy by throwing even more good money after bad in a vain attempt to save their fraudulent scheme. By proposing that Congress adopt higher Social Security taxes to "protect the System's integrity," Carter is essentially sending Congress on a fool's errand — which, come to think of it, is not exactly an inappropriate errand for the U.S. Congress.

As pointed out earlier, there will be hardships and disappointments connected with the termination of Social Security, but this is the price that the American public is going to have to pay for being so gullible as to believe that a collection of irresponsible, self-serving, parasitic politicians could actually fashion a magic scheme to make it socially secure. And, if the experience will have taught the American public that it should never again look to the politicians for economic panaceas, then at least some good will emerge from the inevitable debacle.

Federal Estate Taxes

On page 153, I pointed out how Federal Estate Taxes were "one of the most destructive economic forces in American life" and, on page 33, how inflation had "lowered" the estate tax exemption from $60,000 to $12,000. The rates, shown on page 153, have been superseded by the Tax "Reform" Act of 1976. A new unified estate and gift tax schedule replaces the old $30,000 lifetime and $60,000 estate tax exemptions (while merging in cumulative lifetime taxable transfers — gifts), and establishes exemptions that increase from $120,000 in 1977 to $175,000 in 1981. This may take some of the tax pressure off family farms that were being clobbered under the old exemption but estate taxes will still be as destructive as ever to family run businesses. In any case, given our 17 cent dollar, the current Federal Estate tax exemption will still be effectively lower than the $60,000 exemption established in 1947.

Government Report on Adolescent Education Confirms Author's Contentions

On September 23, 1976, the Office of Health, Education and Welfare released the final report and recommendations of The National Panel on High School and Adolescent Education — a 142 page effort entitled "The Education of Adolescents."

In essence, the report uncovered nothing that many of us did not already know. But, what is important is that its conclusions were developed not by hard nosed lay people who had for so long been critical of the waste (both in money and manpower) in our public school system, but by a panel of fourteen educators backed by a government staff.

This report, in actuality, is a condemnation of our compulsory high school system, and practically calls for the closing of all public trade schools. For example:

> "Investigators report that the graduates of vocational programs tend not to be employed in the field of their training, that their earnings do not exceed those of nonvocational students, that materials and equipment used and skills taught in vocational courses tend to be out-of-date, and that little effort is made to relate training to job needs or to provide help in placement. Little recognition seems to have been given to the fact that 50 percent or more of the high school population is already in the 'labor force.' The evidence indicates that youth are employed heavily in part-time and entry-level jobs. The subtle mechanisms which accomplish this huge job-finding and placement task seem to be informal, through social and familial grapevines, rather than through the ministrations of either

school guidance agencies or the U.S. Employment Service. The latter claims responsibility for 'less than 1 percent of the job placements for employed youth.' " (P.6)

"Given the startling poor results found by cost-benefit studies of conventional vocational education, the Panel recommends that Federal and State subsidies for inschool shop classes be made transferable at local option to various on-the-job training, job placement, and job subsidy programs." (P.11)

"The Panel recommends the creation of a community career education center. This agency would be the vehicle for new forms of vocational education such as reducing emphasis upon job training in the high school and increasing work experience, on-the-job training, job finding resources, and career information activities, all located and carried on in the community." (P.11)

But, U.S. to Get More of the Same

So, even though the Panel established that formalized, vocational programs did not work, while the "subtle mechanisms" and "informal" conditions of the marketplace did (i.e. the market forces of FEAC), the Panel could not break itself of the habit characteristic of "government panels" which is to always recommend new government programs to replace old ones that don't work.

Clearly, what all its findings pointed to is if America is to have enough skilled citizens, they can only be realistically trained and developed within the rich diversity of the community and not in unresponsive and inefficient schools. Both the nation and its adolescent population would be far better off if millions of so-called "students" left school and integrated into society where evidence shows they have a much better chance of acquiring saleable skills. Such a program would also bring relief to taxpayers now staggering under rising property taxes, largely due to "educational" costs.

Naturally, in order to be able to integrate unskilled and untrained adolescents into the community, artificial barriers to employment and training must be removed. The report recognized this and so called for:

"...the removal of those regulations, except for safety and health regulations, including tax and insurance penalties, that handicap and limit the employment of adolescents." (P.11)

Now, after such an observation, I fully expected the report to call for some modification of the minimum wage law, at least as it applies to juveniles, but no, I was to be spared this lapse into sanity since the report went on to state:

"The Panel does not urge the special reduction of the minimum wage law. Using youth to displace the marginally employed, the old, the handicapped or as a competitive source of cheap labor is a disservice to both the economy and to education." (P.11)

So, after specifically calling for the removal of legislative barriers that interfere with the employment of youth, the Panel recommended the retention of the one barrier most destructive to their employment and training.

Towards A Lower Living Standard

As the nation continues to experience sharply higher energy costs, food costs, housing costs, medical costs, etc., etc., and the continued deterioration in public services [For example, while the Post Office now delivers less mail than it did in 1974, Gaylord Freeman, Chairman of the Commission on Postal Service, announced on April 29, 1977 that six-day mail service is now a "luxury that the United States could no longer afford," and predicted higher rates, higher subsidies and *decreased service.* Of course, it's a *government operated postal monopoly that the U.S. can no longer afford,* while, if mail delivery is not opened to private enterprise, it may be that sending letters may soon be a luxury enjoyed only by the rich.], it fruitlessly seeks explanations for each separate phenomenon.

What is really happening is that Americans will be spending more and more of their incomes on necessities, i.e. food, shelter, fuel, utilities, (and, yes — taxes), leaving less to spend on comforts and luxuries. This is merely a manifestation of the voyage that the nation is now taking to ever lower standards of living. GNP figures will, of course, continue to rise (since they make no distinction between dollars spent on necessities or those spent on comforts and luxuries), and will be offered as continuing proof of America's "growth."

And Here's Why

Government expenditures, as discussed in pages 145-147, continued to grow — climbing in 1975 to $585.3 billion or 38.6 percent of our $1.516 trillion GNP; thereby increasing their economic bite by an additional 13.5 percent in only three years. But, to get a better understanding of the ominous growth of government expenditures, please refer to Figure 27 on page 146. The total 1975 GNP value of those listed economic groups was $514 billion, so 1975 government expenditures of $585.3 billion exceeded the total product of these industries (note that the 1972 government expenditures didn't quite equal them) by $71.3 billion or 14 percent! What this means is that between 1972 and 1976, government gobbled up another economic group, Contract Construction —which, in 1975, contributed $66.5 billion to the GNP. So, now you can add the sixth group labeled "F — Contract Construction" to the economic groups listed on page 146 — and ponder the fact that government in the U.S. now takes all that productivity and more. What economic group will be swallowed next? There really aren't too many left.

When, oh when will America realize that all of its troubles stem from the simple fact that the cancerous growth of government is simply destroying its power to produce.

The Energy Crisis

It took an Arab oil embargo to get the government's attention concerning a problem that had been brewing for over 20 years — namely the nations dwindling energy reserves. Well, how has the problem improved in the three years since Washington came out of its stupor and officially "addressed" itself to the problem? Well, while in 1973 we imported approximately 36 percent of our oil needs and produced an average of 9.187 million barrels of oil a day, in 1976 we imported over 42 percent and were producing only 7.79 million barrels a day as of January 1977 (even though oil prices had quadrupled). I suppose only a cynic would ask "Could the situation have gotten any worse even if our government had not, in the interim, spent a penny of the people's money on its many energy investigations, reports, hearings, surveys, and on the Federal Energy Administration?"

In addition, the hardships and dislocations occuring in the winter of 1976-77 from lack of natural gas were clearly predictable. The severe shortages predicted for the winter of 1975-76 (see pages 204-205) did not fully materialize until the following winter, when many politicians, bureaucrats and newscasters actually sought to pin the blame for the "shortage" on gas producers and the consuming public rather than the Federal government. Gas producers were accused of "withholding supplies" while consumers were accused of using natural gas wastefully. It is incredible that the government is still able to escape the blame for the shortage that it alone caused. When government officials complained that natural gas was being "wastefully" used, as in the heating of boilers for instance, it should have been forcefully pointed out that it was precisely because government kept its price artificially low that it was used for these purposes while these same low prices discouraged the development of new reserves. The nation, of course, has been led to believe that the OPEC cartel is responsible for the sharp increase in oil prices — but natural gas prices have risen even more than oil — and it's our own gas! So, who do we blame for that?

If one thing can be proven with absolute certainty, it is that the Federal government created the natural gas shortage and that it is responsible for all the hardships and dislocations this is causing.

The Carter Administration — The Fleecing Continues

Jimmy Carter won the Presidential nomination by campaigning against the Washington bureaucracy; however, once in office he proceeded to enlarge upon it. His withdrawn $50 tax rebate was cut from the same fraudulent political cloth as was Ford's (discussed on page 206). He now promises to give us national health "insurance" which will, of course, not be insurance at all and will prove to be no better at delivering health care than the U.S. Postal Service is at delivering mail. Carter's proposed restrictions on hospital charges to combat "inflation" is indicative of either a misunderstanding of inflation or a willingness to deceive the public. And, if price controls on medical costs could effectively fight inflation, why not controls on everything? Indeed, why not controls on government spending, especially on the salaries and pension costs of Congressmen?

But, while I cannot get into an analysis of why medical costs are rising faster than other expenses (though some considerations are: the inefficiencies created by the increasing incidents of third party medical payments, sharply higher labor costs, extensive pilfering of hospital equipment and supplies, added expenses because of greater preoccupation with malpractice), it should be pointed out that one of the main reasons is the impact of government programs such as Medicare and Medicaid. Carter's attempt to deal with "inflation" by the simplistic method of slapping on price controls shows that he only means to deal futilely with symptoms while allowing underlying causes to deteriorate.

Carter's Energy "Program" or Let's Make Matters Worse

It would be redundant for me to take Carter's energy program apart point by point since my specific criticism of Ford's program applies with equal force to Carter's — since while specific provisions of both programs might differ, their basic thrusts are the same. That is, they both seek to *reduce demand* for oil and gas while providing no realistic provisions for increasing supplies. And, both seek to insanely tax away increases in profits that higher oil and gas prices would create.

The real tragedy of Carter's program is the willingness it revealed in so many to believe that planning by bureaucrats (i.e. socialism) can solve a fundamental economic problem more effectively than America's traditional free market system — relying upon the forces of supply and demand, profit and economic self-interest. And, if government can handle our energy needs better, why not food, clothing, health care, etc., etc.? (But it can't even deliver the mail!) What is so frustrating in this is that it is patently ridiculous to even believe that a government that created our energy mess is even remotely capable of solving it.

The only value to Carter's energy program is that it did impress the American public that the energy crisis is real and not something dreamed up by the oil and gas companies to force higher prices.

The $64,000 Question

The question that needs answering is why did it take a lone Presidential voice to suddenly call the nation's attention to a problem which (in the President's words) ''has not yet overwhelmed us'' but could if ''we do not act quickly.'' How could ''our rapidly shrinking reserves'' so suddenly have created elements of ''a national catastrophe'' if not attended to ''without further delay'' requiring attention ''the 'moral eqivalent of war.' '' How could a situation of such immense gravity and peril have developed apparently undetected and unnoticed by a Congress with its economic and energy committees? How could such a situation have developed, apparently unnoticed by all the economists, experts and statisticians in Washington? How could it have developed undetected by the nation's media? It is as if the President came before us on April 18th and shocked the nation by informing us that there was indeed an elephant in everybody's living room.

Can We Learn A Lesson From A City Besieged?

Finally, President Carter's statement that he would not allow profiteering in connection with the energy shortage reminds me of an incident involving a medieval city under siege.

An enemy force had encircled and blockaded it and, consequently, its food supply was extremely low. Soon food was being smuggled in because of the high prices that could be charged. When word of this reached the reigning Duke, he decreed that he would ''not allow food profiteering because of the city's food shortage'' and that those caught would be arrested and executed. Well, this eliminated food profiteering, but it also eliminated food from being brought into the beleaguered city, since it had only been the prospect of big profits that induced smugglers to accept the risk of bringing it in. With sources of food now effectively eliminated, the city was easily starved into submission.

President Carter's concern with ''profiteering'' due to the energy shortage will prove just as foolhardy and counterproductive as the Duke's

The Myth of Carter's "Jobs Program"

Caping a front page story in its May 14, 1977 issue, the New York Times proclaimed...''Carter Signs Bill for Public Works and Creation of One Million Jobs.'' This kind of ''reporting'' was no doubt duplicated in papers across the country, while similar claims were undoubtedly made by the nation's newscasters. Is it any wonder then that the American public is largely ignorant concerning the real impact of government economic meddling — since not only will Carter's "jobs program" not create, on balance, any new jobs but it will actually *destroy* jobs and *lower* the nation's standard of living.

The reason is quite simple. The $13 million that the government will spend creating "jobs" must obviously be taken out of the private economy, so that's $13 billion private citizens *can't spend* for such things as: automobiles, clothing, houses, furniture, plant expansion, etc., etc. — which obviously destroys jobs in these areas. Carter's "jobs program" merely shifts an additional $13 billion of spending from the public to the government. The reason the government is able to fool the public concerning its ability to create "jobs" is that those put to work by the government on such meaningful projects as raking leaves, washing post offices, etc., etc. are highly visible while *those thrown out of work because of the impact of government taxation are largely invisible.* The government, of course, loves to call attention to the employment it says it "creates" when it *spends* the public's money, but ignores the unemployment it creates when it *takes* the public's money.

Now, some will argue that the government can finance these "jobs" by borrowing or deficit spending in lieu of direct taxation and thus it need not cause a $13 billion *shrinkage* in private spending. Such reasoning, however, is fallacious. First of all, if the government borrows the $13 billion (without actually printing it), it will still draw $13 billion out of the private economy and so again the government simply spends what it has prevented private citizens from spending. In addition, such borrowing would put upward pressure on interest rates (by increasing the demand for borrowed funds) which would have a depressive effect on business expansion and the ability of the private sector to sustain and create real jobs.

If, however, the government simply printed the $13 billion (creating "jobs" by naked inflationary financing), the government would, by forcing up prices, simply lower the purchasing value of all savings and unmoney in the public's hands. With its unmoney and savings now worth proportionately less, the public can only *buy less,* thus again the government has precipitated a decrease in private employment. The destruction of jobs by the government will, in every case, be the same, only achieved differently depending on what mix the government uses to finance the $13 billion expenditure.

If the government, while attempting to create jobs, merely destroyed as many jobs as it "created" that alone might not be so bad — the real tragedy is that the government will actually destroy more meaningful employment in the private sector then the uneconomic employment it "creates" in the public sector, and will thus lower the nation's standard of living. The reason is again quite simple. For the government to merely collect for and administer this $13 billion "jobs program" will itself require the expediture of many millions if not billions in government bureaucratic salaries and overhead — so, right off the bat there is real economic loss as useful, economic, private employment is

IRWIN A. SCHIFF FINANCIAL PLANNING

SPECIALIZING IN TAX SHELTERED AND DOLLAR HEDGE INVESTMENTS

November 23, 1976

Mr. Russell L. Munk
Assistant General Counsel
Department of the Treasury
Office of the General Counsel
Washington, D.C.

Dear Mr. Munk:

I am still confused concerning whether or not I earn any money which can be lawfully taxed under the IRS Code as presently written. Since I have not paid any Federal income taxes since 1974 because of this confusion, I would like to get this settled to see if I incurred any tax liability for 1976.

Is it the Treasury Department's contention that a discontinued promise to pay dollars are dollars themselves? Is it the Treasury Department's view that Federal Reserve notes are, in fact dollars? May I please have a simple yes or no answer to this question?

I call your attention to Section 314, Title 31 of the U.S. Code which defines a dollar in terms of gold and the duty of the Secretary of the Treasury to maintain such parity. I ask you now how has the U.S. Treasury maintained the "parity" required by law?

I also call your attention to the attached letter I recently received from Mr. Norman Bernard, Special Assistant to the Board of Governors of the Federal Reserve. Please note that Mr. Bernard states that "the value of a dollar means what the dollar will buy." If this is true, then it is impossible to define a dollar in absolute terms since prices fluctuate, and if we have a fluctuating dollar, how can wealth be realistically, consistently, and fairly measured? Do you concur with Mr. Bernard that a dollar cannot now be defined in absolute and definitive terms?

In the final analysis, I would like to know what exactly a dollar sign means as it appears on Internal Revenue forms 1040? If it does not mean constitutionally defined dollars but Federal Reserve notes, then why should dollar signs appear? Why not another designation? FRN's--for instance.

I would like a clear and direct answer to this question since if the U.S. Treasury cannot define a dollar as opposed to a Federal Reserve note, then no American can logically and lawfully compute any tax form--be it Federal income tax, estate, or gift, that requests information in dollar totals.

Now--after defining a dollar for me, please tell me where I can get one!

Very truly yours,

Irwin A. Schiff

Irwin A. Schiff

IAS/ve
Enclosure

2405 WHITNEY AVENUE, SUITE 506, HAMDEN, CONNECTICUT 06518 (203) 281-1470

Figure 46

DEPARTMENT OF THE TREASURY
OFFICE OF THE GENERAL COUNSEL
WASHINGTON, D.C. 20220

FEB 18 1977

Dear Mr. Schiff:

This is to respond to your letter of November 23, 1976 in which you request a definition for the dollar as distinguished from a Federal Reserve note.

Federal Reserve notes are not dollars. Those notes are denominated in dollars, which are the unit of account of United States money. The Coinage Act of 1792 established the dollar as the basic unit of United States currency, by providing that "The money of account of the United States shall be expressed in dollars or units, dimes or tenths, cents, or hundredths .." 31 U.S.C. § 371.

The fact that Federal Reserve notes may not be converted into gold or silver does not render them worthless. Mr. Bernard of the Federal Reserve Board is quite correct in stating that the value of the dollar is its purchasing power. Professor Samuelson, in his text Economics, notes that the dollar, as our medium of exchange, is wanted not for its own sake, but for the things it will buy.

Finally, I must inform you that there is no legal basis for an arguement that a taxpayer need not file a return of his income, expressed in dollars, on the ground that Federal Reserve notes are not "dollars" or that only gold and silver coin are lawful money of the United States for tax or other purposes. See Koll v. Wayzata State Bank, 397 F. 2d 124, 127 (8th Cir. 1968); Horne v. Federal Reserve Bank of Minneapolis, 344 F.2d 725-29 (8th Cir. 1965).

I trust this information responds to your inquiry.

Sincerely yours,

Russell L. Munk
Assistant General Counsel

Mr. Irwin A. Schiff
P.O. Box 5303
Hamden, Connecticut 06518

(This two page letter was shortened to one page.)

Figure 47

sacrificed for largely useless, bureaucratic employment. In addition, practically all government created "jobs" will be of a marginal, uneconomic "service" type while the type of employment that government taxes destroy is of a more economic and productive nature related to satisfying real economic need and involving productivity capable of being exported. Will anything be produced by government created "jobs" that can be used, for instance, to help fight the nation's balance of payments problem?

In passing it should be noted how easily the New York Times was fooled by government PR claims, so that it could uncritically report that Washington could indeed create "one million jobs." You might think that so influential a paper would have at least realized that since the average U.S. industrial worker is supported by $37,929 of capital[1] — it would require a capital *investment* of approximately $37.9 billion to create and *sustain* one million legitimate jobs and not a relatively puny, one shot, *expenditure* of $13 billion (and, remember that's *gross* spending, not *net* investment) the government claims will do the job.

The above figure also explains, of course, why America is suffering from a high level of unemployment. The capital really needed to support real employment is simply being taxed away by government in order to fund a variety of wasteful and, in many cases, asinine (such as the "jobs program") government projects. (For more on government created "jobs," see pages 177-178.)

In the final analysis, Carter's claim that his economic "stimulus" program will create "one million new jobs" should be filed with such other government claims as: "Social Security is soundly financed" and "our Vietnamese involvement will only cost $15 billion.

The Tax Rebellion Grows

America is certainly not lacking in organizations and publications seeking to promote limited government and individual responsibility, but, despite the efforts of such organizations, the nation still relentlessly moves towards the cliff's edge. It may indeed be too late to educate sufficient Americans to vote responsibly, since the government has created so many voters with a vested interest in government handouts that responsible voters may, indeed, be licked at the polls even before they start.

It may be that the one stand that understanding and patriotic Americans, who have a clear picture of where the government is taking us, can take, is to simply dig in their heels and say, "Nothing doing, we're not cooperating in our nation's destruction."

If the country is to be spared the fate of England and Italy (and ancient Rome) it may be because of the growing army of tax rebels — now numbering in the millions. It may be that only when Washington politicians see crystal clear evidence of growing legal defiance and legal rebellion amoung more and

[1]According to the 1976 Fortune survey.

IRWIN A. SCHIFF FINANCIAL PLANNING

SPECIALIZING IN TAX SHELTERED AND DOLLAR HEDGE INVESTMENTS

April 15, 1977

District Director
Internal Revenue Service
North Atlantic Region
Andover, Massachusetts 01899

Dear Mr. Director:

The attached letter from Mr. Russell L. Munk, of the Treasury, establishes beyond question that I am not required to file a return; but, I'm doing so anyway so the government can have the benefit of my thinking.

Please note that Mr. Munk clearly states "Federal Reserve notes are not dollars." However, page 5 of "Your Federal Income Tax, 1977 Edition" states:

> "A single individual must file a return if he or she had $2,450 (dollars) or more gross income for the year."

Since I only earned Federal Reserve notes, I obviously did not receive the requisite number of dollars requiring me to file. In addition, I would point out that the last paragraph of Munk's letter is merely rebutable opinion, since the cases cited are no more applicable than is the monetary understanding of a Paul Samuelson.

Further, Mr. Munk's observation that "the value of the dollar is its purchasing power" illustrates how the government violates the Constitution which states that the value of money is to be regulated by Congress--not the marketplace. Now, while I did not earn any dollars, I did earn some notes of the Federal Reserve, and, according to the above IRS manual, the fair market value of "notes or other evidences of indebtedness...is usually the best amount you can get from ...a bank or other buyer of such paper."

Therefore, on December 8, 1976, I went directly to the Federal Reserve Bank of New York and requested that my Federal Reserve notes be redeemed for lawful dollars as defined in Sections 314 and 821 of Title 31 of the U.S. code. They refused and offered only to exchange them for other notes. Thus, one must conclude that Federal Reserve notes have no determinable, real dollar, market value. I admit that private citizens did give me goods and services for these notes, but I don't see how one can list on a 1040 all the goods and services received for notes when the return itself insists that income be shown in dollars and not in goods and services. I am also at a loss to understand how one would convert goods and services received for notes into a dollar total. What kind of dollars would one use? Gold dollars or silver dollars? And, how would their values be determined?

I will be pleased to refile if you can show me how notes, themselves neither redeemable in or exchangable for dollars, can be converted into dollars and thus taxable according to the IRS regulation cited above.

Very truly yours,

Irwin A. Schiff

Irwin A. Schiff

IAS/ve
Enclosures

2405 WHITNEY AVENUE, SUITE 506, HAMDEN, CONNECTICUT 06518 (203) 281-1470

Figure 48

more Americans will it even begin considering reversing the nation's disastrous course.

Tax rebels received some powerful new ammunition when I received a letter from Russell L. Munk, the Assistant General Counsel of the Department of the Treasury (see Figures 46 and 47), officially admitting that "Federal Reserve notes are not dollars." The implication of Munk's admission is contained in Figure 48, the covering letter for my 1976 income tax return.

If you are convinced of the growing danger to our nation from the relentless growth of government, you should seriously look into the tax rebellion movement; since, while the situation isn't hopeless yet, it just soon might be.

Index

(Bold-face figures denote chapter numbers)

PRICE LISTS FOR VARIOUS QUANTITIES OF
THE BIGGEST CON

1-4 copies $5.95 ea.
5-9 copies $4.95 ea.
10-24 copies $4.50 ea.
25-49 copies $4.00 ea.
50 copies and over $3.60

Please add $.50 for postage and handling or 7% which ever is greater.

For those wishing copies sent directly to schools, colleges, libraries, or other institutions or to people in media and government, send us a list, including addresses and we will send such copies for $3.50 each. For those sending in contributions, we guarantee to send out such copies in your name. In addition, copies addressed to students at college will be sent for $3.50.

Those wishing us to send copies to others can send us a list and we will mail books out based on the discounted quantity rate. But be sure to include postage and handling.

To: Freedom Books
P.O. Box 5303
Hamden, Connecticut 06518
(203) 281-6791

Gentlemen:

Please send me________book(s). Payment of $____________is enclosed (check or money order). Add $.50 per copy for postage and handling or 7% which ever is greater.*

Please accept this contribution of $__________. Please send books to:

☐ Institutions of your choice
☐ Per list attached

*Single books will be sent 4th Class U.S. Mail.

For faster, "special handling mail" or UPS service, add 50¢ additional and check here ☐.